IN
FAMED
BREADALBANE

THE RIGHT HON. THE NINTH EARL OF BREADALBANE

In Famed Breadalbane

THE STORY OF THE ANTIQUITIES, LANDS,
AND PEOPLE OF A HIGHLAND DISTRICT

BY

The Rev. William A. Gillies

B.D., HON.C.F., J.P., F.S.A. SCOT.

MINISTER OF KENMORE

Northern Books
from Famedram

In Famed Breadalbane was first published in 1938 under the imprint of
The Munro Press, Perth. The publishers wish to acknowledge
the kind assistance of the Killin Gallery, Killin and Freader's Books,
Aberfeldy in facilitating the production of this facsimile edition.
Famedram Publishers, Ellon, AB41 9EA www.northernbooks.co.uk
ISBN 0905489 82 9
Print: Thomson Press Ltd, C35 Phase II Noida

TO MY WIFE.

CONTENTS.

PREFACE.

THIS book is the result of twenty-six years' residence in the beautiful and historic district of Breadalbane. After being settled as minister of Kenmore, in 1912, I began to gather information with a view to writing a history of the parish. As I proceeded with the work I discovered that the story of Kenmore was intimately bound up with that of the parish of Killin and of the several detached portions of the old parish of Weem lying on Lochtayside and in Glenlochay. I therefore decided to attempt to relate the story of the whole of Breadalbane from Aberfeldy to Tyndrum.

The gathering of information about this ancient and extensive part of Scotland has involved much reading and research ; but the labour has been made a pleasure through the kindly help and encouragement given by numerous persons interested in the district.

I have to acknowledge my great indebtedness to The Right Hon. The Earl of Breadalbane for graciously granting me unrestricted access to the family archives and for photographs of himself and of Auchmore House.

My thanks are due to Mr. William Angus, Keeper of Registers, Register House, Edinburgh, who took a personal interest in the story of a district with which he has a long and honourable ancestral connection. Mr. Henry M. Paton and Mr. Charles T. M'Innes of the Historical Department of the Register House helped me to decipher the obscure script of olden times, and often guided me to unfamiliar sources of information. I shall always recall with pleasure the many hours I passed in the peaceful atmosphere of the Historical Room in association with its genial and obliging staff.

I owe special acknowledgments to Professor W. J. Watson, LL.D., of Edinburgh University, for suggesting at an early stage in my work the lines that I should follow. For such guidance and repeated acts of kindness I record my warmest thanks.

I am indebted to Mr. John Ritchie, Curator of the Natural History Museum of Perth, for copies of papers on North Perthshire contributed over a hundred years ago to the Antiquarian Society of that city, and also for the photograph of the Second Marquis of Breadalbane taken from the portrait in the Perth Art Gallery.

I desire to express my gratitude to Mr. James D. Haggart, O.B.E., Provost of Aberfeldy, for the interest he has taken in my work, and for lending me old maps and books relating to Taymouth Castle.

I have to thank the Council of the Society of Antiquaries of Scotland for the use of blocks with which to illustrate the part of the book dealing with the prehistoric period. The Directors of Taymouth Castle Hotel Company, Limited, provided the illustrations that show the surroundings and the interior of the Castle. I obtained the photographs of the First and Third Earls of Breadalbane from portraits in the Scottish National Portrait Gallery, Edinburgh. Messrs. John Dewar and Sons kindly lent the block for the picture of " The Macnab." For all these favours I am deeply grateful.

I have been fortunate in securing six photographs from Mr. Robert M. Adam, of the Royal Botanic Gardens, Edinburgh, whose superb art is familiar to everyone who knows the Highlands. These magnificent views, along with a few selected from a large collection left by my predecessor, the Rev. James B. Mackenzie, reveal, in a way no words could, the character and surpassing charm of the Breadalbane country.

Several friends who gave me valuable assistance have passed away before my work could be completed. From the late Alexander Campbell of Boreland, Fearnan, the late Miss Jean MacDougall, Milton, Ardtalnaig, and the late James MacDiarmid, Morenish, Killin, I obtained most interesting information about places and old families connected with the district. In this record of a land whose " very dust to them was dear," I have included many of the tales they told me. The late John MacGregor, W.S., of 8 Glencairn Crescent, Edinburgh, placed at my disposal his collection of papers relating to the Macnabs of Glendochart ; while the late J. Graham Callander, LL.D., Director of the Scottish National Museum of Antiquities, Edinburgh, guided me when I was writing the first part of the book, and generously read over and corrected these pages. I hold those departed friends in grateful remembrance.

In this list of acknowledgments it is a pleasure to record my thanks to Mr. David Bissett, Manager of the Munro Press, Limited, and his staff for their unfailing courtesy and the efficient help they have given me with the publication of the volume.

To all the other good friends who aided and encouraged me from time to time in my undertaking I offer my sincerest thanks.

The Carnegie Trustees, having recognised that the writing of this book has involved historical research, have kindly undertaken to contribute fifty pounds in the event of loss being incurred in publication.

In conclusion I desire to say that the labours of those past years will be amply rewarded if I shall be deemed to have added to the historical knowledge of this region in which it has been my privilege to live and labour as a minister of the Church of Scotland.

The Manse of Kenmore,   WILLIAM A. GILLIES.
19th May, 1938.

SOURCES OF INFORMATION AND BOOKS CONSULTED.

The Breadalbane Papers lodged in the Register House, Edinburgh. These Papers consist of charters, and registers of feus and tacks ; bonds of fosterage and manrent ; muster rolls and court books ; household books and inventories ; and a large number of family and other letters.

The Black Book of Taymouth. Bannatyne Club. The history of the House of Glenorchy from Sir Colin Campbell, the First Laird, to Sir Robert Campbell, the third Baronet, was written by William Bowie, tutor and secretary in the family during the first half of the seventeenth century. This book together with the " Chronicle " kept by the vicars of Fortingall from 1424 to 1579, the " Testament " of Duncan Laideus MacGregor, and a selection from the papers in the charter room of Taymouth Castle was edited by Cosmo Innes, in 1855, for the Bannatyne Club, under the title of " The Black Book of Taymouth." Bowie's book is at present in the National Library of Scotland, Edinburgh ; but although there is a transcript of the " Chronicle " in the Register House, the original is not among the Breadalbane Papers kept there.

The Kirk Session Records of the Parishes of Kenmore and Killin.

Papers relating to Highland Clans and Families, collected by the late John MacGregor, W.S., Edinburgh, now in the Register House, Edinburgh.

A Manuscript Description of and Historical Notes on the Tay Valley by Ewen MacDougall, Ardtalnaig, Kenmore, written about 1820.

Proceedings of the Society of Antiquaries of Scotland, especially articles by the following Fellows of the Society :—
Joseph Anderson, LL.D. ; Rev. Odo Blundell, O.S.B. ; J. Graham Callander, LL.D. ; C. G. Cash ; Fred R. Coles ; Alexander Hutcheson ; A. D. Lacaille ; Rev. J. B. Mackenzie ; Rev. Hugh Macmillan, D.D., LL.D. ; T. S. Robertson ; Thomas Ross, LL.D. ; Charles Stewart ; John Stuart, LL.D.

Scotland in Pagan Times. Joseph Anderson, LL.D.

Scotland in Early Christian Times. Joseph Anderson, LL.D.

Transactions of the Gaelic Society of Inverness, especially articles by James MacDiarmid, in vols. XXV., XXVI., XXVII. ; and by W. J. Watson, LL.D., in vol. XXXIV.

The Register of the Great Seal of Scotland.

The Register of the Privy Seal of Scotland.

The Accounts of the Lord High Treasurer of Scotland.

The Exchequer Rolls of Scotland.

The Register of Sasines for Perthshire.

The Reports to the Commissioners for Plantation of Kirks (1627). Maitland Club.

General Assembly Commission Records (1646-52). Scottish History Society.

A Selection of the Forfeited Estates Papers. Scottish History Society.

Scotland and the Protectorate. Scottish History Society.

Scotland and the Commonwealth. Scottish History Society.

The Charters of the Abbey of Inchaffray. Scottish History Society.

Macfarlane's Genealogical and Topographical Collections. Scottish History Society.

Highland Papers. Scottish History Society.

Pococke's Tours in Scotland. Scottish History Society.

Miscellanies of the Scottish History Society. Scottish History Society.

Rentale Dunkeldense, 1505-1517. Scottish History Society.

Liber Ecclesie De Scon. Maitland Club.

Early Scottish Charters. Sir Archibald C. Lawrie.

A Tour in Scotland, 1769, 1772. Thomas Pennant.

Nicoll's Diary. Bannatyne Club.

Memoirs of General Monk. F. P. G. Guizot.

Recreations of an Antiquary. R. Scott Fittis.

The Lairds and Lands of Lochtayside. John Christie.

The Antiquity of Aberfeldy. John Christie.

Scottish Notes and Queries, articles by John Christie.

    John Christie was a clerk in the Breadalbane Estates Office, Kenmore. His book on Lochtayside appeared first as a series of articles in Perthshire newspapers. Christie's information, mostly taken from original sources, is always accurate.

Sketches of the Highlanders. David Stewart.

Records of Argyll. Lord Archibald Campbell.

The Highlanders of Scotland. W. F. Skene.

Celtic Scotland. W. F. Skene.

The Clan Campbell. Sir Duncan Campbell of Barcaldine.

The History of the Clan Gregor. A. G. N. MacGregor.

Scots Peerage, especially article on the Breadalbane Peerage contributed by John MacGregor, W.S., Edinburgh.

Baronage of Scotland. Sir Robert Douglas.

Fasti Ecclesiae Scoticanae. Hew Scott, D.D.

The History of the Kirk of Scotland. David Calderwood.

The Diocese and Presbytery of Dunkeld. Rev. John Hunter, B.D.

Statistical Account of Scotland (1791).

New Statistical Account of Scotland (1845).

Scottish Verse from the Book of the Dean of Lismore. W. J. Watson, LL.D.

History of Celtic Place-Names of Scotland. W. J. Watson, LL.D.

National Records of the Visit of Queen Victoria to Scotland, 1842. James Buist.

Memorial of the Royal Progress. Sir Thomas Dick Lauder.

LIST OF ILLUSTRATIONS.

INTRODUCTION.

"Fam'd Breadalbane opens to my view."—*Burns.*

*T*HE name *"Breadalbane," so suggestive of romance and scenic grandeur, means " The Upland of Alban." The Gaelic word,* braghaid, *upper part, is frequently found in Scottish place-names in the form of* braid. *Alban was the ancient name of Scotland, and to this day it is the name applied to our Northern Land by Gaelic-speaking Highlanders, as well as by the Gaels of Ireland, and by the people of Wales. When the Scots from Ireland settled during the early centuries of the Christian era on the Western coastland from Kintyre to Ross-shire, they called the mountain range that separated them from Pictland, Druim-alban, or the backbone of Alban, and the region immediately beyond that range, Braghaid-Alban.*

The boundaries of Breadalbane have never been defined with any exactness, the reason probably being that the district at no period formed a separate province for administrative purposes. Macfarlane, in his Geographical Collections, published about the middle of the eighteenth century, says,[1] *"Braid Albyn is thirty myl long, east to west, and the breadth bewixt Dalreoch in Glenlyon and Lairig Kylle (Glenogle-head), in Bawhidder is ten myl from north to south." The district comprehends the two large parishes of Kenmore and Killin. Until 1893, when parish boundaries were re-arranged, Breadalbane also included several portions of the ecclesiastical parish of Weem. It would appear that when the parochial system was extended to the Diocese of Dunkeld, these parts were in possession of members of the Clan Menzies, whose Chief resided at Weem. They are now embraced in the parishes of Kenmore and Killin, which together extend westwards from the Point of Lyon to Ben Laoigh on the border line between Perthshire and Argyllshire—a distance of about forty miles.*

(1) Macfarlane's Geog. Coll. II. 563.

The term "Breadalbane" does not appear in old Scottish charters. The earliest recorded reference to the district under this name is in the Book of the Dean of Lismore, where a poem has, "Na fir sin a Braid Albain," " Those men from Breadalbane." The eastern portion around Loch Tay, along with Glenlochay, comprised the Lordship of Discher and Toyer, names which were derived from the Gaelic words, deas *south, and* tuath *north, and signified, " The South-facing Slope," and " The North-facing Slope" of the district, respectively. Glendochart with Strathfillan formed the separate Lordship of Glendochart. At the head of Glenlochay and stretching over the watershed to the shores of Loch Lyon was the Royal Forest of Mamlorn. In still earlier times Breadalbane lay within the Pictish province of Fotla, a name that survives in the modern term, Atholl.*

Breadalbane may, therefore, be taken as that incomparably beautiful region in the very heart of Scotland, extending from the junction of the river Lyon with the Tay to the water-shed at Carndroma, west of Tyndrum. It includes the whole basin of the upper Tay with the noble loch, as well as the two great streams that feed it, the gentle Lochay and the wild, turbulent Dochart. As Perthshire is the fairest portion of Britain, so Breadalbane is the grandest part of Perthshire. It cannot be better described than in these words of Sir Walter Scott,[1] " The rivers find their way out of the mountainous region by the wildest leaps, and through the most romantic passes. Above, the vegetation of a happier clime and soil is mingled with the magnificent characteristics of mountain scenery ; and woods, groves, and thickets in profusion clothe the base of the hills, ascend up the ravines, and mingle with the precipices." It is the story of this favoured region, where, as Scott says, " Beauty lies in the lap of Terror," that I propose to relate in this volume.

(1) " Fair Maid of Perth."

CHAPTER I.

Pre-Historic Period.

FAR up on the western shoulder of Ben Lawers, where the clouds often rest, a copious spring of water, clear as crystal, issues from underneath a great rock. After flowing for a short distance on the surface the stream disappears from sight only to come up again lower down. It thus goes on disappearing and reappearing until at length, greatly increased in volume, it reaches the bed of the corrie below. Here it is joined by a number of other rills, and, flowing over a steep, rocky channel, it may be seen from far as a silver stream rushing down the mountain side to Loch Tay. The history of Breadalbane in some respects resembles this wonderful spring, around which the imagination of the people in the past has woven many a fairy tale. The earliest glimpses that we get of the olden times in this region are few and brief. For centuries the record of the past is hidden altogether from our view, and we are simply left to imagine who the people were that lived here, and how they lived, from their burial monuments and from implements and weapons that have been turned up from time to time by the spade and the plough. In later ages there is a great mass of material from which to construct the story of Breadalbane.

The Age of Stone.

During the most of the time that the Palæolithic or Early Stone Age prevailed on the Continent of Europe, Scotland was covered with a thick crust of ice, and until a few years ago it was assumed that the conditions were so severe as to render human life in this land impossible. Recent discoveries made in the caves at Inchnadamph, Assynt, seem to prove, however, that this assumption was not quite correct. There is definite evidence to show that man was able to make his home in Scotland at a period when animals now confined to the Arctic regions could exist here. So far no human relic has been found in Breadalbane that can carry us back beyond the Neolithic or New Stone Age. Stone axes, flint arrow-heads, and scrapers belonging to this latter period have been recovered from time to time, and examples of them are preserved in the National Museum of Antiquities of Scotland, Edinburgh, and are described in the *Proceedings* of the Society of Antiquaries of Scotland.

A

Among the most interesting and valuable relics of the Neolithic Age found in Breadalbane is a finely formed, and highly polished axe[1] of greenish quartz, which was picked up among the ruins of the ancient native fort on Drummond Hill, Kenmore. It is 8 ins. in length, $3\frac{1}{4}$ ins. across the cutting face, and $\frac{5}{8}$ in. at its greatest thickness.   This beautiful axe

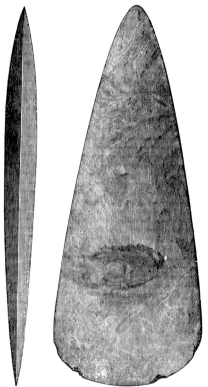

POLISHED AXE FROM DRUMMOND HILL.

belongs to a rare class of triangular, and highly polished weapons usually made of the hardest crystalline stone, such as jadeite, and are usually found in Britain, Brittany, and in some parts of Central Europe.   Both with regard to the British and Continental specimens there is considerable doubt as to the exact localities whence the materials were derived from which they were formed.   It is believed that these very beautiful instruments were intended more for ceremonial than for industrial use, but, so far, no definite conclusion on this point has been arrived at.

(1) Proc. Soc. Ant. Scot., Vol. XXIII., p. 2

Some thirty years ago, while a farmer at Balnahanait, on the north side of Loch Tay was digging a pit for potatoes, he unearthed three stone axes[1] among slabs of stone that may have formed a burial cist. One of the axes was of quite a common type, but the other two were marked and ornamented in such a way as to deserve more than passing notice. The larger of

ORNAMENTED AXE FROM BALNAHANAID.

the axes is of greenstone, measuring $6\frac{1}{2}$ ins. in length by $2\frac{1}{2}$ ins. across the cutting face. Its greatest thickness is $1\frac{1}{4}$ ins. The surface is well polished, and on one face there is an oblique depression or groove, as if it had been used for sharpening the point of an awl. The smaller of the axes is of soft, micaceous stone, and measures 5 ins. in length by $2\frac{1}{2}$ ins. across the cutting face, with a thickness of nearly $1\frac{1}{2}$ inches. The whole surface had been covered with a pattern of crossed lines. On the one side the pattern has been worn away, while on the other it appears as shown in the accompanying illustration.

So far as is known no burial cairns or pottery belonging to the New Stone Age have been identified in Breadalbane, but the stone axes and other remains found go to prove that the people who inhabited this district then were, as elsewhere in

(1) Proc. Soc. Ant. Scot., Vol. XXXV., p. 310.

Scotland, possessed of a wonderful measure of skill and culture. Their implements and weapons were fashioned in a way that combined beauty of outline with the grace of proportion. The polish on the Drummond Hill axe is perfect, and the edge is as finely drawn as if it had been done with modern machinery.

The Age of Bronze.

The earliest bronze implements and weapons found in Scotland carry us back to a period about 1800 years before the Christian Era. From that time bronze gradually replaced stone as the material from which men fashioned their instruments for work and for warfare. The knowledge of copper and bronze was doubtless acquired by the inhabitants of Scotland from abroad, but at a very early part of this period they learned the art of manufacturing for themselves. This is evident, as the moulds for casting flat bronze axes, the earliest form of the Bronze Age axe, have been found in different parts of the country. Later on, axes—flanged and socketed—spearheads, swords, and other articles were also manufactured, as the moulds, sometimes made of stone, and sometimes of clay, in which they were cast, have been recovered.

It seems probable that the first appearance of implements and weapons of bronze in this country was contemporary with the arrival of a new people, who brought with them new burial customs, and a higher state of culture and civilization. These invaders gradually became fused with the ancient people of the land. The relics belonging to this Age that have been recovered throughout the country are wonderfully numerous; but, strangely enough, most of them have been found, not on the sites where the people dwelt in life, but in graves, some of which were enclosed with large round cairns, while others were surrounded with circles of standing stones, and others had no over-ground structure at all. Here the bones and ashes of the dead had been laid, accompanied with pottery, and occasionally, with small implements of bronze, and ornaments of various materials. Articles belonging to this period have also been recovered from sites where there was no evidence of burial. The district of Breadalbane has made a most valuable contribution of the latter class of articles to the large and varied collection of Bronze Age relics preserved in the National Museum of Antiquities of Scotland.

In 1868, while a crofter at Killin, John MacDiarmid, was engaged trenching a gravel hillock on his holding at Monadhmor, he came upon a hoard of bronze articles. They were about a foot below the ground, and had the appearance of having been tied together with some kind of fastening. The mound in which the articles were found was of natural formation, and had always been in pasture until it was turned over on this occasion.

The various articles are thus described in the *Proceedings* of the Society of Antiquaries of Scotland[1] :—

1. A portion of a bronze sword of small size with leaf-shaped blade, having no rivet holes in the handle plate, which is furnished with a somewhat prominent midrib on both sides. The fragment measures $5\frac{3}{4}$ inches in length. This would now be called a knife.

2. A spearhead, $10\frac{1}{4}$ inches in length, the blade leaf-shaped, the socket projecting 3 inches beyond the base of the blade and pierced transversely by a rivet-hole on either side. The

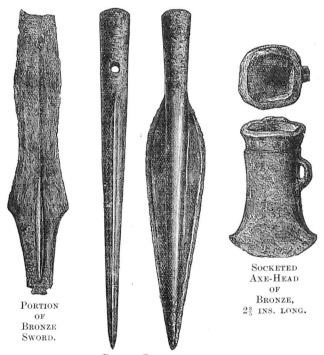

PORTION
OF
BRONZE
SWORD.

SOCKETED
AXE-HEAD
OF
BRONZE,
$2\frac{3}{5}$ INS. LONG.

BRONZE SPEARHEADS.

socket, as usual, is continued as a prominent midrib down the centre of the blade, and cored almost to the point.

3. Two socketed axe heads of bronze. The first is $2\frac{5}{8}$ inches in length, and 2 inches across the cutting face, which is semicircular, and expands considerably as it thins towards the edge. The second is $4\frac{1}{4}$ inches in length, and $2\frac{1}{4}$ inches across

(1) Vol. XVI., p. 27.

the cutting face, which expands to a semi-circular form ; the socket part is long and narrow, with a squarish collar underneath the rim of the socket, and is furnished with a small loop on one side.

4. A socketed gouge, $2\frac{3}{4}$ inches in length. Bronze gouges are of rare occurrence in Scotland, but since the one at Killin was recovered other four examples have been found in different parts of the country, and these are preserved in the National Museum of Antiquities of Scotland.

Left—SOCKETED AXE-HEAD OF BRONZE, $4\frac{1}{4}$ INS. LONG.

Right — SOCKETED GOUGE OF BRONZE.

CIRCULAR HOLLOW RING OF BRONZE.

CIRCULAR HOLLOW RING OF BRONZE.

5. A circular hollow ring, similar in form to the button-like rings found with the bronze swords in Edinburgh and at Tarves, and with spear-heads at Inshoch, near Nairn. In this case there are no loops in the cavity of the ring. It measures $2\frac{1}{4}$ inches in diameter.

6. A penannular ring, or bracelet of bronze, $2\frac{3}{4}$ inches in diameter, with slightly expanded ends.

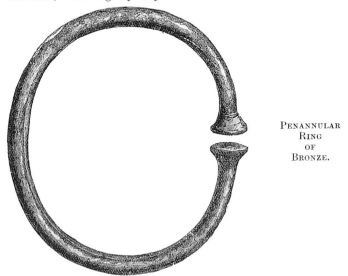

PENANNULAR
RING
OF
BRONZE.

7. Nine plain annular rings of bronze, three of which are $2\frac{1}{4}$ inches in diameter, four are $1\frac{7}{8}$ inches in diameter, and two are $1\frac{1}{2}$ inches diameter.

PLAIN
ANNULAR
RING
OF
BRONZE.

Bronze Age Cairns.

There are innumerable cairns, great as well as small, scattered throughout Breadalbane. The Gaelic word, *carn*, signifying a heap of stones, appears in several place-names. We have one *Acharn* (Cairnfield), near Kenmore, and another at Killin. A field on the farm of Cragganruar, Lawers, used to be known as *Carn Dow* (Black Cairn), while on the farm of Milton, Ardtalnaig, there is *Carn Ban* (Fair Cairn). With the exception of the last mentioned and some cairns recently examined in the neighbourhood of Kirkton, Strathfillan, all the others would appear to be simply accumulations of land stones collected through the centuries of cultivation from the adjacent fields.

The great heap of stones known as Carn Ban at Ardtalnaig is situated immediately below the farm house of Milton, and about two hundred yards from the shore of Loch Tay. A tradition, which was put on record over a hundred years ago, relates that in the time of King Duncan an army under Macbeth and Banquo was sent to suppress the MacDougalls of Lorn. A nephew of the king, who had been wounded in battle, died at Ardtalnaig, and was buried there. His comrades raised this cairn over his grave. The story also stated that a hide of gold was laid in the grave with the remains of the hero. On the south side of the cairn, near the top, there is a hole six feet wide that is said to have been made by two local men who went in the dead of night, hoping to recover the treasure. Disappointed in their first attempt they dared not face the ridicule of their neighbours, and henceforth the cairn was left undisturbed. There is, no doubt, truth in the tradition that this is a burial cairn, but it dates from a much earlier period than that of King Duncan. It closely resembles in shape and size cairns of the Bronze Age that have been examined in other parts of Scotland. The circumference measures about 95 feet, and the diameter about 33 feet. The outer edge seems to have been formed of somewhat large stones which were placed carefully in position. The summit is about 15 feet above the general level of the surrounding field. The stones vary in size, but few of them are larger than 12 inches long by 6 inches broad, and they would appear as if they had been collected from the vicinity. Various articles have been picked up from time to time in the neighbourhood of the cairn, but so far as can be ascertained from descriptions of them obtained from the late Miss Jean MacDougall, Milton, whose ancestors have been tenants of the farm for many generations, none of the relics had any connection with it. They would appear to belong to a much later period, when the early Scottish kings had a hunting seat near the spot.

Several cairns at Strathfillan are supposed to have been burial places of the Bronze Age. The first of these is situated on the farm of Kirkton, about a hundred and fifty yards south of St. Fillan's Chapel. The cairn seems to be intact, except for a slight excavation near the top, where probably treasure-hunters dug into it as at Ardtalnaig. Mr. John Paterson, who was tenant of the farm for over sixty years, never remembered the cairn being excavated, but he stated that the plough had turned up burial slabs on the south margin.

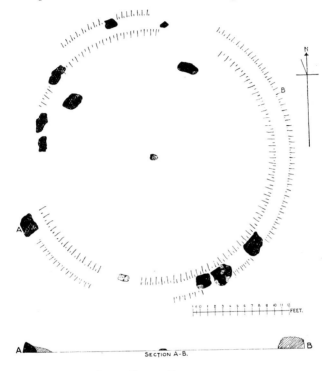

STONE CIRCLE, STRATHFILLAN.

There are remains of a circular cairn[1] to the south of the neighbouring farm of Auchtertyre. Locally the spot is known as *Mod Ceann na Drochaid* (The Mote-hill of the Bridge-end). The centre stones of the cairn have been removed, and all that now remains is an imperfect circle of boulders which were apparently set round the margin of the cairn. Many of them are still in position, owing to the fact that their weight prevented their removal. The circle is raised over practically all its cir-cumference. There are traces of an extension of the cairn to the north for about thirty yards, and it has been suggested that here once on a time was a Long Cairn of the New Stone Age which was disturbed by the people of the Bronze Age, who

(1) Proc. Soc. Ant. Scot., Vol. LVIII., p. 124.

erected a circular cairn at its south end. In a field about three hundred yards to the south-east of this site there is a third small cairn which is very similar to the one described near the Chapel of St. Fillan.

Stone Circles and Standing Stones.

While only a few burial cairns of the Bronze Age have so far been located in Breadalbane, Stone Circles belonging to this period are fairly numerous. Some of these circles are well known, and all of them, with one or two exceptions, have been carefully surveyed and described for the Society of Antiquaries of Scotland by Mr. Fred. R. Coles. Along the valleys of the Tay and Lyon within the neighbourhood of the villages of Kenmore, Dull, and Fortingall there are at least ten sites on which circles stand in a more or less complete form. On some sites no more than a stone or two remain. The others were no doubt removed in the process of clearing the ground for cultivation. As stone circles or, as they are often erroneously called, "Druid Circles," are the objects of much interest and curiosity it may be worth while giving a full description of the monuments of this class that have been discovered within the bounds of our district. These descriptions have been taken for the most part from the *Proceedings* of the Society of Antiquaries of Scotland.

Croftmoraig Circle.[1]

The first of the stone circles to be considered presents one of the most complete groups of standing stones in all Scotland, so far as records of circles have yet been examined. It is situated close by the village of Croftmoraig, and within forty yards of the public road between Kenmore and Aberfeldy, at a point almost opposite the fourth milestone from the latter place. The stones readily catch the eye of the passer-by, and, being easily reached, they are visited every summer by numerous tourists, who are impressed by the general character and completeness of this remarkable monument. The site was briefly described with plans by Mr. Alexander Hutcheson, F.S.A., Scot., in 1889, and in 1910 Mr. Coles made a very careful examination of the stones. Most of the stones are composed of the quartzose schist of the district, and they are remarkably rounded in contour. Perhaps the great sloping block marked D on the plan, which has been polished by the sliding of generations of children over it, may be of a more dioretic variety of mineral : it seems greyer, closer in texture, and harder than the majority.

(1) Proc. Soc. Ant. Scot., Vol. XXIII., p. 356, and Ibid., Vol. XLIV., p. 139.

VIEW OF STONE CIRCLE, CROFTMORAIG.

1. As will be seen from the plan the structural portion of the Croftmoraig circle consists, first, of a roughly circular earthen mound (lettered in small type), some three feet high, which is marked off by a circumference of, approximately, 185 feet. This outermost setting, or *revetement* of stones, is visible now only at certain fragments of the arcs, viz :—it is well defined on the S.W. at **a**, where a long stone, 6 feet 5 inches by 2 feet, lies flat, and bears numerous cup-marks : on the S. arc there are five small stones all earthfast and flattish : on the S.E. are three similar stones : on the E. arc are four . on the N. arc, very slightly to the W., one very large stone flush with the ground at the edge of the bank, and a good deal overgrown with grass, measuring 8 feet 6 inches by 3 feet 3 inches : farther to the N.W. are five stones more, the last three having only very small portions visible : and still farther round, is the last of what appears to be these ridge slabs, close under the edge of the great sloping stone D. Thus the total number of measurable and separate stones on the outermost ring is twenty.

2. The stones of the intermediate ring constitute the imposing feature of the circle. They are thirteen in total number in the present condition of the circle, but they probably numbered eighteen when the circle was complete. Nine of them are the tallest in the whole group : four of these are prostrate on the west arc. By striking a radius from the common centre of the circle through the centres of these great stones, which are erect, to the outermost circumference, we obtain the following measures :—From centre of E. the N.N.W. stone, to the ridge, 14 feet 6 inches : from F, the N.N.E. stone, to the ridge, 13 feet 4 inches : and from I, the S.E. stone, only 10 feet 6 inches. The four fallen blocks, lying as shown, A. B. C. D., no doubt stood on the intermediate ring, the diameter of which, measured from centre to centre, is 38 feet.

Now, it must be observed that between A and B and A and I, there are stones (shaded in the plan) : these two are erect, the one near B measuring 3 feet in length, 2 feet in breadth, and 3 feet 4 inches in height : it is quite vertical and is undoubtedly *in situ*. The other small erect stone, midway between A and I, has much the same size and features. Between B and C there is shown in outline another of these small stones in line with the great pillars which remain on the E. arc : and it is quite clear that if this remarkable and novel feature of alternating each tall stone with a very small, but vertical, block was originally carried out all around the intermediate ring, there would have been eighteen stones in all. Without the most arduous and careful excavation in these interspaces, however, it would be extremely difficult, if not impossible, to prove that these small blocks did once stand on the eastern semi-circle.

As illustrating the general size of the great stones, when fully exposed to view, the dimensions of the four fallen blocks are here

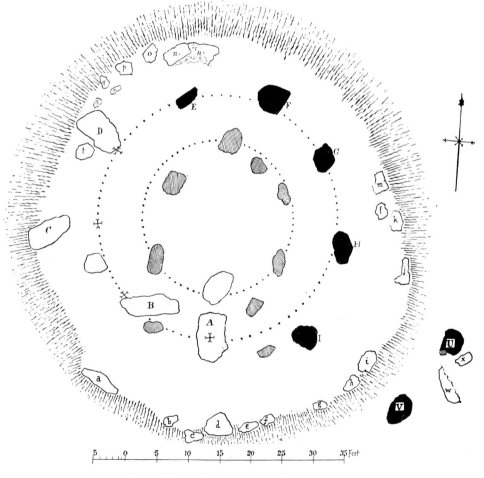

STONE CIRCLE, CROFTMORAIG.   GROUND PLAN.

given :— A, 7 feet 7 inches by 4 feet 10 inches, and fully 2 feet thick : B, 9 feet 2 inches by 3 feet 9 inches (on upper face), and 2 feet 9 inches thick : C, 8 feet by 4 feet, and 3 feet 6 inches thick : D, 7 feet by 4 feet 6 inches, and 3 feet thick at its vertical outer edge.

The five upright stones of the intermediate ring measure as follows :— I, the S.E. stone, 5 feet 6 inches in height, and in girth 11 feet : H, the E. stone, 5 feet 8 inches in height, pyramidal in contour, and in girth 11 feet 4 inches : G, the N.E. stone, 5 feet 3 inches in height, and 11 feet in girth : the next stone, F, 5 feet 7½ inches in height and 13 feet 6 inches in girth : and stone E, nearest to the N. on the W. arc, stands 6 feet 3 inches in height, and measures round the base 9 feet 3 inches.

3. The stones forming the inner ring, which is broad oval in form, are eight in number, quite erect, with one exception : the fallen one (shown in outline) is due south of one set at the north point, and the distance between the two is 23 feet 8 inches. If, however, the distance between the N. stone and the E. one at the S.S.E. be taken, this diameter is 26 feet, as of one of 21 feet taken between the N.W. and the S.E. stone : but between these last two there is a third almost exactly midway.

The fallen stone measures 5 feet 10 inches by 3 feet 9 inches : the N.W. stone is 4 feet 6 inches in height, the S.W. stone 3 feet 6 inches, the N. stone 3 feet 4 inches, and the N.E. one 2 feet 6 inches, and the stone between it and the fallen block, 3 feet 4 inches in height.

4. In addition to the feature above noticed, of tall stones alternating with much smaller ones, Croftmoraig possesses another noticeable arrangement, in the presence of the two great, massive monoliths (U and V on the plan), standing like the remains of a portal, nearly eight feet outside of the boundary ridge on the S.E. Neither of these stones is now absolutely vertical, stone U leaning considerably out towards the S.E., and V having a very slight lean inwards to the circle. The former is 6 feet 2 inches in vertical height, with a basal girth of nearly 12 feet, which is probably an under estimate, for there are two large fragments (w and x) which appear to have been severed from this stone, the edges of which nearest the fragments are rough and sharp. The latter (V) stands 6 feet 4 inches in height and girths 11 feet 8 inches.

Single outstanding monoliths exist in connection with circles at Balquhain and Druidstone in Aberdeenshire, but this is the first site on which two imposing stones fully as high and massive as those composing the circle itself, have been observed grouped together outside the circumference. Reference will be made later on to the cup-markings on this group of stones.

In 1787, when the poet Burns made his tour of the Highlands and visited Aberfeldy and Kenmore, he noticed this circle in passing along the public road, and made the following entry in his diary, " Druids' Temple, three circles of stones, the outermost sunk, the second has thirteen stones remaining : the innermost eight, two large detached ones like a gate to the south-east—say prayers in it."

Newhall Stones.[1]

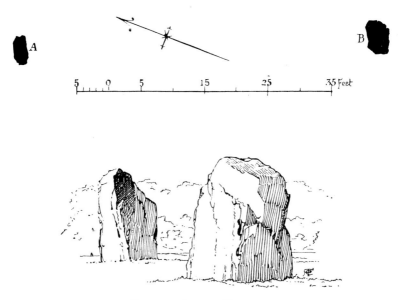

STANDING STONES, NEWHALL.

There are two great standing stones just within the Principal Gate leading to Taymouth Castle. The stone A (see plan) stands at a distance of 54 feet to the N.N.W. of B—a somewhat greater diameter than is common among the Perthshire Circles. These stones are almost equal in height—A 4 feet 9 inches, B 4 feet 7 inches—and they are both rugged blocks of a rough species of diorite. A measures round the base 10 feet 8 inches, and B 14 feet. Local tradition says that at one time there was a paved way connecting the circle, of which these stones are the remains, with the great Croftmoraig circle. The district lying between Cromalltan, the little burn to the west of Newhall, and Bolfracks is called Stix. This name is derived from the Gaelic word *Stuicean*, the Stocks, which no doubt had reference to the standing stones.

(1) Proc. Soc. Ant. Scot., Vol. XLVI., p. 138.

Circle at Dalreoch, Comrie Bridge.[1]

This site is close to the river Tay, on the north bank. The road from Kenmore to Comrie Bridge along the foot of Drummond Hill passes within sixty yards of it. The five stones here are standing, and as shown in the plan they have the following dimensions :— Stone A, 3 feet 3 inches above ground, D is 3 feet, B 2 feet 10 inches, C 2 feet 3 inches, while E is flat and

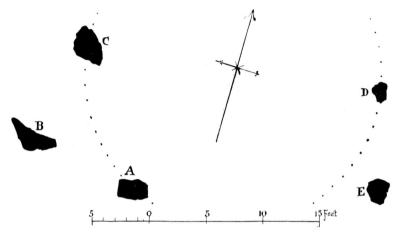

STONE CIRCLE, COMRIE BRIDGE.

only a few inches in thickness. The basal girths, taking them in the same order are respectively, 7 feet 6 inches, 6 feet, 9 feet 2 inches, 8 feet 11 inches, and 6 feet. Three of the stones, A, C, and D rest upon the circumference of a true circle whose diameter is 26 feet, but though B does occupy a symmetrical position on a circle of 31 feet in diameter, concentric with the first, the south-east stone does not fall in with this arrangement. There is no doubt that this circle was at one time much larger and more complete, but standing as it does at the edge of a cultivated field, the majority of the stones have been removed. It is possible that one or more of those remaining have been shifted from their original positions. An examination of the ground was made here recently with the spade, but nothing of any interest was found.

Circle at Greenlands,[2] Remony Hill.

This interesting circle is situated in a plantation about a mile to the south-east of the Acharn Falls, and two hundred yards to the west of Allt Mhucaidh, the burn that

(1) Proc. Soc. Ant. Scot., Vol. XLIV., p. 136.
(2) Proc. Soc. Ant. Scot., Vol. XLIII., p. 272, and Proc. Soc. Ant. Scot., Vol. XLIV., p. 134.

flows past Remony Lodge to Loch Tay. The height above sea-level is 1240 feet, and it is one of the highest recorded sites in Scotland. Before the circle was enclosed by the present plantation some seventy years ago the view from the site was incomparably beautiful. It extended from Faragon on the north-east to Ben Bhreac on the south-west, and took in Schiehallion, the bold heights above the Pass of Glenlyon, Meall Gruidh, and the Ben Lawers range. In the foreground lies Loch Tay, and behind it there rises the steep slope of Drummond Hill which shuts off the valley of Fortingall.

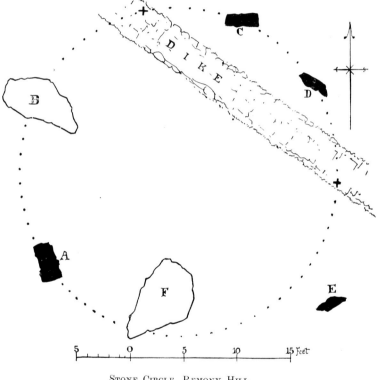

STONE CIRCLE, REMONY HILL.

The stones in this group are seven in number, of which four are erect, and they all appear to be of dioretic schist. There appears to have been one more stone originally. On the south-west is stone A, the tallest, with pointed top, 5 feet 7 inches in height, oblong in contour, and measuring at the base 9 feet 5 inches. Having several deep, horizontal fissures, this stone bears an odd resemblance to masonry. The next stone, B, lies prostrate measuring 7 feet 4 inches by 4 feet, and about 1 foot in thickness above the ground. The little oblong stone, C, on the other side of the dike, stands only 1 foot 10 inches above ground, and is probably a mere fragment of a larger block. At D the stone is 4 feet 3 inches in height, and is a very narrow slab-like piece. Stone E, which has a very decided lean over towards the interior of the circle, is 4 feet 2 inches high, and in basal girth is 6 feet 6 inches. Like the others it is angular and thinnish in proportion to its breadth. Stone F measures 8 feet 2 inches by 5 feet 2 inches, and its position with the narrow end resting almost on the circumference, suggests, as in other cases, the probability that it was this narrow end which was buried when the stone was erected. The seventh stone[1] which was discovered in 1924 underneath a thin layer of turf lies partly below the dike. It measures 5 feet 6 inches by 4 feet 8 inches, and judged by its position, it had fallen outwards from the circumference towards the north-west. The diameter of the circle measuring from stone A to B is 30 feet. Mr. Coles believes that the blocks composing the circle were brought from the low, cliffy ledges near at hand.

Circle at Machuim, Lawers.[2]

This circle is situated on a sloping field, west of the public road to Killin shortly before it crosses the Lawers Burn. It stands at an elevation of over 700 feet above sea-level. The six massive stones originally constituting the circle now occupy the positions shown in the plan, extending over a space of about 22 feet by 19 feet, and rather nearer the west end than in the middle of a long, oval, strongly-defined, artificial-looking mound, which measures 45 feet by 36 feet. The edges, as well as the interior, of the mound are so densely over-grown with a vigorous growth of bracken and small bushes as to preclude a thorough investigation. The diameter of the circle measured through the centres of the standing stones is 19 feet 6 inches.

The dimensions and positions of the stones are as follows :—
Stone A, 4 feet 10 inches high, basal girth 12 feet 5 inches. Stone B, 4 feet, nearly vertical, girth 12 ft. 3 inches. Stone C, 3 feet 7 inches, vertical, girth 8 feet 6 inches. Stone D, 5 feet 7 inches long by 3 feet broad, fallen. Stone E, 4 feet 5 inches, vertical, girth 10 feet. Stone F, 6 feet 5 inches long by 4 feet 10 inches broad, fallen. Between A and B, and between B and C are small earthfast stones about ten inches high, and close to D is an oblong slab too small to have formed one of the standing stones : it may have been moved from a more central spot between D and E. Between E and F there lies part of what appears to be a somewhat large stone, nearly flush with the

(1) Proc. Soc. Ant. Scot., Vol. LIX., p. 75.
(2) Proc. Soc. Ant. Scot., Vol. XLIV., p. 126.

B

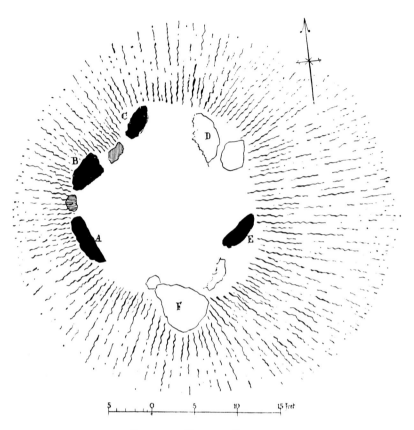

CIRCLE AT MACHUIM, LAWERS.

ground, flat, and with the inner edge running into the grass. The position of stone F suggests that, when erect, its narrow end was embedded, and its broad end stood up perhaps to the height of 4 feet 6 inches or thereby : if so, it would be well in keeping with the others. It is probable that Stone D was originally based close to where the oblong, flat stone now lies. Allow about two feet for depth in founding, and its top would have been about parallel with that of stone C, its nearest companion. The mound on which the stones are set is about three feet above the general level of the surrounding field. A recent examination of the ground around the circle after the crop had been removed from the field suggests that at one time there was an outer circle of stones concentric with the existing one. Most of the stones were removed in order to make more of the field available for cultivation, but there are still large stones lying buried within a few inches of the surface, and here and there they appear above the ground. This circle, as also the next to be described at Kinnell, came under the notice of Pennant when he visited the district in 1772.

Stone Circle at Kinnell, Killin.[1]

This well preserved circle is situated close to the old home of the Macnabs at Kinnell. It is within the policies, and near the corner of a broad, level field called Kinnell Park. It stands in the centre of the magnificent scenery that surrounds the village of Killin. There are six stones, five of which are standing in their original position. From Pennant's reference to this circle it would appear that the six stones were standing when he saw it.

(1) Proc. Soc. Ant. Scot , Vol. XLIV., p. 130.

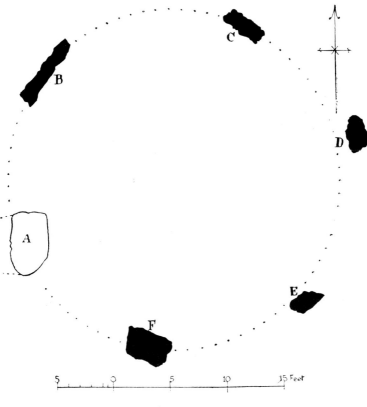

STONE CIRCLE, KINNELL, KILLIN.

Taking the stones in order, their dimensions and characteristics are as follows :— Stone A, 6 feet 3 inches high, springs from an oblong base which girths 11 feet 4 inches, to a rough, irregular top. Stone B, leans forward towards the centre of the circle, and measures along its sloping back 6 feet 9 inches, the present height from the ground to its upper edge being 4 feet. It is of smooth, granitiferous schist, and free from the deep fissures and rifts so common in these stones. Stone C, a very rectangular, but narrow block of schist, has a girth at the base of 9 feet, but tapers up from both ends to a pyramidal summit, 5 feet 4 inches above the ground. Its inner surface is over 6 feet in breadth. Stone D, 4 feet 6 inches high, is a broad, flat-topped, very massive block, measuring 9 feet 5 inches round the base, but near the middle of its height, 11 feet 2 inches. Stone E, the shortest of the group, is only 4 feet high, has a rough, uneven top, and a basal girth of 8 feet 11 inches. Stone F, the tallest, measures 6 feet 4 inches in height, but in girth only 7 feet 3 inches. It is very rough, vertical, fissured in many places, and full of white quartz veins.

Mr. Coles says that, although the circle is comparatively small and well-defined, the positions of the stones do not conform to perfect regularity as points on the circumference. A diameter of 29 feet exactly bisects three of the erect stones, B, C, and F, but leaves the other two untouched. The interspaces of the settings are not all quite equal, yet the stones stand proportionately near enough to each other to give one a satisfying impression that these six megaliths represent the group in its completeness, and that there are no smaller blocks between any two of them. The space enclosed by these stones is quite smooth and level, bearing no indication of having at any time been disturbed.

Stone Circle at Inishewan.

There is an interesting group of five large stones in front of the modern farmhouse of Inishewan, Glendochart, that has hitherto escaped the notice of archaeologists. The arrangement and general characteristics of these rough blocks strongly suggest that at one time they formed part of a stone circle. This house is delightfully situated on a terrace about a quarter of a mile to the north of the river Dochart, and almost directly opposite Luib railway station. The stones stand between the house and the edge of the terrace which runs with a steep slope down to the low-lying field that extends along the river bank.

The measurements and positions of the stones are as follows :— The first stone stands 19 yards south of the front door of the house. It is 4 feet high, and has a basal girth of 11 feet 10 inches. It shows a bore mark on the north-east side where a portion was broken off. The second stone is 20 yards west of the first.

Its height is only 1 foot 9 inches, but its girth is 11 feet 6 inches. The third stone is 12 yards due north from the second. It is a rough, irregular mass, with a sloping ledge on the west side, somewhat resembling a seat. Its height is 3 feet 3 inches, and its basal girth 18 feet 1 inch. From north to south it measures 5 feet 6 inches. The fourth stone is 12 yards north-east from the third, and was included in an old dike that runs along the south-east side of a path that leads to the back door of the house. Its height is 3 feet, and in basal girth it measures 12 feet 1 inch. The last stone in the group is lying on the ground, and rises only 7 inches above the turf. Its length from north to south is 5 feet, and its greatest breadth is 2 feet 7 inches. Inishewan was for many generations the home of a well-known branch of the Clan Macnab. That these stones have been allowed to remain so near the dwelling-house can only be due to the fact that they were regarded with veneration and awe. The present house stands farther forward on the terrace than the old one did, and probably some stones were cleared away when it was built. From the existing stones it is difficult to determine what type of circle they originally formed part of, but some of them are still on the arc of a circle.

Fingal's Stone, Killin.[1]

Both the Old and the New Statistical Accounts of the parish of Killin make reference to a site near the village that had been pointed out from time immemorial as the burial-place of Fingal, the hero of Celtic folk stories. At this point, which is in the middle of a field immediately behind the Schoolhouse, there is a standing stone, 2 feet 8 inches high and 5 feet in girth. The stone had fallen, but in 1889 it was re-erected by Mr. Malcolm Ferguson, a patriotic native of Breadalbane. Without any reference to the original arrangement a smaller stone was fixed on the top, and others were placed near it. The lands in the vicinity of Fingal's Stone used to be known as Stix. The name suggests that here, as at Stix, between Kenmore and Aberfeldy, there were a number of standing stones, of which this one alone remains.

Standing Stone at Acharn, Killin.

Just below the farm-house of Acharn, Killin, a single stone stands in a field close to the public road that leads to Lix Toll. Its height is 3 feet 10 inches and its girth at the base 6 feet 2 inches. Land stones gathered from the field have been thrown around it, and take away somewhat from its height. This solitary stone is possibly the sole survivor of a group that once formed a circle. The site is in full view of Ben Lawers to the north-east and of Ben More to the south-west.

(1) Proc. Soc. Ant. Scot., Vol. XLVI., p. 264.

Standing Stones at Tirarthur.

Mr. C. G. Cash in his notes on this district in the *Proceedings* of the Society of Antiquaries of Scotland, describes a linear setting of stones that stand on the farm of Tirarthur, near the shore of Loch Tay, about two miles from Killin. These large stones do not appear, however, to have any archæological significance. They may have formed part of an old boundary wall. When the wall was demolished they were found too large, and too deeply fixed in the ground to admit of easy removal.

Standing Stone at Croft-an-tygan, Lawers.

The last of these megalithic monuments to be noticed is a great, irregularly-shaped slab which stands on the farm of Easter Croft-an-tygan, Lawers. It is situated at the foot of Ben Lawers, and about half a mile due west from the Hotel, the upper windows of which are visible from the site. In an old map this field is called "An Caisteal Mor," which means, "The Great Castle." The name suggests that near here there once stood a strong erection of some kind. The height of the stone is fully 6 feet 6 inches, and its greatest breadth 6 feet. Its thickness is between 14 and 18 inches. The slab bears no cup-markings, but about 150 yards from it, and in a direct line between it and the Hotel, there is a large boulder which bears six or seven cups.

These great circles and standing stones awaken surprise and wonder in the minds of all who look at them. For two centuries popular imagination associated their origin with the worship of the Druids, and they came to be generally known as "Druid Stones," or "Druid Temples." This explanation, which had no historical foundation whatever, seems to have been entirely disproved by the relics found when the soil around and within the circles has been examined. Such relics consist of incinerated bones, urns, and other articles. When the centre of the circle above Acharn was dug up in 1924, a deposit of burnt bones and charcoal was found at a depth of five inches below the surface. The circles acquired in the minds of men a sacred significance, as burial-places still do, and they were regarded with fear and reverence, a fact that largely accounts for their preservation throughout the long ages of their existence, even in places where they interfered with cultivation. It required no small effort and power of organisation to erect these circles. The stones are everywhere arranged according to a definite plan. The plan was no doubt inspired by ideas of a religious and moral nature, although as yet we cannot say what these ideas were. Dr. Joseph Anderson concludes that our ancestors of the Bronze Age must have attained to a high degree of culture and civilization judging by the character of the monuments that they have left behind them.

The Bronze Age.

Cup-markings on Rocks and Boulders.

The district of Breadalbane is particularly rich in mysterious markings to be found on rocks and stones in many parts of Scotland as well as in England and Continental countries. These markings are generally referred to the Bronze Age, although they have also been found alongside of Christian symbols. One comes across "Fairy Foot-prints," as the old people used to call the cup-markings, in great numbers all the way between Aberfeldy and Tyndrum, and from the lowest levels by the shore of Loch Tay to the height of fully two thousand feet on the slopes of Ben Lawers. The sculpturings consist of a variety of designs. The most common are small cup-shaped depressions measuring from $1\frac{1}{2}$ inches to 4 inches in diameter, and from $\frac{1}{2}$ inch to 2 inches in depth. Sometimes cups are found surrounded by one or more concentric rings, and these again may be connected with another series of the same character by grooves, or channels, cut into the rock surface. Occasionally one finds

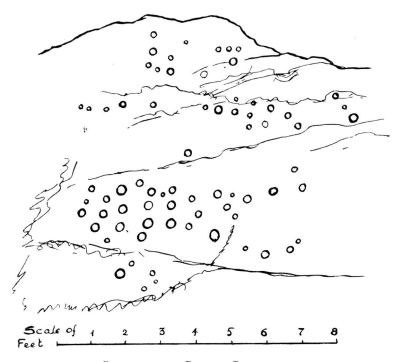

CUP-MARKING ON ROCK AT CRAGGANTOLL.

two large adjacent cups united by a short, broad channel, the whole design suggesting the shape of a human foot. The best known specimen of this kind is Cas-lorg Pheallaidh (Peallaidh's Foot-mark), on a rock in Glenlyon. These different varieties of rock carvings are to be found throughout Breadalbane, and in many instances several designs may be seen on the same rock surface.

The best known example of simple cup-marks in our district is that on the ridge of rock behind the farm-house of Caraggan-toll,[1] Lawers. This knoll, which gives its name, "the Rocky Knoll of the Holes," to the farm, is situated about 150 yards to the south of the public road leading to Killin at a point two miles west from Ben Lawers Hotel. It commands a wide outlook over Loch Tay and the surrounding country. There are at least over a hundred impressions on the rock, some of which have become very shallow owing to the weathering of the ages.

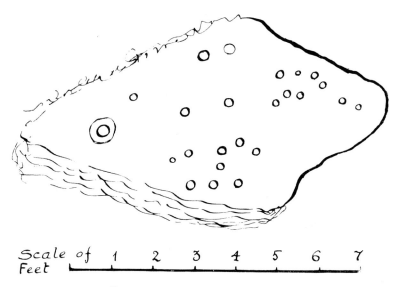

Scale of 1   2   3   4   5   6   7
Feet

CUP-MARKING ON ROCKS IN GLENLOCHAY.

Ringed cup-markings may be seen on a rock right opposite the Keeper's Cottage, on the farm of Duncroisk,[2] Glenlochay, and near the north bank of the river. Fully a hundred yards of rock surface are here exposed, bearing in all 152 cups, seventeen of which have single, and two, double rings around them.

There are twenty-two cups, one of which has a ring round it, on a stone on Mid-Lix Farm,[3] Killin. This stone is situated

(1) Proc. Soc. Ant. Scot., Vol. XLVI., p. 275.
(2) Proc. Soc. Ant. Scot., Vol. XLVI., p. 270.   (3) Ibid, Vol. XLVI, p. 267.

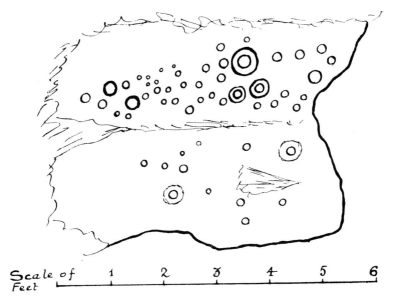

Scale of
Feet   1   2   3   4   5   6

CUP-MARKINGS ON ROCKS IN GLENLOCHAY.

about a hundred yards south of the railway, and about twenty yards east of the road leading from Killin to Glenogle.

At the east end of Loch Tay, on the farm of Balmacnaughton, at an elevation of at least a thousand feet, there is a rocky knoll with a hundred cups. The knoll is situated close to the wall which encloses the plantation on Kenmore Hill, and is about a quarter of a mile due east from the shepherd's house. Here there are simple cups, ringed cups, grooves, and footlike impressions.

Two miles east from this knoll, on the Braes of Balloch above Taymouth Castle, is the well-known Boulder[1] with spiral sculptures. Its position is indicated on the O.S. Map. This type of design is comparatively rare in Scotland. There are altogether nine or ten small centre cups on the Braes of Balloch Boulder, and each cup is surrounded by a series of concentric rings. At the sides there are two oblong grooves. The surface, which is smooth and flat, with a slight incline to the north, is about 4 feet long and 4 feet broad. The Boulder lies about 730 yards north-east of Tombuie Cottage, which stands by the side of the road leading from Kenmore to Amulree.

In the description given above of the Croftmoraig stone circle reference was made to the long prostrate stone in the outermost ring which bears 19 cup-marks. Since the circle

(1) Proc. Soc. Ant. Scot., Vol. XXIX., p. 94.

CUP-MARKED BOULDER, BRAES OF TAYMOUTH.

was surveyed by Mr. Coles it has been noticed that several of the upright stones also show cup-markings on their perpendicular surfaces. Some of these are quite distinct, but others are so worn through weathering that they can only be traced with the fingers.

A few years ago an examination of the ground around Dun-mac-Tuathal on Drummond Hill led to the discovery of thirty cup-marks, two of which are encircled by rings, on a rock situated about a hundred yards to the west of the fort. There are also three cups on rock ridges within the enclosed area of the fort itself. One of these has a diameter of six inches. Boulders bearing marks that must have been made by man are very numerous in the neighbourhood of the Braes of Balloch Boulder, on Clach-an-tuirc, and on boulders within the Cow-park at Fearnan, in a field above Ben Lawers Hotel, and on the farms of Carie, Carwhin, Morenish and Tirarthur.

There are several very distinct markings on a flat stone that lies in front of a ruinous cottage on the farm of Callelochan; on boulders below Cill-ma-Charmaig, Ardeonaig; on rocks near the Old Shooting Range, Killin; and on stones situated near the road between Crianlarich and Tyndrum. So numerous and wide-spread, indeed, are these cup-markings that one is almost certain to find some in every part of the district. A recent examination of a small area on the farm of Carwhin, to the north of the public road, revealed six boulders all near one another, and each bearing five or six cups. The locating and recording of all rock-sculpturings in the Breadalbane district would entail much time and labour; but the work would be well worth doing, and should prove most interesting for anyone able and willing to undertake it.

The fact that rock-carvings are frequently found in association with stone circles and burials of the Bronze Age would seem to indicate that they are the work of the same people. No one has, however, been able to give a satisfactory explanation of cup-markings. It has been suggested that the cups were made for holding libations offered to spirits. This theory is disproved by the cups that are found on the upright surfaces of rocks. It has been also suggested that the markings represent the positions of the heavenly bodies, and that they were made by wise men who brought astronomical lore from the East to these regions. It would be very surprising if it could be proved that the people who inhabited the country when these sculpturings were made could have had such a knowledge of science as this theory presupposes. Some parties maintain that the markings were made by childless wives in order to appease a deity who was believed to be angry with them. It is stated that such a practice still prevails among certain hill tribes in India. This explanation, like the others, presents difficulties owing to the variety and the highly artistic character of some of the designs adopted. For the present, cup-markings and many rock carvings remain among the enigmas of Archæology.

CHAPTER II.

Prehistoric Period—The Early Iron Age.

SOME time between five and three hundred years before the Christian Era, iron began to be used in Scotland for the manufacture of cutting instruments and weapons. The use of bronze was gradually restricted to the composition of articles of an ornamental character. The first appearance of iron was probably contemporary with the arrival in our Northern Land of the earliest wave of the Celtic race. This people had already become masters of South Britain, and now they advanced to the north as an aristocracy of warriors. They belonged to the same branch of the Celtic race as the ancestors of the modern Welsh, and, like them, they spoke the old British language. The invaders brought with them a more advanced culture, as well as the art of smelting and welding iron into implements and weapons. We may therefore be prepared to find great changes taking place with their advent. The Celts vanquished the ancient native people, but they by no means wiped them out, as they are often stated to have done. The conquerors adopted many native customs, and even took over some native place-names.

Our information about the peoples of the Stone and the Bronze Ages has been mainly derived from the cairns and the cemeteries where they laid the remains of their dead, and from the " goods " which they piously placed beside them in the graves. Until very recently few sites inhabited in those remote times had yielded relics ; but the discovery of a house of the Bronze Age in the remote Shetlands, in which swords and axes had been cast, has thrown much light on their metallurgical processes. On the other hand our information regarding the people of the Early Iron Age is chiefly obtained from the sites that were occupied by the living. The Celts were a military people, and when they had subdued the ancient tribes they kept on warring among themselves. They not only knew how to fight on the battle-field, but they had also learned how to defend themselves within strongly fortified positions. They thus combined the knowledge of architecture with the art of war. It is to this combination in their character that we owe the remarkable number of ancient forts to be found in all parts of Scotland—the circular forts of Central Scotland, the strongholds perched on hills, the artificial islands in lakes, and the earth-houses exposed from time to time by the plough. Examination of such sites has shed a flood of light upon the dark centuries that preceded the dawn of history in our land.

Circular Forts.

The Celtic warrior tribes that settled in our region found here a congenial home. The wild mountains and glens of Breadalbane, Glenlyon, and Atholl afforded them splendid bases from which to wage war upon their enemies, and also strong natural defences to which they could retire in times of attack. It is not surprising, therefore, to find numerous traces of these Celtic warriors scattered throughout North Perthshire. Instead of the Brochs of the North of Scotland we have here a remarkable series of circular forts. Between Tyndrum and Pitlochry the sites of over thirty forts have been located, and the existence of many more is indicated by place-names attaching to fields, hillocks and burns.

Legend and heroic Gaelic poetry have associated these round forts with the Fiann, who are believed to have been bands of warriors acting under the rule of a leader, or chief. The most famous of these leaders was Fionn, the renowned Fingal of Celtic tales. The first person to draw attention to the round forts in the Breadalbane district was Thomas Pennant, when visiting Perthshire in 1772. On that occasion he examined three " castles " situated near Pitlochry, and made investigations regarding several others in Breadalbane and Glenlyon. He procured a great deal of information with regard to the strongholds from the Rev. James Stuart at that time minister of Killin. In Glenlyon these defences are called to this day, " Caistealan nam Fiann," the Castles of the Fiann. Pennant quotes a Gaelic saying which he no doubt got from Mr. Stuart, and which gives the local tradition about them :—

" Bha da chaisteal deug aig Fionn,
Ann an Crom-ghleann dubh nan Clach."

" Twelve castles had Fionn,
In the dark bent Glen of the Stones."

Researches carried out by Professor W. J. Watson[1] a few years ago show that the " castles " were widely scattered over the glens and valleys of Central Scotland, and especially throughout the ancient province of Fortrenn, which lay between the Forth and Tay. In southern Perthshire the forts were called " Kiers," and in the northern part of the county " Duns." The walls were built of huge blocks of dry, undressed stones, many of which were six feet in length. They ranged from nine to fourteen feet in thickness. The diameters of the areas enclosed by the walls generally measure from 68 to 95 feet, and, when intact, the height of the walls would vary from twelve to fifteen feet. The low doorway was very narrow at the outside, but broadened inwards. The round forts were not so well built as the brochs, and they would appear to have had neither passages nor chambers in the walls. Unlike the hill forts to be noted later, the circular

(1) Proc. Soc. Ant. Scot., Vol. XLVII., p. 30.

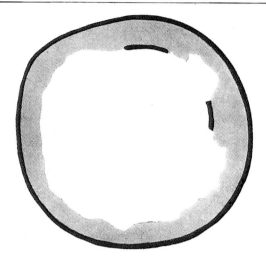

PLAN OF RORO CIRCULAR FORT.

forts were invariably situated on low ground, and well within
the range of what in later times became cultivated land. Indeed,
the disappearance of many of these buildings is due to the fact
that the stones were cleared away and the plough driven through
their foundations.

The forts were frequently grouped closely together, as if
arranged to enable their occupants to assist each other in times
of attack. At Cashlie, in Glenlyon, there are four distinct forts
within the space of one mile, and tradition bears witness to the
existence of a fifth. In the neighbourhood of Aberfeldy, on the
south side of the Tay, the name, " Dun," attaching to several
farms suggests a similar grouping of forts. These names,
beginning with the east-most are, Duntaggart, Duntaylor,
Dun-na-skaig, and Dun-na-cree. The ruins of some of these
forts are still visible, but all traces of others have been removed
by cultivation.

The round forts of Breadalbane have been practically all
demolished, but with the aid of an atlas of the district, made
in 1769, it has been possible to indicate the position of a few
sites. Pennant refers to one that stood on the north side of
Loch Tay, five miles east of Killin, and above the Killin to
Kenmore road. No trace or even tradition of this fort can be
found, but the atlas shows that a " castle " stood in a field on
the farm of Rhynachuilg, which corresponds to the position
given by Pennant. Strangely enough, that careful observer
failed to note the fort that was situated on Dunlochay, the
eminence lying between Finlarig Castle and the river Lochay.
It is probable, however, that by 1772 the site had been cleared

entirely of stones. The name, "Dunchroisg," in Glenlochay, bears witness to the fort that once stood at the southern entrance to Laraig Bhreislich, the pass leading over the mountain to Glenlyon. The atlas gives the locality of another on the farm of Tombreck, Lochtayside, about a quarter of a mile above the public road, and in a field to the east of the burn that flows from the Corrie of Carie. This field had, until recent times, been known to the tenants of the farm as, "An Caisteal." The Tombreck fort, and that known as, "An Caisteal Mor," on the farm of Easter Croftintygan, where the standing stone is situated, no doubt guarded the passes to Glenlyon across the shoulder of Ben Lawers. There do not seem to have been so many forts on the south side of Loch Tay, but two sites are indicated by the old atlas. One fort stood at Callelochan, immediately above the Keeper's House, and to the west of the burn, which still bears the name, Allt an Duin, the "Burn of the Fort." The atlas gives two names in this locality, Tom a Chaisteil, the "Hillock of the Castle," and Leod a Chaisteil, the "Slope of the Castle." This fort, situated six hundred feet above Loch Tay, and at a point where the hillside takes a sharp bend to the south, must have commanded a most extensive view. The old name of a field lying to the east of Dall, Ardeonaig, "Croft Dunard," the "Croft of the High Fort," indicates that at one time there were forts in this neighbourhood which served the inhabitants, and guarded the pass from Glenlednock over the Carn Dearg. According to the atlas of 1769 there were ruins of an "Ancient Castramentation" at Firbush Point on the farm of Auchmore. An examination of this little peninsula revealed the foundation of a very thick wall that at one time ran across its neck, and formed a defence on the landward side. It is probable that the stones were removed for the erection of the small pier and harbour close by.

Reference to a map will show that all the circular forts were situated near passes that lead over the mountains. It is evident from this that they were designed not only as a protection for the rude shelters erected behind the walls, but also for the purpose of providing watch towers along the tracks by which cattle thieves would drive their *creach* before them. Professor Watson excavated a round fort at Borenich, near Loch Tummel, in order to find a clue as to the probable period to which these strongholds belong. The relics recovered were not numerous. They consisted of small shapeless pieces of iron, a bone bodkin a stone spinning whorl, stone discs, the broken half of a much worn quern. Three distinct hearths were disclosed within the enclosure. All this goes to prove that the people who lived within the forts, the Fiann of Gaelic Folk-tales, were acquainted with the working of iron, grew and ground grain, and could spin wool. They belonged to the Early Iron Age, and were engaged in agricultural and pastoral pursuits. For that reason they erected their strongholds near what was then, and in many cases still is, cultivated land.

Hill Forts.

Hill forts, of which a chain of over twenty extends right across Scotland from Killin to Stonehaven, were also erected during the Early Iron Age. These strongholds differ in several respects from the round forts just described. They are generally at a much higher elevation. Some of them are on hills of over a thousand feet above sea-level. The sites were usually chosen with a view to the advantages for defence afforded by rocks, ravines, and steep slopes. The shape is frequently oval, but the plan varies according to the formation of the ground. Two forts of this class fall to be mentioned, Dun-mac-Tuathal, on Drummond Hill, Kenmore, and Caisteal Braigh-an-raoir, near Killin. There are three others just outside the district we are dealing with, namely, Dun Geal at Fortingall, the Dun above Aberfeldy, and the Black Castle of Balnaguard.

Dun-mac-Tuathal, locally known as the "Roman Camp," is referred to by Pennant, who does not appear, however, to have visited the place. It has been surveyed and accurately described by Mr. Alexander Hutcheson,[1] and by Dr. Christison, for the Society of Antiquaries of Scotland. This well known *dun* is

(1) Proc. Soc. Ant. Scot., Vol. XXIII., p. 356.

PART OF WALL, DUN-MAC-TUATHAL.

situated on the eastern spur of Drummond Hill, just above the old, ivy-covered Castle of Comrie. From its elevated position of 900 feet above sea-level it commands a most extensive view of the valley of the Tay. On the south and east sides the rock is steep, and precipitous, but the ground slopes less steeply on the other sides. The walls of the fort follow the contour of the hill, twisting out and in to suit the exigencies of the site. They thus form a somewhat irregular square figure. The area enclosed measures about three hundred feet by two hundred feet. There is a short wall branching off to include a natural platform. The curved wall at the north-east angle encloses a space of about one hundred and sixty feet long, where there is a spur rising towards the summit. On the west, the most vulnerable side, two additional walls have been thrown up on the side of a hollow, some twenty-five feet deep, which separates the fort from the ascending slope of Drummond. At the bottom of this hollow is a spring of water which no doubt supplied the needs of the occupants. The main wall of the fort is much broken down, but in places the outer and the inner faces still stand. The fragments of the walls show that they had been erected of rough and massive unhewn blocks without any mortar or cementing material. The wall is nine feet in thickness, and the outer face is almost perpendicular. On the inside it slopes considerably. It would appear that the ground inside had been raised or filled in at the back of the walls, probably to enable those inside to scale the walls for defence. Judging by the quantity of stones lying about, Mr. Hutcheson estimated that the height of the walls must have been at least from twelve to fifteen feet. Many of the stones are of large dimensions, and, while some of them may have been quarried from the face of the rocks above, no tool mark could be discovered upon any of them. In the Statistical Report of Dull, of 1842, it is stated that the principal access led from the north-east, along the edge of the precipice, and that it was covered on the north-west by the projecting wall. There was also an entrance leading into the enclosure from the south-west. The name of this fort, " Dun-mac-Tuathal," suggests some association with Inchtuthil on the Tay. Tuathal may have been the son of Argusto, the Abbot of Dunkeld mentioned in the Annals of Ulster as having died in 865 A.D.

Caisteal Braigh-an-raoir.

The title of this fort means—the Castle at the upper part of the Outfield. It is situated at the west end of Loch Tay, on the farm of Auchmore. Timothy Pont's attention was drawn to it in the passing, and its position is therefore shown with considerable accuracy in Blaeu's Atlas, on which it is marked as "Bareyra." Pennant, who paid a visit to the place, calls the stronghold, "Caisteal Baraora," and gives the site as being, " on

C

the south side, about a quarter of a mile from the lake, and a measured mile east of Auchmore." The fort occupies the entire summit of a prominent hillock that has the natural defence of rocky precipices some thirty feet high on all sides, except the east, where it is easily approached along a narrow ridge. This vast enclosure is oval in shape, with a length of three hundred and fifty feet, and a breadth of one hundred and fifty. The wall here, as at Dun-mac-Tuathal, was constructed of large unhewn stones. From the foundations remaining, it is evident that the builders ingeniously incorporated projecting rocks into the steep outer face in order to strengthen the defence. Pennant mentions that at the east end of the enclosed area there were indications of a rectangular building some thirty-eight feet long by ten feet wide. The outlook from this fort extends from Drummond Hill on the north-east, far up Glendochart to the west, taking in the magnificent panorama of peaks from Lawers to the Forest of Mamlorn.

Neither of the Breadalbane hill forts has been excavated, but it is probable that an examination of the ground would yield much the same relics as were found when the fort on the Castle Law at Abernethy was exposed by the spade. Here the objects found consisted of articles of stone, bone, bronze, iron, and wood, which go to prove that forts of this character were resorted to for defence over a long period of time.

Artificial Islands of Loch Tay.

The custom of constructing dwellings and places of refuge on marshes and lakes is very ancient. Heroditus, the Greek historian (B.C. 490), tells how the people living on Lake Prasias, the modern Tahinos, in the Struma Valley, Macedonia, were able to avoid being pressed into the army of Xerxes, the Persian King, because their huts were erected on platforms supported by lofty piles in the midst of the lake. Another Greek historian, Hippocritus (B.C. 460), describes how the inhabitants of the Phasis dwelt in marshes and occupied houses of timber and reeds in the midst of the water. They reached their dwellings from the shore in single tree canoes. Pile dwellings are still in use among barbarous tribes in the Malayan Archipelago, New Guinea, Venezuela, and Central Africa.

The Celtic people who brought the knowledge of iron to our land had been accustomed to construct lake dwellings, or crannogs, before they came to Britain. The remains of their erections have been discovered in the lakes of Switzerland, Austria, and other Continental countries. When they arrived in Scotland they found here many lochs with numerous natural islands capable of being converted into places of defence. There were, however, lochs in which islands did not at all exist where they were required, and it was therefore necessary to construct some. Loch Tay was of this character. It afforded no natural defences. The islands in the loch are a further evidence of the enterprise and energy of the people who built the circular forts and the hill forts.

The construction of the islands in Loch Tay must have been a most difficult matter. The water even close inshore is generally deep. Immense quantities of material in the form of tree-trunks, branches, brush-wood, stones, and gravel, would be required to raise a foundation from a depth of twenty or thirty feet, as is often the case. Five of the artificial islands on Loch Tay are marked on the O.S. Map. There are several others that appear only when the water falls to a low level during a long summer drought.

The Isle of Loch Tay.

The first island in importance as in size is the Isle[1] of Loch Tay, anciently known as Eilean nam Ban, the Island of the Women. This island, which was destined to become historic, is situated at the east end of the loch, and a quarter of a mile from the Kenmore Bridge. It is about eighty yards from the north shore. It is oval in shape, the length from east to west being sixty-six yards, and the breadth from north to south forty-six yards. A causeway that joins the island to the shore is within two feet of the surface when the loch is low. A tradition noted by Ewen MacDougall, a native of the district, over a hundred years ago, states that " this island, with twenty-three more of lesser size, was built in the loch at the expense of King Alexander the First of Scotland." The tradition bears out the undoubted artificial character of the island, but its origin is much more ancient than even King Alexander's time. The earliest mention on record of the Isle of Loch Tay is in a charter by King Alexander the First. His consort, Queen Sybilla, a natural daughter of Henry First of England, while sojourning in this quarter, took ill, and died on the island on the 12th of June, 1122 A.D. Here her remains were buried. By charter signed at Stirling, Alexander granted the island to the monks of Scone Abbey, which he had recently founded. The charter was to the following effect :— " Alexander, by the grace of God, King of the Scots, to the Bishops and Earls, and to all faithful of the whole of Scotland, health. I make it known to you that, for the honour of God and St. Mary, and all the saints, I have given for myself, and for the soul of Queen Sybilla, the Island of Loch Tay, in perpetual possession, with all the

(1) Proc. Soc. Ant. Scot., Vol. XLVII., p. 257.

RUINS OF PRIORY ON ISLE OF LOCH TAY.

rights pertaining to the same island, to Holy Trinity of Scoon, and to the Brotherhood serving God there by Monastic Rule, so that a church of God be built there for me, and for the soul of the Queen there deceased, and that this I grant to them for the present, until I shall have given them some other augmentation, so that the place may be renowned for its service to God. Herbert, Chancellor, witness at Stirling."

From this charter it is clear that the Isle of Loch Tay was large enough in the twelfth century to be the site of a royal residence, or of a nunnery, yet it bears every indication of having been artificial in origin. Some forty years ago when the ruins upon the island were being repaired, the soil was examined to a considerable depth, and it was found to consist of small stones and gravel which had evidently been deposited by human agency. At a later stage we shall have to return to the Isle of Loch Tay, and trace its story through the centuries, first as a priory cell attached to Scone, and latterly as the fortified residence of the Campbells of Glenorchy.

Spry Island.

Spry, or Spries Island, marked on the O.S. map as Isle of Spar, and now generally called " Spray Island," is situated

SPRY ISLAND.

almost opposite Kenmore Pier, and within sixty yards of the
south shore of the loch. It appears on a plan of the district
of 1720, and in its origin it was undoubtedly artificial. When
Queen Victoria visited Taymouth in 1842 the Marquis of Breadalbane caused ornamental trees and shrubs to be placed tem-
porarily upon the island, and some time afterwards the Marquis
had it considerably enlarged by transferring stones and soil
from the south shore. It was then planted with firs and alders,
and to-day it makes a decided contribution to the picturesque
appearance of the east end of the loch. The excavation made at
the side of the public road when the island was extended may
still be seen; and some of the stakes that supported the gang-
way over which the material was carried, over eighty years
ago, are standing in their original position.

Croftmartaig Island.

The Island of Croftmartaig lies about half a mile to the west
of Acharn, and thirty yards or so from a small pier that once
served a lime-kiln that has now tumbled into ruins. The channel
between this island and the shore is not more than four feet
deep when the loch falls to its summer level, but on the west
and north of the island the sides descend steeply to a depth

of fifteen feet. The surface, which has a diameter of some thirty
yards, is overgrown with small willows and alders. The map of
1769 shows the position of this island, but does not record its
name.

Eilean-nam-Breaban.

Eilean-nam-Breaban, "the Island of the Boot soles," is a somewhat conspicuous island, situated below the farm of Wester
Carwhin. It is about fifty yards from the north shore of the
loch. The island was formed on the outer end of a long,
irregularly shaped ledge of rock that extends from the shore in
a southerly direction. The channel between the island and the
shore is very shallow for the most part, except at a point where
the rock dips to the depth of five feet. The surface area is
similar to that of the Croftmartaig Island, but the height here
is greater. It is covered with a strong, natural growth of briars,
and crowned with a few alders and ash trees which make it
a prominent object. This island is mentioned in a charter of
1526, by which the superiority of the lands of Carwhin was
transferred from Haldane of Gleneagles to James Campbell of
Lawers; and in subsequent charters relating to this property.
The spelling varies. In 1526 it is "Ila Brebane," in 1546, "Ilane-
brebane," and in the atlas of 1769, "Ellan a Brippan." There
are no signs of any structure on this island beyond eighteen or
twenty large stones, so arranged as to give the appearance of
their once having formed the foundation of a wall. On the
other hand, these stones may have been laid there to protect
the island from the surf which beats strongly upon its western
side.

Eilean Puttychan.

Eilean Puttychan, probably Eilean Sputachan, "the Island
of the little Spout," is situated a short distance to the west of
the Killin Pier. It is about fifty yards in diameter, and its
surface is grown over with green sward, on which stand a few
trees. The passage between the island and the shore has become
silted up. It is referred to in a tack of 1568, by which Sir Colin
Campbell of Glenorchy let the seven markland of Morenish
Wester to Patrick Campbell, brother to Duncan Campbell of
Glenlyon. The reference to the island is in the following terms :—
" And farther he (Sir Colin) sets to the said Patrick, his isle
called Ilan Puttychan, lying in Loch Tay, opposite his lands
of Finlarig, with power to build a stable upon the port of the
said isle, for yearly payment of a sheaf of arrows, if they be
required, also with power to set six small nets upon the loch
ewis to the said isle—it being provided too, that the said Patrick
shall make his residence on the said lands or Isle so long as he
holds them."

EILEAN PUTTYCHAN.

Submerged Cairns.

Besides those five islands, which, even when the level of the loch is at its highest, are to be seen above water, there are at least seven large cairns which are visible only during a long summer drought. These cairns are all situated close to the shore, and generally rise from a depth of twenty feet, or thereby. It is probable that an examination of the sides would reveal the remains of the beams that supported the huts in which the lake-dwellers lived. Anglers on Loch Tay are careful to avoid these sunken cairns, owing to the danger of their lines being caught in them.

Among the submerged islands, with which boatmen frequenting the loch are familiar, are the following :— Cuigeal Mhairi, or "Mary's Distaff," so called because for generations it has been marked by a pole. It is situated about fifty yards from the shore, and about three hundred yards west of the Steamboat Slip at Dalerb, Kenmore. Its summit appears above water when the loch is moderately low, and an area measuring fully sixty feet across is sometimes exposed. On the shore side the water is nine feet deep, but on the other side the foundations of this immense cairn of stones are about thirty feet below the surface. There are two great cairns situated in somewhat shallow water, close to the shore below Fearnan. One is exactly opposite the Hotel, and the other lies about three hundred yards to the east. Three have been located in the neighbourhood of Ardeonaig— one to the west of the spot where the Alltvin Burn enters the loch, the second in the little bay below Dall Farmhouse, and the third in the bay to the west of the Pier. There is another cairn known to anglers near the mouth of the burn at Carwhin, and right opposite those at Ardeonaig. A large sunken cairn that has every appearance of being of an artificial nature is situated about fifty yards to the west of Kenmore Pier. Its summit never comes within four feet of the surface of the water, but, being in the way of the steamers, it must have its position marked in summer by a buoy. The water around it is very deep, especially on the outside.

The old tradition with regard to the existence of twenty-four artificial islands in Loch Tay has not been confirmed; but it is probable that a careful survey would increase the number beyond the thirteen that have been here mentioned. Although crannogs are believed to have been first introduced into this country by the people of the Early Iron Age, there is evidence to show that they were in use during the time of the Roman occupation, and, indeed, as late as the fifteenth century in some places. These little islands acquired a value and an importance beyond anything that their dimensions justified. This probably explains the inclusion of Eilean-nam-breaban, and Eilean Puttychan in charters and tacks of the sixteenth century.

CHAPTER III.

The Roman Period.

THE light of history falls for the first time upon the people who occupied the Circular forts, the Hill forts, and the Lake-dwellings of Breadalbane, in the year 80 A.D., when the Roman legions reached the Firth of Tay. Agricola had led his army across Strathclyde and the Forth Valley without encountering any resistance. Tacitus, the Roman historian, states that the barbarians were so smitten with fear that they did not dare to give him battle. The tribes dwelling beyond the Tay were not, however, going to be overawed by a mere demonstration of Imperial power. While for the next two seasons Agricola was engaged in exploring the Firths of Tay, Forth, and Clyde, and even in planning an expedition to Ireland, the Northern tribes settled all their ancient feuds, and presented a united front to the common enemy. They made successful attacks upon Roman camps, and at last Agricola, finding them troublesome, decided to punish them.

The foremost place in the first fight for the freedom of Alban against the Romans was taken by the Caledonians, who were of Celtic race and spoke the old British language. Tacitus describes them as being red-haired and powerfully built. We learn from Ptolemy's map of Britain, which was based upon information supplied to him by soldiers engaged in the campaigns of Agricola, that the Caledonians occupied the territory extending from Loch Long to the Beauly Firth. Breadalbane lay in the very heart of this wild region, and we may be certain that its warriors were in the army that awaited the advance of the Romans at Mons Graupius. The site of this famous battle has not yet been determined. The leader of the native army was Calgacus, "The Swordsman," and, judged by the address which Tacitus puts into his mouth on the eve of battle, this champion of freedom and the men who followed him, were no mean foes.

"When I reflect," Calgacus said, "on the causes of war, and the circumstances of our position, I feel a strong persuasion that our united efforts this day will prove the beginning of universal liberty to Britain. For we are undebased by slavery, and there is no land behind us. . . We, at the furthest limits of both land and liberty, have been defended to this day by the remoteness of our situation and our fame . . . Those plunderers of the world, after exhausting the land by their devastations, are rifling the ocean, stimulated by avarice, if their enemy be rich—by ambition, if poor——to ravage, to slaughter, to usurp under false titles, they call empire ; and where they make a desert they call it peace. Shall not we, untouched and unsubdued, and struggling not for acquisition, but for the security of liberty, show at the very first onset what men Caledonia has reserved for her defence ? . . Be not terrified with an idle show, and the glitter of silver and gold, which can neither protect, nor wound. . . March, then, to battle, and think of your ancestors, and think of your posterity."

At the end of the day the Romans claimed that they had gained the victory. The enemy had disappeared, retiring to the fastnesses of the mountains. Agricola could not, however, make an effectual pursuit. His scouts told him that the land beyond was desolate and inhospitable, and he thought it better not to send his soldiers through such passes as Dunkeld and Glen Almond, which the brave Caledonians were well able to defend. With the recall of Agricola by the emperor, Domitian, soon after-wards, any garrisons established north of the Tay were with-drawn. During the next hundred years the Roman legions do not appear to have advanced far beyond the camps at Ardoch and Inchtuthil, both of which were occupied for definite periods between the years 140 A.D. and 180 A.D. The southern territory, although defended by means of walls, ditches, and forts, yet provided the Caledonians with a happy hunting ground for pillage and plunder.

In the year 208 A.D. the emperor, Severus, determined to subdue the turbulent tribes of the North. He advanced in person at the head of a great force by the east of Scotland, making roads as he progressed. He managed to reach the Moray Firth, and on his return journey he may have led his army up the valley of the Spey, crossing over Drumochter into the district of Atholl. The result of this expedition was that the tribes to the north of the Forth and Clyde made terms with the emperor, and agreed to cede the region lying between the Tay and Forth. This agreement was, however, terminated by the death of Severus soon after his return to the city of York. With his influence removed, the Caledonians maintained their freedom and independence, and continued their raiding practices as before.

The question as to whether the Romans ever gained a foot-hold in Breadalbane remains to be decided. Bishop Pococke, who visited Taymouth in 1760, refers to the " Roman Camp " near Fortingall, and states that Lord Breadalbane had a copper vase with three feet, which was said to have been found close to the "Camp" in 1733. During his second visit to this district in 1772, Pennant examined the site at Fortingall, and suggested that it might have been a temporary station erected during the reign of Severus. The popular belief in the Roman origin of this mound received confirmation from reports of relics discovered in the neighbourhood from time to time. In papers contributed to the Literary and Antiquarian Society of Perth at the beginning of last century, there are definite references to some bones and a sword that had been dug out of the mound. Dr. A. Irvine of Dunkeld, a native of Fortingall, reported in 1814, the discovery of a slate-coloured stone with the Roman letters T.A.C.I.M.A. inscribed upon it with a rude chisel or stile. He further mentions that some coins of Titus, as well as Roman urns, had been found in the "Camp." All this is, however, very doubtful.

The Scottish historian, Skene, adopted Pennant's view, and concluded that the " Camp " at Fortingall had been established as an advanced station during the expedition of Severus to the North in 208 A.D. The foundation for this belief, which is the popular one, is, however, rather insecure. Sir George MacDonald, the greatest living authority on the Roman occupation of Scotland, maintains that nothing in the character of the mound, or in the relics said to have been found there, proves its origin as Roman. The inscribed stone was probably modern, and if coins were found, they had most likely been part of some plunder. The bones, the sword, and the copper vase were associated with burials of the Bronze Age, which had been made close to the megalith that is lying on the ground hard by the mound.

There are, however, definite records of two finds of Roman coins within the district of Kenmore. Pennant states that " in digging the foundation of a tower near Taymouth, fourteen silver Denarii were discovered ; but none of a later date than Marcus Aurelius." In the New Statistical Account of the parish Dr. David Duff, who had access to charters and other documents at Taymouth Castle, gives the following quotation from a manuscript which he found there, " In the year 1755, in making a road across the hill from Taymouth to Glenquaich, there were found near the crest of the hill, twelve Roman coins, about three inches under the surface of the ground, in what seemed like a bed of charcoal. They appear to be of silver, of the circumference of a sixpenny piece, but much thicker. The dies and the inscriptions of most of them are distinct and legible. They are of the Antonines, and their Empresses. They are at Taymouth." Sir George MacDonald[1] observes that the " bed of charcoal " would, no doubt, be the remains of the wooden box in which the treasure had been concealed. He is inclined to think that, in spite of differences in the circumstantial details, it is more than likely that Pennant's find and that recorded in the Taymouth manuscript are one and the same.

(1) Proc. Soc. Ant. Scot., Vol. LII., p. 263.

The information which later Roman writers give with regard to this region and the brave Caledonians who dwelt here is meagre in the extreme, and what they do tell us is second hand and probably unreliable. They say that the country was covered with woods and marshes. The rivers, no doubt, spread out far beyond their present banks, and the plains that are now in cultivation were densely wooded with trees of native growth. According to reports brought to Rome, the Caledonians had no walled towns, but lived in booths and tents. They did no cultivation, but subsisted entirely by hunting and pillage. They rejected fish, although there was plenty to be had for the catching. They had chariots which were drawn by small, nimble ponies. In battle they fought with dirks and short spears which had a bronze knob on the haft. They rattled this haft against their shields when they charged the enemy. They were swift of foot, and very brave in war. They wore hardly any clothes, so that the beasts depicted on their bodies by tattooing might be seen. The statement that they did not cultivate the soil has to be received in the light of the fact that small hand mills for grinding corn, and even sickles for cutting it have been recovered from sites inhabited during this period. The Caledonians had also their fortified towns.

For at least a hundred years after the expedition of Severus to the North, the Caledonians maintained their supremacy among the tribes of Alban. Their name always appears at the head of the lists given of the barbarians who raided and ravaged the Roman province. Neither walls, ditches, nor forts could hold them back. About the beginning of the century, however, we find a new tribe associated with the Caledonians. In 297 A.D. a Roman writer tells that Picts and Irish were enemies of the Roman Britons in the south; and in 310 A.D. another writer says, " I do not mention the woods and marshes of the Caledonians, the Picts, and others." These are the first references on record to the mysterious Picts, who are the subject of endless controversy. So far as our present knowledge with regard to them goes, the Picts appear to have been a people of Celtic origin also, who had settled in the islands of Orkney and Shetland. From there they moved south to the coasts of Caithness and Sutherland. They were given to piracy and war, and were at home on the sea. They are believed to have built those wonderful brochs in the north, of which no fewer than 362 have been located in the above-named counties alone. The influence of this warrior race gradually extended southwards, until at length they gained the supremacy over the Alban tribes. The Caledonians ceased to hold the foremost place when the Picts crossed the Grampians, and had transferred their capital from Inverness to Abernethy, on the Tay. The country was no longer called Caledonia, but Pictavia.

We are not to suppose, however, that the brave Caledonians were wiped out. They lived on, probably little affected by the change in the name and the government of the land. They continued to retain their language and their ancient customs. West Perthshire, including the district of Breadalbane, was part of the Pictish province of Fortrenn, whose people had been known to the Romans as Verturiones. Professor W. J. Watson[1] derives this name from the old British word, *Fortair*, a fortress, a name which, no doubt, had some reference to the numerous round defences in which the Verturiones lived. Under the new name of Picts, the " Men of the Strongholds " carried fire and sword through the fertile districts to the south of the Roman walls.

When, at length, the powerful arm of Rome was withdrawn in 410 A.D., the Britons within the province were left entirely to the mercy of those wild barbarians. There is evidence to show how great was the terror that their incursions awakened among a defenceless people. Gildas, who wrote about 470 A.D., speaks of the " swarthy columns of vermin from their small caverns of very narrow outlets, loathsome hordes of Scots and Picts." In another place he says, " No sooner were the Romans gone than the Picts and Scots, like snakes, which in the heat of mid-day come forth from their holes, hastily land again from their canoes . . . differing from one another in manners, but inspired with the same avidity for blood, and all the more eager to shroud their villainous faces in bushy hair, than to cover with decent clothing those parts of their bodies which required it. Moreover, having heard of the departure of our friends, and their resolution never to return, they seized with greater boldness than before on all the country to the north, as far as the wall. To oppose them there was placed on the heights a garrison equally slow to fight, and ill-fitted to flee, a useless and panic-stricken body of men, who slumbered away days and nights on their unprofitable watch. The hooked weapons of the enemy were not idle, dragging our wretched countrymen from the wall, and dashing them on the ground."

(1) Proc. Soc. Ant. Scot., Vol. XLVIII. p. 30.

CHAPTER IV.

The Coming of the Scots.

IN the year 360 A.D., Ammianus, a Roman orator, made a reference to the Scots, who along with Picts, Saxons, and Atacotti, were continually harrassing the Britons south of the Roman Wall. This is the earliest mention on record of the great race that was destined to wrest the supremacy of Alban from the Picts, and ultimately to give its own name to our noble land. At the time when Ammianus wrote, the principal home of the Scots was in Ireland, and the part of that island which they occupied was known as Scotia. At their first appearance in the light of history the Scots were a most vigorous and enterprising people. During the course of the third century of our era they had begun to establish settlements along the west of Britain from Wales to Ross-shire. The Scottish colonies on the west of Alban, extending from Kintyre to Loch Broom, were called Oirer-Ghaidheal, the Coastland of the Gael. From this term is derived our modern name Argyll.

These migrations of Scots from Ireland to Alban were followed, in the year 501 A.D., by a great invasion of Argyll by the Scots of Dalriada under the three sons of Erc, named Loarn, Angus, and Fergus. The earlier colonists were pushed northwards by the new-comers, a circumstance which probably explains the differences between the Gaelic dialect spoken in Argyll, and that spoken in Inverness-shire and Ross-shire. Those ancient Scots, like their descendants of to-day, loved to take the place-names of the old home-land with them overseas, and so, when they came to form themselves into a little kingdom in Argyll, they called it Dalriada. When the Scots of Dalriada felt themselves firmly established in Argyll, they began to push their way eastwards across Druim-Alban into Perthshire. The Picts offered a strong resistance, but step by step the Scots obtained a foothold in Breadalbane, Strathearn, and Menteith. In 574 A.D. King Aedan,[1] the son of Gabran, defeated the Picts somewhere in the Mearns, but his own two sons were killed in the battle.

The Pictish resistance to the aggressive warfare of the Scots was greatly weakened by their own continual dissensions. This internal strife was caused chiefly by the peculiar law of succession that prevailed among them. Heirship was traced

(1) Adamnan's Life of Columba, Book 1.

through the mother, and not through the father. The son did not succeed his father on the throne, for the right lay in the mother, and was transmitted through her to her daughter. The heir to a Pictish king was either his own brother, or the son of his sister. Now Pictish princesses from time to time married outsiders, with the result that kings were often foreigners among their own people. On the death of a king, rival claimants almost always appeared, and civil war ensued. Thus in 729 A.D. Angus, the son of Fergus, met his rival, Nectan, king of the Picts, at "the battle of Monith-Carno,[1] near Lake Loogdae." Nectan was slain, and "the family of Angus triumphed." It is believed that this battle was fought at the County March, near Tyndrum, where two hoary cairns still bear witness to some event of long ago. Having got rid of Nectan, Angus next overcame Drust, another rival, who had aspired to the throne. According to an English chronicle Angus was "a sanguinary tyrant." In 736 he invaded the kingdom of Dalriada, laid the land waste, took the fortress of Dun-add, and bound the two sons of Selbach, the king, with chains. Returning to Dalriada five years later he gave it another "smiting," and virtually annexed it to Pictland. Before his death, however, which occurred in 760 A.D., the sovereignty of Angus began "to ebb." The power of the Scots, who had also suffered through internal strife, revived, and under King Aed Finn, who died in 778, they carried on war in Fortrenn, which indicates that they had regained their hold of Perthshire.

Led by a succession of vigorous kings, the Scots pressed steadily and irresistibly into Pictland, until at length the Pictish kingdom received a blow at the hands of the Danes which made its collapse inevitable. The Danes, or Northmen, had plundered Iona in 794, and at the same time laid waste all the Western Isles. In 802 they burned the Monastery of Iona, and put to death the whole "community" of sixty-eight souls.

The Danes continued their piratical attacks upon the Western coastlands and the islands, until they were in a position by 838 to meet and defeat a Pictish army with King Eoganan at its head. In the Annals of Ulster is found the following melancholy record, "Battle by the Gentiles against the men of Fortrenn, in which Eoganan, the son of Angus, and Bran, the son of Angus, and Aed, the son of Boanta, and others innumerable, were killed." The tottering kingdom of the Picts continued to maintain a show of independence for a few years longer, but in 843 it fell an easy conquest to Kenneth, son of Alpin, king of the Dalriadic Scots. Kenneth's seizure of the Pictish sovereignty was made all the easier for him, because, on his mother's side he was a Pict. In the train of Kenneth the Scots poured "with marvellous eagerness into the land of the Picts." They removed

(1) Watson's Celtic Place Names, p. 401.

their headquarters from Dun-add to Scone, to which they brought the Stone of Destiny. There it remained until its transference by King Edward First of England to Westminster, in 1296. For some considerable time after the accession of Kenneth to the throne of Pictland the country continued to be known to outsiders by its old name. Gradually, however, as the Scottish influence asserted itself the name Pictavia gave way to that of Scotia, and the united peoples were known as Scots. Yet for the Gaelic folk this country is still Alban, and its people, Albannaich.

Gaelic culture had been penetrating Pictland, through the Church, for nearly three hundred years, and when the conquering Scots under Kenneth and his successors spread over the country, Gaelic rapidly became the language of the Picts as well as of the Scots. The Pictish language, which is proved from surviving place-names, lists of kings' names, and other names, to have been Celtic in character, and akin to ancient Welsh, perished before a language that was spoken at Court, by the chiefs and nobles, and by the clergy. Gaelic being the fashionable language prevailed much in the same way as English has been doing during the past hundred years throughout the Highlands of Scotland. The suddenness and the completeness of the disappearance of the Pictish language accounts for the fact that, out of several hundred place-names in the district of Breadalbane, scarcely a dozen can be referred with any degree of certainty to a pre-Gaelic origin.

CHAPTER V.

The Celtic Church in Breadalbane.

THE Christian religion, and with it the monastic system, became established in Ireland during the fifth century, and for the next two hundred years that island was the scene of the most amazing missionary enthusiasm and enterprise. The sons of kings, chiefs, and nobles, turned evangelists and monks, and went forth to preach the Gospel, and to set up churches and monasteries among the Britons, the Saxons, and the Picts of Alban. It was from this source that Breadalbane first received the light of the Christian faith.

According to the Venerable Bede, St. Ninian, who founded his monastery at Whithorn about the year 400, induced the Southern Picts to forsake the errors of idolatory and to embrace the truth. To what extent the mission of St. Ninian in Alban succeeded is a matter of much dispute. His name would appear to be associated with more places than he could possibly have visited. It has never been suggested that he entered Breadalbane, although his name is attached to a well near the Parish Church of Dull. According to the New Statistical Account, a chapel that was connected with the ancient religious establishment of Dull was also dedicated to him. The founder of Dull was, however, Adamnan. Tradition is very emphatic on this point, and it is probable that here, as in many other places, the name of St. Ninian was superimposed on the earlier dedication by the Romanising party during the twelfth century, in order to get the people to approve of the new practices that were being introduced at that time.

Before St. Columba landed on Iona in 563, to organise his great campaign against the paganism of Alban, it is believed that fully a score of Irish evangelists had from time to time visited various parts of the country, and preached the Gospel. Among those pioneers was Ciaran Mac-an-t-Sair, who died in 549. His name is preserved in Kilcherran (Islay), in Kintyre, and in Ayrshire.

St. Ciaran.

There were many saints of this name, but it was probably Ciaran Mac-an-t-Sair who built a caibeal, or cell, at Dalchiaran, Fearnan. It stood surrounded by a graveyard, a little to the south of the gate on the roadway leading to the farm-house of Boreland. The graveyard and the site of the cell have long ago been included in the arable land. Fifty years ago the plough turned up the holy water stone, and it was placed near the sacred spot by the proprietor, the late Mr. Alexander Campbell of Boreland. This interesting relic[1] is formed from a rough

(1) Proc. Soc. Ant. Scot., Vol. XXI., p. 372.

D

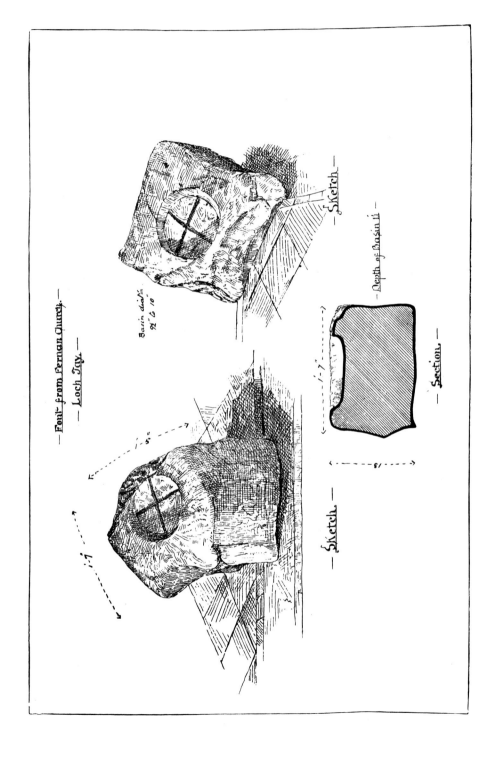

— Font from Fernan Church. —
— Loch Tay. —

Basin diat.
9½" to 10"

— Sketch. —

Depth of Basin 4"

— Section. —

— Sketch. —

boulder of mica slate. The basin is only two inches deep, and on the bottom, which is flat, a rude cross is cut. About three hundred yards to the west of the site of the chapel there is a large, rough stone[1] lying in the very middle of the ploughed field. It resembles a chair, and is believed to have been St. Ciaran's " Seat," or *Suidhe*. This stone, which bears several cup-marks, has a natural cavity in which rain water gathers. The water was regarded as an effectual cure for measles, and there are persons still residing at Fearnan who were taken as children to drink from the water in the hollow of *Clach-na-Gruich*,[2] the Measles Stone.

St. Carmac.

A saint of the name of Carmac is commemorated at Cill-ma-Charmaig, Ardeonaig. The site of his cell, on which was built in later times the Pre-Reformation church of the little parish of Ardeonaig, lies on the hill-slope above the farm-house of Dall. The gable of the church, which was in use until the beginning of the nineteenth century, is still standing. The old font of the church has been set up in the graveyard by Mr. Donald Mac-Dougall, Dall, whose family has had a connection with the district for three hundred years.

The font is roughly hexagonal in shape, and measures fully 30 inches in diameter. It is 11 inches high. The bowl is 19 inches across, and $8\frac{1}{2}$ inches deep. On the rim are two small holes exactly opposite each other, which no doubt kept the lid in position. There is a drain hole through the bottom of the basin. As late as the eighteenth century a market held about the 20th of November was called " Macharmick Mercate."[3] It is not, however, possible to trace the saint whose festival was on that day. It may be his name that is also associated with Coire Charmaig in Glenlochay. The festival of St. Cormac of North Knapdale falls on the 21st June.

Ardeonaig, the name of the district, and until 1617 of the little parish, is apparently derived from Adamnan, the ninth abbot of Iona, who died in 704. The name was formerly spelt Ardewnane (1622), and it was probably given to land bestowed upon the Church of St. Carmac, *Cill-ma-Charmaig*, in the name of Adamnan, the founder of the Church and monastery of Dull.

St. Dabhi.

The little grave-yard on the farm of Morenish, close to the shore of Loch Tay is called *Cladh Dabhi*, thy-Bi's Grave-yard. This has been the burial-place of a branch of the MacDiarmids known as *Rioghal*, Royal. A hillock a little to the north of the graveyard once bore the name of Tom-a-chluig, the "Knoll of the Bell." Within the graveyard, and resting upon an upright

(1) Proc. Soc. Ant. Scot., Vol. XVIII., p. 373.
(2) Proc. Soc. Ant. Scot., Vol. XVIII., p. 370.
(3) Kenmore Kirk, Sn. Rec.

tombstone dated 1817, there used to be two interesting blocks[1] of white quartz. One of them had a socket-hole on each side, $\frac{7}{8}$ inch, and 1 inch in diameter, and $1\frac{1}{4}$ inch deep, respectively. The other had a hole 1 inch deep and $\frac{1}{2}$ inch in diameter. These stones had at one time been used in a mill as socket stones, and through some association acquired mystical powers. They were believed to cure pectoral inflammation, and women came long distances to the graveyard in order to apply the stones to their breasts.

Tradition states that a *Cill Dabhi*, Kildavi, with a grave-yard and well, was situated within the policies of Taymouth, at Stix; but although Ewen MacDougall refers to it in his manuscript, no one to-day can give any information about the place. In an old guide-book published at Aberfeldy over forty years ago there is the following saying :—

> " Cladh Cill Dabhi,
> Thiodhlaic mi mo naoinear ann mar thri :
> An nochd is buidhe Doirbhean,
> An deigh na cloinne caoimh."

> " The burying-ground of Kildavie,
> 'Twas there I laid my nine as three.
> Dear this night is the cross-grained one,
> After the rest so loved are gone."

The explanation of the saying is that this is the wail of a mother of ten children who, during a plague, lost nine of them, and buried them three at a time. The least attractive of them all was the only one left to her.

The chapel, and the well on the ledge in the face of the great Rock of Weem, are also associated with Da-Bhi, now locally called St. David. Professor W. J. Watson suggests that Da-Bhi is a short form of Berach, who was abbot of Cluain Coirpthi. He is commemorated at several places in Scotland.

Carwhin.

Coire-Chunna, Carwhin, may preserve the name of Do-Chunne, an Irish saint whose day is September 6th. There is no trace of a church ever having been here, but a spot in Blairmore wood is pointed out as the former grave-yard of the district. Some members of the Carwhin family of Campbells were buried here. There may be a connection between Coire-Chunna and Cladh-Chunna, Cunne's Grave-yard, near Invervar, Glenlyon.

Killin.

It is uncertain whether the name Killin means White-Church, Holy-Church, or the Church of Fionn. There is no record of a saint of this name, although Killin is found in Ross-shire, and in Sutherland. Dalchill-Fhinn is the name of a farm in Glenquaich, near Amulree. Tradition places the earliest church and graveyard at Killin near the monolith known as Fingal's Stone, behind the village. The fourth Earl of Breadalbane had

(1) Proc. Soc. Ant. Scot., Vol. XVIII., p. 373.

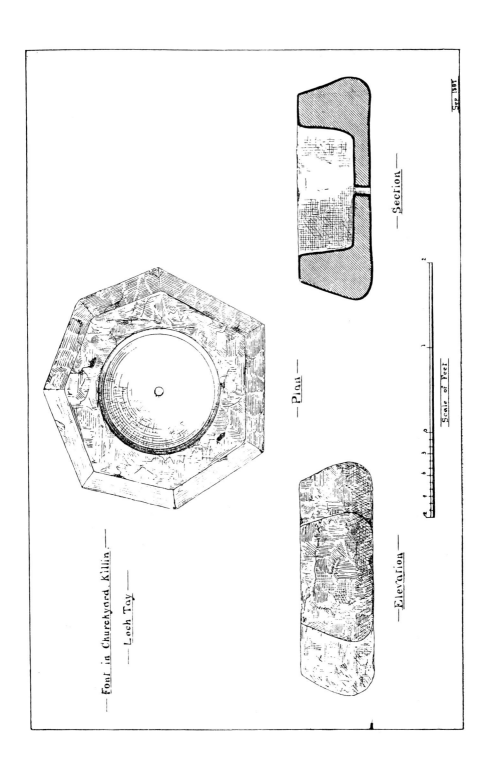

— Font in Churchyard Killin. —

— Loch Tay —

— Plan —

— Section —

— Elevation —

Scale of Feet

Sep 1881

the ground around this stone thoroughly examined, but no
bones were found. The Pre-Reformation church of Killin stood
within the old parish church-yard, and its ruined walls[1] were
still standing in 1842. It is most probable that here also was
the church of Celtic times. People in the olden days did not
readily abandon a site that had been consecrated by centuries
of worship. It was within the old grave-yard that the handsome
stone baptismal font, now preserved in the Parish Church, was
found half buried in the ground. In size it is very similar to
that of Cill-ma-Charmaig, but the workmanship is much finer.
It is the only seven-sided font found, so far, in Scotland. Its
diameter is 2 feet 7 inches, and its height 1 foot 6 inches. Like
the font of Cill-ma-Charmaig it has a drain-hole in the bottom,
and holes on the rim for fixing the cover.

Besides Cladh-Dabhi and Caibeal Chiaran there are other two
ancient ecclesiastical sites on the north side of Loch Tay—Bal-
na-hanaid, and Cladh Machuim.   Bal-na-hanaid is situated
close to Loch Tay, about seven miles east from Killin, and
almost opposite Ardeonaig. The name means the " Town of
the patron saint's Church," and it occurs in Glenlyon, and in
Rannoch. The church probably stood in front of the present
farm-house, and had a grave-yard around it. From time to time
the plough has turned up flat flagstones, such as may have been
laid upon graves.

Machuim.

Cladh Machuim lies close to the shore of Loch Tay, and a
short distance east from the mouth of the Lawers Burn. This
graveyard is still the burial-place for the district. The name
is obscure, but it may mean " The Burial-place of the Field of
the Tomb." The foundation of the Pre-Reformation church
has been disclosed when graves were dug about the middle of
the enclosure. An ancient font fashioned from a rough boulder
used to lie on the shore of the loch, and is now housed in the
little tool-shed at the gate-way to the graveyard.

Kilmory.

It is said that at one time there was a village called Kilmory
at the southern end of Tom-na-croiche, Kenmore. No trace of
it remains, but the name suggests that a saint, Muireach, may
have been commemorated here. We find a Kilmorich, and a
well of St. Muireach at Dunkeld.

Inchadney.

The Pre-Reformation church of the parish of Kenmore, at
Inchadney, or Inchadin, was, no doubt, of very early origin,
but neither tradition, nor the name, gives any clue as to its
founder. An effort was made by Charles Stewart, Killin, who
wrote " The Gaelic Kingdom in Scotland," and others, to
establish a connection between this church and St. Aidan, the

(1) New Stat. Account.

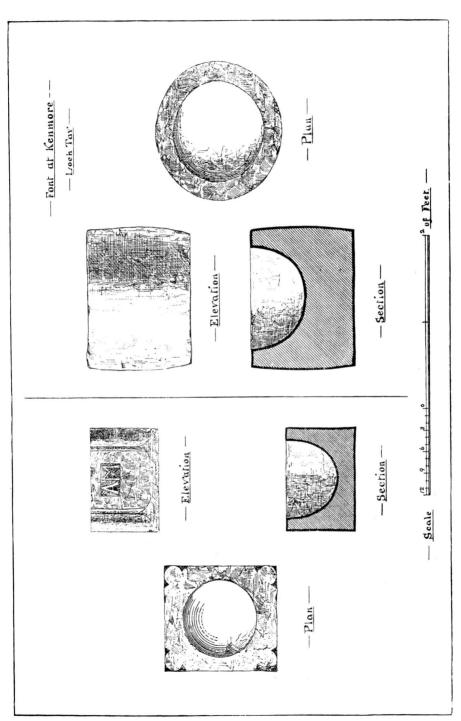

Font at Kenmore —
— Loch Tay —

— Plan —

— Elevation —

— Section —

— Elevation —

— Section —

— Plan —

— Scale —

— 2 of Feet. —

FONTS PRESERVED IN KENMORE CHURCH.

evangelist of Northumbria; but old forms of spelling, as well as the local pronunciation of the name, show that the site was called Innis-chailtnigh, "Keltney-haugh." Less than two miles away, across the river Lyon, there is Allt-chailtnigh, "Keltney-burn," and there is, doubtless, a connection between the two names.

The sites of the vicarage, the church, and the graveyard of Inchadney were at the very apex of the fertile peninsula lying between the foot of Drummond Hill and the river Tay, and opposite the group of houses at Newhall. In olden times Inchadney church was situated beside an important route leading from the North by Trinafour, Glengoulandie, Braes of Balloch, Amulree, and Crieff, to the South. Within the memory of persons still living large droves of cattle used to be taken along this route, and across the Tay at the ford of Inchadney. The points where the road entered and emerged from the river may be still distinctly traced. The church, a small oblong building, lay to the west of the churchyard, and outside it. The vicarage, which was the Manse of the parish until 1760, was immediately below the Star Battery. The Chronicle of Fortingall records the burials of several persons of importance in the district within the church. These included Robertsons of Carwhin, MacGregors of Balloch, and Macnaughtons of Edragoll. Some were buried in the choir, and others on the north and south sides of the great altar. Sir James MacGregor, vicar of Fortingall and Dean of Lismore, who made the earliest collection of Scottish Gaelic poetry, was buried in the choir of the church on St. Lucy's day, 13th December, 1551. The Dean belonged to the MacGregors of Balloch, although his father, Dougal MacGregor, resided at Tullach-a-mhuilinn, at Fortingall. Dougal repaired the sole of the cross at Inchadney in 1526, and three years later he erected a stone cross on Lairig-monadh-marcachd, the pass leading from the Braes of Taymouth into Glenquaich. The summit of this pass is still called in Gaelic, " A Chrois." A short distance to the west of the ford of Inchadney, on the south side of the Tay, there once stood the Inn of Muttonhole. It ceased to be occupied about the end of the eighteenth century. In Gaelic the inn was called " Tigh-an-tuill," the "House of the Hole."

The markets for the district were held at Inchadney until they were removed to Kenmore Green by Sir Colin Campbell of Glenorchy in 1575. At that time the principal market was held on the Nine Virgins' day, the 18th July, and was called " Feill-nam-ban-naomh," "the market of the Holy Women." It was supposed that the market was connected with the nunnery that is believed to have existed at one time on the Isle of Loch Tay, and in his note on the Isle in the " Fair Maid of Perth," Sir Walter Scott states the tradition. This market, however, commemorated the Nine Maidens, daughters of St. Donald, who, after their father's death, retired in the eighth century to the monastery for women at Abernethy. There are several dedications to the Nine Maidens in Angus and Aberdeenshire.

In 1579, when a petition was presented to the commissioners of the Church of Scotland by the parishioners of Inchadney asking for permission to erect a church at Kenmore, the grounds given were that the church at Inchadney was inconveniently situated for the people, and that it was in a ruinous condition. It was put into a condition of repair in 1585, but was only used when the minister was prevented by storms from crossing the ferry to the church at Kenmore. It was not, however, entirely demolished until 1828. The old vicarage was pulled down about the same time.

The churchyard of Inchadney was surrounded by a stone wall, the foundations of which may still be traced. There are two very old oak trees close to the line of the wall, one on the north side, and one on the east side. When the parishioners petitioned for the erection of the new church at Kenmore they " reserved aluayes the place of the auld kyrk and Kyrkyaird for ane buriall for the quhilk use it served of befoir." In 1738 the second Earl of Breadalbane issued an order requiring all parties who had an interest in the graveyard to contribute towards the repair of the wall. His son, Lord Glenorchy, in 1746, forbade burials on the Kirk Green of Kenmore. All graves were to be made at Inchadney, but, strange to say, as third Earl of Breadalbane he closed Inchadney against all burials in 1760, at which time the churchyard of Kenmore was laid out. It is said that earth was taken from Inchadney to consecrate the little graveyards of Ardtalnaig and Stronfearnan, which were laid out for these districts at the time Inchadney was closed. Some old head-stones were taken from Inchadney to Kenmore. The others were thrown aside when the churchyard was planted with trees in or before 1769. Some of these head-stones were taken to Taymouth Castle when it was in course of erection, and laid on places where the constant traffic of the builders had made the ground soft. The desecration of Inchadney was completed when the old church and manse were destroyed in the time of the first Marquis, and every suggestion of its ancient and sacred character obliterated.

About four hundred yards to the north of the graveyard, at the foot of a high bank, there is a holy well, or *tiobairt*, that used to be frequented by great numbers of people on the morning of May-day (O.S.). A few years ago the well, which had been cleaned and its walls repaired by the late Marchioness of Breadalbane. was examined. A rude stone cup[1] and several old coins and pins were found. These were handed over to the National Museum of Antiquities, Edinburgh. The two great oaks, the well, and the ford across the river, remain in this deserted and desecrated spot to tell of the time when Inchadney was the centre of the religious, social, and commercial life of the eastern portion of Breadalbane.

(1) Proc. Soc. Ant. Scot., Vol. LIX., p. 75.

CHAPTER VI.

The Celtic Church (*Continued*).

St. Fillan of Glendochart.

With the settlement of St. Columba and his companions at Iona in 563 A.D., the Christian religion began to spread rapidly over Alban. Prior to this event the lights that had been lit by the pioneers of the Cross were few and feeble. The holy flame flickered, and in many places died away altogether. It is recorded that Columba " taught the tribes of Tay," and tradition associates his name with the founding of Dunkeld. There is no dedication to him in Breadalbane, but there is no doubt that the saint and his fellow-workers frequently passed through Strathtay on their missionary journeys, and crossed over the hill-tracks that lead from the valley of the Tay into Glenlyon and Strathearn.

About the end of the seventh century or the beginning of the eighth the work of Christianising the Atholl and Breadalbane districts received a great impetus through the establishing of Celtic monasteries at the Strath of Dull, and in Glendochart. The name of St. Adamnan, the biographer of St. Columba, is associated with the former place, and that of St. Fillan, the son of Kentigerna, who was a daughter of Ceallach Cualann of Leinster, with the latter district. Tradition relates that these two missionaries crossed Druimalban together into Perthshire, and that when they came to the head-waters of the Tay, at Tyndrum, they cast lots to decide which sphere of labour each should adopt. Glenlyon and Dull fell to Adamnan, while the western portion of Breadalbane, which up to this period would appear to have been neglected, was allocated to St. Fillan. Adamnan is commemorated in Glenlyon at Milton Eonan, where he is said to have set up the first meal-mill in the district, and also at another place lower down the Glen, where a rude stone cross by the wayside marks the spot at which he stopped a plague. A fair that was formerly held at Dull on St. Adamnan's feast-day (September 23rd), was called *Feill Eonain*, and the Church there was dedicated to him. It is said that this Celtic monastery at Dull was succeeded by a seat of learning, the endowments of which were afterwards transferred to the University of St. Andrews. Nothing now remains at Dull to indicate its ancient importance, except a large stone font, and one of the girth crosses that enclosed the sanctuary at Druimdian, the Ridge of Protection. The other two crosses are preserved in the Old Kirk of Weem. The broad, fertile plain, extending from the foot of the bold rock of Dull to the river Tay, is to this day called "Strath-na-h-Apuinn," the Strath of the Abbey-land.

After crossing from Ireland, St. Fillan, along with his mother, Kentigerna, and his uncle, Comgan, settled at Lochalsh, in Wester Ross, where dedications to each of the three commemorate their labours. When St. Fillan came to Glendochart his mother retired to the Island of Inch Cailleach, " the Nuns' Isle," on Loch Lomond, where she died in 734 A.D. The father of St. Fillan was Feradach, a nobleman, who came of the race of Fiatach Finn. Irish legends about St. Fillan tell that he was born with a stone in his mouth, and that his father threw the child into a lake. Angels came, however, and watched over him until he was found by Bishop Ibar, who brought him up as his own child, and had him instructed in the Christian faith. His name, Faolan, Little Wolf, may have suggested the following story. One day, while the saint was ploughing, a wolf came, and attacked his yoke of oxen, killing one of them ; but no sooner had the saint invoked the power of heaven than the repentant wolf returned, and submitted itself to be yoked to the plough, and so supplied the place of its victim. On another occasion, when the saint was in his cell after sundown, a lay brother was sent to call him to supper. The messenger, curious to know what St. Fillan was doing, looked through a chink in the wall, and was astonished to see him writing by means of a light that streamed from his left arm. Next day a tame crane that was kept by the holy fraternity picked out the eye of the lay brother who was guilty of prying upon the saint, and rendered him quite blind, but at the request of the rest of the brethren St. Fillan restored his sight to the erring one. St. Fillan is said to have received the monastic habit from St. Mundu, who was one of St. Columba's companions, and the founder of a monastery at Kilmun, in Argyllshire. His festival falls on the 9th January (O.S.). Struan, in Atholl, Killallan, in Renfrewshire, and Aberdour, in Fife may be associated with the great saint of Glendochart. We must, however, distinguish him from St. Fillan of Rath Erenn, whose chair and well are situated between Comrie and Loch Earn, and who belonged to a much earlier period, and is commemorated on June 20th.

Little or nothing is known of St. Fillan's ministry in Bread-albane, but he has left behind him here an imperishable and gracious tradition, and his memory has given a peculiar charm to every part of the long and romantic glen between Killin and Tyndrum. His mill and healing stones are at Killin ; his seat where he meditated, and taught, is at Suie ; while the broad strath with its beautiful stream from Crianlarich to Carndroma bears his name, Strathfillan.

Priory of St. Fillan.

Tradition assigns the site of his monastic settlement to a spot on the farm of Auchtertyre, in the neighbourhood of the Holy Pool. St. Fillan's Priory, in later times, however, was situated close to the farmhouse of Kirkton, about one mile to the east of the Holy Pool, and on the north side of the river. The stones of the priory were used for the erection of the farmhouse and of the buildings attached to it. Parts of the north and south

RUINS OF ST. FILLAN'S PRIORY.

walls of the chapel, four feet thick, and built with hammer-dressed[1] stones, and excellent lime mortar, are still standing. The foundations of other walls, overgrown with grass, may still be traced. The building which stood to the east was probably the prior's house, and the round part at the end of the foundation a circular tower. Placed in the centre of the Chapel, and resting on a slab, is a schistose boulder, with a deeply cut-out, heart-shaped cavity. This was the font of the Church, and was associated with the rites practised in curing insane persons who

(1) Proc. Soc. Ant. Scot., Vol. XXXII., p. 121.

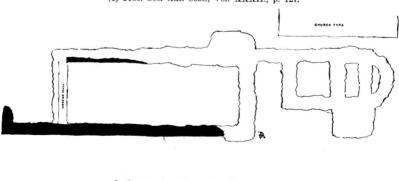

GROUND PLAN OF ST. FILLAN'S PRIORY.

had been immersed in the Holy Pool. The slab is believed to cover the grave of the saint.

A little graveyard, enclosed by four square walls, lies immediately to the north of the ruins. The position of the graveyard in relation to the chapel suggests an older origin for this site than Roman Catholic times, when graveyards were invariably placed to the south and west of the church. Several of the graves are covered with flat stones, which were probably

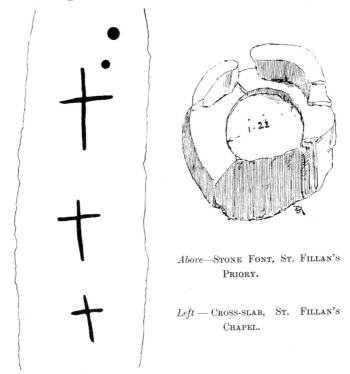

Above—STONE FONT, ST. FILLAN'S PRIORY.

Left — CROSS-SLAB, ST. FILLAN'S CHAPEL.

taken from the floor of the chapel. On two of these slabs Latin crosses[1] are cut, and one of them bears also two small, cup-shaped impressions. The Priests' Well, which supplied the Priory with spring water, is in a hollow by the side of the stream, a short distance to the north. The well was carefully built with stone, and has all the appearance of antiquity. About two hundred yards to the east there is a rectangular enclosure, surrounded by the foundations of a wall. This enclosure is said to have been the garden of the Priory. A bell which was recovered from the river, some forty years ago, is preserved in the Hotel at Tyndrum. It stands about 1 foot 2 inches high, and measures

(1) Proc. Soc. Ant. Scot., Vol. LVIII., p. 125.

4 feet 5 inches round the outside of the rim. It may have been the bell of the Priory during the Roman Catholic period.

The monastery founded by St. Fillan in Glendochart was a centre from which Christian teaching and civilizing influences were spread throughout Western Breadalbane and the neighbouring districts. As at other institutions of the kind, some of the monks devoted themselves to purely spiritual work, such as the conducting of Church services, teaching, and the transcription of manuscripts. Others, called by the name, *scologs*, a Gaelic term still applied to farm servants, were admitted to the tonsure, and given some little instruction on the condition that they worked on the abbey lands. This sacred community, forming one family, and living under one head, was protected from the greed and oppression of a lawless and barbarous age. The members were able to dwell in peace under rules that encouraged Christian culture, and that created an atmosphere congenial to the practice of good deeds and mutual helpfulness. Such a life attracted many persons, and in the course of time the Monastery of Strathfillan became endowed with the revenue of lands in the district.

These lands were vested in the abbot for the time being, but in the course of centuries the office of abbot became secularised, and was hereditary in a powerful family. Thus it is that during the reign of William the Lyon (1165-1174) we find the Abbot of Glendochart appearing with the Earl of Atholl and other Scottish magnates in a list of persons appointed to administer a law made for the recovery of stolen cattle. In the meantime the prior of the monastery as St. Fillan's spiritual successor was invested with the symbols of his office, and administered religious affairs. When, however, the larger and better portions of the endowments of the monastery were alienated, the institution declined in importance and influence. By the time of King Robert the Bruce its condition had fallen so far that we find the eminent King, for reasons that we shall consider later, making a grant of the right of patronage of the church of Killin to the Abbot and Convent of Inchaffray, on condition that the abbot and convent would provide a canon to officiate in the church of Strathfillan. This grant was made under the Privy Seal on 26th February, 1317-18. It was renewed[1] on April 12th following, at Berwick-on-Tweed, but without any mention of the condition stated above. It was understood, however, that the condition was binding, for, in October of the same year, William St. Clair, Bishop of Dunkeld, with consent and assent of his chapter, granted to the Prior and canons of Inchaffray, the church of Killin, with all its lands, fruits, and revenues, saving always the dues of the Bishop and Archdeacon of Dunkeld. The prior of St. Fillan's chapel on the occurrence of a vacancy

(1) Inchaffray Charters, pp. 123-125.

was to be presented by the Abbot and convent, and instituted by the Bishop. The vicarage of Killin was to be served by a canon, or, if more agreeable to the monastery of Inchaffray, by a secular chaplain, who was to receive ten pounds sterling a year, out of which he was to pay the dues of the bishop and archdeacon.

It will be noticed that the King's original proposal, that one canon should serve at St. Fillan's chapel, was enlarged by establishing a priory there, thus maintaining the ancient monastic character of the place. Confirmation of the king's grant was made by Pope Clement VI. at Avignon on November 13th, 1348. It is evident that King Robert the Bruce contributed to the endowment of the priory from the fact that James IV., on October 2nd, 1498, for singular favour towards Dene John Murray, prior of Strathfillan, confirmed a charter of King Robert Bruce to the monastery or chapel of Strathfillan, and to the prior of the same, granting the five-pound lands of Auchtertyre, of old extent, in the Barony of Glendochart and shire of Perth, and incorporating them into the Barony of Auchtertyre. In 1329, the year of King Robert's death, a payment was made from the Exchequer through Sir Robert de Bruys, the King's natural son, of xxlb., *ad fadricum ecclesie Sancti Felani*. At a later date the chapel of St. Fillan is spoken of as " a chapel royal." On February 28th, 1542-3, Dene John Gray, canon regular, prior of Strathfillan, granted the lands of Auchtertyre in feu to James Campbell of Lawers. In this charter, and in the confirmation granted on the second March of the same year, the prior is styled, " of the monastery, or chapel royal of Strath-fillan." The rental to be paid to the prior was to be ten pounds annually. The name of Celestine Johnston, a canon of Inchaffray, who succeeded John of Mortimer as prior of Strathfillan on 16th July, 1414, is recorded in the Papal Registers. Another prior was Sir Hugh Currie, who was one of the executors of Gavin Dunbar, Archbishop of Glasgow. His name appears later in connection with the action raised by the Church for possession of the relics of St. Fillan, in 1549-50.

In the autumn of 1501, when King James IV.[1] went on a hunting expedition to Balquhidder, and Benmore in Glendochart, he resided for part of the time at the Priory of Strathfillan. There he was entertained by " Heland bardis," harpers, and fiddlers who were sent by the chiefs of the neighbouring districts. Before leaving he gave a contribution " for the theking of the Kyrk of Strafelane," and also an offering for the " stok," the vessel containing the holy oil used at the services of the church. A gratuity of 20 shillings was given to the priests. The King returned on a similar visit in 1506, and this time he penetrated as far as the head of Glenorchy, staying at Auch-innis-chalean, at the foot of Ben Doran. Among payments made on his behalf were, " 29th August, in Strafelane to tua pur freris XIIIS., the kingis offerand to the stok thare V s IV d." ; the last day of August, " to the priestis 40 S."

At the Reformation the Priory was regarded as of little importance. The Collector-General's account for the year 1573 gives a list of benefices, " quhilks wes not rentaillit, nor chargit abefoir, but ar new found owt be the comptare." Among these is the following, " the haill priourie of Straphillane the zeir comptit extendis to XL. lib. (forty pounds)." Some time after the Reformation the fruits of the benefice of Strathfillan were granted to a member of the Lawers family. In 1607 we find that the whole Kirk teinds within the precincts of the monastery of Strathfillan were given in tack by the commendator of Strathfillan, Archibald Campbell, to his brother, James, of Lawers, reserving the life-rent of Beatrix Campbell, their mother. Again in 1667, the Priory of Strathfillan, together with the monastery and buildings within the precincts, and all the teinds and other fruits belonging to the Priory, were granted for life to Archibald Campbell, son of John Campbell of Fordew.

St. Fillan's Relics.

The name and the memory of St. Fillan were held in great veneration in Breadalbane and throughout Perthshire. At Killin, a summer and a winter feast were held in his honour, and the rents of some crofts in the neighbourhood, which belonged to the Carthusian Monastery at Perth, were devoted to the provision of lights before his image in the church of Killin. In 1496 an altar to St. Fillan was founded in the Church of St. John, Perth, by Sir Patrick Rae, who endowed it with 20 shillings from a tenement in the Vennel of the Watergate, and £8 11/2 out of lands within the burgh. The patronage of the chaplaincy was vested in the Carthusian Monastery.

A peculiar and romantic interest attached to the relics of the great saint, especially to his crozier, and his bell, both of which have been preserved for us in a most remarkable way. It would appear that at some period not long after his death the relics of the saint were entrusted to the custody of laymen residing in Glendochart, to each of whom was given a free grant of his land from the Crown in virtue of his office. The custodian of a relic of the saint was called in Gaelic, *deoradh*, a word whose original meaning is, stranger or exile. The term came, however, to be applied not only to the person in charge of the relic, but even to the relic itself, from the fact that it was carried as a " stranger " for special purposes to distant districts. When we find such a name as Malise Dewar mentioned in connection with a relic of St. Fillan, we must understand that the man was

Malise, the custodian. In the course of time the office gave rise to the surname, Dewar, so long and honourably connected with Breadalbane.

The five relics of St. Fillan, of which mention is made at one time or another in ancient documents, were handed down from father to son in the several families descended from the men to whom they were first entrusted. These relics had originally been symbols of ecclesiastical offices, but from association with the memory of the saint, and with religious rites, they came to be regarded with awe and reverence, and even superstition. It was believed that they were effective in curing the sick in body and in mind; and an oath sworn with the hand laid upon a sacred relic was regarded as the most solemn oath that anyone could take. In this way the relics of St. Fillan came to serve important public functions long after they had ceased to be the symbols of ecclesiastical offices, or even to express any religious ideas.

The Quigrich.[1]

The crozier, or staff, of St. Fillan is known as the Quigrich, a name that has created much curious speculation, but which is simply the Gaelic word, *Coigreach*, stranger or foreigner. It received this name from the fact that the relic was carried to distant places for the recovery of stolen property. The custom of giving such names to the relics of saints was quite common in the Celtic Church, both in Ireland and in Scotland. The famous Psalter of St. Columba was called *An Cathach*, or The Warrior, and the bell of St. Fillan, at one time connected with Struan in Atholl, was known as *Am Buidhean*, The little Yellow One.

Dr. Joseph Anderson gives the following description of the Quigrich in his book, " Scotland in Early Christian Times." " It is the head of a pastoral staff, commonly, though not with strict correctness, termed a crozier. It stands 9 inches high, and consists of an external casing of silver, enclosing an earlier crozier-head of bronze or copper, ornamented with niello. The external case, which is of silver, gilt and ornamented with chased work, and patterns in filigree-work of silver wire, consists of three parts ; the crook proper, which is cylindrical and curved like the head of a walking stick ; the bulb, or socket, fitted with a collar for the insertion of the wooden staff ; and an ornamented crest, the object of which is to strengthen, and bind together the several parts of which the crozier is composed. The crook is ornamented with eight lozenge-shaped plaques of silver, arranged end to end down the centre, the angular spaces left between them being filled up with plaques of triangular form. No two plaques are exactly equal, and no two are quite alike in their ornamentation. They are implanted on a thin skin of silver, beaten to fit the pattern thus produced, and the spaces left

(1) Proc. Soc. Ant. Scot., Vol. XXIII., p. 110.   Ibid, Vol. III., p. 233.

E

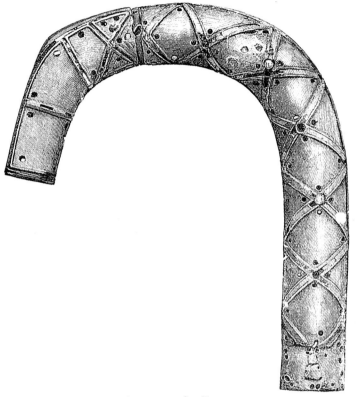

CROZIER OF ST. FILLAN.

between each plaque are slightly chased with a simple cross hatching, rather clumsily executed.

" When we examine these plaques with attention, it is perceived that their filigree-work is of two different varieties. One is an elegant scroll-work formed of a single wire, irregularly placed, but boldly designed, and executed with a precision of curvature and harmony of parts that at once indicates the work of a master of the art. The other is a geometrical pattern, poor in design and feeble in execution. It is wrought with a twisted wire, and appears sometimes as the sole ornament of the triangular plaques, but never occupies the whole surface of any of the lozenge-shaped plaques. Some of these have part of their ornamentation composed of this inferior work, and the large, square plaque, bearing the crystal in front of the pendent part of the crook (which is apparently the latest of the whole) is inferior filigree-work.

" The ornamentation of the bulb, or socket, of the crozier consists of interlaced work, and triangular panels enclosing

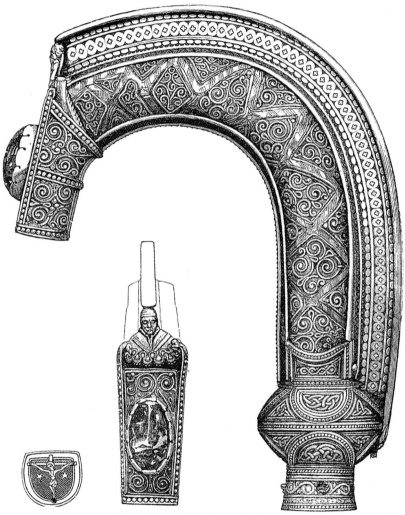

OUTER CASE OF ST. FILLAN'S CROZIER.

triquetra ornaments, separated by a pellet-bordering, which is
continued along the strap under the concave surface of the
crook, and reappears as a bordering on the pendent portion of
the front of the crook. This pellet-bordering and this interlaced work, with many varieties of the triquetra ornament,
appear on the bosses of an Irish crozier preserved at Tedavnet
in the possession of a family of hereditary keepers till the year
1827.

"The crest, which is attached to the bulbous socket, and passes along the ridge of the crook, is pierced by a row of quatrefoils, and terminates at the lower extremity in a rude imitation of an animal's head, the only zoomorphic feature which the art of the crozier presents. A similar termination to the crest of an Irish crozier in the Museum exhibits a more pronounced character of zoomorphism, while the crest of another Irish crozier is entirely zoomorphic, and composed of four lacterine, or dragonesque animals, with their limbs, tails, and crests intertwined in a most elaborate pattern of interlaced work.

"At the upper extremity of St. Fillan's crozier, where the end of the crest overhangs the pendent portion, there is a small bust of an ecclesiastic, probably intended to represent St. Fillan. Underneath the bust there is a peculiar ornamentation, consisting of a wavy ribbon pattern with a pellet in each loop, which suggests an indication of the date of this part of the work, because the same ornament occurs in the privy seal of David II., the successor of King Robert Bruce.

"The result of this examination of the work upon the outer case of the crozier is to show that the filigree-work is distinctly separable into two varieties, one of which is greatly inferior to the other, and is used to patch up deficiences in the plaques along the sides of the crook, while it composes the sole ornament of the front plaque that contains the crystal. We may safely assume that the inferior style, which thus patches up the deficiences, is the later of the two, and that it probably corresponds in date with the time when the body of the crook was bound together by the addition of the crest and strap with the socket to which they are attached, which a comparison of the style of the ornament underneath the bust with the ornamentation of the privy seal of David II. assigns to the fourteenth century. That this binding together of the several parts of the body of the crook really implies the construction of the outer case as it exists, I think is capable of demonstration.

"The meaning of the binding together of the several parts of the outer case became instantly apparent on its being taken to pieces. It was then found that the case had been constructed to contain an older crozier. This venerable relic, which had been deemed worthy of such an enshrinement, was thus restored to view, and it was also seen that not only had the outer case been constructed over it, but that the filigree plaques, which are now the chief ornaments of the outer case, had been originally the ornaments of the older crozier of copper, thus enclosed within it. They fit the spaces between its nielloed straps exactly, and the pinholes at the corners correspond to the pinholes in the copper. Their secondary use also explains the reason why their deficiences were made up with filligree-work of an inferior kind, because, in the re-construction of the crozier, by stripping the enclosed crook of its plaques of filigree-work, and fixing them on the outer covering, it was necessary to make the worn-out work correspond in completeness with the altered appearance of the relic encased in its new shrine. Before the older crozier was thus stripped of its filigree plaques it must have been a work of art of no common order. In style and execution its filigree patterns greatly resemble those on the cover of the Prayer-book of Charles the Bald, preserved in the Louvre, and dating from the first half of the ninth century. It still bears strips of niello-work running down the centre of the raised bands which separate the lozenge-shaped spaces for the insertion of the plaques of filigree-work, and the contrast of the bright silver with the red of the copper, and the dark, lustrous bands of niello must have produced a pleasing effect."

Historical References.

The historical references[1] found in ancient documents to the Quigrich extend over three centuries, and they shed no little light upon the state of society existing in Breadalbane at different periods in the past. In 1336, Alexander Menzies, then lord of Glendochart, addressed a missive to Donald M'Sobrell, dewar Cogerach, confirming to him parts of the lands of Ewich, in Strathfillan. The lands in question had belonged to the Abbey, and being mortified to God and St. Fillan, they were, according to ancient Celtic usage, exempt from all royal and customary charges.

We next find that on the 22nd of April, 1428, an inquest was held at Kandrochid, the Bridgend of Killin, by John Spens, then bailie of Glendochart, concerning the authority and privileges of the Quigrich. At this inquest fifteen persons, whose names are given, all of them resident in the district, gave evidence on oath and declared unanimously as follows :— (1) That the bearer of the relic called the Coygerach ought to receive each year and by inheritance, from each inhabitant of the parish of Glendochart having or cultivating a mark of land, or upwards, whether as proprietor or as tenant, half a boll of meal ; and from everyone having in like manner a half mark of land, a firlot of meal ; and from everyone having a forty-penny land, a half firlot of meal. (2) That the office of bearing the Coygerach was given to a certain progenitor of Finaly Dewar, the present hereditary custodian, by the co-arb, or ecclesiastical successor of St. Fillan. (3) That all these privileges were use and wont in the time of King Robert the Bruce. (4) That for these dues and privileges the hereditary keepers of the Quigrich were bound to render service in the manner following :— If it should happen that goods or cattle were reft, or stolen, from any inhabitant of the parish, and he was unable to follow

(1) Proc. Soc. Ant. Scot., Vol. XXIII., p. 110.

them, whether from doubt of the culprit, or feud of his enemies, then he might send a messenger to the Dewar of the Coygerach, with fourpence, or a pair of shoes, and food for the first night, and the said Dewar should follow the goods, or cattle, wherever they might be found within the bounds of the Kingdom of Scotland.

The Quigrich is next referred to in a deed of confirmation granted by King James III. on 6th July, 1487, at Edinburgh, in favour of Malise Doire, who was to be secured in the peaceful possession of " the holy relic of St. Fillan callit the Quegrich." This document declares that the King understands that Malise and his ancestors had possession of the relic from the time of King Robert the Bruce, and before then, and that they were in no way responsible to any persons, either spiritual or temporal, with regard to the relic. The King commands his subjects to grant all possible facilities to Malise in the discharge of his duties, and in no way to hinder, or impede him passing with the relic through the country " as he and his forbearis were wont to do." The King's subjects " were further chargied to see that Malise was kept unthrallit, and free in the use of the relic under all the hiest paine."

There is no doubt that the clergy regarded the Dewars of Glendochart with no little jealousy, and often wished to secure for the Church the precious relics of which they had legal possession. The relics of St. Fillan stood high in popular favour, not only throughout Breadalbane, but even in districts far beyond. One of them, as we shall see, was associated with the greatest of Scotland's kings, and with the most signal victory that Scotland had ever won. It is quite probable that the Church had challenged the title of Malise, Dewar of Quigrich, when he applied for confirmation of his right to hold it to King James III. In the year 1549, however, Hew Currie, prior of Strathfillan, endeavoured to obtain a decree of court in order to compel " Malise Doir of Quickrich, Archibald Doir of Fergy, and Malcolm Doir Bernane, to deliver and present in the kirkis of Killin and Straphillan certane reliques, and nocht to be tane furth agane without license of the said prioure." Failing delivery of the relics, the three said Dewars were to incur the curses of the Church. The three custodians protested against the unjust claim of the Church, and lodged an appeal in Court. They even employed a procurator to present their case, while the prior appeared in person in support of the claim of the Church. The Lords of Council decided in favour of the Dewars, who were left in possession of the sacred relics, and at the same time absolved them from the imprecations threatened in the letters of the prior. Had the Quigrich and the Bernane passed at this time, when the Reformation was impending, out of the hands of the Dewars, it is probable that they should have been destroyed and thus lost for ever.

The annoyance of the Church at being defeated in its action against the Dewars may account for the fact that in the following year the Crown authorities stepped in and imposed certain charges upon the lands which Malise Dewar of the Quigrich and his ancestors had always held free. It is recorded that on 4th March, 1551, Queen Mary "set in fue farm to Malise Dewar the forty-shilling land of Eyicht, Cryt-in-dewar in Auchincarne, and the half merkland called Cragwokin . . . which have never been computed in the rental, or any payment made from them to the Queen, now to pay 40 shillings annually with a duplicand at the entry of heirs." Twenty-four years later, Donald Deor, probably a son of Malise, made over these same lands by charter signed at Ilanrayne, Killin, to Duncan Campbell, afterwards Sir Duncan, who was notorious for his greed of land, as well as for the unscrupulous methods by which he sometimes acquired it.

THE CROZIER IN CANADA.

Although Donald Deor of the Quigrich parted with his ancestral lands, the relic remained with him and his descendants until the year 1877, when it was acquired by the Society of Antiquaries of Scotland and placed in the National Museum of Antiquities of Scotland. The story of the venerated relic is well worth following until it reached its present safe repository. In spite of the Reformation and the opposition of the Reformed Church to all forms of superstition, the people of Breadalbane still believed in the virtues of the Quigrich and of the other relics of St. Fillan that survived. Although the allowance of meal given from every piece of land in Glendochart to the Dewar of the Quigrich had ceased to be paid, and he was no longer required to go into other districts to recover stolen goods or cattle, still, people came to him for water in which the holy Quigrich had been dipped, and with this they hoped to cure sick friends and ailing cattle. Before leaving they gave an offering to the Dewar. Some time during the reign of Charles II., the fortunes of the Quigrich family of Dewars seem to have fallen very low, and for a money payment they parted with the relic to the MacDonells of Glengarry. The MacDonells had remained Catholics, and consequently had a great regard for the Quigrich. The poor Dewars found, however, that their misfortunes only increased with their breach of trust, and they never rested until they regained possession of the Quigrich, and brought it back from Lochaber to Breadalbane. In the year 1734 they got the letter of King James III. recorded as a probate writ in the books of Council and Session at Edinburgh, at the same time procuring for themselves a certified extract of the document which they ever after retained along with the crozier. This transaction was carried through for them by John Campbell, Cashier of the Royal Bank of Scotland at Edinburgh.

The Dewars of the Quigrich were represented in 1782 by a Malise Dewar, a day labourer, who resided with his sickly son at *Sraid Ghlas* (Grey Street), Killin. It was here that William Thomson, M.A., a student of Oxford, saw the Quigrich, and, being struck by its antiquity and beauty, wrote to the Earl of Buchan, founder of the Society of Antiquaries of Scotland, in the following terms :— " At Killin, July 5th, 1782, in the house of Malise Doire, a day labourer, I was shown what he called the Quigrich. It is the head of a crozier, formerly belonging to St. Fillan. . . A youth of 19, the representative of his father's name, and presumptive heir to the treasure, lay drooping in an outer apartment under the last gasp of consumption. I am induced to advertise the Society of this circumstance lest the relic should at the death of the present owner become a sacrifice to the neediness of his heirs, and find a ready passage to the melting pot." Mr. Thomson's letter was, however, overlooked, and no action whatever was taken to secure the treasure for the nation.

In the year 1795, a Frenchman, M. Latocnaye, who was touring in the district, went to see the Quigrich and was charmed to find such a relic surviving amongst Presbyterians, who came over a hundred miles to Killin to procure water that had been passed through the interior of the crozier.

The failure of the line of Malise Dewar in the person of the consumptive youth seen by Mr. Thomson brought the Quigrich into the possession of his younger brother, Alexander. Alexander discovered that tourists who visited Killin were prepared to compensate him for the exhibition of the Quigrich, and he had an advertisement made out intimating that there was in his custody at Sraid Ghlas, " one of the greatest pieces of antiquity in Scotland. Every nobleman and gentleman desirous to see the foresaid piece of antiquity may be satisfied by calling for a sight of it." Alexander was glad to grant this *gratis*, " unless they were pleased to consider him for his trouble." In 1808 he took the Quigrich to Edinburgh and inserted an advertisement in the " Caledonian Mercury " of January 9th to the effect that there was " to be seen at the first entry below Covenant's Close, on Monday the 11th curt. and for a few days afterwards, a most curious relic of Scottish antiquity, which has been in the family of the proprietor since and before the time of King Robert the Bruce, and was confirmed to them by a grant from King James III. (a copy of which will be shown), being a relic of the famous St. Fillan, under which the Scottish army vowed to conquer or die, previous to the memorable battle of Bannock-burn. Admittance two shillings from 10 o'clock to 4 o'clock."

From Alexander Dewar the Quigrich passed to his son, Archibald, who migrated from Breadalbane to the neighbouring district of Strathearn. For some years he acted as sheep-manager on the Edinchip estate, and later on he occupied a small farm in Glenartney. During the years of agricultural depression that followed the Battle of Waterloo he found it hard to make ends meet, and like a great many Perthshire people he resolved to emigrate to Canada. Archibald Dewar left Scotland in 1818, taking the precious Quigrich with him, and, along with his son, Alexander, who followed a year later, he settled first at Beckwith, and afterwards at Plympton. Here, amid all the contingencies of a remote prairie clearing, the ancient relic was kept. It is told that Canadian Highlanders who had known of its healing virtues in the old homeland used to come occasionally to procure water in which it had been dipped, for the curing of sick cattle. The attention of Dr Daniel Wilson, who was secretary to the Society of Antiquaries of Scotland, was directed to its existence by the Rev. Eneas MacDonell, a Catholic priest in Canada and a descendant of the family who had procured it from the Dewars, in the seventeenth century. Dr. Wilson made several attempts through Father MacDonell to procure the treasure for Scotland, but without success.

Fortunate circumstances led, however, to the appointment of Dr. Wilson to a chair in the University of Toronto, and, once settled in Canada, he got into touch with Alexander Dewar, son of Archibald, who now possessed the Quigrich.

With admirable enthusiasm Dr. Wilson[1] stirred up interest on both sides of the Atlantic for the recovery of the Quigrich for his native land, and after long and tedious negotiations he achieved his aim. On the 30th December, 1876, Alexander Dewar, with the consent of his son, Archibald, executed a deed of transference and surrender of the Quigrich, and all its rights, to the Society of Antiquaries of Scotland, " on trust to deposit the same in the National Museum of Antiquities at Edinburgh, there to remain in all time to come for the use, benefit, and enjoyment of the Scottish Nation." In his letter to the Society, which accompanied the Quigrich and the deed by which it was conveyed to the Society, Dr. Wilson said, " I shall comfort myself with the feeling that my long absence from my native shore has not been wholly purposeless, since it has been the means of securing the restoration to Scotland of an historical relic of such interest and value."

St. Fillan's Bell,[2] or The Bernane.

One of the Dewars, against whom Hew Currie, prior of Strath-fillan, took action in 1549, was Malcolm, who was styled " Doire of Bernane." From a Retour of 1640 we learn that there was a croft at Suie in Glendochart called " Dewar-Vernan's Croft." " *Bearnan*," which means " The Little Gapped One," was a name frequently applied to the bells of Irish saints. The bell

BELL OF ST. FILLAN.

of St. Bridget was known as " Bearnan Bhride," while that of
St. Ciaran was called " Bearnan Chiarain." St. Fillan's bell had,
like the Quigrich, been anciently placed in the custody of a
dewar, or keeper, whose land was at Suie. Of the early history
of this relic we know nothing beyond the fact that it was regarded
of sufficient importance to be borne in the pageant at the
Coronation of King James IV. in 1488. After the Reformation
the office of Dewar-a-Bhearnain appears to have become extinct,
but the bell itself continued to be venerated equally with the
Quigrich, and its subsequent history is scarcely less remarkable.
For centuries the bell lay on a tombstone in the Churchyard of
Strathfillan, near the ruins of the Priory, where it was exposed
to the elements. It was used in connection with the rites observed
in curing insane people who had been dipped in the *Linne
Naomh*, or Holy Pool of St. Fillan in the river.

The Rev. Patrick Stuart, who wrote the Statistical Report
of the Parish of Killin in 1794, states that for some time prior
to his report the bell had been locked up to prevent its being
used for superstitious purposes. Public opinion must have been
too strong for the authority—probably the kirk session—which
had locked up the relic, for by 1798 it was back again in its
wonted place in the old churchyard. In August of that year an
English tourist, who was staying at the Inn at Tyndrum, hearing
of the fame of the bell, went to the churchyard, took it away,
and carried it off to Hertfordshire. When the Rev. Alexander
Stewart, minister of Killin in 1843, wrote the New Statistical
Report, he placed on record the fact that the bell of St. Fillan,

referred to in the previous report, "was stolen by an English gentleman forty years ago." Its whereabouts remained unknown until the summer of 1869, when the Right Rev. Bishop Forbes of Brechin, who happened to be on a visit to the Earl of Crawford at Dunecht, met there a gentleman from England who informed him that the bell of St. Fillan was in the possession of a relation of his in Hertfordshire. The worthy Bishop lost no time in getting into touch with the owner, and he very soon secured it for the Society of Antiquaries of Scotland. The bell is placed beside the Quigrich in the Scottish National Museum of Antiquities, Edinburgh. It is impossible for any Scotsman to look upon these two relics of St. Fillan that have so wonderfully survived the vicissitudes of centuries without being filled with something of the awe and reverence with which they used anciently to be regarded, and without feeling a deep sense of gratitude to the patriotic men who recovered them for "the benefit, and enjoyment of the Scottish Nation."

The identity of the bell as being that of St. Fillan was put beyond all doubt by a note which the man who took it away from the churchyard placed in his diary at the time. This note, which was carefully preserved by his descendants, sheds most interesting light upon the practices observed by pilgrims who resorted to the Holy Pool. The note is as follows :—

"August 9th, 1798. Arrived at Tyndrum by 4 o'clock. Rode after dinner with a guide to the Holy Pool of Strathfillan. Here again is abundant cause for talking of the superstition of the Highlanders. The tradition avers that St. Fillan, a human being, who was made a saint about the beginning of the eighth century by Robert de Bruce, consecrated this pool, and endued it with a power of healing all kinds of diseases, but more especially madness. This virtue it has retained ever since, and is resorted to by crowds of neigh-bouring peasantry, who either expect to be cured of real diseases, or suppose themselves cured of imaginary ones. This healing virtue is supposed to be most powerful towards the end of the first quarter of the moon, and I was told that If I had come there to-morrow night and the night after I should have seen hundreds of both sexes bathing in the pool. I met five or six who were just coming away from taking their dip, and amongst them an un-fortunate girl out of her mind, who came for thirty miles distance to receive the benefits of the waters, and had been there for several months together, but had never derived the smallest advantage, and, indeed, she appeared so completely mad, that, whatever may be the virtue of St. Fillan's Pool, I am sure Willis would pronounce her a hopeless case.

A rocky point projects into the pool. This pool is by no means the fountain head, for the water runs for a long way up the country, yet it is not supposed to receive its virtue till it comes to the very place, on the one side of which the men bathe, and on the other side the women. Strathfillan derives its name from the saint. Near Strathfillan a famous battle was fought between King Robert de Bruce and the MacDougalls, which the former gained owing to the assistance afforded by the prayers of St. Fillan.

Each person gathers up nine stones in the pool and after bathing walks to a hill near the water, where there are three cairns, round each of which he performs three turns, at each turn depositing a stone, and if it is for bodily pain, a fractured limb, or sore that they are bathing, they throw upon one of the cairns that part of their clothing which covered the part affected ; also if they have at home any beast that is diseased, they have

only to bring some of the meal which it feeds upon, and make it into paste
with these waters, and afterwards give it to him to eat, which will prove an
infallible cure ; but they must likewise throw upon the cairn the rope or
halter with which it was led. Consequently, the cairns are covered with
old halters, gloves, shoes, bonnets, night-caps, rags of all sorts, kilts, petti-
coats, garters, and smocks. Sometimes they go as far as to thrown away
their half-pence. Money has often been called the root of all evil, but for
the disease of what part of the body these innocent half-pence are thus
abused I could not learn. However, we may venture to suppose that they
seldom remain there long without somebody catching the disorder again.

When mad people are bathed they throw them in with a rope tied about
the middle, after which they are taken to St. Fillan's Church, about a mile
distant, where there is a large stone with a nick carved in it just large enough
to receive them. In this stone, which is in the open Churchyard, they are
fastened down to a wooden frame-work, and there remain for the whole
night with a covering of hay over them, and St. Fillan's Bell is put upon
their heads. If in the morning the unhappy patient is found loose, the saint
is supposed to be very propitious. If, on the other hand, he continues in bonds,
he is supposed to be contrary.

The Bell is of very curious shape, and has an iron tongue. St. Fillan
caused it to fly to this Church, and a soldier seeing it in the air, fired at it,
which brought it down and occasioned a crack in it, which is still to be seen.
I was told that wherever this Bell was removed to it would always return
to a particular place in the Churchyard next morning. This Church had been
formerly twice as large as it is now, as appears by the ruin of what has been
pulled down, a striking proof of the desecration, either of the population,
or religion in this country. In order to ascertain the truth of St. Fillan's
Bell I carried it off with me to England. An old woman who observed what
I was about asked me what I wanted with the Bell, and I told her I had an

Linne Naomh, HOLY POOL, STRATHFILLAN.

unfortunate relation at home out of his mind, and that I wanted to have him cured. " Oh, but," she says, " you must bring him here to be cured, or it will be of no use." Upon which I told her he was too ill to be moved, and off I galloped with the Bell to Tyndrum Inn."

The famous Bell is composed of bronze, and was cast in one piece. It stands 12 inches high, and at the mouth it measures nine inches by six inches. The ends are flat, the sides bulging, and the top rounded. In the middle of the top is the loop-like handle, terminating where it joins the Bell in two dragonesque heads with open mouths. It is cracked and has a hole at the top which impairs the sound. The Bell was probably rung by being beaten with some object that worked on a pivot outside of it. Its weight is eight pounds fourteen ounces. The late Marchioness of Breadalbane had an exact model made of St. Fillan's Bell, and this may be seen at Tyndrum Hotel.

The Fergy.

The third relic of St. Fillan claimed for the Church by Sir Hew Currie in 1549, along with the Quigrich and the Bernane, was termed " Fergy." The hereditary Dewar of this relic had a croft at Auchlyne, in Glendochart, which is referred to in 1632 as Dewar-na-fargs-croft. At Auchlyne there stand the roofless walls of the chapel in which the relic was preserved in Pre-Reformation times. This chapel is 25 feet long and 15 feet wide. The walls are about 9 feet high. The door is near the middle of the north side, and on the south side there are two windows faced with hewn stone. The soles of the windows are $5\frac{1}{2}$ feet above the ground level. There are four niches on the inside of the west wall and one on the south side. The chapel used to be known in Gaelic as *Caibel-na-Fairge*. It is impossible to say what the Fairge was. Dr. W. J. Watson[1] suggests that the name is derived from the Irish word, *airce*, a shrine. During the seventeenth and eighteenth centuries the chapel was used as a burial-place by the Campbells of Auchlyne. The last burial took place there over a hundred years ago.

The Mayne.

In the retours of 1640 and 1670 mention is made of a Dewar's croft at Killin, which was called Dewar-na-Mans-croft, or Dewar-na-Maynes-croft. The word " man " or " mayne " suggests that in this relic we have the left arm-bone of the saint, in the light of which he was seen to be writing by his servant. Like the crozier, the arm-bone would be enshrined at an early period, and it was probably this relic that was carried to the field of Bannockburn by Maurice, abbot of Inchaffray, and venerated by King Robert on the eve of battle.

We are told that on the night before the battle the king was very tired and extremely anxious for the well-being of his

(1) Watson's Place Names of Scotland, pp. 264-265.

army. He could not rest and kept turning over in his mind the chances of the morrow. Sometimes he went to his devotions, offering up prayers to God and to St. Fillan, whose arm, as he believed, enclosed in a silver case, was within the tent. In the meantime the case was heard to give a sudden crack while it lay still, with no one near it. The priest, who was astonished at the sound, went to the altar where the case was lying, and when he found the arm-bone in the case he cried, " Here is a miracle." Then he confessed that he had brought the case empty to the field, being afraid that the relic might be lost amidst the confusion of battle. The king rejoiced at the great miracle and accepted it as an omen of success. He then passed the rest of the night quietly at his prayers, with good hope of victory.

The interest shown by King Robert in the Priory of Strathfillan, and his remarkable devotion to the saint himself, are explained by the experiences through which he and his army passed while taking refuge in this remote and wild region after the Battle of Methven in 1306. Barbour tells us that, crossing from Aberdeenshire, Bruce and his little band came to the head waters of the Tay. Here they lived as outlaws among the hills. They had no shoes on their feet, and they had little food to eat. It is probable that the king and his gallant company received in their sad plight such shelter and hospitality as the poor priory could afford. While sojourning here Bruce became acquainted with the traditions regarding St. Fillan ; he was attracted to his relics and developed a strong faith in the saint's power to aid the righteous cause for which he and his followers were fighting.

Battle of Dalree.

The place of Bruce's retreat was made known to Alasdair MacDougall of Lorne, whose wife was a daughter of Comyn, whom Bruce had slain at Dumfries. MacDougall vowed to avenge the murder of his father-in-law, and he mustered the barons of Argyll.[1] With a thousand men he crossed Carndroma, intending to surprise the king. The royal party were, however, made aware of the approach of the MacDougalls and met them at Dalree, the King's Meadow, by the bank of the river, about a mile below the village of Tyndrum. Bruce's army numbered only five hundred. Along with him were his own brother, Edward, the Earl of Atholl, and Sir Neil Campbell of Lochawe. When the king saw that his enemies were too numerous for his little army, he advised a retreat, and the royalists therefore withdrew across the river. The king himself rode behind, bravely defending his retreating men from the attacks of their pursuers. Again and again he turned and successfully drove them back. Daunted by the defence of Bruce, the men of Lorne slackened in their attack, and when the chief saw that his enemy was likely to

(1) Barbour's Bruce, Book 2.

LOCHAN-NAN-ARM, DALREE, WHERE BRUCE'S COMBAT TOOK PLACE.

escape he became intensely enraged. Three of his hardiest followers, noticing his chagrin, swore that they would die, or slay the king. They planned a simultaneous attack upon him at a narrow place between a steep bank and the edge of a small loch,[1] where the king could not turn his horse round. The first man caught hold of the bridle of the king's horse, but with one blow Bruce cut off his arm at the shoulder. Another leapt on to his horse behind, but him Bruce dragged forward and slew. The third had seized hold of the king's leg, but when Bruce felt his hand he spurred on his horse. The man was thrown to the ground, where he was killed by a blow. Terror-stricken by such feats of valour, the MacDougalls withdrew from further attack. One of Bruce's assailants had seized hold of his mantle and held it in his dying grasp. In this mantle was found fastened the famous brooch of Lorne, long treasured by Alasdair Mac-Dougall's descendants as a memento of the historic combat. An old local tradition tells that as Bruce's men passed the loch in their hasty retreat they threw their arms into the water in order to lighten themselves. There is no doubt that King Robert ascribed his wonderful deliverance on this occasion to the good

(1) *Note.*—Lochan-nan-arm, Loch of the Weapons, near Dalree. There is a steep bank on the east side of this loch.

services of the gracious saint at whose shrine he had been so
kindly received, and eight years later, when he was facing a
more formidable foe, he addressed his prayers to St. Fillan of
Glendochart, believing that he could again aid the cause of
freedom. In this pious belief the King was greatly encouraged
by the presence of the precious arm-bone, the Mayne, within
his tent.

The Meser.

A fifth relic of St. Fillan is referred to in an ancient document
relating to a claim for rent made by Lady Margaret Stirling,
the wife of Sir Colin Campbell, of Glenorchy, against John
Molcallum M'Gregor. In the court of the Bailie of Glendochart,
held at Glendochart, Killin, on the 9th February, 1468, the said
John stated publicly that he did not hold the tack of the lands
of Corehynan from the said Margaret, but from the " Deore of
the Meser." It is impossible to discover from the name what
this relic was. Dr. Joseph Anderson suggests that the " Meser "
may have been the manuscript which St. Fillan wrote with the
aid of the light that streamed from his left arm in the dark.
On the other hand, Dr. W. J. Watson derives the word from
meise, a portable altar, such as was often carried about by the
attendant of a priest for the celebration of Mass.

The Healing Stones of St. Fillan.[1]

The Tweed Mill, at the north-west corner of the Bridge of
Dochart, Killin, which used to be a meal mill, stands on the

(1) Proc. Soc. Ant. Scot., Vol. XIV., p. 107.
    Ibid, Vol. XLVI., p. 264—seq.

HEALING STONES OF ST. FILLAN.

traditional site occupied by a succession of meal mills, the earliest
of which is said to have been erected by St. Fillan. Close by
the mill there used to grow a large ash tree, under which stood
St. Fillan's seat. This was a stone where he sat, and taught
the people who gathered round. The seat was swept into the
river by a great flood in the year 1856, and disappeared for
ever. The tree, however, survived until blown down by a gale
in 1893. The natives of Killin looked upon the tree as sacred,
and no one dared touch any of the branches. One man who
had the hardihood to cut off a branch with which to repair his
house had it soon afterwards burned to the ground. In the popular
mind his loss was regarded as a punishment for sacrilege. The
mill, which was in olden times busy milling all the year round,
ceased operations on the saint's festival day, the 9th of January
(O.S.). The present occupier maintains the ancient custom out
of respect for the memory of the patron saint of his establishment.

Within a small recess in the loft of the mill, and protected by
iron bars and a padlock, there are preserved eight stones, of
various sizes and shapes, associated with the saint's name, that
were formerly used for the purposes of healing. Seven of the
stones are water-worn, and two of them are "socket stones"
with highly polished holes, once used in connection with the
machinery of the mill. The largest of the stones weighs about
nine pounds. Each stone had its own particular part of the
body assigned to it in the process of healing. In 1836 the stones
were in the custody of an old woman whose ancestors had charge
of them for centuries back. In virtue of her "office" she had
a house at Killin rent free, and, although she charged no fees
for working the cure with the stones, she might receive presents
from her patients. Each stone bore some kind of resemblance,
fanciful, or real, to the part of the body to which it was applied.
For example, the stone used for the head is shaped somewhat
like a skull. The old woman rubbed the head with it, first three
times one way, then three times the reverse way, and finally
three times right round the head. At the same time she repeated
a Gaelic incantation. The "socket stones" were applied to
the nipples of the breasts of women who had pectoral inflammation. A quaint ceremony, which is still maintained by the
villagers of Killin, was observed in connection with the stones
on the 5th of January, Christmas Eve (O.S.). The stones are
then taken out and replaced on a fresh bed of straw, reeds, and
grass gathered from the river bank. Thus resting in their
accustomed niche in the wall, these old stones, to which the simple
faith of long ago attached strange mystical virtues, may be seen
by all who inquire at the Mill.

St. Fillan would appear to have had a great liking for stone
seats. Besides the one already mentioned, which stood at the
Killin Mill, there is another flat stone on the top of a knoll about

F

a mile to the west of the village, and on the north side of the river, on which he is said to have sat and taught. His name is associated with an earth-fast boulder at Killallan, Fillan's Cell, in Renfrewshire. At Suie, the saint's "Seat" in Glendochart, there is an ancient burial-place situated on a prominent mound, a short distance to the west of Luib Hotel, and about half way between the public road and the river Dochart. The mound rises to an elevation of about eight feet above the general level of the field surrounding it. The foundations of a wall, that at one time enclosed a circular space about twenty yards in diameter, may still be traced. Occupying the summit of

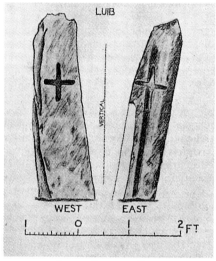

STONE CROSS AT SUIE.

the mound is a small, square erection or *caibeal*, which was built in 1759 by John M'Nab, " Possessor of Inchoane." Within the enclosure are several gravestones of Macnabs, belonging to the early nineteenth century. It is probable that this chapel is a reconstruction of a much older building, similar to that at Auchlyne, in which a relic of St. Fillan was preserved. Outside at the south-east corner of the building there is a stone[1] on which is carved a rude Latin cross that may very well carry one right back to the days of St. Fillan himself.

(1) Proc. Soc. Ant. Scot., Vol. LXIII., p. 346.

CHAPTER VII.

Early Lairds.

IN olden times most of the lands of Breadalbane were vested in the Crown, and the rents were paid into the royal exchequer. The kings themselves appear to have been frequent visitors to the district, coming in order to fish for salmon on Loch Tay and to hunt in the forests of Ben More and Mamlorn. Holinshed, the English chronicler, states that Donald IV., who was an intimate friend of King Oswald of Northumbria, was drowned in Loch Tay by the swamping of his boat in the year 647. An old tradition asserts that a royal castle once stood near the shore of Loch Tay on the farm of Milton, Ardtalnaig. If it ever existed this castle was probably a hunting seat, similar to that erected for King James II. at Loch Fraochie, in 1459.

The Crown lands were administered by a bailie, or chamberlain, who collected the rents, paid all necessary charges, and submitted an annual return to the Exchequer. The bailie also decreed justice throughout the district for which he was responsible, and the numerous knolls on Lochtayside and in Glendochart associated with the words, *croich*, gallows, and *crochair*, hangman, testify to the grim character of his jurisdiction. A field at Ardtalnaig, which had been used by the bailie when he visited the south side of Loch Tay, is still known as *Am Baillidh*, The Bailie. The district chamberlain was assisted in his work by local mairs, or officers, each of whom received an annual fee and a free croft for his services. It is interesting to find that the mair of Discher and Toyer in 1456 was paid a higher fee than that given to the mair of Dull, in respect of the fact that the former had the custody of the boat of the Isle of Loch Tay. In the Exchequer Rolls of 1266 and 1373 there are entries showing the amounts received by the Crown from farms in Glendochart. Prior to 1480 the payments made for Discher and Toyer to the Crown are given only as a slump sum, but in that year the bailie, who was Sir Duncan Campbell, the second Laird of Glenorchy, submitted a detailed rental in which the names of the farms and the tenants are given. Four of those farms were held by Sir Duncan himself. At one time part, at least, of Discher and Toyer was included in the ancient Earldom of Atholl.

From time to time lands in Breadalbane were granted to court favourites, and also to the Church. In this way the revenues gradually decreased until, at length, during the Reformation period, Sir Colin Campbell, the sixth Laird of Glenorchy, converted his leases of the Crown and Church lands in the district into feus. From henceforth the tenants in Breadalbane had no direct contact with the Crown. They had to pay their rents and render their service to their feudal lord.

Ancient Land-holders.

Among the tenants mentioned in the rental of 1480 are three names representative of families that had a very ancient connection with the district of Discher and Toyer. The oldest of these were probably the Macnaughtons, who are said to have been thanes. In 1480 Donald Macnaughton was tenant of a forty-shilling land in Eddergoll, near the east end of Loch Tay, and to this day the *Da Fhichead Sgillinn*, or Balmacnaughton, is held by a member of that clan. Macmillans also appear in the rental, which fact goes to bear out the tradition that the Macmillans of Argyllshire went there from Lochtayside, where they held the lands of Lawers until they were driven out by a Crown favourite named Chalmers, to whom they were given during the reign of David II. In Glenlochay the Macarbres held lands of the Crown in the fifteenth century ; and General Stewart of Garth states that at this period there were no fewer than twenty-four wadsetters of that name in the district. By the next century the name had entirely disappeared, probably because they exchanged it for an *alias*.

The Menzieses.

The Menzieses of Weem, who had been loyal supporters of King Robert the Bruce, acquired lands and considerable influence in Breadalbane during the fourteenth century, and continued to be lairds in the district for the next three hundred years. We have seen that in 1336 Alexander Menzies, who was then Lord of Glendochart, granted a missive to Donald M'Sobrell, dewar of the Quigrich, and confirmed him in the lands of Ewich. Before that year the thanage of Crannich on the north side of Loch Tay was granted by the Earl of Atholl to Robert Menzies, along with the lands of Auchmore, Easter Kenknock, and part of Morenish. The Menzieses held these lands until 1604, when they were made over to Sir Duncan Campbell of Glenorchy, along with the Tosachachdership of Ardtalnaig, by Alexander Menzies of Weem. The possessions of the Menzieses in Breadalbane and Glenlyon were included in Weem, and all of them, with the exception of Edramucky and Morenish, still pay teind to the minister of that parish. In 1891, when parish boundaries were re-arranged, Crannich and Auchmore were annexed to Kenmore parish, while Easter Kenknock was included in Killin.

The Drummonds of Stobhall.

At the beginning of the fifteenth century, the ten merk land of Finlarig was in possession of Sir John Drummond of Stobhall,[1] the ancestor of the Earls of Perth. Sir John was Justiciar of Scotland, and died in 1428. His descendant, another Sir John, was created Lord Drummond in 1487 by James III. He built Drummond Castle in Strathearn, and sold the lands of Finlarig to Sir Duncan Campbell of Glenorchy in 1503. The Drummonds had erected a castle at Finlarig in their time, and the possession of this stronghold made the position of the Campbells secure in Breadalbane. Finlarig henceforth became one of their principal seats.

The Napiers of Wester Ardeonaig.

While King James I. was a prisoner in England, the Earl of Lennox seized the Crown lands of Discher and Toyer, Glenlyon, and Strathtay, of which he had been hereditary bailie ; and he dealt with them as if they were his own legal possession. When, however, the King was restored to his throne, he took these Crown lands from the Earl, with the exception of the twenty-pound land of Ardeonaig. Duncan, the eighth earl, had three daughters, the eldest of whom was Isabella, Duchess of Albany, whose husband and two sons were executed at Stirling in 1425. Margaret, the third daughter, was married to Sir Robert Menteith of Rusky, and she bore him a son, Sir Murdoch. This Sir Murdoch married Christian Murray, of Tullibardine, and had one son, Patrick, and two daughters, Agnes and Elizabeth. Patrick died without issue, and the lands of Ardeonaig were divided between his two sisters. Napier of Merchiston married Elizabeth, the younger daughter of Sir Murdoch Menteith, and through her he acquired the wester half of Ardeonaig, which included Tullochcan, the middle third of Ardeonaig, and the ten merkland of the wester half of the Haugh, along with the fishings in Loch Tay, opposite these lands. From the Napiers these lands passed, at the beginning of the seventeenth century, to John Campbell of Invergeldy, in Glenlednock.

The Haldanes of Easter Ardeonaig.

Agnes, the elder daughter of Sir Murdoch Menteith, married Sir John Haldane of Gleneagles, and she brought to him the easter half of the lands of Ardeonaig, together with the fishings opposite these lands, half the multures of the mill, and the alternate patronage of the church. Along with this property there went the superiority of Carwhin and Carie, Eilean nam Breaban, and the shealings of Rialdt, in Discher. In 1526 John Haldane of Gleneagles parted with the superiority of Carwhin to James Campbell of Lawers, and in 1609 James Haldane made over all his possessions in Ardeonaig to Sir James Campbell, then Laird of Lawers.

(1) Christie, Lands and Lairds.

The Robertsons of Carwhin.

Two branches of the Clan Donnachie possessed lands on the north side of Loch Tay as early as the fifteenth century. These were the Robertsons of Carwhin, and the Robertsons of Strowan who held the land of Fearnan. It is impossible to say when the Robertsons acquired Carwhin, but in the Chronicle of Fortingall the following obituary notices of the family appear :—

1483, February 4. Death of Donald Robertson of Keirquhin.

1529, September 29. Death of Donald Robertson of Kerquhwin, at that place on the day of St. Michael, the Archangel, and he was buried in the nave of the church of Inchaden.

1553. Death of Katherine Neyn Dowyll vc Ayn, spouse of the Baron of Kyrquhwin, and afterwards spouse of Alexander Maxton of Cultoquhay, who died at Cultoquhay on the last day of April, 1553.

1559. Malcolm, Baron of Keyrquhon, died at Balloch, on 10th day of March, in the year of the Lord, 1559, and was buried at Inchaden.

When the superiority of Carwhin was transferred in 1526 to James Campbell of Lawers, the proprietor of these lands was William Robertson. Malcolm Robertson, who died at Balloch in 1559, would appear to have been the last of the barons of Carwhin. In 1546 the lands of Carwhin were included in a charter that was granted to Duncan Campbell of Lawers ; and in 1596 John Robertson, who sold the two merk-land of Murlaganbeg to Sir Duncan Campbell of Glenorchy, is referred to as " *alias* Baron, brother german of the late Malcolm Robertson in Carwhin."

Robertsons of Strowan.

The thirty merk-land of Fearnan, extending from the west march of the Port of Loch Tay to Allt Phaderley, along with the pendicle of Kinghallen, which lies on the northern slope of Drummond Hill, was held by the Robertsons of Strowan before 1451. In that year Robert Robertson, Laird of Strowan, received from King James II. a charter erecting his whole lands, which included Fearnan, into a free barony, as a reward for assistance rendered by him in capturing the assassins of King James I. King James V. granted a charter at Stirling in 1541, by which he confirmed to Robert Robertson of Strowan, and to his wife, Mariot NcAne, the lands of Fearnan. At the beginning of the seventeenth century the Robertsons were forced to assign their lands to creditors. At this time Sir Duncan Campbell acquired the four-merk land of Stron-fearnan, the tenants of which then were Hugh McKermeit, Jo. McIntaillour Moir, and Alexander Mc. O'Neill Vc-Eane, *alias* Robertson. In 1619 the Strowan lands in Rannoch and the barony and lands of Fearnan, were made over to Sir James Campbell of Lawers in consideration of debt. The Fearnan property was formally restored to the family in 1636, when the king granted anew to Margaret Grahame, daughter of George Graham of Inchbrakie, then wife of Alexander Robertson, fiar of Strowan, in liferent the thirty merk-land of Fearnan, with manor, mill of Fearnan, fishings, lakes, forests, grazings, and shealings ; reserving to Robert Robertson of Strowan, and to said Alexander, his son, in their liferents, the barony, and to Agnes M'Ranald, spouse to said Robert, liferent of the part granted to her. The manor-house of Fearnan was situated above the little graveyard of Stron-fearnan, and courts were held at *Tom a mhoid*, a short distance to the west.

The last Laird of Strowan to own Fearnan was Alexander, the eccentric poet and ardent Jacobite, who has made the name of the family so familiar. He was born in 1668. During his career the Strowan estates were forfeited three times. After the battle of Killiecrankie he fled to France, where he joined the court of the exiled King James VII. He was pardoned and returned to Scotland, but he supported the rising of 1715 and was taken prisoner at Sheriffmuir. He, however, managed to escape. By 1745 Strowan was too infirm to take the field himself, but his heart was with the Prince, and many of his men went out. His death took place at Carie, Rannoch, on 18th April, 1749. With his passing, the family became extinct in the male line.

The following characteristic letter written by Alexander Robertson of Strowan to Mr. John Hamilton, minister of Kenmore, is preserved in the Kirk Session records of that parish :— " Kenmore, December 30, 1730. This day Angus M'Donald, officer to the Laird of Strowan, & Donald M'Grigor, & Malcolm M'Grigor, elders there, presented a letter from the Laird of Strowan, dated December 11, 1730, the tenor whereof follows :—
Sir,
Since my Tenants, I do not know by what Inspiration, are willing to hear a person of your persuasion, I hope you will not see them dispossessed. Their seats in the Kirk are well known, pray let them sit easy, and have elbow room, Least a dispossession may Cause a rupture among you, not for the Honour and Interest of that Unity which ought to be visited in the people of God. You, who are a kind of Exorcist, cast out the spirit of oppression, hatred, and malice from amongst us, That every Man may possess his Paternal Inheritance from The Throne in Westminster Abbay to the Cobler's sate in the Kirk of Kenmore. In doing this be Rever'd by Sir,
Your most humble servt.
Alexr. Robertson, of Strowan."

The lands of Fearnan were administered by the Commissioners for the Forfeited Estates until they were disposed of in 1767 by Act of Parliament, to John, third Earl of Breadalbane, in excambion for part of the lands of Pitkellony, in Strathearn.

CHAPTER VIII.

The Macnabs of Bovain.

FOR nearly a thousand years Glendochart was the home of the famous, and once numerous, Clan-an-Aba, or Macnabs; yet to-day there is only one occupier of land bearing that name in the stretch of twenty miles between the head of Loch Tay and Tyndrum. Skene says that we may recognise in the Macnabs the descendants of the lay abbots of Glendochart. This appears to be a much more probable descent than that assigned to them by Buchanan of Auchmar, who claims that they were descended from the first abbot of Inchaffray, whose surname was MacDonald, in the beginning of the reign of Alexander the Second. Inchaffray, however, was founded in the reign of William the Lion, and the first abbot was Malis, presbyter and hermit.

The genealogy of the Macnabs, given in the Gaelic Manuscript of 1450, and printed in the Transactions of the Iona Club, " Collectanea de Rebus Albanicis," is quite absurd. This

BOVAIN, THE ORIGINAL HOME OF THE MACNABS.

genealogy traces the origin of the family back to a period prior to the founding of St. Fillan's priory in Glendochart.

The Macnabs, the Mackinnons, and the MacGregors appear to have had a common ancestry, and evidence of their kinship is found in two curious bonds of friendship that were drawn up between the chiefs of these respective clans in the seventeenth century. The first of these bonds is dated 12th July, 1606, and was entered into between Lauchlan Mackinnon of Strathordel, in Skye, and Finlay Macnab of Bovain, who happened " to forgether with certain of the said Finlay's friends in their rooms, in the Laird of Glenurchy's country, and the said Lauchlan and Finlay, being come of ane house and being of ane surname and lineage, notwithstanding the said Lauchlan and Finlay this long time bygane oversaw their awn dueties till adderis, in respect of the long distance betwixt their dwelling places," agreed with the consent of their kin and friends to give all assistance and service to each other ; and are " content to subscribe the same with their hands led to the pen." Mackinnon signs his name—" Lauchland, *mise* (i.e. myself) MacFingon."[1] The other bond of friendship, dated at Kilmorie, Skye, in 1671, was between Lauchlan Mackinnon of Strathordel and James MacGregor of MacGregor, and it is therein stated that " for the special love and amitie between these persons, and condescending that they are descended lawfully fra twa brethern of auld descent, wherefore, and for certain onerous causes moving, we wit ye we to be bound and oblesit, likeas by the tenor hereof we faithfully bind and obleise us and our successors, our kin, friends, and followers, faithfully to serve ane anither in all causes with our men and servants, against all who live or die."

A Fantastic Genealogy.

The genealogy of the Macnabs has presented much difficulty owing to the absence of family papers. It is said that the Macnab writs were destroyed on two occasions, first in the time of King Robert the Bruce, and again when the castle of Ellanryne was burned down by the English during the Commonwealth. The genealogy given in the Douglas Baronage is fanciful and fictitious and has an extraordinary history behind it. When Sir Robert Douglas of Glenbervie was collecting material for his book, in 1768, he wrote to John Macnab of Bovain, then chief of the clan, for information concerning his family. Macnab prepared a genealogy, which Douglas stated to be pretty good so far as it went, and he himself undertook " to make it fuller and better." At the same time the historian asked Macnab to furnish him with further details regarding his immediate ancestors and their children, and any anecdotes concerning the clan that he could recollect. John Macnab thereupon wrote

(1) Skene's Highlanders, p. 342 and 343.

to his brother, Archibald Macnab, then a colonel and afterwards a general in the British Army, in the following terms :—
" Dr. B. yours of the 6th June I had, and wou'd be extreamly
happy how soon your affairs would admitt of your being here.
You see I lost no time in writting Mr. Douglass, and sent him
the accompt of our Family in the very manner you sent me.
On perusing it frequently with all attention I found you justly
took care not to Incence or Raise the ill nature and Umbrage
of the B.[1] family against us. You are, as well as I am, sensible
the doing it att this time of day answered no ends, nor would
Monk's Letters being so very recent add any Antiquity To the
Family, and placing them or any pairt of them of course behoved
to rip up old sor's and Disgrace B's family. Mr. Douglass may
indeed mention his having by him letters from Monk will prove
that the Great Family keeped possession of the whole of our
Estate during the length of the Usurpation, and still hes some
of it to this day, but does not incline to insert them at this
juncture ; this I intended to have inseart in the skeath, but
delayed doing it till I had your thought thereon. I was also
for Two or three days Endeavouring, but in vain, to get rid of
the Etimologie of our name, I mean Abbot's son, Fearing that
when published the Readers might Infer therefrom wee were
bastards ; Because noe Abbot or Kirkman in Orders befor the
Reformation were allowed by their Canons marriage. To obviate
this my Intention was to putt it on this footing, viz :—That
as the Abbots of old amassed a deall of Riches, That this Abbot
of Glendochard had given all the lands he had acquired of
Temporalities to his Nevay, or nearest Heir, and had got thereby
the Appellation of M'nab *Eyre* (i.e. heir) ; by this we get quyt
clear of the Imputation of bastardy, which to the utmost of
our power wee ought to guard against. I have just now write
to Mr. Douglass that I sent you a Coppy of what was sent him,
and desyred he would print nothing till he heard from us, not
knowing but we might make some alterations. If I send him
what he wants I shou'd mention Achalader and Achlyne come
of our Grandfather ; let me have your opinion of this also. If you
approve of thir remarks I have made, and as I believe you have
keeped by you a Coppy of what you sent me, you may att
conveniency Extend it a new and remit to me. Frank is just
now at Ednr. pushing and procuring of some £100 pounds mentioned in my last. I expect he'll meet with success. Wee are all in
good health, and Jamie is become a Father, but I doe not think
his son will live any Time. My wife, Rob, and Don. Campbells
wife, who is here, joyne in compliments To you, and I ever
remaine,

Your affect. Brother,

Kinnell 3d July, 1768 "   John Macnab.

(1) B—Breadalbane.

The fantastic genealogy prepared by John Macnab and his brother in this remarkable way bears on its face the marks of inaccuracy ; yet, strange to say, it has been accepted as true by historians, and has received the approval of John Macnab, Callander, who wrote a book entitled " The Clan Macnab," published in 1907. In 1768 John Macnab, in making up his genealogy, reckoned himself to be eleventh in descent, tracing from father to son, from Gilbert Macnab to whom a charter was granted in 1336. This allows a period of possession of thirty-nine years and three months for each of his predecessors, and if each chief was twenty-one years of age when he succeeded, each must have attained an average age of sixty years. Between the years 1488 (when King James III. was murdered), and 1606, if we are to credit this genealogy, there were only three Macnabs in succession as chiefs. As a matter of fact, however, there were six chiefs during that period.

For much of the following genealogy of the Macnabs of Bovain, as well as for the interesting letter of John Macnab to his brother here produced, I am indebted to the late Mr. John MacGregor, W.S., Edinburgh, who placed at my disposal the results of his long and careful searches for information concerning the clan among the charters and papers of many Highland families.

During the time of William the Lion (1165-1214) the Abbot of Glendochart was associated with the Earl of Atholl in the government of the neighbouring part of Argyll. This goes to prove that even at this early period the Macnabs had attained to a position of considerable influence and power in West Perthshire. During the Scottish War of Independence the Macnabs supported the MacDougalls of Lorn in their opposition to Robert the Bruce. They fought against him at Dalree (1306), and at Bannockburn (1314). When Bruce gained control in Scotland, it is said that he punished the Macnabs by depriving them of the greater part of their lands and by burning their houses ; but in the reign of Bruce's son, David II., the Macnabs were reconciled to the Crown, and they remained loyal to the Throne ever after.

The Chiefs of Bovain.

I. GILBERT MACNAB. In the reign of David II. (1329-70) there is mention of a charter (" Index of Missing Charters ") to Gilbert Macnabbe (printed M'Nable) of the lands of Bothmachan, in the sheriffdom of Perth. The date of this charter is 1336 ; and it may have been in existence in 1768, as it is stated in the article in the Douglas Baronage to have been *omnibus et singulis terris de Bovain in dominatu de Glendochard infra vic. de Perth anno* 1336.

From the date of this charter, in the reign of King David, until the year 1406, there is no evidence as to the succession of the Macnabs of Bovain. It is true that the article in the Douglas Baronage assigns to Gilbert a son, Finlay, who lived in the reign of King James I., and who was father of Patrick Macnab of Bovain ; but no evidence is given for this statement. King James I. began to reign on 4th April, 1406, but at that time he was a prisoner in England, and on the death of King Robert III., Robert Duke of Albany, Earl of Fife and Menteith, was appointed governor of the kingdom. The after-mentioned charter was obviously granted prior to Albany's appointment as governor, or regent, and subsequent to his marriage with Margaret, Countess of Menteith, the dispensation for which marriage is dated 9th September, 1361.

II. ALEXANDER MACNAB. For his useful service rendered, and to be rendered, Alexander Macnab had a charter ('' Breadalbane Papers '') from Robert, Duke of Albany, Earl of Fife and Menteith, and Lord of Glendochart. It is not dated, but the lands conveyed were Ardekelechyr, Invermonekel, Bothmeghan, and Dovniche, which may be indetified as Ardchyle, Inver-monichele, Bovain, and Downich. This was not the original grant of these lands. They had belonged to Alexander Macnab before, for they were resigned by him into the Duke's hands in his chamber at Stirling, and they were regranted, to be held by the said Alexander, and John Macnab, his son, and the heirs male of his body, whom failing by Maurice Macnab, also son of the said Alexander, and the heirs male of his body, whom failing by Alexander Macnab, the son of the foresaid Alexander, and the heirs male of his body, whom all failing, by the lawful heirs whomsoever of the said Alexander, of the said Duke and his heirs in fee and heritage, as is set down more at length in the charters of the said lands. Not only does this charter preserve the names of Alexander's heirs, but it shows that there were older charters of which there is now no trace. The Lairds of Macnab at that time did not hold of the Crown, but of the Earl of Fife and Menteith, who is also styled " Lord of Glen-dhochir." The probability is that Robert, Duke of Albany, acquired right to lands in Glendochart through his wife, Margaret, Countess of Menteith, who had married Robert, as her fifth husband, and he therefore designed himself Lord of Glendochart in respect of that right. Alexander[1] Macnab was dead before 18th September, 1407, and is designed in the sasine to John, his son, as " the deceased Sir Alexander Macnab." His wife's name is unknown ; but he had three sons mentioned in the above-quoted charter :—1. John ; 2. Maurice ; 3. Alexander.

III. JOHN MACNAB.[2] On 16th September, 1407, the said Earl of Fife, now Governor of Scotland, granted a precept of sasine to his bailie of Glendochart, who was also named John Macnab, to give sasine of the lands of Bochvane, Ardeqhulley, Duffince,

(1) Not in Douglas Baronage.   (2) Not in Douglas Baronage.

with their pertinents, and of the office of " Farbaleschip " of
Auchlyne in the barony of Glendochart to John Macnab, the
son of the deceased Sir Alexander Macnab. He received infeftment four days later.   John McAlastair Macnab[1] was one of
the jurymen who made a declaration with regard to the rights
and privileges, and also the duties of the hereditary Keeper
of the *Coygerach* at Kandrochid (Killin) on 22nd April, 1428.
John Macnab survived 21st September, 1428, when in a court
held at Logierait, Walter, Earl of Atholl and Caithness, after
calling all parties interested, ordered a transcript to be made
of the last mentioned precept of sasine. Why this precept was
not in John's possession, and who the other interested parties
were, is not known. Whether John was succeeded by his son
is not known, but it seems probable that the next Macnab of
Bovain was Finlay Macnab.

IV. FINLAY MACNAB. On 24th August, 1450, a notarial instrument was taken by Finlay Macnab, who is not designed, in the
Chapel of St. Martin in the parish church of Perth. He insisted
that he and Edana of Abercromby had agreed in the last Sheriff
Court of Perth to meet on the said day and place, and settle
their disputes by certain arbiters, and that the party failing to
appear should lose his case, and be held liable in amerciament,
and therefore, protesting on the non-appearance of the said
Edana, that he had gained his case, and was entitled to the
stipulated fine. What was the nature of the dispute between
them does not appear. Finlay may have been the father of
Patrick, the next Laird. The authority of the Douglas Baronage,
such as it is, would support this view.

V. PATRICK MACNAB.[2] On the 18th November, 1464, " Patrick
Mackynab of Bochtuane " was confirmed by the Prior of the
Charterhouse in the office of Ferbaleschip of Auchlyne in such
wise as he and his predecessors held the same. This office had
been in the family for at least three generations. On 30th September, 1474, Patrick took an instrument that he had lost his
titles of the lands of Auchlyne, and that having desired a new
charter thereof with clauses and privileges as full as in his old
deeds, his desire was granted, and on the same day he confessed
before Patrick Russell, the Prior of the said Monastery, that
he held the lands of Auchlyne, in the Lordship of Glendochart,
of the said Prior and Convent in chief, in the same manner as
his predecessors held them of any persons prior to the grant
of them to the said Prior and Convent. The Prior and Convent
granted a charter dated 1st October, 1474, to the said Patrick
and his heirs male of the lands of Auchlyne, to be held of the
Prior and Convent in fee and heritage, for the yearly payment
to them of the sum of ten merks Scots, with a stockmart in

(1) B.B.T., page XXXV.
(2) Not in Douglas Baronage.

manner used and wont. Apparently the lands of Auchlyne were held of the Monastery, while Bovain and other lands were held of the Crown.

The probability is that Patrick Macnab married considerably before the year 1483, for on 26th June of that year, at Perth, he granted a liferent charter of the lands of Easter Ardchyle in favour of " Marion Campbell, daughter of Duncan Campbell, the son of Charles Campbell." The grandfather of this lady was probably one of the Strachur family of Campbells, who about this time held Glenfalloch.

On 1st January, 1486-7, Patrick Macnab[1] disponed to his son and heir, Finlay, the lands of Bovain, Ardchyle Easter, and Downich, and King James III. confirmed this charter on 21st March following. According to the Dean of Lismore's Book and the Chronicle of Fortingall, Patrick Macnab died at Auchlyne in the year 1488 ; but the Prior and Convent of the Charterhouse had granted a precept of *clare constat* in favour of his son and heir, Finlay, in the lands of Auchlyne, on 25th September, 1487. Whether Finlay was his son by the above Marion Campbell, or some former wife, is not known.

VI. FINLAY MACNAB, Patrick's heir and successor, received from his father the conveyance above mentioned of Bovain, and had the precept of *clare constat* from the Prior and Convent of the Charterhouse, as his heir in the lands of Auchlyne. He was infeft in the lands held of the Crown, and in Auchlyne. The latter infeftment was on 25th September, 1487. " Finlay Maknab of Bowayne " was a witness at Inverness to a charter on 29th January, 1497. He was dead before 6th July, 1499. There is no evidence as to his wife.

*VII. JOHN MACNAB had a precept from King James IV., as heir of the deceased Finlay Macnab of Bovain, on 6th July, 1499. This precept covers the lands of Bovain, Craigchur, Downish, and Easter Ardchyle, security being taken for the sum of £8 6s. 8d., being the rents of said lands at the last term, and for two silver pennies for the doubling of the blench farm.

VIII. FINLAY MACNAB, son of John Macnab of Bovain, is designed " of Bovain " on 5th January, 1502-3, when he had from Patrick M'nabe of Monzie a procuratory of resignation in his favour of the lands of Ewer and Leiragin, extending yearly to four merks, and lying in the barony of Glendochart, and on the 9th day of the same month Finlay had a Crown charter of these lands. It does not follow from the above resignation that his father was then dead. On 3rd April, 1506, Finlay had a charter from the Prior and Convent of the Charterhouse

(1) Reg. Mag. Sig. II., 1668.
(2) Thanes of Cawdor, p. 88.
* *Note*—In Douglas's Baronage after Patrick four Finlay Macnabs are shewn in succession, and Finlay's son, John, is omitted altogether.

of an acre, or croft, in the town of Killin. He is named as the first witness to a charter signed at Isle of Loch Tay on 18 September, 1511.[1]

Finlay Macnab married Mariot Campbell, and on 18th January, 1522-3, he gave her a charter in liferent of the lands of Ewer and Leiragan. She died at Perth[2] 9th July, 1526.

On 11 December, 1524, Finlay granted letters of baliary over his lands in favour of John Macnab, his son and heir. Again on 20 March, 1524-5, he granted a twenty-five shilling land out of the lands of Ewer and Leiragan to John Macnab, his " second son." On 1 April, 1525, with his wife's consent, Finlay granted a charter of the whole said lands of Ewer and Leiragan to the said John Macnab ; and on the same day John granted a charter of the whole of the said lands to Mariot Campbell, his mother. It is probable that Finlay's eldest son was killed with Duncan Campbell of Glenorchy, and his brother, John Campbell of Lawers, at Flodden. There are poems in the book[3] of the Dean of Lismore ascribed to a Finlay Macnab. The author was probably this Finlay who was contemporary with the Dean, in whose Chronicle both his own death and the death of his wife are recorded. It has even been suggested that the Dean was inspired to take up the work of preparing his book by Finlay, and that the poem entitled, " The Sluggard's Book of Poetry," was intended to encourage him with the undertaking. Finlay died[4] at Ellanryne, 13 April, 1525, and was buried at Killin.

IX. The ninth Laird was JOHN MACNAB, the second son of Finlay. At Perth, on 3 July, 1525, John was retoured by ten jurors, whose names are given, as lawful and nearest heir of the deceased Finlay, his father, in the lands of Bovain which had been in the hands of the Crown for three months. On the 8th of the same month the sheriff issued a precept for his infeftment, which was duly carried out on 11 July ; but the Crown apparently raised a summons against the jury who had served him heir to his father, for on 30 December, 1529, John and five or six of the jurors granted a procuratory to answer the summons. John Macnab granted a tack for nine years of the two merk-land of Auchessan, on 9 April, 1545, to John Campbell of Glenorchy. He died before 10 July, 1558, and left a widow, Eleyn Stuart. John had at least two sons, Finlay and Alexander Macnab.

X. FINLAY MACNAB, the tenth Laird, appears to have been a man of mature age at the time of his father's death, for on 3rd November, 1552, he bound himself under a penalty of 500 merks Scots, at the ensuing feast of St. Andrew, to resign in the hands of the Regent at Edinburgh all his lands in Glendochart holden of the Queen, for new infeftment of the same, in

(1) Reg. Mag., Sig. II., 3646.   (2) B.B.T., p. 119.
(3) " Scottish Verse from Book of Dean of Lismore," Prof. W. J. Watson, pp. xvi-xvii.
(4) B.B.T., p. 119.

favour of himself and his heirs male of him and his " moderne " (present) wife, Katryne Campbell, natural daughter of the deceased John Campbell of Glenorchy, and failing these heirs, in favour of Colin Campbell of Glenorchy and his heirs ; and providing that he, the said Finlay, shall have heirs as above specified, he should pay to the said Colin the sum of 300 merks Scots ; and further leasing to the said Colin Campbell all the said lands, together with the feu and tack lands which the said Finlay held of the Prior of the Charterhouse within the said bounds of Glendochart, and that for the life-time of the said Finlay, and for the rent which his father, John Macnab, got out of these lands ; the said Colin binding himself in return to defend the said Finlay, his heirs male above written, his friends and his kinsmen, in all their just causes. This agreement was either departed from, or Finlay was circumvented, for in the following charter, which is not a lease, nothing is said about it being only for Finlay's life-time.

Finlay granted a charter on 24th November, 1552, in favour of Colin Campbell, sixth Laird of Glenorchy, his heirs and assignees, of the lands of Ewer, Leiragan, and the lands of Bovain, Ardchyle Easter, and Downich, for a pair of gloves yearly in blench farm, for a sum of money paid to him in his great and known necessity. Following thereon Colin Campbell had a charter under the Great Seal, dated 27 June, 1553, confirming this charter, and as he had already taken sasine there was a clause inserted in the charter of confirmation declaring it as valid as if granted prior to the sasine. Having now acquired the lands of the Laird of Macnab, Colin Campbell of Glenorchy disponed these lands to the said Finlay on 8 April, 1559.

The marriage contract of Finlay Macnab and Katherine Campbell, natural daughter of John Campbell of Glenorchy, is preserved among the Breadalbane Papers. It was drawn up at the Isle of Loch Tay on 13 March, 1547-8. There is a stone in the Macnab burial enclosure at Inchbuie, which may be taken as marking the grave of Finlay and his wife. This stone is 3 ft. 10 ins. by 1 foot 10 ins., and is of a coarse, hard material. Towards one end there is a hole, 3 ins. in diameter, drilled right through it. The central panel on the stone is occupied by a shield, which bore the arms of Macnab of Bovain (now defaced). The initial letters " F.M." and " K.C." are carved above and below the shield respectively. Below are symbols of death, and surrounding the central panel is the inscription, "THIS BURIEL APERTINES TO FINLAY MACNAB OF BOVAIN."

Finlay, the tenth Laird, appears to have had a son, John, who is described in the charter of 8 April, 1559, as his son and heir, but who must have predeceased Finlay, his father. The last reference to Finlay is in a Court[1] case on 12 November,

(1) Breadalbane Court Books.

1573, when he sued John Bane Macnab for the rents of Sleoch and Acharn. The claim was not disposed of on that day, and when it came up again on 12th October, 1574, the pursuer was

XI. ALEXANDER MACNAB, Finlay's brother, who succeeded as the eleventh Chief. Alexander Macnab obtained a precept of *clare constat*, as heir to his brother, Finlay, of the lands of Ewer, Leiragan, Bovain, Downich, Achessan, and Craigchur, from Colin Campbell of Glenorchy, on 21 and 22 July, 1574. He continued the practice, begun by his brother, of disposing of his lands to the Campbells of Glenorchy. On 2 November, 1577, having borrowed from Colin Campbell, the sixth Laird, and Patrick, his third son, the sum of 500 merks, he interdicted[1] himself to them anent his lands of Kinnell and others. On the same day he also interdicted himself with respect to Bovain, Ewer, and other lands, to Colin Campbell, the second son of the Laird of Glenorchy, on account of another sum of 500 merks borrowed from him. Again, on 12 May, 1578, Alexander granted a charter of Ardchyle Easter and Downich to Katherine Ruthven, wife of Colin Campbell of Glenorchy, in liferent, and to Colin Campbell, the second son of Colin Campbell of Glenorchy, and to the heirs male of his body, whom failing, to Patrick Campbell, his brother german, and the heirs male of his body, whom also failing, to Archibald Campbell, likewise his brother german, and to the heirs male of his body. It will thus be seen that Alexander Macnab involved himself hopelessly with the Glenorchy Campbells, and for his foolish actions his descendants had to suffer severely.

Alexander Macnab of Bovain signed a document[2] at Kenmore on 10 April, 1585 relating to the repairing of the Kirk of Inchadney, and on 12 November, 1587, he witnessed a band of manrent,[3] also at Kenmore. There is no evidence as to his wife, but he had at least two sons, Finlay, by whom he was succeeded, and Patrick.

XII. FINLAY MACNAB, the twelfth Laird, was the last of his line to bear the favourite family name of Finlay. He married Katherine Campbell, who is described in an incomplete Glenorchy genealogy of the end of the seventeenth century as "first daughter to Sir Duncan Campbell, seventh Laird of Glenorchy, of his other children." The term, "other children," is evidently a euphemism for natural children. There is no mention of this marriage in the Black Book of Taymouth, which records the marriage of another natural daughter, also a Katherine, of Sir Duncan. Tradition says that Finlay had twelve sons, the weakest of whom could drive his dirk through a two inch board. The only sons whose names appear in records are John, the eldest,

(1) Books of Council and Session Vol. XVI., Dec. 1577.
(2) B.P's.
(3) B.B.T., p. 243.

G

and Duncan in Tullichcan. The Glenorchy genealogy above referred to states that Finlay had three daughters, one of whom married Finlay Mac-Alastair Macnab of Innishewan, and another married John Dow Macfarlane, son of the Laird of Macfarlane. Finlay is styled as a "sheriff of that part" (Glendochart) in a sasine[1] granted on 25 February, 1619. The earliest reference to him as "of Bovain" is in a charter[2] which he witnessed on 20 November, 1601, when Sir Duncan Campbell gave the lands of Mochaster to his second son, Robert Campbell. Finlay Macnab was entirely in the power of the Campbells. On 16 December, 1613, his brother, Patrick Macnab, renounced his title to Bovain and Wester Ardnagaul in his, Finlay's, favour ; and on the following day these lands were granted in wadset to Robert Campbell of Glenorchy. On the same day the charter[3] of the superiority of the Campbells over the Macnab lands was confirmed. In 1618 Finlay Macnab of Bovain and his kinsmen, Alastair Macnab of Innishewan and Duncan Dow Macnab in Acharn, were arrested[4] for the illegal carrying of arms, hakbuts, and pistols. Finlay was imprisoned within the Burgh of Edinburgh until he was released on the security of Sir Duncan Campbell of Glenorchy. In the Muster Rolls[5] for 1638 Finlay Macnab is stated to have possessed one sword and target, one hakbut, and one steelbonnet ; while his son, John, fiar of Bovain, who was then resident at Auchlyne, had one sword, target, bow, arrows, and one hakbut.

The Macnabs and the Civil War.

Finlay Macnab's career as chief extended over the troublous period of the Civil Wars, in which he and his clan were deeply involved on the side of Charles I. under the Marquis of Montrose. Finlay survived 28 July, 1656, when he signed an agreement anent the lands of Inneshewan and Bovain with John Campbell apparent of Glenorchy. While the Macnabs no doubt united with the Campbells in support of the National Covenant in 1638, they deserted to Montrose in 1644. This action brought them into direct conflict with the Laird of Glenorchy and his family, to whom they were bound by feudal and financial obligations. The consequences for the Macnabs, as we shall see, were ruinous ; and although they were able to survive as land-owners in Breadalbane for another century and a half, they were always at the mercy of their powerful neighbours, the Campbells.

The appearance of Montrose in Perthshire in August, 1644, was the signal for the Macnabs to rise under Finlay's eldest son, John Macnab, fiar of Bovain, who was called in irony Iain *Mìn Macanaba*, or Smooth John Macnab. According to the well-known Macnab legend[6] Smooth John was the leader

(1) Perth Sas. Vol. II. Folio 201.   (2) Reg. Mag. Sig. XI., No. 1277.   (3) B.P.'s.
(4) Reg. Priv. C.   (5) B.B.T., p. 401.   (6) Notes & Queries, 10 Ser., Vol. XI., p. 375.

in the fierce and murderous attack upon the remnant of the clan Neish, who after their defeat at Boltachan, near Comrie, took refuge on the Isle of Lochearn, at St. Fillans.

John Macnab married Mary Campbell, daughter of Duncan Campbell, fourth Laird of Glenlyon. On the 15 October, 1633, she had a charter[1] from her father-in-law, Finlay Macnab, investing her in the liferent of Kinnell. In this charter Mary Campbell is described as the " betrothed spouse " of John Macnab. John Macnab and his wife had a family of four sons, Alexander, Patrick, Archibald, and James, and six daughters, three of whom married. Of the sons, Patrick and Archibald died unmarried; James married Katherine Macfarlane, daughter of George Macfarlane of Rosneath, and lived at Auchessan. On 6 September, 1676, the Laird of Glenorchy was commissioned to arrest James Macnab in Auchessan, Finlay Macnab in Innishewan, and Archibald Macnab of Acharn, and imprison them "until they presented John, Callum, and Duncan McGibbon." Margaret Macnab, John's eldest daughter, married Gregor MacGregor in Ruskich, Glenlyon ; another daughter married John MacGregor, while Agnes, the third daughter, married Alastair Dubh Campbell of Achallader, who was known as " Black Sandie," and was father of John Campbell of Achallader, for fifty years chamberlain to the Earls of Breadalbane.[2]

According to the account of the Macnabs in the Douglas Baronage, John Macnab was of great service to Montrose at the battle of Kilsyth, and immediately afterwards he was appointed to garrison Montrose's own castle of Kincardine, which held out against General Leslie until provisions began to fail. John Macnab then managed to get the whole garrison of 300 men clear away ; but he himself and one private were captured. John Macnab was sent to Edinburgh, where he was tried, and condemned to death. He, however, contrived to escape from prison on the night before the day appointed for his execution.

There is a tradition in Breadalbane to the effect that, when Finlay Macnab saw the terrible destruction that was being wrought by the wild host that followed Montrose through the district, he intervened on behalf of the poor people who were burnt out of their houses, while their cattle were driven away and they themselves chased to the hills to perish in mid-winter. This tradition receives some support from the fact that on 21 January, 1645, immediately after the historic raid, an agreement[3] was drawn up at Finlarig between Alastair MacFinlay Macnab and his sons, Duncan and James, on the one side, and John Campbell, eldest son of Sir Robert Campbell, on the

(1) Gen. Reg. Sas. XXXVII, 103.
(2) Glenorchy Genealogy.
(3) B.P's.

other. By the terms of this agreement the keys of Ellanryne were to be delivered to John Campbell, while the Castle of Lochdochart was to be placed in the custody of Alastair Macnab, so that he himself and his sons with their families might remain there until the present troubles were over. They were to regard themselves as the Laird's men and to hold the castle for his use. The Laird of Glenorchy on his part was to procure remissions for the sons of Macnab.

It would appear, however, that the above agreement was not observed. The Macnabs, on gaining possession of the island of Lochdochart, held it for themselves against the Campbells. In the Black Book of Taymouth it is stated that John Macnab, fiar of Bovain, and Alexander MacFinlay Macnab in Inchewan, with the whole Clannab, joined with the enemies and took " the isle of Lochdochart, which isle of Lochdochart was violently tak from them again in 1646, and burnt through their default."[1]

The above record receives confirmation from coins and various articles found among the ruins of the castle when they were explored[2] by the late Mrs. Place of Lochdochart some thirty years ago.

(1) B.B.T., p. 101.
(2) Proc. Soc. Antiq. Scot., Vol. XL., p. 358.

THE CASTLE OF LOCH DOCHART.

Death of John Mìn Macnab.

According to the notice in the Douglas Baronage of the Macnabs, John Mìn Macnab was killed at the battle of Worcester on 3 September, 1651, and this statement has been accepted by the clan historians ever since. From a memorandum anent the lands of Croftchoise and Ellanryne, which was evidently written at the end of the seventeenth century, and entitled "the oldest writs the Macnab hes by him," it appears that the writer had before him discharges for feu duties on the Macnab lands paid to the Laird of Glenorchy by the Macnabs. Among the items detailed is one to the effect that Sir John Campbell discharged "John Macnab, fier of Bovain, for 1651 and 1652 of the sum of £7 11s. 8d. as the yearlie dutty on the whole of lands." There is no mention of any payment being made for 1653, the reason for which will appear later, but the discharge for 1654 was granted to "Marie Campbell, relict of John Macnab, fier of Bovain." The memorandum proves that John Macnab survived till 1652, and could not therefore have been killed at Worcester, but evidently he was dead by 1654. How then did he meet his end?

The circumstances of John Macnab's death at the hands of the English are revealed by reports of the activities of the Commonwealth troops in Scotland during 1653. In the spring of that year some Highland chiefs and Lowland noblemen began to stir in the Royalist interest, and during the last week of May they held a meeting at Killin to resolve upon the movement that led to the rising under the Earl of Glencairn. Colonel Daniels, commander of the Commonwealth troops at Perth, having heard of the Royalist rendezvous, led a company of soldiers into Breadalbane and came into conflict with the Macnabs. It was in this encounter that John Mìn Macnab was killed.

Colonel Lilburne,[1] commander of the Commonwealth army in Scotland, writing to Cromwell on 9 June, 1653, from Dalkeith, makes the following reference to the incident, "That little baffle which was put upon the Highlanders by Col. Daniells' partie hath much discouraged them, and was very seasonable to us, there being at that time in those parts divers great Lords and others complotting mischief, who since are discovered to us, and I hope to have some of them by the craigs; yet your Lordship may believe that many of them are in so desperate a condition that they would be glad to lay hold of the least opportunity to disturb us." In another communication[2] written two days previously, Colonel Lilburne gave the following details of the incident:—"Last week a partie of horse and foot being

(1) Scotland and the Commonwealth. p.p. 142-3.
(2) Ibid. note.

sent forth from St. Johnstons (Perth) towards the Highlands, in Athole, to arrest the collector, the Lord MacKnab, one of the great Montrossians, with his whole clan, did rise upon our partie ; and coming to them, after some little parley (we having got some of their cattel together) they offered our partie free quarter, if they would lay downe arms and return in peace. But our men, not willing to be so affronted, stood upon their defence ; which the Highlanders perceiving, sent a flight of arrows and a volley of shot among them ; and ours letting fly again at them, killed MacKnab, the great chieftain of that wicked clan, with four more, and fell upon them and routed them all." There can be no doubt that the " great Montrossian " who thus met his death was the fierce and dauntless warrior, John Mìn Macnab, who by his deeds added Neish's head, the boat, and the motto, " Timor omnis abesto," to the armorial bearings of his clan.

General Monk and the Macnabs.

The Macnab's castle of Ellanryne, with a half merk of land attached to it, stood on the east bank of the river Lochay and within half a mile of the Laird of Glenorchy's stronghold at Finlarig. The presence of a hostile clan at their very door had been a source of much trouble and annoyance to the Campbells during recent years ; and they no doubt gave every encouragement to the English, when in 1654 the latter gained control in Breadalbane, to burn and destroy the ancient castle, and to carry away the Macnab writs. General Monk gave over the Macnab lands to the Laird of Glenòrchy and his people, granting them full permission to help themselves to the property of the rebel clansmen. On 21 November, 1654, Monk sent the following letter[1] to the commanders of the garrisons at Finlarig, Balloch, and Weem, instructing them to assist Glenorchy in the work of spoliation :—" In regaird of the manie insolences and depredations off the Maknabs and ther pairtie and uther under ther Comand upon the Laird of Glenorquhay, and his tenents, thes ar therfor to authorize you to be assisting unto the said Laird of Glenorquhay to mak up his said Losses out off the chieffs of the Maknabs estaits, and also quhatt farder Losses they sall sustene ; to be Lykwise assisting unto the said Lord Glenorquhay to put the haill Macknabs out off the countrie till such tyme they give good securitie off Low Countrie Gentlemen, that the said Laird Glenorquhay sall be in securitie in tyme coming : unto all ther presents sall be your warrant ; given under my hand and seall att Dalkeith,"

The Campbells, in their merciless attack upon the Macnabs, seem to have awakened strong resentment in certain quarters, and very soon after the above orders were given representation

(1) Nat. Lib. Edin.

was made to Monk on behalf of the widow of John Macnab and her children and other members of the clan. The result was that on 18 December following Monk[1] wrote as follows to the Laird of Glenorchy :—" Understanding that by virtue of my late order for your having satisfaction out of the estates of the McNabbs you are proceeding against the widow of the Laird of McNabb deceast, I desire you will forbeare to trouble her, in regard shee has paid sesse, and lived peaceably since her husband's death ; nor would I have you extend that order to any that live peaceably at home ; but such as are obstinate and continue out in arms against the Commonwealth. I desire you also to forbeare to meddle with any of the Magriggors."

Monk followed up this communication with an order to Captain Gascoigne, in charge of the garrison at Finlarig, commanding him to see that Lady Macnab and her children were protected from the Campbells. The order to Gascoigne, sent from Dalkeith, dated, 18 January, 1654-5, was in the following terms:— " I do hereby declare that it was not intended by my order for repairing of the Laird of Glenorchy's losses by the Macnabs out of their estates that the same should extend to the molesting or intermeddling with the estates of any of the Macnabs who live peaceably. And forasmuch as I understand that the widow of the Laird of Macnab hath lived peaceably, you are hereby authorized and I desire, in case any vexation be offered to the outing or dispossessing of the said widow and her family of the said lands or anything that belong to them under colour of said order to preserve the rights that to them belong, as if the said order had never been made, and to enter and to receive them into their lands ; and this favour also is to be extended to Archibald Macnab of Acharn[1]." By 1655, Alexander, eldest son of the deceased John Macnab, fiar of Bovain, attained his majority. In that year we find him being put in possession of his ancestral lands by his grandfather, Finlay. On 14 September, 1655, at Kinnell, Finlay Macnab of Bovain gave charter[2] to Alexander Macnab, his grandson, of all and whole the lands of Kinnell, Ardnagaullbeg, Bovain, Auchessan, Ewer, Suie, Acharn, and the half-merk land of Ellanryne, all lying in the Lordship of Glendochart and parish of Killin. On 23 September following, Archibald Macnab of Acharn, as bailie of Finlay Macnab, gave sasine to Duncan Macnab in Tullochcan, Finlay's lawful son, as attorney for Alexander in the above mentioned lands. There is no evidence as to the date of Finlay's death, but, as already stated, he signed an agreement with John Campbell, apparent of Glenorchy, anent the lands of Innishewan and Bovain, on 28 July, 1656.

(1) Nat.. Lib., Edinr.

(2) Perth Sas., Ser. 4 ; Vol. III., Fol. 20.

The Appeal to Parliament.

Alexander Macnab, who succeeded his grandfather as thirteenth Laird of Macnab, had no charter to prove that his lands belonged to him.   His writs had either been destroyed or were in possession of the Laird of Glenorchy.   He was therefore compelled to submit a petition[1] to the Scottish Parliament on 14 March, 1661, craving Parliament to force the Laird of Glenorchy to invest him in the Macnab lands in terms of several acts that had been passed by Parliament for assisting Royalists who had suffered during the period of the Commonwealth. The commissioners ordered the Laird of Glenorchy to be called before them, and in May, 1662, Glenorchy and Alexander Macnab submitted the differences between them to lawyers, the Earl of Glencairn, Chancellor of Scotland, being oversman, but no decree ensued on the submission.

Alexander had to deal with John Campbell younger of Glenorchy, afterwards first Earl ; and he found that the latter would make no concession until the feu duties outstanding for the years from 1656 to 1661 were paid.   When these had been discharged, John Campbell, acting for his father, granted Alexander Macnab a charter of his lands, on the narrative " that his father, John Macnab, fiar of Bovain, had been killed by the English and his writs destroyed, it was not reasonable that the said Alexander should be depryved of the loss thereof through a public calamity[2]" The half-merk land of Ellanryne, which Finlay had made over to Alexander, in the charter of 1655, was not included in the charters.   John Campbell evidently did not wish to see the Macnabs rebuilding the ruined castle of Ellanryne, or having any possession on the east side of the river Lochay.

On the 29 April, 1660, Mary Campbell,[3] widow of John Mìn Macnab, married Malcolm MacGregor, Tutor of the Clan MacGregor, who had been associated with her late husband in the Royalist army.   By an agreement[4] with her son, Alexander Macnab, Mary Campbell renounced her liferent of the six-merk land of Kinnell, which had been secured to her.   In return Alexander disponed to her and her husband in conjunct liferent, and to himself (her son) in fee, the lands of Ewer, in Glendochart.

Alexander Macnab married Elizabeth Menzies,[5] third daughter of Duncan Menzies of Weem.   Their marriage contract is dated 14 November, 1662.   Alexander must have died before 16 August, 1683, for by that date Elizabeth Menzies, his widow, was the wife of Duncan Campbell,[6] brother to Mungo Campbell of Kinloch, one of the Earl of Breadalbane's bailies.   Alexander Macnab's family consisted of two sons, Robert, who succeeded,

---

(1) Macnab Memorandum, Rev. A. T. Grant's Papers.   (2) B.P's.
    (3) Buchanan Par. Reg.   (4) Perth Sas., 10 Feb., 1664.
(5) Menzies Papers.   (6) Reg. Privy Counc., Third Series, viii p. 549.

and John, who died without heirs before 23 January, 1689 ; and two daughters, Jean and Agnes, neither of whom appears to have married.

XIV. ROBERT MACNAB, who succeeded as Fourteenth Laird of Macnab, was apprenticed to Colin Campbell of Carwhin, Writer to the Signet, Edinburgh, the Earl of Breadalbane's man of business, on 1 February, 1686. Robert Menzies of that Ilk was his cautioner.[1] It would appear from the Glenorchy genealogy, already referred to, that Robert married, as his first wife, a daughter of Robert Campbell of Glenlyon, by whom he had a son who died young. Robert's second wife was Anna, daughter of Sir John Campbell of Glenorchy by his third marriage. Robert was thus brother-in-law to John, first Earl of Breadalbane. He and Anna Campbell were proclaimed[2] at the Kirk of Killin on 10 October, 1697. They had a family of seven sons and five daughters. John, the eldest son, born in 1698, succeeded as fifteenth Laird.

Archibald Macnab, Robert's second son, died at Edinburgh, 2 January, 1790, after having had a long and honourable career, as a soldier in the British army. He was commissioned a lieutenant in the Marine Regiment of Foot, 26 January, 1740; appointed captain in the Highland regiment, 7 December, 1745; and promoted to the rank of Colonel of the 41st Regiment of Foot, 29 August, 1777. He was commissioned a Major-General in the army, 19 October, 1781.

Allan Macnab,[3] the sixth son of Robert, was a soldier in Sir Duncan Campbell of Lochnell's Independent Company, and died 9 March, 1735, at the age of 19 years. He was buried in the churchyard of Tarland, Aberdeenshire, where a stone marks his grave. On the stone is the following inscription, " Humanity with pity, both virtues shining clear, and those indeed are in a youth of birth and worth lies here." Of Robert Macnab's daughters. Mary,[4] the eldest, married John Campbell younger of Baleveolan. Their marriage contract is dated 8 June, 1720. According to the account of the family in Douglas' Baronage, only two sons. John and Archibald, survived in 1769. Robert Macnab died before 17 November, 1725 ; but his widow survived until 6 September, 1765.

Litigation and Increased Debts.

XV. JOHN MACNAB, who succeeded as Fifteenth Laird, served as a soldier in the Hanovarian army at the Forty-five, with the rank of major. He was taken prisoner at Prestonpans, on 21 September, 1745, and confined in Doune Castle until the rebellion was well over. It has been said that while the Laird of Macnab and his brother, Archibald, took the side of the government, the clan rose in support of Prince Charlie and

(1) Menzies Papers.   (2) Killin Par. Reg.
(3) Scot. Notes & Queries, March, 1893.   (4) Argyll. Sas. Vol. IV. fol. 502.

fought at Culloden with the Duke of Perth's men. In the list
of persons who were involved in the rebellion, and who were
wanted afterwards, there are only two Macnabs mentioned, and
neither of them belonged to Glendochart. With the Laird and
his brother opposed to the rebellion, it is unlikely that many
of their kinsmen and tenants would respond to the call of the
fiery cross when it was sent round Loch Tay by Archibald
Menzies of Shian and John Campbell of Glenlyon.

  John Macnab married Jean Buchanan, only daughter of
Francis Buchanan of Arnprior.   Her brother, Francis, who
joined the army of Prince Charlie, was executed at Carlisle on
18 October, 1746.   John Macnab had a precept[1] of *clare constat*
for his lands on 17 November, 1725. During his time the family
debts went on accumulating, but this fact did not prevent him
from carrying on many lawsuits against his powerful cousin
and neighbour, the Earl of Breadalbane.   Macnab disputed
with the Earl about the maintenance of the banks of the river
Dochart. He raised actions in the Court of Session over the
rights and multures attaching to the meal mills of Auchlyne,
and Millmore, at Killin. He further contended that the Earl
had still part of the Macnab lands in his possession. At length
John Macnab decided that he must give up the fight against
his powerful opponent, and on 24 June, 1756, he sent the following
letter[2] to John, the third Earl of Breadalbane :—" My Lord,
I am sorry that so many suits and disputes are subsisting betwixt
your Lordship and me, and to put an end to all these, I am
perfectly willing to enter into a general submission of all disputes
betwixt your Lordship, your wadsetters, tenants, tacksmen,
and me. And if agreeable to your Lordship, to be determined
by Mr. James Ferguson of Pitfour, your Lordship's lawyer.

    My Lord,

  Your Lordship's most obedient and most humble servant,

                                              John Macnab."

John Macnab and Jean Buchanan, his wife, had a family of
two sons and two daughters. Francis, the elder son, succeeded
as sixteenth Laird of Macnab. Robert was a doctor, and resided
at Bovain. Elizabeth, the elder daughter, married Dick Miller,
and Marjory, the younger, married Colonel Campbell of
Baleveolan. John Macnab died at Kinnell on 19 February,
1778, at the age of eighty years. His widow survived until
20 April, 1789.

Francis Macnab.

XVI. FRANCIS MACNAB, the sixteenth Laird, was born in 1734,
and died at Callander on 25 May, 1816. The grim face and
massive form of the Laird of Macnab have been made familiar by

<hr>

(1) Perth Reg. Sas. Vol. XIX. fol. 284.   (2) B.P's.

"THE MACNAB"—FRANCIS, THE LAIRD OF MACNAB.

From a painting by Raeburn, the property of Messrs. John
Dewar & Sons, by whose courtesy the picture is reproduced.

Raeburn's famous full length portrait,[1] which was painted at
Taymouth for John, fourth Earl of Breadalbane. Francis
inherited the family debts and estate burdens, but he sat
lightly under the weight of his financial obligations and treated
with contempt the numerous demands that came to him for
payment. He went on living the life of a feudal lord at Kinnell,
waited upon by a few faithful retainers, as if he were the greatest
man in the kingdom. His habits and eccentricities provided

Note.—There is also an etching of Macnab in Kay's Portraits, Vol. 1.

much amusement for his own generation ; and numerous stories about him have been preserved.

Francis Macnab remained unmarried, but he is reported to have had numerous natural children. On 8 August, 1786, Janet Buchanan, daughter of Robert Buchanan, sometime of Leny, and her son, Francis, raised an action[1] of declarator of marriage against the Laird of Macnab, on the ground of an alleged marriage, which took place by mutual declaration on 2 November, 1781. Macnab was, however, assoilzied by the court. Mrs. Murray of Kensington, in her book[2] describing a tour in Scotland at the end of the eighteenth century, referring to the Macnab burial-ground on Inchbuie, says, " It belongs to a Highland chief hard by, who once on laying his pretensions and possessions at the feet of a fair lady, whom he courted for his bride, told her as an irresistible charm that he had the most beautiful burying-ground in the world. Whether the lady preferred beauties she could enjoy in life to those offered her after death, I cannot say, but the chief was not accepted ; nor has he ever worn the chains of matrimony, though he has added to his family thirty-two children."

Francis Macnab, discovering that he could not find sale for surplus barley that he grew at Kinnell, started a distillery of his own at Killin, and according to Heron, who toured Perthshire in 1792, he produced the best whisky to be found in Scotland. He held the rank of Lieutenant-colonel in the Royal Breadalbane Volunteers, and on the parade ground at Taymouth he used to give his commands to his men in voluble and forcible Gaelic.

The Last Laird of Macnab.

XVII. On the death of Francis Macnab in 1816, the chiefship of the clan and the Macnab lands with their heritage of debt devolved upon his nephew, Archibald Macnab, only son of Doctor Robert Macnab, who died at Killin on 8 June, 1814. Robert Macnab had been married to Anne Maule, and besides Archibald he had a daughter, Anne, who married Robert Jameson, Advocate, on 28 July, 1811.

Four years before his death, Francis Macnab had made a disposition of the Macnab lands in favour of his nephew, Archibald, who is designed in the deed as of Easter Torry, a property which the Macnabs had acquired about 1778. Archibald Macnab had married Margaret Robertson, whose father was a Writer to the Signet, and a clerk in the Register House, Edinburgh. They had a family of three sons and three daughters, two of whom appear to have died in infancy. Of the others, Alexander died at Edinburgh on 20 May, 1828, in his eleventh

year ; William died at Pisa on 23 November, 1833, at the age
of twenty years ; Margaret died at Florence on 31 January,
1834, aged eighteen years ; Sarah Anne, the eldest born of the
family, survived until 19 January, 1894, when she died at
Florence at the age of eighty-six years. Alexander was buried
in Greyfriars Churchyard, Edinburgh, and the last three
mentioned members of the family were interred in the Protestant
cemetery at Florence, where their mother, who died there on
20 June, 1868, was also laid. A stone marks, their graves.

The career[1] of Archibald Macnab, the Seventeenth and last
undoubted chief of his clan, was remarkable and strange in the
extreme. He had been brought up with the expectation of being
a Highland chief, inheriting lands that had been in the possesion
of his ancestors for at least six centuries. When he came to
succeed as Laird he discovered that his lands were mortgaged
beyond redemption, the chief creditor being John Campbell,
fourth Earl of Breadalbane. By 1823 Archibald Macnab's
position had become desperate. The Court had issued a writ
of foreclosure, and numerous creditors were threatening to
imprison him for debt. He took refuge for a time with his cousin,
Dr. Hamilton Buchanan of Leny ; but his retreat was discovered,
and he had to flee. Macnab made his way to Dundee, where he
boarded a ship that was sailing to London. In London he
borrowed sufficient money from some friends to pay his passage
to Canada. On his arrival at Montreal the Macnab was given
a great welcome and entertained to a dinner by some of the
best people in the city. As he moved about the country he was
honoured everywhere for the sake of the name that he bore.
Through Bishop MacDonell of the Roman Catholic Church,
who had founded the settlement of Glengarry in Canada, Macnab
obtained introductions to persons of authority in the government.
The Governor-General at the time was Sir Peregrine Maitland,
who was greatly attracted by the chief's personality and engaging
manners, and when Macnab asked for a grant of land on which
to settle clansmen, whom he intended to bring out from Glendochart, he was given eighty-one thousand acres in the valley
of the Ottawa river. He lost no time in taking possession of
the estate, to which he gave his own name of "Macnab." He
then built for himself a villa[2] on a charming site commanding
a view of river, lake, and mountain scenery, such as would
appeal to the heart of a Highlander. In the meantime he got
into communication with his former tenants in Glendochart
and others in west Perthshire, through his cousin, Dr. Buchanan
of Callander. The bright prospects and wonderful advantages
offered to settlers on the Macnab's lands were widely advertised,
and some eighty-five men, women, and children arrived at

(1) See *Perthshire Advertiser*, Feb. 21, 1934   Article Chambers Journal, July, 1928
(2) Macnab's villa was destroyed in 1936 by a clanswoman in order to prevent it
being converted into a museum.

Montreal on 27 May, 1825, bound for the land of promise. They were met on landing by the chief himself, who had brought his piper with him to give them a right Highland welcome.

The journey from Montreal to their destination was slow and toilsome and took them two months, although it is covered to-day by train in a few hours. On arrival the Macnab allocated home-steads to the emigrants, and they proceeded to erect shacks and to clear the land of timber. It was altogether an arduous task, and when the chief failed to fulfil his promise to provide them with a year's food, they began to regret that they had ever left Scotland. For the winter they had to subsist on flour and potatoes, and not too much of that. The more independent men among the settlers began to grumble and complain of the treatment they received ; and as they dis- covered from other settlers near them that Government land in Canada was free, while they had bound themselves to pay rent to the chief, discontent became more wide-spread and intense. The protests of the Highlanders were met by the chief with acts of tyranny and oppression, and it was apparent that he was endeavouring to transfer the feudalism of Scotland to the free lands of Canada.

Macnab was on very friendly terms with the governing powers, and being himself a Justice of the Peace, with authority to hold courts, he was able to deal in a summary way with those of his tenants who gave signs of disloyalty. With the arrival of a new company of settlers the spirit of insubordination spread, and at length one man sent an anonymous communication to the Governor-General, complaining of the Macnab's acts of oppression. The letter was sent to the chief, and he at once concluded that it had been written by a certain Alexander Macnab, who had been giving him trouble. Without delay he sent the following extraordinary epistle to the suspected man :—

Kinnell Lodge,
"Alexander Macnab,   13 March, 1829.

Degraded Clansman,—You are accused to me by Sir John Colborne of libel sedition and high treason. You will therefor compear before me at my house of Kinnell, and there make submission ; and if you show a contrite and repentant spirit, and confess your faults against me, your legitimate chief, and your crime against his Majesty King George, I will intercede for your pardon. Your offended Chief,   Macnab."

It turned out, however, that the man accused was not·the writer of the offending epistle ; but he answered his chief's summons, and appeared at his house. Alexander Macnab protested his innocence, but all to no purpose. He was convicted in the chief's court and sent to his prison. On getting out the aggrieved man went to an able lawyer, who appealed against the conviction, and had the man cleared of all blame.

The Macnab was indignant, but his position became more and more difficult with the arrival of each new company of emigrants from the home-land. After the passing of the Reform Act of 1832, democratic ideas, that had found expression in that act, spread to the Canadian settlers, and they rebelled against the government of the proud and tyrranous Macnab. When Lord Durham arrived in Canada as Governor-General in 1838, a petition setting forth the grievances of the Macnab settlers was presented to him. He at once ordered an inquiry to be made, with the result that the illegal and oppressive rule of the Macnab was exposed. It was shown that he had wrongfully withheld the land patents from the people ; he had exacted rents from them, when none was due ; and he had restricted their freedom. He was compelled to refund the rents and to make restitution to those whom he had wronged ; and by the time he had done this Macnab was a ruined man. He remained in Canada until 1853, when he returned to Scotland to find himself landless and friendless in his native country. His wife and surviving daughter, who had refused to share in his Canadian adventure, were living in Florence, and for some years he was left to live a lonely and miserable life. His wife at length made him a small allowance, and with this he went to live at Lanion, Cotes du Nord, in France, where he died on 12 August, 1860.

Disposal of the Macnab Lands.

After the departure of Archibald Macnab for Canada in 1823, his creditors proceeded to dispose of what remained of the Macnab estate. Some of the lands had already been sold ; Ewer had been purchased by Mr. Edward Place of Lochdochart ; Suie by Mr. Colin Macnab ; and Craignavie by Dr. Daniel Dewar. The remaining portions consisted of Kinnell with the grounds and parks around the mansion-house ; the farms of Sleoch and Acharn, and the houses in Grey-street, all on the south side of the River Dochart ; Mill-more and several houses in the village of Killin, and the farms of Bovain and Craitchur on the north side of the Dochart. These subjects were all let and yielded an annual rental of £942 15s. Each tenant was under obligation to lead a load of coals from Stirling to the House of Kinnell. The burdens on the lands and the family debts amounted to the sum of £35,000. Although the estate was advertised for sale in June, 1823, it was not until 1828 that the properties, along with the superiorities over Ewer, Suie, Craignavie, and Arnfinlay, were sold to the fourth Earl of Breadalbane. The islands in the river Dochart, Garbh-innis, and Inchbuie, also became the property of Lord Breadalbane. The old burying-ground of the Macnabs is on the latter island.

THE HOUSE OF KINNELL.

Kinnell House.

Kinnell House is a plain building of some ten rooms, situated on the south side of the River Dochart, almost opposite the village of Killin. It faces the south, and the front walls are covered with ever-green creepers. The oldest part of the house probably dates from the seventeenth century, and, after the destruction of the Castle of Ellanryne, Kinnell became the seat of the chiefs. The ceilings of the house are very low, and it is probable that the rooms have undergone little or no alteration since they were occupied by Francis Macnab. The house was vacant for many years after it came into the possession of the Breadalbane family. Gavin, the third Marquis, and the Marchioness had the house re-furnished, and they resided there for a few weeks each year. They collected various articles of furniture and other antiques, that had at one time been in the possession of the Macnabs, and displayed them in the rooms and on the walls of the staircase. The family sideboard stood in the dining-room. Beside it was a brass candlestick that was said to have been in the family since the days of Iain Mìn. Silver shoe-buckles, spectacles, and a snuff-box that had belonged to

Note.—Kinnell House was renovated, and part of the Macnab relics sold, October, 1935.

Francis, were also shown, as well as several relics that had been associated with the name of Rob Roy. At the front of the house there used to be a large collection of mill-stones, querns, knocking-stones, and one or two ancient baptismal fonts, all of which Lord and Lady Breadalbane had gathered in from the district around. For most of the year the house was thrown open to visitors, and large numbers came to view the house that was once the home of the chiefs of Bovain. At the west end of the House of Kinnell is the famous Kinnell vine,[1] which was planted by the second Marquis of Breadalbane in 1832. This black Hambro vine rivals the celebrated vine at Hampton Court and has never been known to miss a crop.

Inchbuie.

Inchbuie, or *Innis Buidhe*, the Yellow Island, situated in the River Dochart, has from time immemorial been the burial-place of the Macnabs. It is approached down a flight of stone steps from the east side of the Bridge of Dochart. The whole island measures some two hundred yards from east to west. Near the steps are two massive pillars, and a little beyond them is a high wall that stretches across the island, having in it three open arches. The entire island[2] is divided into three sections by two artificial earthen mounds that run parallel to each other across it, at a distance of about one hundred and fifty yards apart. These mounds were no doubt thrown up at some remote period in the past, when the island was used for defensive purposes. The burying-ground proper is in the eastmost section of the island. Here within a walled enclosure are the graves of the chiefs. On a great slab of mica-schist there is carved the effigy of a warrior. The art is rude and primitive. Tradition says that this slab was taken from the shoulder of Ben Lawers, and that it marks the grave of one of the earliest chiefs. Another stone, also recumbent, covers the grave of Finlay Macnab, the tenth Laird, and his wife, Katherine Campbell. The ordinary members of the clan admitted for burial to Inchbuie were interred outside the enclosure to the east. Here there are many grave-mounds, some of them covered with rough stone slabs. There are two erect head-stones, with quaint carvings and inscriptions, dating from the end of the eighteenth century and the beginning of the nineteenth.

As the visitor treads upon the soft, golden turf that has given the name, *Innis Buidhe*, to this sacred spot, and proceeds under the shade of the sombre firs to the graveyard, he cannot but be filled with regret at the failure and almost entire disappearance of the wild warrior clan which for so many centuries dominated Glendochart, and played so prominent a part in Scottish history. The Macnabs are now scattered to the ends of the earth, but the traditions of the chiefs and their clan will cling to this beautiful and romantic countryside so long as the waters of the Dochart continue to surge and roar around the rocky foundations of the island where the dust of their dead reposes.

(1) Ferguson's Rambles in Breadalbane, p. 78.   (2) Proc. Soc. Antiq., Vol. XLVI., p. 265.

Genealogy of the Lairds of Glenorchy and the Earls of Breadalbane.

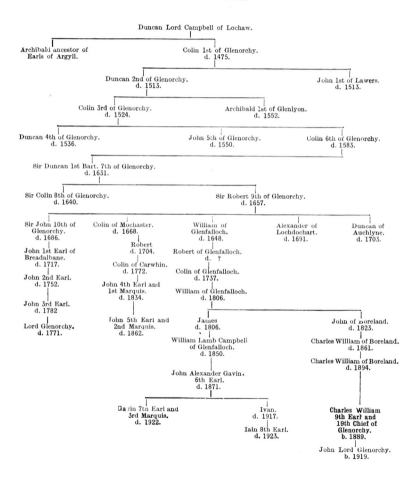

CHAPTER IX.

Coming of the Campbells.

THE Campbells of Glenorchy entered Breadalbane as land owners during the fifteenth century, and the greater portion of the district is still in the possession of a lineal descendant of that long line of chiefs, who, like the Campbells of Argyll, belong to the Mac Cailein branch of the family of Diarmaid o Duibhne[1]. The common ancestor of these two powerful Scottish houses was Sir Duncan Campbell of Lochaw, who was raised to the dignity of Lord Campbell in 1445. Sir Duncan's first wife was Marjory Stewart, daughter of Robert Stewart, Duke of Albany, who was regent of Scotland during the long imprisonment of King James I. in England. By her Sir Duncan had a son, Archibald, whose son, Colin, was created First Earl of Argyll in 1457. On the death of his first wife, Sir Duncan married again into the Royal Stewart family, this time taking Margaret Stewart, daughter of Sir John Stewart of Ardgowan, who was a natural son of King Robert III. By this marriage he had a son, Colin, born about 1406, who became the ancestor of the Campbells of Glenorchy, whose head in the person of Sir John Campbell was raised to the peerage in 1677, under the title of Earl of Breadalbane.

There is little information to be gleaned regarding the career of Colin Campbell, but tradition has associated his memory with tales of travel, adventure, and romance. He is said to have visited Rome three times and to have been made a Knight Templar at Rhodes. To succeeding generations he was known as *Cailean Dubh na Roimhe*, Black Colin of Rome. He is described as being "a man of high renown for military prowess, and for the virtues of social and family life. He was a stream of many tides against the foes of his people, but like the gale that moves the heath to those who sought his aid." His father granted Colin the lands of Glenorchy on the 20th October, 1432, and, being a knight, he came to be styled Sir Colin Campbell of Glenorchy. He appears to have been married five times, and by two of these marriages he added considerably to the lands with which his father had endowed him. His first wife was a Royal Stewart, being Mariot, daughter of Walter Stewart, son of Isabella, Duchess of Albany and Countess of Lennox. Along

(1) Diarmaid o Duibhne. (The genealogy of Mac Cailein has one ancestor Duibhne—Skene Vol. III. Appendix. The supposed descent from D. o D. is, of course, mythical.

with Mariot Stewart, Colin obtained certain lands in the district of Lennox from the Countess. The marriage contract[1] of 4th October, 1440, shows that these lands were conveyed to him under the grim stipulation that all thieves convicted there should be hanged on the Countess's own gallows at Faslane. A document among the Breadalbane papers reveals the fact that nullity of marriage was granted to Sir Colin against Janet Borthwick, Lady Dalkeith, in 1449, yet he appears to have married Janet Stewart, one of the three daughters of John Stewart, Lord Lorn, in 1448. With her he received the lands of Letterean and the Brae of Lorn by a charter dated 2nd March of that year. Sir Colin's next wife was Margaret, daughter of Robert Robertson of Strowan, and his last wife was Margaret, daughter of Luke Stirling of Keir, who probably survived him. He died at Strathfillan in 1475 and was buried at Kilmartin.

Sir Colin's first possession in Breadalbane was probably the lands of Auchreoch in Strathfillan. He next secured tacks of various other lands in the district for a period of years. He rented Auchmore from Menzies of Weem, Balloch from the Stewarts of Ardgowan, and part of Ardtalnaig from the Carthusian Monastery at Perth. For the part that he played in apprehending the murderers of King James I., Sir Colin was granted by James III., the grandson of that monarch, the Barony of Lawers, which was conveyed to him and Margaret Stirling, his spouse, and their heirs on 17th December, 1473. Lawers had previously been in the possession of Thomas Chalmers,[2] one of the assassins of the king.

Sir Colin further obtained the heritable title of the lands of Port of Loch Tay, along with the adjacent Isle on which was situated the ancient priory. He resolved to make the Isle his residence in the east end of Breadalbane, and had the priory buildings converted into a stronghold by the erection of a " barmekyn wall,"[3] or rampart, around the Isle. Here his successors resided from time to time until the Castle of Balloch was built by his great-grandson about 1560. Sir Colin also erected a tower in Strathfillan. Thus established at both ends of Breadalbane, Sir Colin laid firm foundations for the future prosperity of his family ; and we shall see how well his successors followed his example by making fresh conquests and keeping " things conquest."[4]

During his travels abroad Sir Colin carried on his person a charm stone which was described in an inventory[5] of jewels kept at Balloch in the seventeenth century as " ane stone of the quantitye of a hen's eg set in silver, whilk Sir Coline Campbell first Laird of Glenurchy woir when he fought in battell at Rhodes agaynst the Turks, he being one of the knychtis of

(1) B.Ps.   (2) Reg. G. S. 16 June, 1525.   (3) B.B.T.
(4) See photograph on page 36.   (5) B.B.T.

Rhodes." There may be more legend than truth in this statement, but a jewel answering to the above description is still preserved in the Breadalbane family. Tradition states that it was during a prolonged absence from home that his wife built the Castle of Caol-chuirn (Kilchurn), at Lochawe, devoting upon its erection the rentals of seven years from the estates.

An old tale relates that while at Rome on one occasion Sir Colin, who had been a long time away, dreamt a strange dream and, being much disturbed by his vision, he consulted a priest, who told him that he ought to return instantly to Scotland, as only his own presence could avert a serious domestic calamity. He made all haste for home, and when he arrived at Succoth, disguised as a beggar man, he craved food and shelter from an old woman who had once been his nurse. She recognised him, and informed him that an atrocious act of villainy was being perpetrated by MacCorquodale, an Argyllshire chief, who was besieging the Castle of Caol-chuirn, in order to carry away and marry Sir Colin's lady. MacCorquodale had intercepted every message that had been sent to Sir Colin, and had also spread a report to the effect that he had been killed in battle. Sir Colin hastened on, and arrived at Caol-chuirn in time to assist his son and clansmen in their fight. The wicked suitor was slain, and Sir Colin received a joyous welcome from his wife, his family, and his people. This legend was made the subject of a long poem published anonymously in 1840, under the title, " The Chief of Glenorchy," with a dedication to the second Marquis of Breadalbane.

Sir Colin's name recurs in the Exchequer Rolls from 1455 until the time of his death, in connection with an annual payment that was made to him by royal favour from the Crown lands of Discher and Toyer. Among the Breadalbane Papers there is an interesting document written in Latin, granting permission to Sir Colin to have a portable altar. It is dated March 27th, 1437, at Edinburgh, and is in the following terms : "Licence by Antonine,[1] Bishop of Urbino, Pope's legate in Scotland, to Colin de Cambel, Laird of Glenhurcha, in diocese of Argyll, for his known devotion to the Roman Church, to have a portable altar upon which at places convenient to himself he may have masses and other divine offices celebrated in presence of him and his whole family, by a fit priest."

Sir Colin was succeeded as Laird of Glenorchy by his eldest son, Duncan, whose mother was Janet Stewart of Lorn. He left Lawers to his youngest son, John, from whom are descended the Campbells of Lawers, Loudon, Murthly, Aberuchill, and Schian. Sir Duncan married Margaret, daughter of George Douglas, Earl of Angus, and by her he had a family of four sons and three daughters. Colin, the eldest son, succeeded himself,

(1) B. Papers.

while Archibald inherited Glenlyon, and became ancestor of the Campbells of that glen. John, Sir Duncan's youngest son, was Bishop of the Isles, an office that was also held by his nephew of the same name.

Soon after his father's death Sir Duncan was appointed to the office of king's chamberlain in Discher and Toyer, and in 1498 he became bailie of Glenlyon and of the Barony of Glendochart. In 1492 he acquired a feu charter of the lands of Port of Loch Tay, part of the lands of Eddergoll, and of Balloch from the Crown. He secured a tack of the lands of Crannich, a district lying to the west of Lawers and formerly a thanage, from Sir Robert Menzies of Weem. At the beginning of the sixteenth century the lands of Finlarig were held by two proprietors, James Muschet of Tolgarth, and John, Lord Drummond of Stobhall. Sir Duncan bought out the former in 1506, having already acquired the Drummond portion with the castle and the barony by a charter dated 22nd April, 1503. The several lands on Loch Tay, which Sir Duncan feued from the Crown, were incorporated into the barony of Finlarig on the 16th May, 1513. For several years previously he had held tacks, with power to sublet, of such lands in Discher and Toyer as he did not hold in fee. It will thus be seen that the second Laird of Glenorchy had attained to a position of supreme power and influence in Breadalbane.

During Sir Duncan's time the buildings on the Isle of Loch Tay were burned down. According to the Chronicle of Fortingall this took place on Palm Sunday, 1509, and is said to have been due to the carelessness of servants. The Laird reconstructed the old religious house, erecting "the great hall, chapel, and chalmeris." It is probable that the greater part of the walls still standing were built by Sir Duncan. There are Gaelic poems in the Book[1] of the Dean of Lismore attributed to Sir Duncan.

It would appear that he was accused of being involved in the Highland rebellion of 1504 against the king, but the charge may have been raised by enemies jealous of his influence at Court. His name was included in the list of chiefs summoned to answer for a charge of treason. There is no record of the result of the charge, and it was probably dropped. That the Laird lived on intimate and friendly terms with King James is evident from the fact that when the royal party was hunting in Strathfillan in September, 1501, he sent him presents. Again, while the king was staying at Ach-innis-chalain, at the foot of Ben Douran, in August, 1506, Glenorchy's bard was sent to cheer him with Gaelic songs. It is recorded in the books of the Lord High Treasurer that Sir Duncan joined the king and Sir William Murray at the pastime of "schutand at the schell." In 1513 he supplied spars for the great ship that the king was then building. Along with his brother, John of Lawers, and Archibald, Earl of Argyll, Sir Duncan fell at Flodden[1] on the 9th September, 1513. In the Black Book it is recorded that " he was bureit with his chief, Archibald Campbell, then Erle of Ergyle, in Kilmun, because in the foirsaid field they deit valiantlie togidder."

Sir Colin, who succeeded as third Laird, at the age of forty-five years, married Marjory, daughter of John Stewart, Earl of Atholl. During the struggle for the bishopric of Dunkeld in 1515 Sir Colin supported his cousin Gavin Douglas, who had been nominated to the office by the Queen Regent. The canons of the Cathedral, however, acting under the powerful influence of the Earl of Atholl, elected Andrew Stewart, brother-in-law to Sir Colin, but this fact did not prevent the Laird of Glenorchy mustering his men, and making an attack upon the servants of Andrew Stewart, who had garrisoned the palace and the steeple of the cathedral. Stewart had to abandon his claim, and Gavin Douglas was able to enter upon his duties as bishop.

It is recorded of Sir Colin by the family chronicler that " he kepit bayth conques and takis left to him. And was ane great justiciare all his tyme." Assured that the Campbells of Glenorchy had obtained a firm foothold in Breadalbane, and that their future was to be bound up chiefly with this region, Sir Colin erected a burial chapel at Finlarig " to be ane burial for himself and his posteritie." The present mausoleum of the Breadalbane family is on the site of Sir Colin's chapel. He died on the 26th July, 1524, and was buried at Finlarig, in his own chapel of the Blessed Virgin. He left three sons, Duncan, John, and Colin, each of whom was destined to be Laird of Glenorchy.

Sir Duncan, the fourth Laird of Glenorchy, married Elizabeth daughter of Sir John Colquhoun of Luss. His only son had died young, and thus at his death on 5th September, 1536, the succession devolved upon his brother, John. Of Sir Duncan it is said that he preserved intact the family possessions " keeping all thingis left to him be his worthy predecessors."

Sir John, the fifth Laird, married Mariot Edmonstone, daughter of the Laird of Duntreith, and had two daughters, Christian and Mariot, but no male heir. In 1532 he had been outlawed for failing to appear before the Justice in response to an order convocating the lieges. In the year of his succession Sir John was a member of the escort that accompanied King James V. to France for his marriage with Madeline de Valois, which was celebrated in the Cathedral of Notre Dame, Paris, on 1st January, 1537. Letters of protection for their property and interests were issued under the Privy Seal on the 28th August, 1536, in favour of the Earl of Argyll, his kinsmen, and their retainers.

(1) A poem of incitement addressed to MacCailein, preserved by the D. of Lismore, was most probably composed just before Flodden.

The list included John Campbell of Lundie ; John Campbell of Glenorchy, and Colin, his brother ; James Campbell of Lawers, and John, his brother ; Archibald Campbell of Glenlyon ; Finlay, Donald, John, and Duncan MacCarbre, who hailed from Glenlochay (Killin) ; Duncan MacGregor of Roro, and Gregor his son ; Gregor Dougalson of Balloch, and his brothers Dougal and John. From the fact that MacGregor of Balloch and his brothers went with Sir John Campbell it is evident that he was on friendly terms with them. As their superior he received the rents of Balloch, and allowed them to live in peace. It was to be otherwise when Sir John's brother, Colin, came to rule in Breadalbane.

Among the Breadalbane Papers there are several bands of manrent between Sir John and tenants on his lands, by whom he was accepted as chief and protector ; while they, on their part, undertook to serve him, and to give him or his successors a portion of their estates at death. The family historian relates of Sir John that " besyde keeping of the auld leving haill, he conquesit the twelve markland of Ardbeich on Loch Earn, quhilk he left to the house, with great riches and stoir." Sir John died on the Isle of Loch Tay on the 5th July, 1550.

Colin the Grey Laird.
(1550-1583).

Cailean Liath, Grey Colin, the youngest son of Sir Colin, the third Laird, came into the family possessions on the death of his brother John. He was born in 1499, and had thus passed middle age at his succession ; yet his career as laird extended to thirty-three years, and covered one of the most eventful periods in the history of Scotland. Through the changes that took place in Church and State, Sir Colin was able to strengthen the position of his house, and greatly to enlarge its possessions.

At the age of eleven years Sir Colin was sent by his grandfather to be fostered with a family of MacGregors at Stronfearnan. Fosterage was an ancient Celtic custom by which the child of a rich family was handed over to a family of lower rank to be nursed and brought up. When the child was sent to his new home a certain number of cattle was given by his father, and to this the foster parents added an equal number. This small herd was given free pasturage, and became the child's property. At the death of the foster parents part of their estate fell to the child. In return for fostering the child and granting him a share of the foster parent's inheritance, his father undertook to protect the foster parents. This curious custom has long since fallen into disuse, but at one time it bound the different classes of society together in bonds of the strongest affection. The closeness of the ties formed under fosterage is expressed by a Gaelic proverb, the meaning of which is—Fostership to a hundred, and blood relationship to twenty (degrees). Among the Breadalbane Papers there is a document recording an agreement that was entered into on 29th April, 1510, between Sir Duncan, the second laird, and two brothers of the Clan Gregor, John McNeill Vreik (Speckled), and Gregoure, his brother, at Stronfearnan, under which the MacGregors were to receive Colin, Sir Duncan's grandson, to be fostered. The MacGregors promised to give the boy " a bairn's part of gear," and to give " to the said Sir Duncan and his heirs their bonds of manrent and calps, that is the best aucht in thair housis the tymes of thair deceiss ; the said Sir Duncane and Coleyne, his son, being bound to defend the saids John and Gregoure in the lands of Stronferna, and the rest of the rowmis they possess as law will."

When Grey Colin became laird he showed little consideration for the kinsmen of his foster parents. Two years after his succession he turned Gregor Dougalson out of Balloch, where his ancestors had lived as tenants of the Crown for many generations. The long connection of this family of MacGregors with the lands of Balloch had indeed passed into a saying, " Bealach nan laogh aig deagh Mhac Griogoir," " Balloch of the calves in the hands of the worthy MacGregor." The curate of Fortingall recorded the tyrannous deed in his Chronicle in these words, " Expultio Gregorii Dougallson de Belloch per Colinum Campbell de Glenurquhay, Anno Domini Mv^clij at Vtsunda." The aged MacGregor crossed the Tay to the Carse of Dull, where he died three years later. The curate again put on record an event that deeply affected the countryside. " Gregor Dougallson died at Carsedall, near Dull, on first May, and was buried in Inchadin the second May with a great congregation of people and women, in the year 1555."

Building of Balloch.

As soon as he secured entire possession of Balloch, Sir Colin proceeded to build a castle. The Isle of Loch Tay afforded little room for this ambitious laird. It is said that the first site he selected was a prominent mound on the west bank of the Acharn Burn, just above the Falls, at a place called Tom-a-voulin. His men had levelled the ground, and the masons had begun to build, when an old woman who kept a few goats near the spot intervened. The old tale[1] translated from Gaelic runs thus :—" When Cailean Liath wished to build a castle at the east end of Loch Tay, Acharn was the first place that he selected, and his men had begun to work at a hill for a foundation. A place was levelled, and they began building the wall of the castle. An old woman who had goats dwelt at the place, and she knew that when the castle should be built, she would not be allowed to remain in the place any longer, or keep goats in it.

(1) Lord Archibald Campbell's Records of Argyll.

CASTLE OF BALLOCH, BUILT 1560.

So she said to the men, ' Cold is the place where you are building the castle. It will be exposed to every wind and storm.' ' And where would you build it ? ' they asked her. ' Where I should hear the first thrush,' she answered. Cailean Liath told them to ascertain where the first thrush should be heard. Now there was a field where MacGregor was wont to keep his calves. It was enclosed with blackthorn and hawthorn, and there was a pass called the Pass of the Calves, through which the calves were put in, and brought out. That was the first place where the men heard the thrush. The castle was built there, and it was called Caisteal Bhealaich, the Castle of Balloch, by the common people, but Taymouth by the gentry." The Castle of Balloch appears to have been occupied by the Laird of Glenorchy some time before 12th October, 1560, as the earliest document among the Breadalbane Papers to be signed at Balloch bears that date. At the time that the castle was built, and indeed for many years after, the property of the Lairds of Glenorchy scarcely extended to the eastward for more than a quarter of a mile beyond its gate. It is said that when Sir Colin was asked why he built his castle so near the margin of his lands his reply was, " Ou we maun just birze ayont." This answer was characteristic of his inordinate feudal ambition, and his insatiable lust of land.

Sir Colin took a leading part in promoting the Reformation. He was a member of the Parliament of 1560 when the Protestant doctrines received the sanction of law, and he acted on commissions that directed the policy of the Church. In May, 1561, he installed Mr. William Ramsay as minister of the parish of Inchadney, and in 1579 he promoted a petition asking permission to erect a church at Kenmore, as the church of Inchadney was inconveniently situated and was in a ruinous condition. He intended at the same time to transfer the manse and glebe to Kenmore, but this change had to wait for nearly two hundred years. In 1572 Sir Colin built a hostelry on the Coble, or Ferry, Croft, at Kenmore. This house, which was " loftit," and had chimneys, doors, and windows, was let on lease[1] to two trusted servitors of his own, Hew Hay and Christian Staness, his spouse. Sir Colin laid it down, as a condition of the lease, that Hew and his wife should have in their house at all times sufficient ale, bread, and other provisions, as were procurable within the bounds ; and to serve the country for reasonable payment. In the event of Hew's death before the termination of the lease, his widow could not marry again without the " special advice and consent of the Laird, or his heirs." Another reform that the Grey Laird effected at the east end of Loch Tay was the transfer of the markets from Inchadney to the Green of Kenmore. The Curate of Fortingall thus records a change that he

(1) B.B.T.

did not seem to favour, " Item the yer of God MVᵉ sexte XV yeris on the Nyn Virgines day the prasyn and the margat was haldin and begwn at the Kenmor at the end of Lochthay, and there was na margat nor fayr haldin ay Inchadin quhar it was wynt til be haldin. All this doin be Collyn Campbel of Glenurquhay." With the hostelry, the markets, and the kirk set up at Kenmore, the " Model Village " began its history.

Sir Colin recovered the lands of Port of Loch Tay and Eddergoll from the daughter of his brother, Sir John, to whom these lands had been left. He acquired the superiority of the Macnab lands, and through his influence in Church and State he was able to convert tacks and leases of lands that he held from the Abbey of Scone, from the Carthusian Monastery at Perth, and from the Crown, into secure feu tenures. Besides building the House of Balloch, he erected the Castle of Edinampill in Balquhidder, and added the four corner towers and the north chamber to the family stronghold of Caol-chuirn, Lochawe. He was twice married. His first wife was Margaret, daughter of Alexander Stewart, Bishop of Moray, and widow of Patrick Grahame of Inchbrakie. By her he had two daughters, Beatrix, who married Sir John Campbell of Lawers, and Margaret, who married MacDougall of Ragray in Lorn. Sir Colin's second wife was Katherine, daughter of William-Lord Ruthven. By her he had a family of four sons and four daughters. The eldest of the sons, Duncan, succeeded himself, while Colin inherited Edinampill. Margaret, the eldest of his daughters by this marriage, became the wife of the Earl of Glencairn. Sir Colin died at Balloch on 11th April, 1583, in the eighty-fourth year of his age. His latter years were disturbed by family troubles. A bitter dispute existed between himself and his son and successor, Duncan, although at Duncan's marriage in 1573 with Jean Stewart, daughter of John Earl of Atholl, his father endowed him with several lands on Lochtayside and in Glenlochay.

CHAPTER X.

The Lairds of Glenorchy and the Clan Gregor.

IN the Black Book of Taymouth it is said of Sir Colin, the sixth Laird, that he was " ane great justiciar all his tyme, throch the quhilk he sustenit the deidlie feid of the Clangregour ane lang space." This reference to the prominent part that the Grey Laird took in the persecution of the romantic clan, among whom he was fostered as a boy, leads us to trace briefly that tragic and melancholy chapter in Highland history. The misfortunes of the MacGregors during this period made them famous. As one reads the story of the persistent and relentless war that was waged against them one is filled with amazement at the indomitable spirit that they showed, and at the tenacity with which they maintained their separate existence as a clan.

Although the early Chiefs of Glenorchy had gradually come to possess the greater part of Breadalbane, and had acquired from the Crown the bailiaries of Discher and Toyer, and of Glendochart, they were yet looked upon in the district as outsiders. So far as Breadalbane was concerned the Chiefs were, even in Sir Colin's time, without a clan to follow them. The native population of the district included MacGregors, Macnabs, Robertsons, MacMillans, MacCawishes, MacCarbres, MacNaughtons, MacEwens, and several minor septs. For generations the majority of these families had held their farms of the Crown, or from the Abbey of Scone, or from the Carthusian Monastery at Perth, and as " kindly tenants " they enjoyed considerable freedom. The MacGregors were the most powerful clan in Breadalbane, but their chief resided at Glenstrae, in Argyll. The earlier Lairds of Glenorchy were themselves tenants of Crown and Church lands, but when the sixth laird attained to the dignity of a feudal lord, it was necessary for him to secure from his tenants not only their rents, but also an undertaking to render military service. The smaller septs readily accepted Sir Colin as their chief and overlord ; and when the Laird of Macnab in 1552 sold to him the superiority of his lands he and his clan came under obligation to serve the Laird of Glenorchy, and his heirs. The submission of the MacGregors could not, however, be so easily secured. Through the " greed of the Campbells," their kinsmen in Argyll had been robbed of most of their ancestral lands, and they regarded the intrusion of the Lairds of Glenorchy into Breadalbane with keen resentment. They were bound by the ties of clan loyalty, as well as by a proud tradition, to serve their Chief of Glenstrae and in war to fight under him alone.

In order to overcome these difficulties, Sir Colin adopted the wily policy of attaching individual members of the Clan Gregor to himself and his heirs by securing their bands of manrent. This policy explains the undertaking that was given on 10th July, 1550, by Alasdair Odhar McPhadrick V' Condoqhuy in Morenish, by which of his own free will Alasdair became a faithful servant to Sir Colin, and promised to go on horse, or on foot in the Highlands, or Lowlands, at Sir Colin's expense. In the event of a dispute arising between Sir Colin and the Chief of Clan Gregor, Alasdair was to adopt a neutral attitude. Sir Colin and his heirs were appointed executors of Alasdair's estate, should his own children not survive him.

This agreement was fraught with fatal consequences for Alasdair Odhar, and it proved to be the beginning of the deadly feud that disturbed the peace of the Central Highlands for nearly one hundred years. Alasdair's submission to the Grey Laird of Glenorchy brought down upon him the wrath of his fellow clansmen, by whom he was regarded as a traitor. From that day on which he signed the deed he became a marked man. Four months later Duncan Ladasach MacGregor, along with his son, Gregor, went on a dark November night to Morenish, and slew Alasdair Odhar,[1] taking his purse and forty pounds that it contained. Thereafter they proceeded to Killin, where they broke into the house of John MacVean, who was probably a friend of Alasdair, and, dragging him out to the front of the door, they struck off his head.

Duncan Laideus.

The career of Duncan Ladasach was a most remarkable one. For over forty years prior to the murder of Alasdair Odhar he had been the terror of the Central Highlands. From his youth he had been a robber. As long ago as 1510 he was hunted for his crimes through Lorn, Menteith, Atholl, and Breadalbane, and found refuge by fleeing to the wilds of Lochaber. The Earl of Argyll, acting on royal authority, chased him out of the country of the Camerons, and at last he fell into the hands of Sir Duncan, the second Laird of Glenorchy. He was cast into "dungeon deep," but while he lay in prison waiting trial, the Earl of Argyll and Sir Duncan were killed at Flodden. Their deaths brought him freedom. He was immediately joined by his former associates, and under his leadership the desperate band became the scourge of the countryside. They even induced the young Chief of Glenstrae, Alasdair MacGregor, to join them in their raids upon the Laird of Glenorchy's property. The

(1) B.B.T.

Chief was also with them when, in 1545, they set fire to the House of Trochry in Strathbran, took Robertson of Strowan prisoner, and slew four of his servants. Soon after this raid Alasdair, the Chief, died, and Duncan Ladasach was appointed the guardian of the young chief, Gregor of Glenstrae. The duty, therefore, of punishing the degenerate Alasdair Odhar devolved upon Duncan Ladasach, and we may be sure that he was not unwilling to undertake it.

When the murder of Alasdair was reported to the Privy Council the Government ordered Sir Colin to bring the outlaw to justice. He thereupon entered into an agreement with Stewart of Balindoran and the Drummonds of Drummond-Ernoch " to pursue after Duncan Laideus, his son, and their compleises, in all bounds and countries, wherever they shall happen to make residence, be reason that thai are our deidlie enemies, and our Souerane Ladie's rebellis." The commission to James Stewart and the two Drummonds was signed at the Isle of Loch Tay on 10th March, 1551 ; but within six weeks events took a strange and inexplicable turn with regard to the attitude of Sir Colin towards Duncan Ladasach and his associates. The spirit of revenge gave way suddenly to one of forgiveness. Had the Laird of Glenorchy come within the power of the desperate Duncan when, on the second of May, 1552, another agreement was drawn up by which Grey Colin moved by " the zeill of luf, and gude conscience, received Duncan and his son in his main-tenance " ? The deed further declares that Sir Colin had " for-given the said Duncane and Gregour, their servandis, complices, and partakeris, all manner of actionis, and faultis, that ony of thame hes comitit to me—providing alwais that the saidis Duncane and Gregour fulfil, their band and manrent to me and my airis in all pointis." This full and free pardon did not for long save Duncan Ladasach from the block. The curate of Fortingall records that on the 16th June, 1552, little more than a month after the signing of the deed of remission, there took place " the slaughter, and execution of Duncan M'Gregor, and his sons, Gregor and Malcolm Roy, by Colin Campbell of Glen-orchy, Duncan Roy Campbell of Glenlyon, and Alexander Menzies of Rannoch." The circumstances of the capture and execution of the wild freebooter and his sons are not known, but the entry in the Chronicle suggests that they were put to death with some show of trial and ceremony, probably at Ken-more.

The singular career and remarkable character of Duncan Ladasach made a deep impression upon the generation in which he lived. The adjective " Laideus " attached to his name in English probably represents the old Gaelic word *ladasach*, meaning " bold " or " stern." His career was made the subject of an anonymous poem of considerable length which was found written on the blank pages of a manuscript book, " The Romance of Alexander,"[1] that had been transcribed by Sir Duncan Campbell of Glenorchy, Sir Colin's son and successor. The poem is entitled " Duncan Laider *alias* Makgrerouris Testament," and the author represents the free-booter as telling the story of his life of crime, while waiting for death, and reflecting in a moral and religious mood upon the outstanding events of his turbulent past. In satire he disposes of his " spiritual goods," bequeathing negligence to the Curate, rapacity to the Vicar, oppression to the Parson, gluttony to the Prior, pride and arrogance to the Abbot, his " free-will " to the Bishop, and flattery to the Friars. Cosmo Innes, who directed attention to the poem, showed that it referred to a man who had been only too well known throughout Central Scotland, and not, as some were inclined to think, to an imaginary character. Innes says of the poem, " Some of the verses show a breadth and intensity of satire worthy of Lindsay. There is poetry in the wild wail of the chained robber, and, moreover, a sense of natural beauty, and a tenderness of feeling, which we do not look for in writers of that age." Bidding a last adieu to his former haunts, Duncan is represented as saying :—

> " Fair weill Glenloquhay, with thy forest free ;
> Fair weill Fernay, that oft my freind hes bene ;
> Fair weill Morinche, alace, full woe is me ;
> Thow wes the ground of all my wo and tyne ;
> Fair weill Breadalbane, and Lochtay so scheyne ;
> Fair weill Glenurquhay and Glenlyon baith,
> My daith to yow wil be bot litill scaith."

Gregor Roy.

When the control exercised by Duncan Ladasach over the MacGregors was removed, many members of the clan granted their immediate submission to the Laird of Glenorchy. Within six months of the freebooter's death no fewer than nine influential families signed bands of manrent by which they renounced Gregor of Glenstrae as chief, and undertook to follow and serve Sir Colin and his heirs. Gregor himself became a ward of the Campbells. He was placed under the charge of Duncan Roy, the Laird of Glenlyon. Here he grew to manhood, and was taught to read and write. He found congenial companionship in his guardian's family, and a strong affection developed between himself and Marion Campbell, a daughter of Duncan Roy. The alliance was approved by all parties concerned, and in due course the lovers were married. It looked as if peace had been established for evermore between the Campbells and the MacGregors.

The truce was, however, of short duration. When Gregor Roy came of age about 1560, he put forward to Sir Colin a

(1) B.Ps.

request for his ancestral lands of Glenstrae. He was met with a blank refusal, and instantly the whole clan rebelled. They felt that their honour as a clan had been grossly insulted, and even families that had given their solemn promise to adhere to the Laird of Glenorchy treated their bands of manrent as scraps of paper.

The MacGregors reverted to their old practices of raiding and plundering the Laird of Glenorchy's lands. At length he appealed to the Privy Council for protection, with the result that a commission of Highland noblemen was appointed to slay the MacGregors, and to burn them out of their homes. Glenorchy himself obtained special powers by which he might punish persons who gave shelter to members of the outlawed clan. He also entered into private agreements with the Earls of Argyll, and Atholl, under which they were to combine their forces in the war. Among the Breadalbane Papers there are several letters that passed from Argyll to Glenorchy relating to the movements of the MacGregors during this period. Alexander Menzies of Rannoch was unable to maintain order within his own bounds owing to the number of broken men that sought asylum in that region. In despair he made over Rannoch to Sir Colin, who entered into a bargain with MacDonnell of Keppoch. MacDonnell undertook to reside in Rannoch, expel the MacGregors, and plant his own men there. Queen Mary, however, intervened, and told the Laird of Glenorchy that he and his confederates must evacuate Rannoch and the Castle on the Isle of Rannoch. Sir Colin employed bands of ruffians who went about robbing and murdering the MacGregors and any persons suspected of giving them food, or lodging. Prominent among those hired assassins was James Mac-an-Stalker Rioch (Grizzled) in Ardeonaig. This man was so strong and dexterous that he could shoot an arrow from one side of Loch Tay to the other. Among the Stalker Rioch's victims were the sons of James MacGregor, Dean of Lismore, who resided at Fortingall. The murder of these gentlemen gave a shock to many hearts, and the young chief and his clan resolved that the crime must be avenged. On the 25th July, 1565, Gregor went with a company of his men to Ardeonaig, and put the Stalker Rioch and several of his followers to death. In his note recording this act of revenge the Curate of Fortingall says, " They were wicked and oppressors of the poor, and the said malefactors could not be suffered to live upon the earth."

The war against the Clan Gregor was a source of annoyance to Queen Mary and her government ; but when she came to understand the position of the hunted clan she showed greater wisdom than her counsellors. She ascertained the facts for herself by a visit[1] to Castle Menzies, at Weem. Her womanly

(1) " Arrow of Glenlyon," Ramsay.

I

heart was touched with pity for the persecuted fugitives, and in a letter to the Laird of Weem she pled that the MacGregors might be allowed to occupy the lands that they held of him before, and be given tacks upon reasonable terms. Among the Breadalbane Papers there are three undated letters that Gregor Roy wrote about this time, two of them to Sir Colin, and one to his Lady, pleading for consideration and kindness for himself and his friends.

The Grey Laird of Glenorchy would not, however, relent. He was determined that Gregor Roy must die. In May, 1569, when Queen Mary was a prisoner in England, he procured

WHERE GREGOR ROY LEAPT THE LYON WHEN PURSUED BY THE
CAMPBELLS AND THEIR BLOODHOUNDS.

authority to capture and execute the chief of Clan Gregor. The Earl of Atholl, the Laird of Lawers, and, strange to say, even Duncan Roy of Glenlyon, Gregor's father-in-law, agreed to join in the pursuit. Poor Gregor was chased from one hiding place to another for three months. Bloodhounds were used to track his steps. From time to time he visited his wife and boys at her father's castle of Carnban, but his movements were watched. At length, in August he was captured and thrown into the dungeon at Balloch. There he was left to languish until 7th April, 1570, when he was executed at Tom na Croiche, Kenmore. His wife was a witness of the execution, and she gave expression to the anguish of her grief and bitterness of soul in a song of weird, wild beauty that she sang to her infant son. The following free translation of some of the verses will show the spirit of the song :—

> " I was daffing with my loved one,
> Early on a Lammas morn,
> But ere noontide I was weeping,
> For my heart with grief was torn.
>
> Ochain, ochain, ochain, darling,
> Sad at heart am I ;
> Ochain, ochain, ochain, darling,
> Thy dad hears not our cry.
>
> Curses on chieftains and kindred
> Who have pained me so,
> And bereft me of my Gregor,
> Causing thus my woe.
>
> On an oaken block they laid his head,
> And made his blood to flow ;
> Had I there a cup to hold it,
> I'd sip of it, I know.
>
> O that Finlarig were blazing,
> And Balloch burning low,
> And that I round my Gregor Fair
> My arms could fondly throw."

Gregor Roy's infant sons, Alasdair and Iain Dubh, were placed under the charge of their uncle, Ewin MacGregor, at Stronmelochan. Ewin was also appointed Captain of the Clan until the chief should come of age. At Stronmelochan the boys grew to manhood, well instructed in all manly sports and exercises, but, unlike their father, ignorant of all school education. After Gregor Roy's execution, his clan maintained a guerilla warfare for a time against their enemies, inflicting serious losses upon the Laird of Glenorchy's tenants. As the years went on, however, conditions improved, and there was comparative peace in Breadalbane. Sir Colin died in 1583, and was succeeded by his son, Duncan. In the traditions of the Highlands the name of *Donnachadh Dubh a' Churraic*, "Black Duncan of the Cowl," is recalled with feelings of revulsion and horror.

Clever, scheming, unscrupulous and cruel, Sir Duncan resorted to the most sinister means to attain the aggrandisement of his already rich and powerful family.

When Alasdair came of age in 1588, and applied, as his father had done before him, for possession of the lands of Glenstrae, he was met with opposition from Sir Duncan. The young chief had no alternative but to assert his rights to his ancestral lands with the sword, and many of his Clan were ready to support him. The law was, however, on the side of the feudal lord who had secured written titles to these lands, and the resumption of the war could have only one end, the crushing of the MacGregors. Alasdair and his followers were undeterred by all considerations of prudence and caution. "Revenge! Revenge!" was their cry.

Glenfruin.

Driven to desperation, some of the outlawed MacGregors, among them the descendants of Duncan Ladasach, betook themselves to the mountains. Some bands of those broken men committed revolting crimes. The most shocking of all their deeds of vengeance was the murder of John Drummond of Drummond-ernoch, in the Forest of Glenartney. The story of the atrocious deed and its terrible consequences, is told by Sir Walter Scott in the "Legend of Montrose." For this crime and the support that the Clan Gregor gave to the perpetrators of it, Alasdair MacGregor and one hundred and thirty members of his clan scattered over the counties of Dunbarton, Argyll, and Perth, were proscribed by the Privy Council in 1589. Commissioners were again appointed to search for, take, and apprehend the persons named in the black list. The principal commissioner was Sir Duncan Campbell, who procured full powers to set up courts for the trial of the MacGregors. The lands and property of all those who were convicted were sold, and the proceeds divided between the Crown and the parties who brought them to justice. If any of the MacGregors were hurt, mutilated, or slain while they were being arrested, the commissioners were not to be held in any way responsible. Fire and sword were carried through the districts of Lennox, Lorn, Strathearn, Rannoch, and Breadalbane. The hunted MacGregors fled from their pursuers to other parts of the Highlands, and there survived until a general pardon was granted to the chief and his clan in 1596. On the 17th July of that year Alasdair MacGregor appeared before King James VI. at Dunfermline, and obliged himself as chief of his clan to keep the king's peace and good rule in the country, and in no way to invade, trouble, or oppress his Majesty's subjects.

The chief was no doubt willing, and even anxious, to keep the peace, but his broken men were not. The feudal lairds had encroached upon their ancient rights, and Alasdair could

not restrain them from raiding the lands of their enemies.
During 1602 the MacGregors made several incursions into
Dunbartonshire, and wasted the lands of Colquhoun of Luss.
Alexander Colquhoun complained to the king.   An act of
Parliament had been passed some time before forbidding the
carrying of arms, but King James, in consideration of the great
losses incurred by the Colquhouns, granted the chief and his
tenants liberty to wear various kinds of offensive weapons.
The arming of the Colquhouns was accepted by the MacGregors
as a challenge.   The situation was aggravated by many acts of
aggression on both sides.

At length the Clan Gregor mustered, and with the chief at
their head they set out for Loch Lomond, arriving at Glenfruin
on the 7th February, 1603.   They had a force of between three
and four hundred, and every man was a hardened warrior.
The Colquhouns had received some warning of their coming,
and were prepared for an attack.   The town council of Dunbarton
had issued an order instructing the burgesses to provide themselves with armour and weapons, and to be ready to muster
at any moment.   The forces at the disposal of Colquhoun numbered some three hundred horse, and four hundred foot, among
whom were the burgesses of Dunbarton.   The MacGregors
furiously charged the Laird of Luss and his men.   For a time the
Colquhouns bravely maintained their stand, but they were
ultimately pressed back, and thrown into disorder.   About a
hundred and twenty of them were slain, and the Laird himself
had to flee for Ross Dubh, with the MacGregors at his horse's
heels.

Immediately after the battle of Glenfruin, messengers were
sent by the Privy Council with letters to the sheriffs of Perth
and Stirling, and to the Laird of Glenorchy, ordering them
to assemble all men able to bear arms within their bounds
and to keep their bounds from invasion by the Clan Gregor,
under pain of being reputed to be " art and partakers with them
in all their wicked deeds."   An Act of the Privy Council was
passed on April 3rd, 1603, by which it was ordained that " the
name MacGregoure suld be altogidder abolisched, and that the
haill persounes of that Clan sulde renounce thair name, and tak
them some other name, and that thai nor nane of their posteritie
sulde call thame selffis Gregoure or M'Gregoure thair efter
under paine of deade."

Black Duncan of the Cowl and his second son, Robert Campbell, played a most active part in stamping out the name and
the race of Gregor at this time.   The latter, at the head of his
father's forces, followed up a large body of MacGregors who had
laid waste and burned several properties in Breadalbane and
Menteith, and, overtaking them on the Moor of Rannoch, he
thoroughly routed them.   Among the MacGregors slain on this

occasion were Duncan Abrach, grandson of Duncan Ladasach, and Gregor in Ardchyle, the grandfather of the " Bold " Rob Roy.

The story[1] of Alasdair MacGregor after the Battle of Glenfruin makes sad reading. His fate was bound up with intrigues and conspiracies in which the Laird of Glenorchy played a satanic part. At length poor Alasdair was betrayed by the Earl of Argyll, tried, and condemned to death at Edinburgh in February, 1604. He was not only hanged, but quartered. Many prominent members of the Clan suffered with him, but to him was accorded the "honour" of being "hung on ane pyn about an eln heichar nor the rest." Bowie, who was a servile creature of Sir Duncan Campbell's, adds in his story of the family of Balloch, " besydis the forsaidis that were hangit at the Mercat Cros of Edinburghe, thair wes sundrie hangit thair and in uther places quhais names were superfluous to wrett."

Without a chief to lead them, and with all the forces of the country ranged against them, the Clan Gregor became broken and scattered. So effective had the edicts of 1603 and 1604 been, that there was a lull in the persecutions for want of objects to arrest. Between 1610 and 1613 a new series of fulminations was issued against the doomed Clan. This time the Earl of Argyll was the leading commissioner. He and other landlords were empowered to bring to trial all persons who were suspected of affording shelter to MacGregors, their wives or their bairns. Parties who were found guilty paid fines in proportion to the assessed value of their estates. According to Privy Council papers the persons convicted of " resetting " MacGregors during these years resided in the districts of Inverness, Elgin, Perth, Strathearn, Menteith, and Dunbarton, and the amount imposed as fines was returned at £115,068 (Scots). More than half that sum was due from Inverness and Elgin. It was impossible for the Crown to recover the whole amount, but £44,665 (Scots.) was actually paid into the Exchequer. So wretched had the condition of the orphaned MacGregor children become that in 1615 we find Sir James Campbell of Lawers coming forward and pleading for them before the Privy Council. He proposed that for the maintenance of three or four score of them the sum of two thousand merks a month should be levied upon the landlords. The reply of the Laird of Glenorchy was that " he had gotten more skaith of Clan Gregor than all the subjects of the Kingdom." The scheme of the Laird of Lawers came to nothing, and the MacGregors and their bairns were left to starve. For the next three decades the persecution of the MacGregors was maintained, but, at length, when the Marquis of Montrose took the field for King Charles I., the scattered remnant of the Clan rallied round him, happy at the opportunity of joining under such a leader with others who had a feud with the hated houses of Argyll and Glenorchy.

(1) See that excellent biography, " The Arrow of Glenlyon," by Miss A. A. W. Ramsay, M.A., Phil. D. (1930).

CHAPTER XI.

The Black Laird of Glenorchy.
(1583-1631).

SIR Duncan, the seventh Laird of Glenorchy, was born some time between 1552 and 1555. He succeeded his father in 1583, and died in 1631, so that his career as laird covered a period of nearly half a century. So vast were the additions that Sir Duncan made to the estates already held by the family of Glenorchy that he has sometimes been erroneously regarded as its actual founder. In 1583 he acquired Ewich, Croftindewar, and Craigwokin, in Glendochart, from Donald Dewar. In 1598 he bought lands in Menteith from Alexander Balfour of Boghall. The following year he procured the lands of Glenfalloch from the Campbells of Strachur, and, at the same time, the lands of Duneaves and Culdares, near Fortingall, from William Moncrieff. He made extensive purchases of land in Menteith in 1618. By acquiring the little property of Wester Stix and other lands in Strathtay and Atholl from the Earl of Atholl, he was able to realise his father's ambitious intention of pushing on towards the east. From the Laird of Weem, Sir Duncan procured new charters for the lands of Crannich, Morenish, Auchmore, and Kenknock, which he had held previously on tack. For these charters he paid the Laird of Weem the sum of 28,000 merks. Owing to the low state of the royal exchequer Sir Duncan had to re-purchase the Lordship of Discher and Toyer from the Crown at a price of 2,000 merks.

He was commissioner for the smaller barons of Argyll in the Parliament of 1593, and again in 1599 he represented them at the Convention of Estates. In 1617 Sir Duncan was appointed to the office of keeper of the royal forest of Mamlorne, an office that was to continue in his family. He was knighted about the time of the marriage of King James VI. in May, 1590, and in 1625, he was created a Baronet of Nova Scotia.

Sir Duncan was determined to advance his power and influence by every means, whether fair or foul. He either erected or extended seven houses on different parts of his estates, and thus gained for himself the title of "Black Duncan of the Castles." At Balloch he spent a large sum of money to prevent the river from flooding the castle. He made extensive improvements at Coal-chuirn, and at Finlarig. He built the Castle of Loch-

SIR DUNCAN CAMPBELL, Bart. OF GLENORCHY ("Black Duncan of the Cowl.")

dochart, and after he had cleared the Fletchers out of Achallader, he erected a tower on the property. He also built two great houses in Lorn, one at Benderloch, and another at Barcaldine. On these undertakings he spent large sums of money, much of it gathered by oppressing the poor and conspiring against the rich.

Murder of Calder.

Sir Duncan was deeply involved in the nefarious plot through which Sir John Campbell of Calder[1] and the " Bonnie Earl

(1) See " Arrow of Glenlyon "—Ramsay.

of Moray " were murdered in 1592, and an attempt was made at the same time upon the life of the young Earl of Argyll. The political movements of that period in Scotland were complicated by court intrigues, and by religious and clan feuds, and are somewhat difficult to follow. The circumstances that led up to the plot were these :—When the sixth Earl of Argyll died in 1584, his son and heir, Archibald, seventh Earl, and afterwards father of the great Marquis, was only a boy of eight years of age. He was, therefore, placed under the guardianship of six Campbell cousins, among whom were the Laird of Glenorchy, Sir John Campbell of Calder, Sir James Campbell of Ardkinlas, and Archibald Campbell of Lochnell. Calder gained the trust and confidence of the young earl's mother, to the exclusion of the other guardians, who were seldom consulted about affairs relating to the Argyll estates. This led to jealousy on their part, and their feelings were aggravated by the fact that Calder was far in at Court and a friend of Maitland of Thirlstane, the Chancellor of Scotland. Argyll and the " Bonnie Earl of Moray " were closely related, and were regarded as the leading representatives of the Protestant movement in Scotland. Opposed to them was George Gordon, Earl of Huntly, the leader of the Roman Catholic party, who had lost his ancestral lands in Moray to the father of the " Bonnie Earl." Between Huntly and Moray and their respective parties there was an irreconcilable feud. Calder, as the friend of Argyll, supported the " Bonnie Earl." Sir Duncan at this time was busily engaged with his war against the Clan Gregor, and he was much annoyed to find that as soon as he had chased them out of Breadalbane they received shelter in Argyll through Calder's influence with the Earl. Lochnell, who was a weak, vain creature, happened to be the next heir to the peerage and the estates of Argyll after the young Earl and his brother, and, no doubt inspired by the evil advice of Black Duncan, he encouraged himself in the hope that one day he might be Earl of Argyll, and owner of the estates. Sir James Campbell of Ardkinlas, one of the guardians, had died, and was succeeded by his son, John, who was married to a sister of the Laird of Glenorchy. Sir Duncan resolved that Calder should be cut off, and he induced young Ardkinlas to promise that he would have this done. Lochnell undertook to dispatch Argyll. Sir Duncan then agreed to support Huntly against the " Bonnie Earl " and his party. The result of these several pacts was that Sir John Campbell of Calder was shot through a window by an agent of Ardkinlas while he was sitting in his own house in Lorn. The " Bonnie Earl " was lured under promise of royal protection to his castle of Donibristle in Fife, and there attacked and murdered by Huntly. Ardkinlas and Lochnell tried to poison Argyll at Stirling by bribing his servants. Argyll had a serious illness, but never suspected the cause at

the time. He, however, discovered the diabolical conspiracy
soon after, when he went at the head of a force of Highlanders
to punish Huntly and the other Catholic earls, who were en-
couraging Philip of Spain to invade Scotland. Lochnell was one
of Argyll's lieutenants, but all the time he was trying to betray
Argyll and his army to the enemy. The two armies met at
Glenlivot, and, acting upon instructions from Lochnell, Huntly
concentrated his attack upon the point where Argyll was
stationed. Lochnell hoped that an enemy's bullet would open
the way for him to the earldom. A bullet, however, found
himself, and the traitor fell on the field. Argyll and his army
were defeated, but he learned of the treachery of his faithless
guardians, and took immediate action. Lochnell was dead, but
others were at large. Ardkinlas was arrested, tried, and for a
time imprisoned. Under the terror of torture the miserable
creature made a confession, with the result that the part taken
by MacEllar and Iain Og Campbell, Lochnell's brother, in the
murder of Calder was revealed. Argyll had them both hanged.
In the end Ardkinlas was liberated. Glenorchy, the blackest
villain of them all, was trembling, but he declared that he
knew nothing of the plans or the doings of the conspirators.
The King, who had favoured Huntly's party because of his
jealousy of the "Bonnie Earl," was forced to support Argyll
and the Protestant party. Sir Duncan found that he had been
on the wrong side, and he was now afraid of Argyll, who was
Justice General of Scotland. On the 4th January, 1594,
Glenorchy managed to procure a band[1] from the Earl to the
following effect :—"Obligation by Archibald Earl of Argyll
on the occasion of certain rumours spread by evil disposed persons
having raised coldness between him and his loving cousin Sir
Duncane Campbell of Glenorchy, knight, promising never to
act deceitfully to the said Sir Duncane, or to misuse him in his
possessions or body, and that in case any misreport should
breed offence, he shall first advertise the said Sir Duncane
thereof fifteen days before he shall be holden to answer thereto,
and thereafter shall appoint a convenient place of trial thereof
in the lowlands before himself and his friends, the Earl of Mar
and the Sheriff of Air being present ; the said Sir Duncane
binding himself to behave kindly to the said Earl as his superior,
and to believe no evil reports of him in the future without first
reporting the same and giving up the reporter to the Earl."

In the evidence given at the trial of Campbell of Ardkinlas[2]
before the Privy Council for his part in the plot, some
strange revelations were made with regard to his own
and the Laird of Glenorchy's trafficking with witches and
wizards in order to secure their evil ends. The widow of Iain Og
Campbell, who was hanged with MacEllar, told how Ardkinlas

(1) B.B.T.
(2) Celtic Review, Vol. XII., No. 27.

consulted her about the practices and the powers of the witches of Lorn. He informed her that he was acquainted with a minister of the name of Patrick MacQueen who was a far better enchanter than any of the Lorn witches. This Patrick was indeed so skilled in his craft that " he could mak up and big ane castle " between sunset and sunrise. He had told Ardkinlas and the Laird of Glenorchy that they should both be arrested, but that they would be liberated through his (Patrick's) art. Ardkinlas had said to Margaret Campbell that Patrick was the enemy of Argyll, and given time he would compass the Earl's death by witchcraft ; and when the house of Argyll had fallen Ardkinlas and Glenorchy would have the estates between them.

This degenerate minister belonged to a family of MacQueens, or MacEwens, who occupied the farm of Duneaves, near Fortingall. They were in reality MacGregors, and in 1574 Sir Colin Campbell executed Donald Dow MacQueen at Kenmore, and appropriated his goods. Sir Duncan, however, restored the farm to Donald Dow's nephews, and when they died he entered into an agreement with Patrick MacQueen, Donald Dow's grandson, who was minister at Rothesay.[1] This was in 1594, and in the band the minister stated that he had proof of Sir Duncan's goodwill in giving him possession of the lands, " which he could not enjoy without the assistance of the said Duncan."

In the course of a few years, however, Sir Duncan had no further use for the wizard and his enchantments, and, wanting Duneaves for his illegitimate son, Patrick, he sent agents to turn Patrick MacQueen out. Patrick MacQueen, who was by this time minister of Monzie,[2] near Crieff, complained to the Privy Council in 1601 that he had sustained great trouble " through certain broken men and other evil disposed persons." They had taken from him his lands and possessions which fell to him at his father's death. They had destroyed all his houses, and " had given himself sundrie bloody wounds, and left him for dead." The injuries inflicted upon him were so serious that he was unable any longer to pursue his calling as a minister of the Kirk. The Privy Council listened with sympathy to the story of his grievances, and advised the King to grant MacQueen a third of the vicarage of Kingarth in Bute " for the better support of his wife and family." The Council received at the same time another complaint against Sir Duncan from Donald Menteith, Baron of Carwhin, Lochtayside, who charged the Black Laird's agents with the destruction of his house and property. Sir Duncan was called to task, arrested, and imprisoned in the Castle of Edinburgh until he paid a fine of forty thousand merks Scots, a sum equivalent to £2,000 sterling. Bowie, the chronicler of the family, who would find no fault in his chief, states that the charges were false, and had never

(1) Clan Campbell, Vol. VII.   (2) Scott's Fasti.

been proven. They were, however, accepted as truth by the poor and greedy courtiers of the time. No sooner was Sir Duncan free than he gained access to the King, and was commissioned by His Majesty to " enquire into the burning of Carwhin."[1] We hear no more of the Baron of Carwhin, or of the warlock minister of Monzie.

A Royal Favourite.

In spite of all his scheming Sir Duncan never seems to have forfeited the king's favour. When arrangements were being made in August, 1594, for a royal baptism, he received an invitation to the ceremony and a request to send on a consignment of venison and wild fowl for the feast. In 1609 Sir Duncan sent a present of two eagles to Prince Henry, and in return the Prince gave him a stallion, one of the best in the royal stables. This " fair Cursour " was killed along with forty brood mares and their followers by the MacGregors in a raid that they made two years later upon " the Cosche " of Glenorchy. The king came to hear, in 1622, of a white hind that had been seen in Coiricheba, Black Mount, and was very anxious to secure her for himself. With this end in view he sent John Scandoner,[2] one of his servants, with two attendants from London, giving them a letter to Sir Duncan. The royal messengers arrived in Breadalbane on the 13th February, 1622, having taken nearly a month to the journey. Sir Duncan gave the Englishmen a right Highland welcome, and sent a company of his own men with them to assist in the capture of the coveted hind. The weather, however, was very severe, and the country difficult to traverse, and although Scandoner got a sight of the hind, he failed to capture her. He duly reported his failure to London, but, instead of bringing him home, the King commanded Scandoner to proceed with his men to the Forest of Glenartney, which then belonged to the Earl of Perth, and there to capture red deer and roe deer, which were to be sent alive to London. By such practice in the wilds of Glenartney, the king expected that Scandoner and his men would be better able to take the white hind the following year. Scandoner appears to have returned to London by July, and on his arrival at Court he related his experiences, and was loud in praise of the kindness he had received in Scotland, especially from the Laird of Glenorchy. This moved the king to write in the following terms to Sir Duncan :—" Your entertainment of Scandoner hath given him occasion to speak of our kingdom in general, and of you in particular, as of a people dutifully devoted to their Prince, and well affected to strangers."[3]

In many ways Sir Duncan was ahead of his age. He was a pioneer of afforestation, and made laws requiring all tenants and cottars to set down and plant young trees, oak, ash, and

(1) B. Ps.   (2) B.B.T.   (3) B.B.T.

plane, every year in their "kailyards," in proportion to the size of their holdings. The saplings were to be supplied by his own gardener in each district at the rate of " twa pennies the piece," and as soon as they were ready to take up again, they were to be set in the most " commodious place of each occupation." He laid down extensive plantations himself, and formed avenues at his several houses. He planted the avenue of limes behind Taymouth Castle in the shape of the letter D. This avenue used to be called "The Dark Walk." The group of Spanish chestnuts, of which three still survive, at the bridge opposite Taymouth Castle, belong also to his period. These trees were admired for their girth by Thomas Gray, the poet, when he visited Kenmore in 1765.[1] Sir Duncan formed the stately avenue of lime trees called " the Cathedral " that leads

(1) Letter to Wharton.

FINLARIG CASTLE.

to the Castle of Finlarig.   In order that his woods should be protected a fine of twenty pounds was to be imposed on any one cutting, or in any way destroying young trees, and a reward of ten pounds was offered for information against the offender. Sir Duncan introduced fallow deer and rabbits into the Highlands, putting them, to begin with, on the island of Innisail, in Lochawe.   He built a bridge over the river Lochay at Killin to the " great contentment and weill of the country."

Strange as it may seem, the Black Laird of the Cowl was a lover of books.   Among the books that he left are two manuscript copies of a ponderous work, " The Buike of Alexander the Conqueroure."   " The Testament of Duncan Laideus," already referred to, is written on the last pages of one of these books. On the blank pages of other books that had once belonged to Sir Duncan, some verses of a moral and religious character were found, and it has been suspected that he was the author. He lived the life of a feudal lord, surrounding himself with a large retinue of followers, among whom was a bard, MacAlasdair, who sang the praises of his chief and the renown of his ancestors.   Sir Duncan's vast estates and the affairs of his household were managed with the utmost care and method.   Detailed accounts were kept of everything that was brought into and consumed in his house.   At the beginning of each weekly summary in the household books, there is usually a list of the guests who were entertained during the period, the workmen who were fed, as well as the " sindrie uthers commers and goers."

Sir Duncan married for his second wife Elizabeth, daughter of Henry Lord Sinclair.   By his first wife, Jean Stewart of Atholl, he had seven sons and four daughters ; and by his second wife, two sons and four daughters.   He was thus the father of seventeen legitimate children.   Besides these he had numerous natural sons and daughters, to several of whom the King granted letters of legitimacy.   By the time Sir Duncan died in 1631, the Campbells of Glenorchy had become a numerous clan in Perthshire, and they possessed a large portion of the county.

CHAPTER XII.

The Lairds of Glenorchy and Civil War.

SIR Duncan was succeeded by his eldest son, Colin, who was born in 1577. He married Juliana, second daughter of Sir Hugh Campbell of Loudon, and had no family. In character and tastes Sir Colin presents a marked contrast to his father and to his younger brother, Robert, who succeeded him. While Robert had assisted his father in hunting the Clan Gregor, Colin had pursued the arts of peace. He was a good Latin scholar, and knew both French and Italian. It is probable that he had travelled extensively on the Continent. While he continued his father's policy of extending the family residences, he adorned the interiors of the houses by introducing rich furniture, silk hangings, tapestry, and even silk beds. He was the first Scottish nobleman to encourage painting. In 1633 Sir Colin gave a thousand pounds (Scots) to a German painter whom he employed for eight months at Balloch painting " thirty broads of the kingis of Scotland, and of Great Britain, France, and Ireland, and twa of their Majesties queins of gude memorie, and of the said Sir Colin his own and his predicessors portraitis, quhilkis portraitis ar sett up in the hall and chalmer of daes of the house of Balloch."[1]

Much more important than the production of fanciful portraits of ancient kings was Sir Colin's patronage of George Jameson of Aberdeen, Scotland's earliest portrait painter. Jameson was brought to Balloch in July, 1635, and remained there until the end of September. During that time he painted over twenty portraits. For this work Sir Colin paid Jameson over four hundred pounds (Scots). Jameson's portraits were hung at Taymouth until the Castle was sold. They included those of many contemporary members of the Glenorchy family and other Scottish noblemen.

The last year or two of Sir Colin's life were disturbed by the War of the Covenant. He joined with his great kinsman, Archibald, Marquis of Argyll, in upholding the cause of Presbyterianism in Scotland against King Charles I., and was no

(1) B.B.T.

doubt present at the meeting held in Perth on 17th July, 1638, when steps were taken for the mustering of the armed forces of the county. It was resolved at that meeting to ascertain from each landowner the number of men able to bear arms that he could call up, the character of the arms in their possession, and also the number of horses available. To this inquiry Sir Colin made the following reply:—[1]"The Laird of Glenorchy for himself and his domestic servantis ar sufficientlie provydit with muskets, thair rests and bandeliers, with poulder and lead, some steill targetts, some horsemen and footmen armes, headpieces and steilbannetts, some hakbuts of found (cast metal), and twa fielding pieces on thair cariages.

"The Laird of Glenorchy and his vassillis within the parochines of Killin, Straphillan, Inchaddin, Dull, Weyme, hes about ane hundrethe ablemen or thereby to bare weapons, and ar alreadie provydit, some with hakbuts, some with swords and targetts, some with bows and arrows, and some with syclik swordis, so that ther is non of them for the present but ar provydit with some of thir sortis of weapons.

"The Laird of Glenorchy intendis, God willing, with all convenient diligence not onlie to provyde these of his tennentis within the parachinis forsaides with sick weapons and armour as is expedient for them to vse, but likwyse to be carefull that all the rest of his tennentis within quhatsumevir parochine they be of may be tymouslie and weill provydit."

Following upon this communication a muster roll was submitted giving the names of the men, as well as the weapons that each possessed. These lists include 129 names from Sir Colin's Perthshire estates, and 59 from Glenorchy.

Sir Colin died at Balloch on 6th September, 1640, at the age of sixty-three years, and was succeeded by his younger brother, Robert, who had married Isobel, daughter of Sir Lauchlane MacIntosh of Dunachton. Their family consisted of eight sons and nine daughters. Three of the sons died young. Of the others, John succeeded as tenth Laird of Glenorchy, and was the father of John, first Earl of Breadalbane ; Colin settled at Mochaster, and became the head of the Carwhin family of Campbells, from which the first and the second Marquises were descended ; William had the estate of Glenfalloch from his father until he was killed at Stirling in 1648; from him was descended the sixth Earl who succeeded to the peerage and the estates on the failure of the Carwhin family in the male line ; Alexander, Sir Robert's seventh son, was the founder of the Campbells of Glendochart ; while Duncan, the youngest son of the family, inherited Auchlyne and Wester Ardchyle.

Several of Sir Robert's daughters married Highland chiefs, and during the next generation these alliances had considerable

(1) Muster Rolls, B.B.T.

influence upon political events in the North. His daughter, Juliana, married Murdoch MacLaine of Lochbuy, Margaret married John Cameron of Lochiel, Jean married Archibald Campbell of Glenlyon, Isobel married James Campbell of Ardkinlas, and Catherine married Andrew Tosach of Monzievaird.

Sir Robert was Member of Parliament for Argyll from 1639-41, and again from 1643-49, and was thus brought into the very centre of the military, political, and ecclesiastical movements of that stormy period. He went himself along with the Marquis of Montrose and General David Leslie in 1639 on the expedition against the opponents of the Covenant in Aberdeenshire. During the following year he supported the Marquis of Argyll, who was sent with a force to compel the Earl of Atholl and the Earl of Ogilvie to support the Covenanting movement. Argyll came with an army of four thousand men to the Ford of Lyon, and the Earl of Atholl made a peaceful submission. Terms were arranged at Balloch during the first week of July, 1639, and from there Argyll proceeded to the burning of the " Bonnie House of Airlie."

Raid of Montrose, 1645.

John Campbell, fiar of Glenorchy, was Colonel of the Perthshire Foot Regiment, and along with a large number of Breadalbane men went with the Scottish army to England. Over two hundred of the Laird's men were killed during the English campaigns. Although Sir Robert received the estates free of debt, various circumstances soon involved him in financial difficulties. He had to provide for a numerous family, and pay large annuities to the widows of his father and brother. He had to find equipment for, and pay the expenses of, the men raised for the army from his estates. His rentals were reduced by the disturbed condition of the country at the time. He might possibly have been able to overcome these troubles, but when the Marquis of Montrose and Alexander MacDonald, with their following of lawless Irishmen and Highland clansmen, who had many grievances against the house of Glenorchy, invaded Breadalbane during the autumn and winter of 1644-45, Sir Robert was brought to the verge of ruin. The Irish troops first appeared in Breadalbane in August, 1644, when the family were in residence at Finlarig. A guard was set up in the castle, and by the end of the month the Marquis of Argyll, MacLaine of Lochbuy, and a number of other gentlemen arrived. Fresh muster rolls were prepared, and it was found that over two hundred men between the ages of sixteen and sixty years of age were available as soldiers from Breadalbane.

Sir Robert placed garrisons in all his strongholds. Even the Isle of Loch Tay, which had been abandoned for over eighty years, was put into a state of defence. The Glenorchy household removed from Finlarig to Balloch during the first week of

J

November.   In the meantime Montrose with his main army
was engaged on his campaign in Aberdeen and Angus, but
wandering bands of Irishmen were crossing the Ford of Lyon,
and raiding Lochtayside.   In December Montrose himself with
his whole host descended upon Breadalbane like a whirlwind.
Balloch, the Isle of Loch Tay, Finlarig, and the Isle of Lochdochart were all attacked.   MacDonalds, MacGregors, Macnabs,
and others were let loose upon the countryside.   They killed
every man found with arms, they burned all the houses, destroyed
the corn stacks, and drove away the cattle.   Even the Kirk of
Kenmore did not escape.   Its door was broken, and the basin
for baptism was stolen.   As the Royalist army swept along both
sides of the loch towards Argyllshire it left a trail of desolation
behind it.   Tradition says that on the south side of Loch Tay
only one house was left standing, and the reason for its escape
was that it was concealed by trees.   When the Kirk Session
of Kenmore met on the 12th January, 1645, " it was regreted yt
yr wer many poore people who wer burned and spoyled, and
hed nothing to live on."   The poors' box of the church had
somehow escaped the thieves, and out of it the session were
able to make a distribution of money to relieve the distress.
Sir Robert's garrisons, with the exception of the Isle of Lochdochart, which was taken by the Macnabs, were able to hold
out, but he and his tenants were reduced to desperate straits.
The damage done on his estates from the Ford of Lyon to the
Point of Lismore was estimated at £66,000 sterling.

A Stricken Land.

Sir Robert was compelled to borrow large sums of money
with which to procure seed-corn for his tenants.   He also gave
them grants to aid them with the re-building of their houses,
allowing forty shillings (Scots) for every couple erected.   A
tardy Parliament in 1646-47 came to his aid with a grant of
£5,000, and later he received a small payment out of the sum
voted by the English Parliament to the Scottish army.   The
last page that Master William Bowie, who took such a pride
in recording the " conquests " of Sir Robert's predecessors,
wrote, shows that the house of Glenorchy had fallen upon evil
days.   The loyal chronicler ceases writing after giving a list of
the creditors who were pressing his master for payment of
debts due.

The distress throughout Breadalbane was acute in the extreme.
A petition[1] from " Elizabeth and Marjorie Campbells for themselves and other poor wedowes and orphans " in Breadalbane
was received by the Commission of the General Assembly on
16th December, 1646, and recommended to the Estates of
Parliament.   The Commission resolved to raise a voluntary

(1) General Assy. Commission Records, Vol. II., p. 147 and 219.

contribution for those people who had suffered at the hands
of the enemy throughout Argyll and Breadalbane. Collectors
were appointed in every synod of the Church, and committees
were set up for the distribution of the fund in the distressed
areas.   The Laird of Glenorchy and other heritors of the parish
of Kenmore sent a petition[1] to the Commission on 20th January,
1647, representing the lamentable condition of themselves and
their tenants, by which they were unable to " give that maintenance and provision which is due to Mr. William Menzies,
their minister."   The Commission thereupon wrote to the
presbytery of Dunkeld as follows :—" Our desire to yow is
that the vaking fruits and stipends of any kirks within your
bounds, which by an act of Parliament printed ar appoynted
to be employed upon pious uses, may be given to Mr. William
Menzies, or some competent portion thereof, for his present
subsistence, and that the patron, titulars, heritors, and others
adebtit in payment therof, be dealt with for that purpose, and
that notwithstanding the destination of the Act in favours
of youths that have the Irish toung for their breeding at schooles
and universities."

Encouraged by their success under Montrose, the MacDonalds
of Lochaber returned in 1646 to raid Sir Robert's lands at the
west end of Loch Tay.   They had probably heard that his
plundered tenants had gathered a little gear, and the thieves
came along to " lift " it. It was on the 4th June, and the garrison
at Finlarig was making merry over a christening.[2]   Hasty news
was brought to the revellers that the MacDonalds were in the
act of driving a *creach* over Sron a' Chlachain, the high ridge
above the village of Killin.   The festivities came to a sudden
end, and the Campbells, contrary to the advice of Crowner
James Menzies, an experienced soldier who was one of the
party, ascended the hill with thoughtless bravery, and were
completely overpowered.   John Campbell, the captain of the
garrison, John Campbell of Criachens, Balquhidder, Captain
Hew Campbell, Duncan M'Arthur, brother to M'Arthur of
Inschstrynie, all nephews of the Laird, besides thirty-six of
the Laird's ablest tenants, were killed, and twenty-one men
were dangerously wounded.   The fight took place in a hollow
known as *Coire nam Bonnach*, the " Bannock Corry," and tradition
says that the stream that flows from the corrie ran red with
blood.   It is called, *An t-Allt Fuileach*, the " Bloody Burn."

News of the disaster soon reached Balloch, and a strong body
of men armed with guns was dispatched with all haste.   The
MacDonalds were overtaken before they could get across the
hills between Glenlochay and Glenlyon, and the majority of
them were slain, among them Angus, son of Alasdair nan Cleas

(1) General Assy. Commission Ibid, p. 179.
(2) Pennant's Tour, and Breadalbane Papers.

of Keppoch, for whom Iain Lom,[1] the Bard of Lochaber, composed a lament. Iain Lom was himself present at the battle,
and he tells how his heart was rent at the sight of his chief's
fair son lying wounded and dead in " the little house of Coire
Charmaig." He had left his father dead in Glenlochay, but
sore as was the loss of his father, even sorer was the leaving of
Angus of the " pleasant countenance." The cattle were driven
home to their owners, and the MacDonalds of Lochaber and
Glencoe kept to their own bounds for some time to come.

The Royal Honours at Balloch.

With the return of the Scottish army from England in February,
1647, most of the Breadalbane soldiers were able to settle down
at home. The country began to recover from the effects of the
recent raids, but poverty was still so acute that the Church
had to modify the fines imposed upon dilinquents who " had
been spoyled by the enemies." Property was insecure. The
poors' box of Kenmore had to be kept for safety in the House
of Balloch, and brought to the church by an elder on all occasions
when it was required. During the bitter quarrels of the factions
into which the Scottish Parliament was divided at this period,
William Campbell of Glenfalloch, Sir Robert's son, and forty
of his men were killed in a fight at Stirling in September, 1648.
They were probably engaged in defending the Marquis of Argyll
against an attack made upon him by the forces of the Committee
of Estates. The Marquis saved his life by riding with all haste
to North Queensferry, and crossing from there to Edinburgh.

After the proclamation of Charles II. as king on the 5th
February, 1649, some measure of unity was restored into Scottish
national life ; but the appearance of the Marquis of Montrose
in the North of Scotland in January, 1650, as the champion of
a king who should be untrammelled by the conditions of the
Covenant, created fresh fears in Breadalbane. Therefore,
when news arrived that the Marquis had been captured and
executed, there was a feeling of intense relief, and the people
gathered into the churches on 26th May for a public and solemn
thanksgiving " for the merciful deliverance from the intended
violence and oppression of that excommunicat traitor, James
Grahame." This sense of relief was, however, short-lived.
Charles agreed to subscribe to the Covenant, and he was brought
from Holland to Scotland, landing at the mouth of the Spey
on 3rd July, 1650. Within three weeks of his landing, Oliver
Cromwell crossed the Border with an army of five thousand
cavalry and ten thousand infantry, many of them soldiers who
had been on service during the previous eight years. Thanksgiving now gave way to fasting. On August 11th a public fast
was observed at Kenmore[2] for " the present calamities on the

(1) Turner's Collection.   (2) K. S. Records.

Kingdome be the incoming of the English." Military preparations were hurried on for opposing this invasion, but the
effort ended in the disaster of Dunbar on the 2nd September.
Argyll, with Charles and the Covenanting leaders, withdrew
immediately from Edinburgh to Perth, taking the Scottish
Regalia with them. For the greater safety of the Royal Honours
Argyll resolved to entrust them to his cousin, the Laird of
Glenorchy,[1] and sent them by Lieut. Colonel Menzies to Balloch
on the 17th September. Meantime Charles became restive
under the preaching of the ministers, and under the restrictions
imposed upon him by Argyll. He tried to escape to his Royalist
supporters, the Earls of Atholl, Ogilvie, and Middleton, on the
4th October, and managed to reach the Grampians, where he
spent an uncomfortable night. Next day he was captured,
brought back to Perth, and censured. This incident, which
came to be known as "The Start," alarmed Argyll, and he
wrote from Inveraray three weeks later to Sir Robert, urging
him " to be careful of these things quhilkes ar conceidit to your
custody." Before another month passed, Argyll and the other
leaders had come to terms with the Royalists, and with sympathy
running strongly in favour of the king, preparations were made
for his coronation. The Royal Honours were brought back to
Perth on November 19th, and Charles was crowned at Scone
on January 1st, 1651.

(1) B. Papers.

CHAPTER XIII.

The Glencairn Rising.
(1652-1654).

WHEN the Royalists and the more moderate section of the Covenanters, who were known as Resolutioners, became reconciled, plans were made for the invasion of England. While Cromwell held Edinburgh, the Lothians, and Fife, the Scottish army had a way open to the south by Stirling and the west of Scotland. Charles, encouraged by his own counsellors, and by promises of help from English Royalists, resolved upon the daring adventure. Argyll, however, who had fallen into disfavour with all parties, was against the scheme, and retired to the seclusion of his own castle at Inveraray. Sir Robert Campbell, who had attended the meetings of the Commission of the General Assembly from March 19th to 22nd, 1651, did not return again to its sittings. He also appears to have disapproved of the English campaign. When the elders of Kenmore church went round their bounds seeking a voluntary collection[1] for the army in obedience to an order of the Commission of Assembly, they reported on August 3rd that they " could get nothing." The Laird's attitude was no doubt that of his people.

The Scots suffered a terrible defeat at Worcester on September 3rd, the anniversary of Dunbar. Of the twenty thousand men whom Charles led away from Stirling very few ever saw their native land again. Many were slain, six or seven thousand were taken prisoners, some of whom died from starvation and disease, while others were shipped to the plantations, and sold as slaves. Charles himself, after several romantic adventures, managed to escape to the Continent, where he was joined by exiled Royalists. Meanwhile, the English left in Scotland were gaining command of the country. On 28th August a number of the members of the Committee of Estates and of the Commission of Assembly were surprised at Alyth, and sent as prisoners to the Tower of London. Scotland was left in a helpless condition with no government to maintain a resistance to the English. When the news of the defeat at Worcester arrived

(1) Gen. Assy. Commission Records, Vol. III., p. 449.

" all men almost everywhere lost heart and hand."[1] The responsibility for taking action devolved upon Lord Loudon, the Chancellor of Scotland. The Earl was one of the Campbells of Lawers, who had married the heiress of the house of Loudon. He was, therefore, cousin to the Laird of Glenorchy, and closely related to the Marquis of Argyll. Loudon induced Argyll to help him in setting up some semblance of Government in the land. At a meeting which they held with a few others at Rothesay it was decided to call a meeting of Parliament to be held in Finlarig Castle[2] about the middle of November. The English had not as yet penetrated as far as Breadalbane. The proclamation calling Parliament together was duly made at Killin, and to it was added the notice that though the meeting " could not by reason of the enemy be proclaimed at the Edinburgh Cross as formerly, yet it should be as effectual to all intents and purposes."[3] When the appointed day came only three members of Parliament appeared at Finlarig, and all they could do was to sympathise with the Chancellor, and tell him that he had done everything that could be expected of him. They expressed the opinion that it was hopeless to attempt to maintain for the present an independent Government in Scotland.

As the dreary winter of 1651-52 wore away, the spirits of the Royalists began to revive. The country was to a large extent occupied by the English ; but in the Highlands the chiefs were stirring. Some of them had got into communication with King Charles, and he gave his approval to any attempt they made to oppose the Commonwealth. He promised to send Lord Middleton to command them, giving him the title of Lieutenant General. Middleton, however, turned ill, and for some time nothing was done. The Royalists became restless, and the Earl of Glencairn, who was second-cousin to Sir Robert Campbell, was appointed by the King Commander-in-Chief until Middleton should arrive in Scotland.

The Standard Raised.

A secret meeting was held in the Kirk of Killin[4] on the last day of May, 1652. This meeting was attended by Lord Glencairn, Lord Balcarres, Sir Arthur Forbes, and many others. Lord Lorn was not present, but he gave the movement his ardent support, much against his father's will. Lord Loudon sent a representative. Glencairn produced his commission from King Charles, and all those present bound themselves by a secret vow to stand by one another. The leaders separated in order to stir up the country and to recruit their forces. They fixed upon Killin as the place of rendezvous, and groups of volunteers began to gather there from the Lowlands as well

(1) Firth, Scotland and the Commonwealth, p. 25.   (2) Nicoll's Diary, p. 73.
(3) Burton, Vol. VII., p. 48.   (4) Scotland and the Commonwealth, p. 144.

as from the Highlands. When the party had gained some strength they raised the royal standard on 27th July, and then proceeded to give trouble to the English commanders, who became thoroughly alarmed. At length the Royalists moved north to Dornoch to await the arrival of General Middleton, who was expected to bring men, money, and stores from the Dutch, who were then at war with the English Commonwealth.

During this time the position of Sir Robert Campbell was an extremely difficult one. He was an aged man, and his lands had suffered grievously from the war. Much as he might sympathise with the Royalists, common prudence advised him to keep apart from them. Several of the leaders were related to himself. Glencairn was his cousin, Lochiel and Lochbuy were his sons-in-law, Lorn had been fostered in his family, Kenmuir was cousin to Lorn. Sir Robert, however, resolved to be guided in his policy by Argyll and remain on friendly terms with the English. Colonel Lilburne sent him the following on 29th August, 1653 :—" For your better security and defence . . . I desire you will place such strengths in your several houses which are defensible as you shall conceive necessary, and further to secure the peace of the country as you shall be able ; and when you have put yourselves into a posture of defence I shall desire to hear from you to know what your demands may be about some consideration for your paines and charges in securing the peace of that country."[1] That Sir Robert complied with this request is evident from the fact that Lilburne issued an order on September 14th for the abatement of the tax due by him for the six months to May, 1653.

Wogan's Gallantry.

While still waiting at Dornoch for Middleton, the Royal army received a great accession of strength and inspiration by the arrival of Colonel Edward Wogan[2] with a troop of well trained and fully equipped men. Wogan had had an adventurous career, and his character was singularly attractive. He came of an English family that had settled in county Kildare, Ireland. He was originally engaged in the service of the Parliament, and fought in the New Model army, but in 1648 he deserted to the Royalist side, taking his whole troop over with him. At Worcester Wogan rallied the Royalist horse and after the battle escaped to France. When he heard of the effort that was being made by Scottish nobles and Highland chiefs for the cause he loved, Wogan pleaded before the king, even with tears in his eyes, to be allowed to go and join the loyal band. Obtaining the king's sanction he crossed to Dover with a few companions, and found his way to London. There he assembled a body of cavaliers, and made a dash for the North. The party

(1) Scotland and the Commonwealth, p. 197.
(2) Dict. Nat. Biog. and Scotland and the Commonwealth, pp. 296-8.

escaped undetected until it reached Durham, where a brush with Commonwealth troops took place. They got safely across the Border, and joined the Royalist army at Dornoch about the middle of December.

Without waiting any longer for Middleton the Royalists decided to move south. They made north Perthshire their headquarters, and, taking possession of the castles of Blair-Atholl, Weem, Balloch, and Garth, they placed garrisons in them. Wogan was stationed at Balloch. The Royalists began a guerilla warfare with the Commonwealth troops, who operated from the city of Perth as a base. Wogan's skill and daring won him the highest reputation, and he was adored by his own troopers and by his Scottish comrades. He had, however, the misfortune to be wounded[1] in the shoulder during a sharp conflict which took place near Drummond Castle, Strathearn, on January 14th, 1654. Skilled surgical assistance was not procurable at the time, and although he was taken to Balloch in the course of a few days and there attended by his own surgeon[2] Holan, he died on 4th February. The grief of his fellow officers and of his own men was intense. According to Heath's "Chronicle of the Civil War," Wogan "was buried in great state and much lamentation with a military funeral in the Church of Kenmore." A month after the funeral the following minute appears in the Kenmore Kirk Session records, "12 March, 1654. This day the minister (Mr. William Menzies) and elders did declare that burial was made in the Kirk, so farre as they know without consent either of the heritors of the paroch, or yet without consent of the Session, and they did much regrate that burial should be made thairin at this tyme, whereas thair has never been such thing befor, and found that this was done be one heritor's foolish facilitie, and contrair to the law of the Kirk of Scotland."

In spite of the Kirk Session's protest the fact of Wogan's burial in the church passed out of people's memory, and when Sir Walter Scott told the story of the gallant hero in "Waverley" he created a romantic tradition to the effect that Wogan's grave was under the branches of the great oak-tree that overspreads the ancient churchyard of Inchadney. This tree was called "Wogan's Tree" by old people in the district. In 1871, when workmen were engaged in re-flooring the Kenmore church, human remains[3] were found, and no doubt they were those of Wogan. No one at the time suspected this, and they were taken by the beadle and buried somewhere in the churchyard. Heath, in his panegyric on Wogan, takes farewell of him in these words, "Here we must leave him till some grateful, learned Muse shall sing the honourable achievements, and most laudable

(1) Spottiswoode Miscell., Vol. II., p. 170.
(2) Breadalbane Papers and Household Books.
(3) Christie, Lairds and Lands of Lochtayside, p. 28.

high actions of this famous and renowned Captain."[1]   Scott fulfilled this prophecy by giving Wogan a place in his immortal story, and in a poem of six stanzas apostrophizing the Oak-tree, are these verses[2] :—

> " Thy death's hour heard no kindred wail,
>   No holy knell thy requiem rung ;
> Thy mourners were the plaided Gael,
>   Thy dirge the clamorous pibroch sung.
>
> Yet who, in Fortune's summer-shine
>   To waste life's longest term away,
> Would change that glorious dawn of thine,
>   Though darken'd ere its noontide day."

Monk at Balloch.

Middleton landed in Sutherland about the end of February, 1654, but his arrival did little to strengthen a dejected army, whose leaders were quarrelling among themselves.   General Monk entered Scotland eight weeks later, and after making his position secure in the south he resolved to advance boldly into the Highlands.   He divided his forces into two bodies, one of which he commanded himself.   The other he placed under General Morgan.   As the English army advanced, the generals took care to plant a garrison in every house that was capable of defence.   When Monk arrived at Balloch he saw that the Castle was fitted to receive a small garrison, but when he mentioned the matter to the Laird, Sir Robert, it is said, refused to yield up the house.   " Well," said Monk, " I shall not violate your hospitality," and with that he ordered his officers to evacuate the Castle immediately.   When Monk saw that they were all outside he turned to the Laird and said, " Now, look to your defences, for we are about to attack."   We are told that although the Laird was surrounded by a considerable number of friends, and had a large body of soldiers in the house at the time, he thought it wise to yield, and he agreed to receive a garrison on condition that part of the house should be left at his own disposal.[3]

When General Monk arrived at Balloch he discovered that the Isle of Loch Tay was occupied by a company of Royalists under Captain Donald Robertson.   Monk immediately called upon Robertson to surrender, offering him and his men lenient terms on condition that they should evacuate the island at once.   Robertson at first adopted a defiant attitude, and sent a message to the effect, " that hee would keepe itt for his Majistie's service to the expence of his laste droppe of bloud " ; but when he saw preparations being made for the storming of the place he surrendered the garrison.   Monk thus reported[4] upon the incident to the Protector from Balloch on 14th June,

(1) Heath's Chronicle of Intestine Wars.   (2) " Waverley," Chap. XXIX.
(3) Guizot's Monk, pp. 28-29.
(4) Scot. and the Commonwealth.   Trans. Gaelic Soc , Inverness, Vol. XVII., p. 75.

ISLE OF LOCH TAY LOOKING FROM KENMORE BRIDGE.

1654 :—" Wee are now gott thus farre into the Hills. Uppon my coming hither on Munday last, understanding that the Enemy had a garrison in an Island in Lough Tay, I sent a summons for the rendition of it, to which the Governor at first returned a resolute answer. Wheruppon I gave order for the fetching uppe of some boates several miles from the place, the Enemy having seized uppon all the boates in the Lough. Two were gott uppe (against the streame) into the Lough, and the floates were appointed for the carrying over our men ; but the Enemy perceiving some preparations were willing to submit to terms, which I granted, and the place was rendered this day. They had some store of provisins, but nott much amunition in itt, and 7 prisoners of ours were releast."

When passing through Breadalbane, Middleton, who suspected that Sir Robert sided with the English, burned and harried some of the lands.[1] The small force of Royalists was chased from place to place, and, at last, wearied and half-starved, it was overtaken by General Morgan at Dalnaspidal in July, and defeated and scattered. Monk became master of the Highlands, and by erecting forts at various points of vantage he held a tight grip of the country so long as he was governor. A garrison was placed in Finlarig Castle with Captain Gascoigne[2] in command. A party of English soldiers was also stationed on the Isle of Loch Tay, and to them is given the credit of having introduced the habit of tobacco smoking into Breadalbane. The local tradition to that effect was confirmed by the discovery of a number of small clay pipes, when walks were being laid out on the Island some fifty years ago. During the summer of 1650 Colonel Daniel, who was in command of the Commonwealth troops at Perth, visited Kenmore. From the Kirk Session records we find that on 22nd June of that year Thomas Whyt " was ordained by the Session to present their supplication to Colonel Daniel for reparation of the losses done by the armie to the Kirk, and 31 shillings allowed therefor."

Sir Robert Campbell died on 17th November, 1657, at the age of eighty-two years. He had lived through one of the stormiest and most trying periods in Highland history, and the fortunes of his house and of his people had suffered severely. It is a pity that the venerable chief had not lived to see the family delivered from its debts and raised to honour in the next generation.

(1) Gen. Assy. Commission Records, Vol. I., p. 585.
(2) Douglas Baronage.

CHAPTER XIV.

A Fortune and an Earldom.

JOHN Campbell, fiar of Glenorchy, succeeded as laird on his father's death. His position was an extremely difficult one. The family exchequer was empty. His lands were heavily mortgaged, and creditors were pressing for payment of debts and overdue interest. His tenants were just beginning to recover from the wasting of their farms during the recent raids. To aggravate the new laird's troubles a quarrel[1] arose between himself and his eldest son, John, who wanted to secure for himself control of the estates. As we shall see this vigorous and ambitious young man gradually eclipsed his father, with the result that Sir John's career as laird appears comparatively uneventful. He had, however, played a prominent and distinguished part as an officer in the Scottish army during the Civil War. He was a member of the Committee of War for Perthshire from 1644 to 1649, and served in a similar capacity for Argyllshire during 1648. He was member of Parliament for that county from 1661-1663.

Sir John was married[2] three times. His first wife was Mary, daughter of William Graham, Earl of Airth and Menteith. By her he had a family of six sons and eight daughters. When she died he married Elizabeth Campbell, daughter of Patrick Dow Mor Campbell of Edinchip, a cousin of his own. She bore him four sons and three daughters. His third wife was Christian Mushet, daughter of Robert Mushet of Craighead. By her Sir John had two sons and four daughters, one of whom, Anna, married Robert Macnab of Bovain. Although several members of this numerous family died young, it was no easy matter for the laird, embarrassed as he was with debt at the beginning of his career, to provide for the survivors. Before he died, however, in 1686, he had the satisfaction of seeing his eldest son and successor raised to the peerage, and become one of the wealthiest and most powerful of Scottish nobles.

A Romantic Marriage.

John Campbell younger of Glenorchy was born about 1635. For the first ten years or so of his life he came under the influence of Master William Bowie, the author of the Black Book, who was tutor and notary in the family from the days of Sir Duncan

(1) B. Ps.   (2) Scots Peerage.

JOHN CAMPBELL, FIRST EARL OF BREADALBANE.

the seventh Laird. Master Bowie must have found in John Campbell an apt pupil, eager to follow in the footsteps of his ancestors, and to make it his chief duty to " Conques, and to keip thingis conquest."

John Campbell's first " conquest " was the beautiful and wealthy Lady Mary Rich, daughter of Henry Rich, first Earl of Holland, who had been executed in 1649 for his attachment to the cause of Charles I. How the young Glenorchy made his way to London and secured such a prize for his wife, when he was as yet only twenty-two years of age, is not easy to understand. The couple were married on 17th December, 1657, in the church of St. Andrew, Wardrobe. Writing to his father a fortnight later, the gallant bride-groom says :—" Right Hon. I have wrett several tymes to yr honr, but hes had no return concerning my then intended marriage, which now by the Lord's blessing I have accomplished. Ther was many reasons for my speedy carying it on by reason of oppositions which wer put in the way to break it off. I wrett lastly to you of all the particulars, so that I need not in this. I hope the business is so satisfactory to all my friends that the dispatching of it is concluded to be noe prejudice, and so soon as I have settled my business here I doe lay my accompt to come home."[1]

It was said that John Campbell received the sum of ten thousand pounds with his wife, and he was no doubt anxious to see his fair lady and her vast fortune safely lodged within the walls of Balloch. There is an old story[2] about the strange fashion of the home-coming. It is related that John Campbell had two Highland ponies sent all the way to London. When they arrived he mounted his bride behind himself on the one, and on the back of the other he placed their treasure, all in gold. On each side of this precious horse-load two Highlanders, fully armed, trotted on foot as guard. In this manner the little company proceeded on their way until at length they came to Balloch, where the romantic adventure was long remembered, and the room in the old castle that the young couple occupied on their arrival used to be shown to visitors.

Once settled at home John Campbell proceeded to take an active part in the business of the Kirk, and in the management of his father's affairs. We find him at the presbytery of Dunkeld in December, 1659, in order to secure the appointment of his cousin, Mr. Patrick Campbell, as minister of Kenmore. After reporting upon his success to his father, who was then in Argyllshire, he adds in his letter, " We hear great news ; the General Monk gon into England ; and of Lord Fairfax joining with him." His interference with the administration of the estates and his dealings with the creditors were strongly resented by his father, who accused his son of ambition and covetousness. Sir John compared himself to King David when Absolom rebelled against him, and he solicited the sympathy of the Marquis of Argyll and other kinsmen in his distress. At length the differences between father and son were composed, probably because the latter was allowed to manage things pretty much as he pleased.

Expedition to Caithness.

An expedition that John Campbell undertook in 1669 at the request of the Privy Council led him on to secure another notable " conquest." William Sinclair of Dunbeath in Caithness had

(1) B. Ps.   (2) " The Picture of Scotland," Chambers, Vol. II., p. 284.

gathered some 1,200 men under arms, and with them he invaded Sutherland, robbing, plundering, and killing wherever they went. Strathnavar suffered severely at their hands. The Privy Council " satisfied with the ability and fidelity " of John Campbell, younger of Glenorchy, gave him a commission to pursue after, apprehend, and imprison William Sinclair, with powers to proceed against anyone who should receive or give shelter to him or his supporters. In addition to the forces that he raised himself, John Campbell had at his command three hundred men of the King's Guard and also a party of Lord Linlithgow's Foot Regiment. On reaching Sutherland he was joined by George, sixth Earl of Caithness. The company reached Dunbeath and took the castle, but the people had departed, clearing the countryside of everything needed to feed an army. John Campbell's men ran short of rations, and for some time they were in great straits. He, however, carried out his instructions, returned home, reported diligence to the Privy Council, and was duly thanked for his services. In the following year, when John Sinclair of Ratter and others lodged complaints with the Council as to the oppressive and illegal manner in which John Campbell had treated them by keeping them in close confinement for three months, they were simply told by the Council that he had only acted in accordance with his commission.[1]

The Peerage of Breadalbane.

John Campbell's association with the Earl of Caithness, which, as we have seen, began as early as 1669, had a most interesting and extraordinary sequel. The Earl, who was married to Mary, daughter of Archibald, Marquis of Argyll, was heavily in debt. John Campbell advanced money to him from time to time, and at length he became the Earl's principal creditor. The Earl had no family, and on the 8th October, 1672, he conveyed to John Campbell his dignities, landed estates, and heritable jurisdictions. This transaction was confirmed by a Crown charter of 11th January, 1673, and was followed by infeftment on 27th February of the same year. Under the terms of the conveyance John Campbell was under obligation to allow the Earl of Caithness and his wife £1,000 sterling a year during their lifetime. So long, however, as the Earl lived Campbell did not enforce his rights, being content to live in family with him and his lady ; but on the Earl's death in May, 1676, he put forward his claim to the Caithness titles, and, strange to say, his claim was admitted, and on 28th June, 1677, he was created Earl of Caithness, Viscount of Breadalbane, Lord St. Clair of Berridale and Glenorchy, and directed to assume the name and the arms of Sinclair. Strong protests were immediately made against what appeared to many to have been an outrage, and it was declared that John Campbell had secured his titles " upon gross and false representations." When the

(1) Registers of the Privy Council.

rightful heir, George Sinclair of Keiss, came forward asserting his claims, Charles II. realised that a mistake had been made. He annulled the patent of the Earldom in favour of Campbell, and confirmed George Sinclair in that dignity.[1]

On the 13th August, 1681, John Campbell was compensated for his loss of the Caithness titles by being given a new patent with the former precedency, and was created Earl of Brea D'Albane and Holland, Viscount of Tay and Paintland, Lord Glenorchie, Benderaloch, Ormelie, and Wick, in the Peerage of Scotland. He was granted special power to nominate, as his successor in the titles and the estates, whichever of his sons he should design by a writ given under his hand.

A Battle.

John Campbell found it no easy matter to take possession of, far less hold, the Caithness estates. George Sinclair laid claim to them, and strenuously disputed the legality of Campbell's title. At length with the sanction of the authorities Glenorchy mustered an armed force of over seven hundred men, and with this array he marched into Caithness. A battle was fought with the Sinclairs at Allt nam Mearlach, where the Breadalbane men won the victory. Glenorchy then quartered his men on the Caithness lands in order to collect the rents and taxes. The Sinclairs, however, so harassed the invaders, that they were forced to withdraw, and George Sinclair was left in undisputed possession of the estates until his death in 1698. John Campbell then acquired them, and drew the rents during his life-time. After his death the lands of Caithness were sold by the commissioners appointed under his will, and thus arose the saying in Breadalbane, *Or Ghallaibh air bòrd Bhealaich,* " The gold of Caithness on the table of Balloch."

It has been said that when the Breadalbane men were being recruited for the expedition to the North, the test to which each man was subjected before being selected was, that he should be able to leap, fully accoutred and in marching order, over a double plaid (four feet nine inches).

A curious story is also related of how the Campbells, while the two armies faced each other at Allt nam Mearlach, dispatched a convoy, carrying a quantity of whisky, along a track by which it was sure to fall into the hands of the enemy. The stratagem succeeded, with the result that when the battle began the Sinclairs were so drunk that they could not put up a formidable resistance.

This battle, which was one of the last of its kind fought on Scottish soil, is commemorated by the pibroch that was composed on the field by Finlay MacIvor, Campbell of Glenlyon's piper, while the fight was in progress, and which is still known as the

(1) Scots Peerage.

K

" Breadalbane Salute."   The Gaelic words which were afterwards composed to the tune used to be very popular in the Highlands among the Campbells, and were as follows :—

" Tha píob agus bratach,
A Bealach 'toirt caismeachd,
Beinn Labhair 'na lasair,
'S na gaisgich ag eirigh.

" The pipes and the banner,
From Balloch give warning,
Ben Lawers is aflame,
And the heroes are swarming.

A bhodaich nam briogaisean,
Nan lúireach, 's nam briogaisean,
A bhodaich nam briogaisean,
'S mithich dhuibh eirigh.

Carles of the breeches,
The *lurachs*[1] and breeches,
Carles of the breeches,
'Tis time you were rising.

'S áillidh, ge gruamach,
Borb chomhlan nam fuar-bheann,
Do Ghallaibh a' gluasad,
Chur Tuathaich nan eiginn.

Lovely, yet grim-set,
The bold band from the cold bens,
Marching to Caithness,
To put Northmen in straits.

'S ann aig Inbhir na h-Abhann,
A dhúin sibh 's an sgathadh,
Dh' fhág ioma fear-claidhimh,
Na laighe gun eirigh."

'Twas at Inver-na-havon
You closed in the conflict,
That left many a swordsman,
Lying silent for ever."

The Earl of Breadalbane's wife, Lady Mary Rich, had died on 8th February, 1666, and on 7th April, 1678, he married as his second wife, Mary, widow of the Earl of Caithness. By this step he saved the payment of the annual alimentary allowance due to her for the period of her life from the Caithness estates.

(1) The *luireach* was a padded coat used for protection in battle instead of armour.

CHAPTER XV.

Lord Breadalbane Negotiates with the Highland Chiefs.

THE first Earl of Breadalbane bears a most unenviable reputation in history. He was much distrusted in his day. One contemporary said that " he was cunning as a fox, wise as a serpent, but as slippery as an eel,"[1] while another[2] declared Breadalbane to be the cunningest temporiser in Britain. Lord Macaulay[3] describes his character in the following epigrammatic sentences :—" John, Earl of Breadalbane, ranked high among the petty princes of the mountains. He could bring seventeen hundred claymores into the field ; and, ten years before the Revolution, he had actually marched into the Lowlands with this great force for the purpose of supporting the prelatical tyranny. In those days he affected zeal for monarchy and episcopacy ; but in truth he cared for no government and no religion. He seems to have united two different sets of vices, the growth of two different regions, and of two different stages in the progress of society. In his castle among the hills he had learned the barbarian pride and ferocity of a Highland chief. In the Council Chamber at Edinburgh he had contracted the deep taint of treachery and corruption." It is true that the Earl lived at a time when it was no easy matter for a man in his position to save his head from the block, or his property from confiscation. He had seen both his cousins, the Marquis of Argyll and the Earl, his son, executed ; their lands and houses plundered and destroyed ; and their people shipped off wholesale to the Colonies. These noblemen paid the penalty of adhering to their religious and political principles ; Breadalbane, however, never lost sight of his own private gain and advantage while professing to serve the public interest.

Breadalbane had gained favour at the court of King James VII., and was an important member of the Privy Council of Scotland. When the position of the King was becoming insecure in October, 1688, he contributed a hundred men to the militia that the Earl of Perth, Chancellor of Scotland, summoned to Stirling.[4] In the following month Breadalbane was appointed by the Council to proceed to Stirling and disband half of the thousand men there assembled. When the Council had to

(1) MacKy Memoirs of Secret Service, p. 119. (2) Gen. Hugh MacKay Memoirs.
(3) Hist. Chap. XVIII. (4) Breadalbane Papers.

decide between the claims of the fugitive King and those of the Prince of Orange, Breadalbane joined with Viscount Tarbet, the Marquis of Atholl, and Sir John Dalrymple in supporting William ; yet during the following summer (1689), while Viscount Dundee was organising an army in the Highlands he was counting upon Breadalbane's assistance. In a letter written from Moy, Lochaber, on June 23rd, to MacLeod of MacLeod, Dundee wrote, " I had almost forget to tell you of my Lord Breadalbane, who, I suppose, will now come to the feelds."[1] Breadalbane, however, gave no support to Dundee, and after the battle of Killiecrankie he handed the castle of Finlarig over to General MacKay, who made it one of his military posts.

When the government of William and Mary became established, Breadalbane was able to secure influence at their Court, and being on intimate terms with Sir John Dalrymple, then Secretary of State for Scotland, he was appointed to negotiate with the Highland chiefs who had been in arms against the Government. Breadalbane's own account of these historic proceedings is given in a statement[2] which he drew up four years later when he was confined as a prisoner in Edinburgh Castle. The Earl says that during the year 1690 he was living retiredly in his own house ; but, acting on the advice of some friends, he went to Edinburgh, where he had several interviews with the Lord Privy Seal, who at the time was considering how he could reduce the expense of keeping up a large army in Scotland for the suppressing of the Highlanders. He was further affected by the distressed condition of the greater part of the Kingdom which " lay exposed to the invasion and insults of the Highlanders." After discussing methods by which the Highlanders might be persuaded to lay down their arms and submit to the government, Breadalbane was recommended to place his plans before the King. Before, however, he could wait upon him, the King had gone to Ireland, and the Earl " gave over meddling further in affairs " until he went to London with his family in May, 1691. The King was at that time in Flanders, and the army in Britain was very small. He found that the Queen and her ministers were most anxious to avoid internal trouble, and were willing to bestow £12,000 among the Highlanders " for taking of them off." Breadalbane says, " I was employed and commissioned very unexpectedly to come down, and use my endeavours for effecting that design."

Achallader Meeting.

The Earl proceeds to relate how he met with the Highland chiefs, and, after they had considered the government's proposals among themselves, and with the officers of King James, they came to a resolution that they would grant their bands and keep the peace till October, provided that Breadalbane

(1) Browne Hist. of the Highlands, Vol. II., p. 148.   (2) Breadalbane Papers.

should obtain for them the sum of money that the King was willing to bestow, and that the officers should get passes to enable them to go overseas. Breadalbane says that he and the chiefs parted on good terms. " They left in good hopes to receive the money and an indemnity when they disbanded and dismissed all their men, and I went straight to London, where I gave the Queen and the ministers an account of what passed. From thence I went to the King in Flanders, and represented the whole affair in its true and full state wherewith his Majesty was well pleased."

Breadalbane then goes on to say that when he returned to London he was surprised to hear from the Highlands that the chiefs had been influenced to break the agreements they had made with him. He was also informed of papers that had been circulated under the name of private articles that had been reported to have passed between the chiefs and himself. Copies of these articles, which differed from each other, had been sent to the Queen and her ministers. Breadalbane regarded them as " malicious coffee-house stories." He found it difficult to believe that the chiefs could allow themselves to be moved to reject such good terms as he had been empowered to offer, and he, therefore, hastened back to Scotland. He sent invitations to the chiefs, asking them to meet him, and he went and stayed several days in the Highlands before he could induce any of them to come near him.

" Yet, at last," Breadalbane says, "some of them did come, who declared that after my parting with them at Achallader, and their treatie with me was made public, there was great pains taken upon several of them to prevent them not to lay down their arms as dishonourable, nor to accept any conditions I was to bring them ; and deluding others by telling them that they were not to get a higher proportion of the money. Glengarie was made to believe that he was to have only one thousand pounds, whereas I had warrant to give him £1,500 stg. to his account. These reports and insinuations did so far prevail with them as to engage by their oaths not to stand by their treatie with me ; and they did trifle over their time until the days appointed for their accepting the benefit of their Majesties' indemnity was elapsing, or elapsed, then they repented their folly, and lost the money, which was returned to the Treasury in England."

The difficulties that Breadalbane encountered were due in some measure to the fact that he was distrusted and feared by the chiefs, especially by such as knew him best. Even his cousin, Lochiel, could not be sure of Breadalbane, and believed that he might keep to himself a good share of the money promised by the Government. At the Achallader meeting on 30th June, Breadalbane used threatening words to MacIan of Glencoe because his men had " lifted " some cattle from Glenlyon and Glenorchy on their way home from the battle of Killiecrankie.

On 27th August the Government issued a proclamation, promising pardon and an indemnity to all who had been in arms on the condition that they would take the oath of allegiance before a sheriff, or a sheriff-depute, on or before the 31st December, 1691. The chiefs were, however, slow in responding The one waited for the other to move. Glengarry, the Captain of Clanranald, MacLean of Duart, Keppoch, and Glencoe appeared determined to hold out.   During the autumn letters passed between Sir John Dalrymple and Breadalbane in which they discussed measures to be adopted against the defiant chiefs and their people. Writing on 27th October, Dalrymple said to Breadalbane that they would " root out such as stood out." They were going " to pull down Glengarry's nest " that winter, so that the King might be able to withdraw four regiments from Scotland for his war in Flanders. Dalrymple wanted to see Glengarry and his clan destroyed, and his house converted into a military post half-way between Inverlochy and Inverness. He wished to know from Breadalbane the methods he thought best suited for the reduction of Glengarry, and " what regiments of foot would be necessary to take the house and ruin the clan."

The Massacre of Glencoe.

The Earl of Breadalbane went to London at the end of December, and he remained there until 13th April, 1692. During this period he was kept informed of all that was going on in the Highlands by his own cousin and man of business, Colin Campbell, of Carwhin, Writer to the Signet, Edinburgh. Carwhin received regular reports from the Earl's three chamberlains, Alexander Campbell of Barcaldine, Mungo Campbell of Kinloch, and Duncan Tosach of Monzievaird, all kinsmen of his own. Sir John Dalrymple and the Earl of Argyll were also in London, and by the 16th January Lochiel arrived there, and took up his quarters with the Earl of Breadalbane.   Breadalbane's letters to Carwhin from 9th January until he left in April have been preserved, and they contain numerous references to current events. His character stands revealed as vain and ambitious; but it is difficult to believe that he was so black a villain as he has been made out to have been. His vanity made him a ready tool in the hands of Dalrymple and Argyll, who concealed from him their plans for the murder of the MacDonalds of Glencoe. Breadalbane had set his heart upon securing peace in the Highlands, and he took no little pride in the scheme by which he hoped to bring it about. He believed besides that it would be a patriotic action to have £12,000 transferred from the Exchequer in London to Scotland. He was grievously disappointed at the miscarriage of his plans ; but he was satisfied that he had been the means of preventing a rising of the chiefs

during the summer and autumn of 1691. He naturally resented
the behaviour of chiefs who had so bitterly opposed and
maligned him, and would not have been sorry to see them
punished. At the same time he appears to have disapprov̧ed of
drastic and precipitate action on the part of the Government.
He came to believe that such measures would only make matters
worse.

The Massacre took place on 12th February, and when Breadalbane came to know of it from Carwhin on 27th February, he
expressed his astonishment at the affair, and deeply regretted
that Robert Campbell of Glenlyon should have been involved
in it. Glenlyon and his estate had been a source of great
anxiety and worry to the Earl. The wretched creature's affairs
were in a hopeless muddle. He was beset by creditors on every
side, and his wife and children were likely to be thrown out of
house and home. Through Carwhin the Earl had been trying
to help " Robine," but the shiftless man could not be helped.
The Earl came to the conclusion that Glenlyon's ruin had now
been completed, and he advised Carwhin to see that he went to
Flanders. It is quite apparent that on receiving the first reports
of the Massacre, Breadalbane never imagined for a moment that
any blame for the deed would attach to himself, and when Carwhin
informed him later that his name was associated with the Massacre
he protested his innocence. However wily and crooked Breadalbane may have been in his ways, it is impossible to read his letters
through without arriving at the conclusion that he knew much
less about the Government's designs than he is generally supposed
to have done. He could not have been the prime instigator
of the crime, or have been even consulted about the plans for
its execution. This becomes evident from the references to
political events in these letters, which were written with his
own hand, chiefly to give instructions to his friend and trusted
advisor, Carwhin, regarding matters of estate business anf
family affairs.

On 9th January Breadalbane refers to Sir John MacLean of
Duart " who had ruined his chances by not coming in " ; and
on the same day he wrote a letter to Lochiel in which he said,
" Honored Cusine, I receaved your two letters of the 20 from
Lochaber last night's post, which brought with it ane accompt
to severalls here that you and diverse wer come in, and that
you wer coming hither. But in regard that ther was no word
come from you nor from Ardkinlas to Edinburgh on the fifth
ĩnstant, it's feard by yr Friends & hopt by yr enemies that you
ar the old man still, and not kept to what you wreat to me."
Two days later the Earl tells Carwhin to " see that Bar : (Barcaldine) keep weekly correspondence, and give ane account
of the motion of the forces. Send the proclamations which is
to be made to Bar: and Kinloch to prevent my men's harbouring

of the goods of those who ar to be prosequte by the forces.
They may do it cairfully and discreetly. We judge none to be
standing out but Glengarie, Glencoe, and the Captain of Clanranald, except McLane . . . I am impatient to have Lochzeall
here."

By 14th January Carwhin had sent a list of such as had " come
in " in Perthshire, and Breadalbane wrote in reply saying,
" All things that ar already determined ar kept secret. We
know as little as you do until they be done. Endeavours ar
used to mak such as cam not at the day to be as acceptable as
such as did, but both without money." Writing on 16th January
he wished Carwhin to tell him how Glenlyon's " curatorie "
was going on.

Sir John MacLean had agreed to submit, and had written
asking for an annuity, and in a letter of 23rd January, Breadalbane
says, " McLane's letter was shown to the King and E. of Port-
land, and they asked why he had not come sooner. Another
said it was a question if the King would give £500 a year to
a single man, seeing his clan had already taken the oath, to
keep him from going to France. . . . . Ther was orders to
fall on such Highlanders as stood out, and whoever reseat
their goods to treat them as enemies. Therfore I had reason to
warn, which I still do. I expect to hear daily what Glengarie
has done, and Keppoch."

Breadalbane was evidently finding that the Government was
not now prepared to pay over the money promised, and on
January 28th he writes, " I had this day a reckoning about
such as cam in in time for their money, but without success,
except to break any court I had ; they admiring of my speaking
for such as had done me so egregious ane injurie ; for all who
wer their friends for my sake ar become their bitter unfriends,
and little under it to me for my now insisting for them ; so
am I regirt on all hands ; and yet I thank God I do not repine
for all the trouble and charges and danger I have been at for
them and the nation, which is my dewtie and interest to
endeavour that it be in peace and prosperitie." In this letter
there is a reference to Glenlyon's curators. Two days later
(30th January) the Earl says, " It's from you that all news here
is expected, even so as it was during the Highland treatie.
Col. Hill wreats that Lochaber is as peaceable as the streets of
London, and Argyll's men quartered at Keppoch."

Breadalbane's Defence.

In seven letters covering the fateful period from 2nd February
to the 25th of that month there is little reference to politics.
The Earl's correspondence deals with a variety of matters,
among them Glenlyon's debts, and the necessity for economy
in his households. " Wreat," he says, " to Mungo to cause tak

cair of and look well to my servants at Balloch and Finlarig ; they consume meal and money." On the 25th February he states that he was surprised to find Keppoch in his dining room the previous day, and mentions that so soon as he can have him put " in order " he will present him at Court. Keppoch had evidently left Scotland before the news of the Massacre had got abroad. Writing on the 27th February, Breadalbane says, " I am to present Keppoch to the King tomorrow ; Bar : knew of his coming ; he came to me so soon as he lighted. . . . . What Bar : wreat to you astonisht me. I have espostulat about for the unseasonable and mad measures taken in it, and that E.A's (Earl of Argyll's) men be the executioners, and that after they had taken the oath. I fear innocent persons be the sufferers in the same measure. When I told E.A. he said he hopt the King would protect them. I said it was a far cry to Lochow. He had not got any notice of it. I pray God preserve my friends who are in that neighbourhood, and very free from accusation : it cannot be so ill as that ; Bar : says many hav escapt, as will do mischief and revenge, I fear, on such as ar as displeased as themselves, which works great trouble to the countrie. . .

" I doubt not Bar : has sent you a 2nd accompt of that affair; he would express my inclinations about it ; it was ane destructiv advice to put E.A.'s men and not the garrison on it. It's not believed the party was quartering peaceably among them. O ! how it will reflect, and needed not if wisely managed. I am exceedingly concerned about it." By 5th March fuller accounts of the Massacre had reached London, and Carwhin had informed Breadalbane that he was being blamed. In a letter of this date he replies, " You hav be this time my opinion about that precipitate action in Glencoa, and all the Court here have heard my resentment, and prophecie of the event that it will produce, which are contrarie to what I have ventured my life and fortune to have completed in the Highlands, and that is peace. Ane ill and miraculous fate follows unfortunat Glenlyon in the whole tract of his life. He is not to be mended. I hope he will go to Flanders. I wish his relations and children pay not for it. . . . Find out the certaintie and particulars of that affair. It makes no noise here ; nor was it noticed by the Court even at the first report. . . . Argyll tells me that my men hav bought the Glencoa cows for a dollar the peace. I told his Lordship that if it be true I'll mak them restore them to the widows and fatherless. I did expostulate that affair with him, and yet it may tak that lying turn you mention, but that is nonsense to have so contrived it, when a profound peace was best and intended, and bygones to have been bygones. E. A. goes from this on Monday, a very well pleased man with the King and Sir J. D. (Dalrymple). He has got his regiment to Flanders, and money advanced here for their clothing."

There are two letters dated 8th March. Carwhin had informed Breadalbane that McIan's two sons and fifty of his people had escaped, and he fears that " they will do mischief." "I have," he says, " in great men's company expresst my public dissent and disapproving of it as neither legal nor honourable, as I heard it, and I told E. A. this day that it will entail a new, and renew the old quarrel to his family, which he seemed to neglect." In his second letter of the 8th, the Earl again refers to Glencoe, and the charges being brought against himself. He goes on to say, " It's villanie to accuse me for Glenlyon's madness, and it's the height of malice if these people chase the poor woman and children out of the countrie. It's done by design. You have my mind alreadie of these well laid plotts for settling the Highlands ; such as hav been the obstructors ought to be chargt with such acts so agreeable to their designes, and so destructiv to mine. I wish I had known of it. I told the ministers here if I had, I would hav warned them, and thereby prevented all the mischief they will commit, which scarcely will be got done by the Government. I wish they would for a short time garrison Megernie. E. A. is in hopes to get them to go abroad . . . he will get them remissions. Keppoch has engaged Lochbuy to him to be ane ensign, providing he get men to him. . . . Glenlyon is the most unfortunat man that I ever heard of. I wish he wer gone ; but he's left ane ill farewell with his wife and bairns."

The Glencoe affair and its probable consequences to himself and his people gave Breadalbane much concern. He had, besides, arranged for two Londoners to come to extract turpentine from fir trees on his Argyllshire estates, and he feared that he could not afford them protection from the enraged MacDonalds and their friends.

On 17th March he wrote, " I had yours of the 10th last night. . . . They ar malicious and calumnious who blame either Lochzeall, or me, in the least accessory to that unhappy and inconsiderate action in Glencoe. It was ordered or eyther of us cam hither, and lay so long by Col. Hill until he saw, as he thought, his opportunitie, so was it mismanaged exceedinglie in execution. It never entered my thought, nor was it my interest to hav the least accessation to the thing to bring trouble on myself and familie. . . . Lochzeall goes from here to-morrow with Keppoch, both alyk well pleased. The money is all ordered to be brought up again, but I suppose to be there, or this can be done." By 12th March Breadalbane was thinking of returning to Edinburgh, and gave instructions to Carwhin to procure lodgings for him in the Canongate. The " projectors for extract of fir " were to follow him down, and he adds, " I shall be troubled to protect them if ther be not a profound peace, as we hear ther is." He wrote on the 15th March to say that, as he and Lord

Tarbet were in his coach in the public street in the town, they were stopped by messengers, who had a warrant for Breadalbane's arrest in connection with a bond of security that had not been paid. He found the sum charged, and the matter ended. He felt, however, deeply affronted. On the 22nd March, and again on the 31st, he referred to the Massacre, and asserts his blame-lessness. " I am as free of accession," he says, " as the man in Spain. It was ordered or I cam here, and lay so long with Col. Hill until he thought fit to execute it, which he did by others than his own regiment. . . . I neither know Col. Hill's orders first or last about Glencoa ; but I see a letter from him after that valiant, wise action that was acted, valuing himself on it as his deed, and regraiting the storm that hindered all to be cutt off."

Robert Campbell of Glenlyon and his affairs continued to be a source of trouble to Breadalbane. He felt sorry for the plight of his wife and children ; but he wished Glenlyon himself well out of the way. Glenlyon wanted to leave the country, and hesitated between going with Argyll's regiment to Flanders, or joining some Argyllshire gentlemen who were proposing to take up farms in Ireland. He wrote to Breadalbane asking for permission and assistance for the latter project. Breadalbane was inclined to approve ; but he first wanted Carwhin to get Barcaldine and Kinloch to report upon the prospects of the scheme. He left London on 12th April, and hoped to arrive in Scotland about the early days of May, when he wished Carwhin and his chamberlains to meet him in the Lowlands.

Breadalbane in Prison.

The Commission appointed in June, 1695, to inquire into the Massacre of Glencoe attached no blame to Breadalbane in the conclusions of its report ; but the feeling against him in the country and in Parliament was very strong. That feeling found vehement expression when the report was submitted to Par-liament, and although he could not be accused of having been a party to the Massacre, he was charged with high treason in connection with statements he was alleged to have made, while negotiating with the chiefs during the summer of 1691. He was committed for trial, and confined a prisoner in Edinburgh Castle. His friends set themselves immediately to secure his release. The King had, however, gone to Flanders, and was too busily engaged with the siege of Namur to trouble over Scottish affairs.

John Lord Glenorchy, the Earl's second son, went to England, and laid his father's case before the Duke of Devonshire and Lord Godolphin. From London he crossed over to Flanders, where he had to wait for nearly three months without attaining his purpose. He was, however, compensated for his enforced absence from home by being present at the siege of Namur. He witnessed the dramatic surrender of the Castle, and saw the garrison of 5,000 men marching out with drums beating and ensigns flying, while their commander, the proud Marshal Boufflers, and his staff closed the procession. Writing to his father on the 5th September from Namur Lord Glenorchy says, " I am glad I have seen this siege, nothing belonging to war but was in it.[1]" The King, who had not signed one paper relating to Scottish business all that summer, was at last able to give attention to the appeals for the liberation of Breadalbane. He sent a communication to the Commissioners of the Court of Justiciary at Edinburgh, to the effect that he did not expect the Earl of Breadalbane should have been prosecuted in Parliament in relation " to a negotiation he had been employed into by our allowance, and for which he had our exoneration and approbation, without representing the matter first to us." A few weeks later Breadalbane was set at liberty.

Breadalbane has been blamed for appropriating to his own personal uses part of the money offered by the Government to the chiefs. He is reported by tradition to have said, when called upon to submit a statement of his transactions, " The money is spent, the Highlands are quiet, and this is the only way of accounting among friends." There is, however, no ground for the belief that he appropriated this money, or that he uttered the words attributed to him. The money never seems to have left London ; and Breadalbane had some time afterwards to lodge a claim against the Government for the sum of two thousand pounds which he laid out during the negotiations.

Breadalbane and the Rising of 1715.

Breadalbane remained at heart a Jacobite. At the union of Parliaments in 1707. he refrained from voting. By 1715 he was too aged and infirm to take the field in person, but he did all in his power to further the movement under the Earl of Mar. He was represented at the Mar " Deer-hunt " at Aboyne, in August, by Colin Campbell of Glendaruel ; and later Glendaruel, with a party of Breadalbane men, marched under General Gordon through the north-west of Scotland mustering the clans. Acting on Glendaruel's advice, this force, which numbered over four thousand men, entered Argyll and advanced to Inveraray. When the Earl of Islay, brother to the Duke of Argyll, heard of the threat to the town and the castle, he assembled the county militia and procured arms and ammunition from Glasgow. Gordon contented himself with making a demonstration against Inveraray, and retired into Perthshire.[2]

The clans under Gordon had no sooner left Inveraray than a detachment of the Earl of Breadalbane's men under John Campbell of Glenlyon, son of the notorious Robert, invaded Argyllshire.

(1) Letters in Breadalbane Papers.   (2) Browne's Hist. of Highlands, Vol. II., p. 269. seq.

The Earl of Islay sent a party to drive them out, and the two forces met at the head of Lochnell, in Lorn. They prepared immediately for a fight, and both parties threw away their plaids and other encumbrances. There they stood facing each other, waiting for the command to attack. The leaders, however, recognising their kinship and reluctant to see Campbell blood shed, decided on a conference, which was held midway between the lines, while the men looked on. It was agreed that the Breadalbane men should be allowed to march safely out of the country on the condition that they laid down their arms. The terms, on being communicated to both sides, were received with great joy. Soon afterwards the Earl of Islay arrived with the remainder of his forces, and was much displeased at the easy terms granted to the invaders. He was, however, persuaded to approve of them, and the articles of agreement were honourably observed by both parties.

The Breadalbane men returned to Perthshire, and were able to join the Earl of Mar at Moulinearn, in Atholl, about the middle of September, when he proclaimed the Chevalier. The Earl of Breadalbane himself had been summoned by the Government to attend at Edinburgh along with some other sixty suspected persons ; but, instead of appearing, he forwarded a certificate from a physician at Perth, and another from Mr. Alexander Comrie, minister of Kenmore, stating that he was too aged to travel and was lying in bed suffering from several diseases. The very next day, however, the Earl joined Mar, and conferred with him at Moulinearn.[1]

During the weeks of inactivity that the Jacobite army spent at Perth the Earl of Breadalbane kept in close touch with Mar ; and when at length the forces began to move on towards Dunblane, the old Earl repaired to Drummond Castle, Strathearn. Here he had an interview with Mar on the eve of the Battle of Sheriff-muir. By a strange fate the Campbells were brigaded with the MacDonalds at the battle, and it is said that when Glengarry looked over their ranks he thought of Glencoe with some bitterness, and turning to Glenlyon he said, " Your father has deprived me of the use of an arm." To this Campbell replied, " Of that I am sackless, the only rivalry I shall have with a MacDonald is, which of us will best wreak upon yon ranks the injuries of our King." With that Glengarry grasped Glenlyon by the hand, and begged to be accepted as a brother.

It was this brigade, composed mostly of Campbells and MacDonalds, that secured the victory for Mar's right wing. Rae, the historian of the Rebellion, thus describes the achievements of the Campbells, " Four hundred of the Earl of Breadalbane's men and two hundred of the clans, making in all a confused body of six hundred men, fell on with incredible resolution

(1) Browne Hist. of Highlands, Vol. II., p. 282.

upon the three regiments of foot which were on the left of the
royal army, while they were forming. And although they made
all the resistance it was possible for them to make in that
situation ; yet they were broken, and a great many of them cut
to pieces, and those that were not killed, or taken, were driven
in among the dragoons, and put them likewise into confusion."

The gallant part played in the battle by the Breadalbane men
received due praise from the Gaelic bards. MacIvor[1] lauded
them thus :—

> " Thogainn fonn, thogainn fonn,
> Thogainn fonn, thogainn fonn gu foirmeil,
> Thogainn fonn gu farumach
> Air lasgairean Bhraid-Albann.
>
> Dh-innseadh latha Sliabh-an-t-Siorraim,
> Nach robh sibh anns an iomairt cearbach,
> Gun do theich na bleideirean,
> Ach sheas iad fir Bhraid-Albann."

> " I'll raise a tune, I'll raise a tune,
> I'll raise a tune full cheerful,
> I'll raise a stirring tune
> About the gay gallants of Breadalbane.
>
> The day of Sheriffmuir showed
> You were not in action blate ;
> Though the cowards ran away,
> Fast stood the Breadalbane men."

The stand taken and maintained by the Earl of Breadalbane
throughout the Rebellion won for him the favour and even the
admiration of his former enemies, the MacDonalds. Silis
MacDonald,[2] the bardess of Keppoch, in her poem on the battle,
celebrates the fame of the noble company, who fought under
" the gold-spangled banner." She wished that the Earl had been
in his fifties, and could have commanded the French cavalry.
Then had King George's men been chased home to their door-
steps. At last Iain Glas, to give Breadalbane the name by which
he was known in the Highlands, had become popular.

After Sheriffmuir, although Lord Glenorchy was detained a
prisoner in Edinburgh during the spring of 1716, the aged Earl
was allowed to remain at Balloch. Small garrisons were placed
both there and at Finlarig. A story is told to the effect that an
officer was sent to arrest Breadalbane, and was shown into
the room where he was lying in bed, in a semi-conscious condition. The officer touched him gently on the shoulder, at the
same time saying, " Sir, you are my prisoner." When the old
Earl realised the position, he looked at the officer with mingled
pity and scorn, and said, "Your prisoner ! I am the prisoner of
God Almighty, and eighty-one years of age." Turning to the
attendant, Breadalbane said, "Duncan, take that poor man

(1) Campbell's Lang. and Poetry of Highlands.   (2) Turner's Collection, pp. 303-304.

away, and get him out of the country before my people get to
hear of the insult he has offered me."

Proclamations were read in the churches ordering all arms to
be surrendered. Soldiers went about searching the houses; and
the cattle of those who were found with arms concealed were
driven to Finlarig. The house of Kinloch was plundered, and
the Laird of Turrerich was taken prisoner. Every parish in the
district had to raise money to provide the garrisons with food
and fuel. The ministers were enjoined to pray for King George
" in express terms." The country was sorely oppressed, and
John Campbell of Achallader, writing to Lord Glenorchy in
Edinburgh, in May, 1716, says, " I know few men can look
on themselves with safety."[1] Such were the consequences
of the '15 Rebellion for Breadalbane. The old Earl himself
survived the rising by only a year. He died on 19th March, 1717.

The Earl of Breadalbane's wife, Lady Mary Rich, whose
fortune had made him wealthy, died on 8th February, 1666.
By her he had two sons, Duncan, who was styled Lord Ormelie,
born about 1660; and John, Lord Glenorchy, born on 19th
November, 1662. The Earl took as his second wife, Mary,
daughter of Archibald Marquis of Argyll, and widow of George,
sixth Earl of Caithness. This marriage took place on 7th April,
1678. By his second wife he had a son, Colin, who was styled
"of Armadie." A bond of provision amounting to £96,000 Scots
was settled upon him in 1694. When Lord Glenorchy crossed
to Flanders in 1695 Colin was at the Hague, probably a soldier
in King William's army. He died unmarried in London on
31st March, 1708.

Colin of Armadie left one hundred pounds to the poor of Kenmore parish. According to tradition he was the father of John
Campbell, cashier of the Royal Bank of Scotland, Edinburgh,
who was a man of much importance in his day and who died
in 1777.

Some time after the death of his second wife the Earl took for
his mistress Mrs. Mildred Littler, housekeeper at Balloch. Mrs.
Littler bore him a daughter, Mary. On 8th December, 1716, a
few months before his death, the Earl made a settlement upon
" Lady Mary Campbell, my daughter by Mrs. Littler." Lord
Glenorchy referred to Lady Mary as " my sister." Lord
Hailes[2] relates a story that receives confirmation from a tradition
existing in Breadalbane, to the effect that after Mary was
grown up, the governess of Lord Glenorchy's daughters said
she was an impudent bastard to take place of them in going into
a coach. When the old Earl heard this, he said she would take
place of them, and accordingly acknowledged her mother as
his wife. If any ceremony of marriage took place, there does
not appear to be any record of it. Lady Mary Campbell married

(1) Breadalbane Papers.   (2) Scots Peerage.

Archibald Cockburn, son of Sir Archibald Cockburn of Langton, on 11th April, 1719, and she died with issue in 1725.

Lord Ormelie.

When John Campbell was created Earl of Breadalbane he was given power to nominate as his successor in the peerage and the family estates any one of his sons whom he should design in writing. The reason alleged for this peculiar provision in the patent was that Duncan, his elder son by Mary Rich, was feeble minded. On Duncan's own statement he was easily deceived through the " facility of his nature and want of knowledge," and he therefore concurred in the conveyance of the titles and the estates to his younger brother, John Lord Glenorchy, at the same time reserving to himself an alimentary allowance.

There was, however, in the Highlands a strong and persistent tradition that Duncan, Lord Ormelie, was not by any means weak minded, and that the Earl had other reasons for passing him over in favour of his younger brother. It is said that, as a young man, Duncan fell in love with Marjorie Campbell, daughter of the Laird of Lawers, and that he eloped with her, dressed up as a fiddler. The couple were married, and had two sons, the elder of whom was Patrick, whose great grandson, Donald Campbell,[1] Fort William, came forward claiming the peerage and estates in 1863. According to this tradition the Earl's real reason for passing over Lord Ormelie was that he and his two sons were ardent Jacobites, and that at Sheriffmuir they were instrumental in securing victory for the Breadalbane men by their skill and bravery. It was said that the wily old Earl feared that if he nominated Lord Ormelie as his successor, the estates might be confiscated to the Crown. He, therefore, made the titles and the estates over to John Lord Glenorchy, who was sympathetic to the Hanoverian cause. It was stated that after Sheriffmuir Duncan and his sons went to reside on his own estate of Ach-innis-chalain at the head of Glenorchy. It is difficult to explain how such a story could originate, but it was made the foundation for Donald Campbell's claim ; and was stated in a pamphlet published in 1866 in connection with the Breadalbane case. The evidence brought forward is based upon the tradition, and upon verses quoted from Gaelic ballads ; but it is not such as would be likely to carry much weight in a court of justice. There were, however, many persons ready to believe in the validity of Donald Campbell's claim, and to declare that he should have been granted the peerage and the Breadalbane estates in 1867 on the ground of his descent from Duncan; Lord Ormelie.

(1) Statement of Breadalbane Case—Sinclair, 1866.

CHAPTER XVI.

The Second and Third Earls of Breadalbane.

(1717-1782).

THE second Earl of Breadalbane was twice married. His first wife was Frances, daughter of Henry Cavendish, the second and last Duke of Newcastle. She died without issue while she was travelling with the Earl on the Continent in 1691. His second wife was Henrietta, daughter of Sir Edward Villiers, and sister of the first Earl of Jersey. While her father-in-law, the first Earl, was in prison in 1695, she used all her influence to secure his release. By his second wife the Earl had one son, John, who afterwards succeeded him, and two daughters, Charlotte, who died before her father, and Henrietta, who survived until 1766. In 1736 the latter was appointed one of the Ladies of the Bedchamber to the Princesses Amelia and Caroline, daughters of King George II.

The second Earl was of a retiring disposition, and had no desire for public life, but in 1721 he was elected a Scottish representative peer in succession to the Earl of Annandale. The election was keenly contested, and the right of the Earl to the peerage was called in question on the ground that his elder brother, Duncan, Lord Ormelie, was living. It was contended that the disposition granted by his father in the Earl's favour could not convey the honours and dignities of the Earldom ; and, further, that even the Crown could not effectually grant a peerage to any person and at the same time leave it to him to name his heir. Such a patent, it was argued, was inconsistent with the very nature of the peerage, and entirely without precedent. The objections were, however, overruled, and at the later elections in 1736 and 1741 Lord Breadalbane was again chosen a representative peer. The second Earl was Lord Lieutenant for the County of Perth. He died at the Palace of Holyrood House on 23rd February, 1752, in the ninetieth year of his age. By his political adventures the first Earl had burdened the estates with debt to the extent of half their value, and he ended his career as a life-renter receiving £500 a year out of his property. After his death the estates were placed under the management of commissioners, who included Lord Monzie and Lord Polton, and the second Earl was not served heir to his father until 26th December, 1733.

L

The unhappy experiences of the Fifteen had taught the second Earl that it was necessary to put his loyalty to the government beyond doubt. He, therefore, used all his influence to discourage his tenants from joining attempted Jacobite risings ; and he further helped the authorities to suppress the rebels. The garrison at Finlarig was maintained there until January, 1718 ; diligent searches were made for arms ; and suspected persons were placed under arrest. The Earl and his commissioners were splendidly aided in their task of placing the estates in a solvent condition, and of bringing law and order to prevail throughout Breadalbane, by John Campbell of Achallader, who acted as chamberlain, and who resided at Auchmore, Killin. This gentleman was succeeded in the same office by his son, and the factorships of father and son extended to over ninety years. Both were men of great administrative ability and wisdom ; they were trusted by their superiors and by the tenants alike, with the result that during their tenure of office matters under dispute between tenants were settled by them in such a way that appeals to law courts were very rare.

For some years after the Fifteen, Breadalbane, in common with other parts of the Highlands, suffered severely from raiding and cattle-lifting. The country was in a lawless condition. The garrison at Finlarig was quite incapable of affording protection to life and property. The situation was aggravated by the fact that persons attacked could not defend themselves owing to their arms having been surrendered to the authorities. In a series of letters written at this time to Lord Breadalbane at Edinburgh, John Campbell of Achallader describes the pitiable state of matters. In a letter of 14th June, 1717, Achallader says : " The state of the Highlands will soon be rendered desperat by stealing which is now beginning very fast both south and north, for companys of armed men are seen in the hills, who cross this country to Strathearn and braes of Menteith, and take cows and horses in small droves of ten or a dozen. When the night turns longer, and the cows stronger for driving it will be much worse, for a dozen armed men may robb and plunder the whole side of a country, since there is no arms to oppose them, which these loose fellows know very well. The garrisons of regular troops are no ways fitt to curbe them. The sogers that are sent from Finlarig with letters are sometimes seized betwixt the head of Lochearn and Tombea, and searched for letters." A month later Achallader informs Lord Breadalbane of steps that he had taken to check the thieves :—" They begin to steal horses, particularly on the sides of the Loch. Those I suspect most are the people of Rannoch and Glenlyon, and some within ourselves. I know very well that there is none come to give us any trouble from the north and Lochaber. I have appointed a watch of 18 men of the loose fellows in the country, John Macnab to command the one half, and Duncan Roy the other. They are to carry arms with the permission of the governor of Finlarig, to be paid every month ; and laid equally on the country, which will come to about £70 to 1st December from 1st instant. A month's pay is to be given in advance." The action taken by Achallader proved effective so far as the district of Breadalbane was concerned. He was able to report to Lord Breadalbane in February, 1718, that only one cow had been stolen in that region since the watch was set up. So successful did this method of dealing with the "mischievous trade of stealing" prove, that in 1719 the Earl of Atholl wrote to Lord Breadalbane suggesting that they combine with some smaller proprietors north of the Grampians in stamping out the evil from the Central Highlands.

Rob Roy.

Among the Breadalbane Papers there are at least four letters bearing the signature of " the brave Rob Roy." The earliest of these letters, written to the first Earl of Breadalbane from Portanellan, Glendochart, is dated 17th December, 1697, and refers to cattle that had been stolen, and to Rob's services in recovering them. The second, bearing the date, 4th September, 1711, was sent from the same place to give information to his Lordship with regard to " a ploy " of a somewhat serious nature that had occurred between John Campbell of Inverardoran and the sons of Campbell of Glenfalloch, the Earl's own kinsmen. It was about this time (1711) that Rob became involved in financial difficulties owing to his speculations in the cattle trade ; and the third letter, addressed from Corriechaorach, at the foot of Benmore (where the ruins of his house still stand), on the 14th September to his Lordship, reveals the fact that Lord Breadalbane was using his influence on Rob's behalf with such creditors as Campbell of Lochdochart and Lord Drummond of Perth.

In 1713 the first Earl appointed Rob to act as a bailie on his estates in Argyllshire with power to hold courts. When the news reached Lord Glenorchy in Edinburgh he was indignant at his father's action, and wrote in the following terms, protesting against " the indecencie of making use of such a man to be a judge " :—" Ednr. 6 January, 1714. My Lord, I did flatter myself I should have no occasion of complaining to your Los., but am heartily concerned to be undeceived by finding that yr Los. has given orders to Rob Roy to hold courts in Argyllshire. This is a great surprise to me upon many accounts. Yr Los. knows by settlements upon me no commissions of any nature there can be given without me ; and to make use of such a person as Rob Roy to be a judge upon our estates is what I could hardly believe, after the many advices you have

AT THE SOURCE OF THE TAY—CORRIES OF BEN LUI.

given me never to make use of any of them in our lands, but only to keep well with them otherwise, which method I did incline to follow. And now yr Los to make use of him at a time you design leaving the country doth appear to me as if you intended he should command in your absence, which forceth me to tell your Los., he nor no man ever shall, as long as I am living, and in this notion, and for my own honour I am obliged to write to forbear meddling in any public business in the countrie . . . . . so that I expect your Los. will be pleased to recall yr commission, and discharge his further appearing in any business." At the same time Lord Glenorchy wrote to Rob himself by John Campbell of Achallader, and on the 17th January Rob replied, " My Lord, I had the honour of your Lor.'s qth was not off ye nature I expected . . . The poor family I have come of have upon all occasions given proof of their being still in the interest of the house of Glenorchy qth I do not dream your Los. would now reject, because of my accepting a commission of baliary in this country from ye Earle by qth he was pleased to show his favour and protection from the unjust persecution off oyr great men ; nor would his Los. allow me to have my dependence upon others of ye first rank in ye nation, who att ye tyme I com in to this country prest it. But if yr Lors. discharge me ane office, I have no gaine by, nor does not pretend to make any, only untill I get my private affair put in some order. And the Earle on ye oyre hand charging me nor to demitt untill he think fitt to recall his commission, which if I did, his Lors. would be my greatest enemy. This would be the highest injurie don to me imaginable, qth I hope is in no ways your Los designe." All four letters were written by another person at Rob's dictation, but they bear his signature " Ro. Campbell." When John Campbell of Achallader handed over Lord Glenorchy's letter he had a talk with Rob about his position, and, writing to his Lordship, the chamberlain said, " The truth is I neither advised him to it, nor forbid him, being reproached before when he was prosecute (be the whole country people) as the author of the ruin of himself and family."

Although Lord Glenorchy might disapprove of Rob as a bailie, the latter appears to have been popular among the tenants. Rob's term of office soon came to an end, and he was forced to resort to less honourable methods of securing a live-lihood. Achallader continued to take an interest in Rob's doings, and kept his chief informed of his various escapades. In a letter of June 14th, 1717, he tells Lord Breadalbane of how Rob was induced to go to the Boat of Dunkeld under promise of pro-tection from the Duke of Atholl, but when he got there he was surprised to find himself surrounded by armed men, and forced to surrender. Rob begged to be sent to the prison at Logierait, and this request was granted. Meanwhile a message was sent to Perth asking for 100 men to take Rob thither. When the party from Perth arrived at Inver they learned that Rob had made his escape a few hours earlier by drinking his guards drunk. He and his servants made their way up through Strathtay and the Appin of Dull, giving out as they went that the Duke was Rob's best friend, and that he was to make him his chamberlain until he got him a better post.

A month later Achallader wrote saying, " All I hear of R. R. is that there is above ane hundred men of the forces quartered in Inversnaid, and that he very lately disarmed 40 or 50 of the Duke of Montrose's tenants that were in pursuit of 30 cows taken out of the parks of Buchanan ; and in two days thereafter went in daylight to Montrose his girnel, and ordered a chalder of meall to be weighed to him, which he carried off. He does not come near this country any time, and since the many small garrisons in Menteith can do no service against him, the garrison at Finlarig can do far less since he does not come within 20 miles of it."

The last reference in the Breadalbane Papers to Rob Roy is in a letter written by Achallader on 14th October, 1725, six months after Duncan Forbes' Act for the disarming of the Highlanders had been passed. General Wade had made a survey of the Highlands during the summer of the previous year, and now he returned to Scotland as Commander-in-Chief. He had power to give effect to the Disarming Act, and to build forts wherever he pleased. Wade sent Colonel Peers, whom Achallader describes " as a very civill gentleman," to Finlarig in order to receive the arms from the districts around. Achallader reported to Lord Breadalbane as follows :—" Seven or twenty-eight guns was the bulk of all the arms given up in yr Lordship's interest ; Glenlyon gave in 11 guns and the like number of dirks ; Culdares 19. Ther cam non out of Rannoch, and very few from the Duke of Atholl's people. Balquhidder non, except what the MacGregors brought, who cam in to the number of 40, each of them having a gun or a sword, Rob Roy's son and John Og's boys marching before them, and their piper playing. Rob was along with them, and was guide to Peer's and his men to the Kirk of Callander." Such was the dramatic manner of Rob Roy's exit from the story of Breadalbane.

Note contractions :—Los. for Lordship ; Lors. for Lordship's ; yr for your ; ye for the ; qth for which.

The " Forty-Five."

During the thirty years that separated the rebellion of 1715 from that of 1745 the district of Breadalbane had an opportunity of recovering somewhat from the disastrous effects of the civil wars and turmoil of the preceding century. Under the cautious administration of the second Earl and his counsellors peace prevailed, and there was a considerable measure of security for both life and property. The religious and political sympathies of the people also underwent a great change. At the Fifteen the ministers of Kenmore and Killin were Episcopalians and ardent Jacobites ; but in 1716 Mr. Alexander Comrie was deposed from Kenmore for refusing to conform to the Revolution Settlement ; and in 1728 the presbytery of Dunkeld insisted on the appointment of Mr. Adam Fergusson as assistant and successor to Mr. Robert Stewart of Killin, who had grossly neglected his spiritual duties while busily engaged in securing landed estates in Strathtay for his sons. So strong was the feeling for Prelacy and for the Stewart cause in Breadalbane after the deposition of Mr. Comrie, that five years elapsed before the presbytery could find a minister who would face the opposition of the people ; and when at length Mr. John Hamilton of Blair Atholl was settled at Kenmore, in 1723, he encountered many difficulties, and could gather very few of the parishioners to his services. Mr. Hamilton, however, persevered, and by his earnestness and diligence he won the esteem and affection of his people. Before his death, which took place in 1742, the great majority of them had become sound Presbyterians and loyal supporters of the government. Mr. Hamilton was succeeded by Mr. John Douglas, also a strong Hanoverian ; while at Killin, Mr. James Stuart continued the religious and educational reforms that had been begun by Mr. Fergusson, who removed to the parish of Moulin. The character and spiritual teaching of these ministers, who were well supported by their respective sessions, worked mightily against the influences that were brought to bear upon the people of Breadalbane when they were summoned by the fiery cross to rise and follow Prince Charles Stewart.

At the Forty-five the second Earl was aged and infirm, and the management of the estates had fallen into the hands of his capable and accomplished son, Lord Glenorchy, who afterwards succeeded as third Earl. Lord Glenorchy was baptised on 10th March, 1695-6, and at the age of fifteen he entered Christ's Church, Oxford. By his character and attainments he won a splendid reputation for himself at the University. The first Earl took a deep interest in the educational career of his promising grandson, and was most anxious that with all his attainments he should keep up his knowledge of the Gaelic language. Young John Campbell assured the aged nobleman that he was by no means forgetting the language of the Highlands. In a letter written from Oxford on 21st July, 1713, he said, " I still take care about my Irish, and sometimes meet with Sir Donald MacDonald's son, who is here, and another Gentleman, when we talk nothing but Irish."

The brilliant qualities of Lord Glenorchy early attracted public attention, and, attaching himself to the Whig Party, he became an intimate friend of Sir Robert Walpole. In 1718

JOHN, THIRD EARL OF BREADALBANE.

he was appointed Master of the Horse to the Princess Royal, and two years later he was sent as British minister to Copenhagen. He went to the court of St. Petersburg as ambassador in 1731. He entered Parliament as member for Saltash in 1727, and continued to represent that constituency until 1741. Lord Glenorchy was one of the Lords of the Admiralty in 1741-42. He was married on 20th February, 1718, at St. James', Westminster, to Amabel, daughter and co-heiress of Henry Grey, Duke of Kent. Lady Glenorchy died at Copenhagen in 1727.

She bore him a son, Henry, who died in the same year as herself, at the age of six years ; and one daughter, Jemima, who married Viscount Royston, afterwards the second Lord Hardwicke. In 1730 Lord Glenorchy married as his second wife, Arabella, third daughter of John Pershall, who was the son and heir-apparent of Sir Thomas Pershall, Baronet, of Great Sugnall, Staffordshire. By her he had two sons—George, who died at Moffat in 1744, and John, styled Lord Glenorchy, who was born in 1738, and died 14th November, 1771, eleven years before his father.

By his political experience and high social standing in the country, Lord Glenorchy was well qualified to advise and assist the king and his ministers, when, in 1745, the nation was threatened with invasion from abroad and insurrection in the Highlands. In a series of letters written at this time by Lord Glenorchy to John Campbell of Barcaldine, son of Alexander Campbell, who had been chamberlain to his grandfather, the active part taken by himself in opposing the rebellion is revealed. The correspondence begins after the battle of Prestonpans was fought, from which fact it appears that Lord Glenorchy had come down from London after that event. Before his arrival at Taymouth, John Campbell of Glenlyon and Archibald Menzies of Shian had made a bold attempt to raise the Breadalbane men for the Prince. The fiery cross was sent round Loch Tay, a distance of over thirty miles, in the incredibly short time of three hours, but the response was not what the leaders had hoped for. At the instigation of Alexander Robertson, the poet chief of the Clan Donnachaidh, who was himself too infirm to take the field, the Fearnan men went out. Tradition relates that the feeling for the Prince was so strong among the Fearnan people that some women from there who were crossing from Kenmore church in the ferry-boat along with Mr. John Douglas, the minister, attempted to throw him overboard and drown him, after he had preached against the movement and prayed for its speedy overthrow.

Once settled in Breadalbane, Lord Glenorchy set himself to do all within his power to oppose the rebellion. He was kept well informed as to the movements of the Highlanders, and this information he passed on to the Government. At the same time he sent reports which he received from England about the advance of the Hanoverian troops to leading men on his own estates and in other parts of the Highlands. In this way he was able to discourage many waverers from joining in the rebellion. Writing to John Campbell of Barcaldine on 14th October, 1745, Lord Glenorchy said, " Shian finds a great deal of difficulty in raising Struan Robertson's men again. About 130 soldiers taken at the Battle, who were committed to the care of Shian and were listed by him, have escaped from his guard, and are gone into Stirling Castle." On the 25th October he informed Barcaldine that eight regiments ordered from Flanders had landed on the 11th October, at Newcastle, and had come to Berwick. The army coming from the south was estimated at 8,000 men. In this letter Lord Glenorchy stated that Young Cluny had brought the McPhersons into Atholl and had gone back to fetch more men. Two hundred of Cluny's men had gone into Glenlyon, and had been forcing Menzies of Culdares' men to rise. Culdares was, however, " too cunning to expose himself, and prevailed upon Duncan, Duneaves' brother, to head them, with whom they went willingly. Shian has, at length, with the assistance of the McPhersons, forced out the Appin of Dull men much against their will, and yesterday they all marched."

By November, 1745, the Duke of Argyll had resolved upon raising the county Militia. When intimation of the Duke's action reached Lord Glenorchy, he wrote to Barcaldine in the following terms, " When the Militia is raised, all in my estate must be on the same footing with the rest of the shire, and I hope my friends who are to command them will qualify, as the Law directs, especially if the Duke's friends do it ! " The castles of Caolchurn and Finlarig were garrisoned, as was also Kingshouse, which had been erected after the Fifteen rising. In this way the passes on the west were held against the Jacobites, and when they returned from England they were compelled to take the eastern route to the North. At this time the lead mines at Tyndrum were in full operation. They had been wrought by Sir Robert Clifton, an English gentleman, who was a keen Jacobite. When the Argyllshire Militia were marching past the mines on their way to Finlarig, they destroyed the mining apparatus and other furnishings. Sir Robert afterwards submitted a claim for damages to the Crown.

In his letters to Barcaldine Lord Glenorchy stated that great numbers of Highlanders were passing north, twenty and thirty of them in a body. They gave out that they were appointed to form a " body of Observation " in the North, but his Lordship believed that they were deserters. He told Barcaldine that " Old Glenlyon " had come to Taymouth, but that he had declined to see him. He was told to go away immediately. Glenlyon had no information regarding the Jacobite army. As Lord Glenorchy closed his letter of 11th November, he intimated to Barcaldine that he had just received information to the effect that General Wade had 11,000 men with him in Yorkshire, and that 30 ships had arrived from Flanders with forces. " I hear," he continued, " there is great unanimity and high spirits in London, being in no ways apprehensive of an invasion." These ten letters[1] written by Lord Glenorchy during the critical period between 9th October and 26th December, 1745, reveal his activities in the Govern-

(1) Trans. Gaelic Soc., Inverness, Vol. XXI., pp. 148-166.

ment's cause, and the invaluable services that he rendered to the Crown. Through his influence his own tenants and many others besides were prevented from rising in support of the Jacobites. In his efforts he was strongly aided by the ministers of Kenmore and Killin. At both places a fast day was observed on 17th April, 1746 " upon account of the present unnatural Rebellion." Culloden had been fought and lost the previous day by the Jacobites, but the news had not yet reached Breadalbane. The people of both parishes were again summoned to the churches on 26th June for " a service of solemn thanksgiving to God for the Defeat and Dispersion of the Rebels." It was due to Lord Glenorchy that the district of Breadalbane was spared the miseries that befell other parts of the Highlands that had thrown in their lot with the Prince.

Development of Industries.

The second Earl of Breadalbane, who was a man of simple tastes and inexpensive habits, devoted his life to paying off the debts that his father had so foolishly contracted. In his worthy and successful efforts he was greatly aided by the wise and careful administration of his chamberlain, John Campbell of Achallader. The second Earl planned and effected considerable improvements on the estates. In 1739 the lead mines on the lands of Auchinturin, Tyndrum, were started ; and before this time he brought wool-workers from England to teach the people of Breadalbane the arts of spinning and weaving. Flax was first raised about the year 1728, and in 1734 his tenants began to sell lint yarn at the Kenmore markets. Under the fostering care of the third Earl spinning and weaving developed until they became a thriving industry in the district. When Thomas Pennant visited Breadalbane in 1769, he was able to state, " The north side of Loch Tay is very populous ; for in sixteen square miles are seventeen hundred and eighty-six souls ; on the south side, about twelve hundred. The country, within these thirty years, manufactures a great deal of thread. They spin with rocks, which they do while they attend the cattle on the hills ; and, at four fairs in the year, held at Kenmore, above sixteen hundred pounds worth of yarn is sold out of Breadalbane only ; which shews the great increase of industry in these parts, for less than forty years ago there was not the least trade in this article. The yarn is bought by persons who attend the fairs for that purpose, and sell it again at Perth, Glasgow, and other places, where it is manufactured into cloth." The third Earl set up spinning schools in different parts of the district, and gave away a certain number of spinning wheels each year. Thus the slower method of spinning with the rock or distaff, was gradually superseded.

In 1770 the amount of flax dressed at Lawers lint mill was 460 stones, and at Killin mill, 954 stones. These scutching mills were the first of their kind to be erected in the Highlands, and were constructed by Ewen Cameron, a native of Breadalbane. This remarkable man was born in 1705 and died at Lawers in 1817 at the extraordinary age of 112 years. It was he who taught the people of Breadalbane how to use spinning wheels and jack-reels. He settled down at the Shian of Lawers, and from there he travelled all over the Highlands constructing lint mills. Cameron also designed the first mill for the shelling of barley to be set up north of the Forth. Prior to his time barley, which was much used for broth, was shelled in the *clach-chrotain* or mortar stone in which the grain was pounded after being moistened. Many such hollowed stones may be seen about the doors of houses in Breadalbane still. Ewen Cameron's mills filled the people of the district with amazement, and many came from far to watch them working. His fame was celebrated in a Gaelic song composed by John Campbell or Macglasserig, the bard of Morenish.

Before 1769 a waulking or fulling mill was started at Remony near Kenmore by William Murray. Encouraged by Sir John Sinclair of Ulbster, the great pioneer of Scottish industries, the fourth Earl of Breadalbane extended the Remony mill, and introduced plant for carding and spinning wool, and for dressing and dyeing cloth. The weaving was done by hand-loom weavers, of whom there were a great many throughout the district. In 1792 the tenant of the Remony mills was Alexander Macnaughton whose great great-grandsons are the owners of the well known Tweed and Tartan mills at Pitlochry.

James Haggart, a native of the district of Acharn, entered the employment of Alexander Macnaughton as an apprentice in 1808. After becoming fully acquainted with the various processes of manufacturing cloth, James Haggart took up the tenancy of the meal mill at Keltneyburn, to which he added machinery for wool-carding and dyeing. Here he carried on a successful business until his death, when he was succeeded by his sons, Peter, and James. They greatly extended the business until they were able on the Keltneyburn premises to carry through all the processes of manufacturing cloth from the fleece to the finished article. About 1880, Messrs. P. & J. Haggart acquired the unexpired portion of the lease of the Aberfeldy Woollen Mills in order to be nearer the rail-head ; and ten years later they transferred their entire business to the Aberfeldy premises which they enlarged. They introduced new and improved machinery for the manufacturing of the high class tweeds and tartans that are now known all over the world. The firm has held the Royal Warrant for many years, and annually supplies tweeds, tartans, and rugs to the King and Queen Elizabeth, and to many other members of the Royal Family.

The sole partner of the firm of Messrs. P. and J. Haggart

is Mr. James Dewar Haggart, O.B.E., the son of the late Mr. Peter Haggart. When the eastern portion of the Breadalbane estates was sold in 1922, Mr. J. D. Haggart acquired the lands of Aberfeldy, Duntaylor, Duntuim, and Dunskiag, along with the superiority of the Aberfeldy feus. He is joint-director of the Taymouth Castle Hotel Company along with Mr. J. Mactaggart of Newton Mearns. Mr. Haggart has been Provost of the burgh of Aberfeldy since 1914.

Roads.

It was during the time of the second Earl that Marshal Wade was engaged upon his great road-making schemes in the Highlands. By 1734 he had constructed the two main arteries leading from Stirling to the North—one by Crieff and Tay Bridge (Aberfeldy)—and the other by Callander past the Kirk of Balquhidder to the east side of Loch Dochart, thence through Strathfillan and over the Black Mount to Fort William. These two high-ways were connected by a road which crossed Breadalbane. It went from Lochearnhead over the hill to Ardeonaig, along the south side of Loch Tay, and on to Taymouth Castle and Tay Bridge. The third Earl, at his own expense, made a road from Kenmore to Glendochart, along the north side of Loch Tay, in the construction of which he had to build no fewer than thirty-two bridges on the Lochtayside section alone. In 1769 Pennant says, " I must not omit that on the north side of the lake is a most excellent road, which runs the whole length of it, leading to Tyndrum and Inveraray, and is the route which travellers must take, who make what I call the *petit tour* of Scotland. They will find the whole country excel in roads, partly military, partly done by statute labour, and much by the munificence of great men." The third Earl built the handsome bridge over the Tay at Kenmore. It took two years to construct, and was completed in 1774. The commissioners for the Forfeited Estates contributed the sum of one thousand pounds sterling towards its cost.

The Village of Kenmore and Taymouth Policies.

Before 1760 the village of Kenmore consisted of the church, the inn, the school which occupied the site of the low building attached to the Estate Office, and one or two houses. About that year the third Earl formed the present village by erecting several neat little cottages on the north and the south sides of the square, thus giving it the appearance of an English village. Pennant observes " Lord Breadalbane permits the inhabitants of the village to live rent-free, on condition that they exercise some trade and keep their houses clean ; so that by these terms, he not only saves the expense of sending on every trifling occasion to Perth, or Crieff, but had got some as good workmen, in common trades, as any in His Majesty's

KENMORE BRIDGE. Built 1774.

dominions." About the middle of the eighteenth century the policies of Taymouth underwent a great change at the hands of the second and third Earls. The public road through the grounds was converted into a private drive to the Castle, and a new road was constructed from Kenmore to near the foot of the Balloch Burn, where it joined the old road. The line of the new road admitted of a considerable addition being made to the policies, but it certainly was a peculiar one. Running along the end of the loch, the new road ascended the hill for some distance, and then, turning sharply eastward, it passed the old houses of Balnaskaig or Big Raw, and thence down the hill till it joined the old road at the village of Ballivouline, where the Power Station now stands. Before 1786 the present highway from the Kenmore cross-roads over the Fort Hill to Aberfeldy was constructed.

Numerous walks and footpaths were laid out within the policies ; and here and there, both within and without the walls enclosing the Castle grounds, a number of ornamental summer houses were erected on knolls that commanded wide views of the loch and the surrounding mountains. The flower and kitchen gardens of Balloch, which were situated to the east of the Castle, were transferred to the east of Newhall, beside the nursery for rearing trees. The old Chinese bridge across the Tay behind the Castle, the first tower above the Fort, and the Hermitage at the Falls of Acharn were all erected about this period.

Afforestation.

Letters written by John Campbell of Achallader to the second Earl about 1726 reveal the interest of the latter in afforestation. In this respect he was following the example set by his ancestor, Sir Duncan Campbell, the seventh Laird. Plantations were formed by enclosing areas of waste ground on different parts of the estates with stone walls, sowing them thickly with seeds, and placing them under the charge of a diligent forester. This was found to be the least expensive method. About 1738 James Menzies of Culdares brought the first larches to Scotland from the Tyrol, and it is said that some of them were planted at Taymouth. The giant larch tree that was felled on Drummond Hill after the Great War was not, however, one of these imported larches. It contained 700 cubic feet of timber, and was declared by forestry authorities to have been the largest larch tree in Britain at that time. By the year 1754 the southern slope of Drummond Hill, from Comrie to Rhevard, had been planted ; and there were also extensive plantations on the opposite side of the valley. Maps of this period show that the plantations around Taymouth extended to over 500 acres ; and by 1786 the area under trees had been increased to 1103 acres. Many of the trees planted by the second and third Earls

KENMORE CHURCH AND VILLAGE.

were cut down after the Great War ; and some of them were
of stately proportions. There were larches within the policies
that ranged from 100 to 120 feet in height, with girths of from
10 to 12 feet ; on the southern slopes of the valley spruces
were felled of 100 feet in height, and over 21 feet in circumference. Some magnificent silver firs were 120 feet high, and
over 20 feet in girth.

The third Earl took much pride in beautifying Taymouth
and its surroundings ; and in his time the place became famous.
Tourists to the Highlands made a point of paying it a visit.
Thomas Pennant resided at the Castle on two occasions, and has
given us most interesting and valuable accounts of all he saw
within and without the great house. In September, 1765, Thomas
Gray, the poet, stayed for a night in Kenmore Inn.   In
his description of Taymouth, Gray says, " Lord Breadalbane's
plantations and woods rise with the ground on either side of the
vale to the very summit of the enormous crags that overhang it.
Along them, on the mountain side, runs a terrace a mile and a
half long, that overlooks the course of the river. From several
seats and temples perched on particular rocky eminences you
command the lake for many miles in length, which turns like
some huge river, and loses itself among the mountains that
surround it.   At its eastern extremity, where the river issues
out of it, on a peninsula, my Lord has built a neat little town
and church with a high square tower, and just before it lies a
small round island in the lake covered with trees, amongst
which are the ruins of some religious house. I saw four old
chestnuts in the road, as you enter the park, of vast bulk and
height.   .   .   .   Of the house I have little to say, it is a very
good nobleman's house, handsomely furnished and well kept,
very comfortable to inhabit, but not worth going far to see.
Of the Earl's taste I have not much more to say, it is one of
those noble situations, that man cannot spoil ; it is however
certain that he has built an inn and a town just where his
principal walks should have been, and in the most wonderful
spot of ground that perhaps belongs to him. In this inn, however,
we lay, and next day returning down the river, we passed it
over a fine bridge, built at the expense of the government, and
continued our way to Logierait."

First Earl's Line Fails.

The third Earl of Breadalbane by his second marriage had
two sons, both of whom predeceased himself. George, the elder
son, died at Moffat, on 24th March, 1744, aged twelve years.
John, the younger son, who was styled Lord Glenorchy, was
born 20th September, 1738.   He married Willielma Maxwell,
daughter and co-heiress of William Maxwell of Preston, on 26th
September, 1761. Lord Glenorchy died without issue on 14th
November, 1771, in his thirty-fourth year. He had inherited

M

the estate of Sugnall, Staffordshire, through his mother, but he sold it, and bought the property of Barnton, Midlothian, where he died. It has been stated that his death was the result of a duel in which he had engaged. His widow, who was a woman of refined tastes, great charity, and genuine piety, survived until 17th July, 1786, when she died at George Square, Edinburgh. She was buried in the city within a church which she founded, and which still bears her name.

With the death of Lord Glenorchy, the right of succession to the Breadalbane peerage and estates passed to a third cousin of the third Earl—John Campbell, whose father, Colin Campbell of Carwhin, was a great-grandson of Sir Robert Campbell of Glenorchy, the ninth Laird and third Baronet. A curious and interesting story relating to the marriage of the fourth Earl's father is told by Burke in " The Vicissitudes of Noble Families."

In 1758, according to the story, the Earl had an English visitor at Taymouth, who, in exploring about the place, fell in with a fine-looking lad in the Highland garb, attended by a gillie. The stranger asked who the boy was, and was told he was " The Young Breadalbane." After dinner that evening, when the Earl and his guest were sitting together, the latter related the circumstances, with the reply given, and asked, " Now, who could the boy be ? " " Oh," replied Lord Breadalbane, " I know who that would be, that was young Glenfalloch," savagely adding, " So he called him, ' The Young Breadalbane,' did he ? "

SPANISH CHESTNUT TREES AT TAYMOUTH. Planted about 1600.

At that time Lord Glenorchy was unmarried, and Colin Campbell of Carwhin, the next heir, was an elderly, confirmed bachelor who had retired from business in Edinburgh to his little Lochtayside estate. The handsome and popular son of the next heir—the laird of Glenfalloch—was, therefore, considered by many as likely one day to become Earl of Breadalbane —hence the designation "The Young Breadalbane."

That he should be so named, however, appeared to rankle in the mind of the old Earl, who continued the whole evening in a fit of abstraction, repeating occasionally, "So he called him 'The Young Breadalbane.'"

Next morning, at break of day, a messenger was sent from Taymouth to summon Colin Campbell of Carwhin, the retired bachelor, who had settled down to end his days in peace. When he arrived, and had been welcomed, Lord Breadalbane said to him, "Now, Carwhin, you can't guess why I sent for you." "Oo, onything to please your Lordship," was Carwhin's reply. "Well," said Lord Breadalbane, "I'll tell you what it is. I want you to marry." "Me marry, your Lordship, I hae naething to marry on," Carwhin answered. "Oh, I'll make that easy for you, Carwhin," Lord Breadalbane said. "Well, but if I were ever so well inclined, I dinna ken onybody that would take me," the old bachelor replied. Lord Breadalbane assured him that he had a remedy, and said, "You'll go to Inveraray, where the Circuit Court meets soon, get introduced to Miss——, daughter of Lord —— one of the judges, who is to be there; and I'll warrant she'll take you." "Well, Breadalbane, onything to please your Lordship," answered Carwhin. In due time he set off in his best trim, arrived at Inveraray, got introduced to the young beauty, danced with her, took her to supper, and proposed, as he had been directed to do. Carwhin was, however, rejected, and, much disconcerted, he appealed to a bosom friend, and explained the position. His friend said, "If all you want is to please Lord Breadalbane, try Betty Stonefield. I'll warrant she'll no refuse you." This was a maiden sister of Archibald Campbell, Lord Stonefield, the other judge on the Circuit, but she was neither young nor handsome. Carwhin took the advice, went through the same form, and was gladly accepted. The son and heir of this curiously planned marriage was no other than John Campbell of Carwhin, who eventually succeeded to the exclusion of Young Glenfalloch, as fourth Earl of Breadalbane. Burke goes on to observe that events are not to be controlled. The fourth Earl's son, John, the second Marquis, died childless, and some time after his death in 1862, the great-grandson of "The Young Breadalbane" became the sixth Earl, in spite of the jealousy of the third Earl, and the canny courtship of old Carwhin.

CHAPTER XVII.

The Fourth Earl and First Marquis of Breadalbane.

(1782-1834).

THE third Earl of Breadalbane died at the Palace of Holy-rood House on 26th January, 1782; and on 13th August of the same year John Campbell, who had succeeded his father in the little property of Carwhin ten years earlier, was served heir to the peerage and the family estates of Breadalbane. The fourth Earl was born on 30th March, 1762, and was thus in his twentieth year. He had been educated at Westminster, and resided for some time at Lausanne. Two years after his succession he was appointed a representative peer for Scotland in the House of Lords, a position that he held until 1802. On November 13th, 1806, the fourth Earl was created Baron Breadalbane of Taymouth Castle; and at the coronation of King William IV., on 12th September, 1831, he was made Earl of Ormelie and Marquis of Breadalbane, in the peerage of the United Kingdom. The fourth Earl married Mary Turner, eldest daughter and co-heiress of David Gavin of Langton, Berwickshire, in London, on 3rd September, 1793, and had a family of one son, John, who succeeded as second Marquis, and two daughters, Elizabeth, who married Sir John Pringle of Stitchill, and who died 17th February, 1878; and Mary, who married Richard, Marquis of Chandos and Duke of Buckingham, and died 28th June, 1862.

The Beadle's Grand-daughter at Taymouth.

A romantic interest attaches to the fourth Earl's marriage with Mary Turner Gavin. Some time in the early eighteenth century a Dutch ship was wrecked off Lunan Bay, near Montrose, and the crew were sheltered by Alexander Gavin, beadle of Lunan Church, whose father had held the same office before him. The skipper of the ship, David Smith, fell in love with Margery, Alexander's sister, and in 1742 they were married in Holland, and settled down there. In due time they sent for David Gavin, Alexander's son. David became a prosperous merchant in Middleburg, Zealand. In the course of a few years he amassed a large fortune, and in 1758 he was able to leave his brother, Benjamin, to look after the business, while he himself returned to Scotland. He bought the estate of Langton, Berwickshire, from the Cockburns. David Gavin had married Christina Maria Hearsey, daughter of Andrew Hearsey, who was a member of the English congregation at Middleburg, in 1751, and she bore him one child, a daughter, who died at the age of seven years, in 1765. Two years later Mrs. Gavin herself died at Langton House. In 1770, David Gavin married as his second wife, Elizabeth Maitland, daughter of the seventh Earl of Lauderdale, by whom he had three daughters. The eldest of these daughters, Mary Turner, born on 6th March, 1771, became Countess, and afterwards Marchioness of Breadalbane.

Lady Breadalbane was a woman of great kindness and charity, and gave freely of her wealth to poor people on the estates. Her husband was devoted to her, and during her life-time he erected a monument on the north bank of the Tay, to the east of Kenmore Bridge, to commemorate her good deeds. This monument occupies the site of an old summer-house, called Maxwell's Building. Surmounted by a stone cross, it stands about thirty feet high, and is well proportioned. It is approached by a flight of steps, which enclose the building. A heavy door of chlorite slate—of which stone the monument itself is built—gives admission to a spiral stair, which leads to a small arched gallery that runs round the structure. On a brass mural tablet is the following inscription :—

" THIS BUILDING IS DEDICATED TO MY FAITHFUL FRIEND
AND FELLOW-LABOURER,
MARY, COUNTESS OF BREADALBANE,
WHOSE MATERNAL CARE HAS BEEN LONG EXTENDED TO ALL
AROUND THIS PLACE—ANNO DOMINI 1831."

Miss Elizabeth Gavin, sister of the Countess, who frequently resided at Taymouth, was also deeply interested in the poor of the district, and she gave to the kirk session of Kenmore the sum of one thousand pounds, which is secured over a portion of the Breadalbane estates, and yields fifty pounds annually. This sum is divided half-yearly among the necessitous poor of the parish of Kenmore.

Agricultural Improvements.

The settled condition of Breadalbane in the eighteenth century led to a considerable increase of the population during that period. Small-pox, typhus fever, and other maladies, as well as the sword, which had formerly checked the growth of the population, took a much smaller toll. Tradition still preserves the fearful memory of many a *galar mor*, or great plague, that devastated the countryside in olden times. The population of Kenmore had risen from 3,067 in 1755, to 3,463 in 1794 ; and that of Killin increased at the same rate until it had reached 2,360 in the latter year.

The increasing population created a serious problem for the proprietors. Under the antiquated system of agriculture that existed, the country could not carry so many people, and provide them with even a modest standard of living. In common with other parts of the Highlands the run-rig system of farming prevailed in Breadalbane. The houses of the several tenants on a farm, usually built of dry stone, were grouped closely together beside a stream, or good spring of water. The arable land was held in common, and the fields were so divided that the alternate ridges, or rigs, were worked by different tenants. The rigs changed hands from time to time, so that there was little incentive for improving the land. The cultivated land was divided into infield or croftland, and outfield. The former received practically all the manure, and was cropped yearly. The latter, on the other hand, consisted of patches of poorer land, usually situated higher up the hill-slope. They were enclosed with stone, or turf walls, within which cattle had for some time been folded at night. These enclosures received no manure at all, but they were cropped as long as they would bear a crop and then abandoned to weeds, while other patches were enclosed and the same process followed. Under such methods the yield per acre was exceedingly small. Black cattle and horses were kept in numbers far in excess of the provision made for their wintering. In 1769 there were 193 tenants on the south side of Loch Tay between Auchmore and Kenmore.

OLD COTTAGE AT ARDEONAIG.

Among them they had 1,545 head of cattle, 369 horses, and 443 harrowers or young unbroken horses—a total of 2,357 animals that would require more or less hand feeding in winter. Sheep numbered only 4,097, and goats, 202. On the north side of the loch there were 180 tenants between Finlarig and Fearnan, and probably even a larger stock than on the south side. In both districts there were many cottars, or cow-holders besides. Other parts of Breadalbane were similarly over-stocked with cattle and horses.

The third Earl of Breadalbane was familiar with the more advanced methods of farming on his wife's estate in England, and with a view to the introduction of reforms in Breadalbane he proceeded with careful surveys of his estates in 1769. Every bit of land was carefully measured and its character and quality were noted. Most accurate maps were prepared by the surveyors, giving the location and acreage of croftlands, outfields, meadows, pastures, and woodlands, below the head-dykes that separated the farms from the hill-grazings. These various details and measurements, along with the stocking and sowing of each farm, were set down in tabular form. In this way it was possible to ascertain the conditions then existing, and to decide upon a policy for the improvement of the estates.

There is no evidence to show how far the third Earl was able to carry out his contemplated reforms. By the time the fourth Earl succeeded the population had greatly increased, while black cattle and horses were more numerous than ever. The land and the people were impoverished. The fourth Earl, acting on the advice of experienced agriculturists, proceeded to introduce reforms. He had the run-rig system done away with ; and compact farms were laid out, suited to the capacity of the tenants. The infield and outfield arrangement was brought to an end. In these ways causes of bitter disputes between tenants were removed. Leases of fifteen years duration were granted ; thus the farmers were encouraged to improve their land by draining marshes, clearing it of stones and scrub, and building dykes. The Earl sent the sons of tenants to Norfolk and Leicestershire to learn farming, and to bring new ideas back to Breadalbane. A system of rotation of crops was introduced ;. and as fields came to be enclosed increasing areas of turnips and sown grass were laid out. Potatoes had been introduced into Breadalbane before the middle of the eighteenth century. By 1770 Pennant discovered that they were grown in every cottage garden, and in fields. The most successful variety was the "London Lady," which yielded a return of from seven to ten-fold. At that time potatoes were made into starch, and even into bread. Some were distilled into a spirit which was found to be stronger than that made from grain. Potatoes had now became more plentiful, with the result that swine increased. Tenants who were struggling in high-lying farms were brought to more fertile places, and sheep-runs were formed on the uplands. The sheep introduced were mostly of the Linton breed. The souming of all farms was restricted. Over-stocking was discouraged, and so the number of black cattle was reduced to what could be easily wintered. The result of these reforms was that in a few years the quantity of grain grown was doubled. The rental of the land increased, but for the first three years the proprietor divided the difference between the old rent and the new, amounting to £1,200 a year, among the tenants. He gave prizes to the best cultivators, and expelled those tenants who would not conform to his regulations. The system of subsetting parts of farms to cottars was forbidden, as this had caused much oppression of the weak and poor by the strong in the past. No tenant could hold more than one farm, and the Earl made it a condition of every lease he granted that the holder should reside upon his land. To show that he meant to have his reforms carried out the Earl served notices to quit upon forty-eight defaulting tenants on his Perthshire estates alone, in the year 1795. Many of those who were removed ultimately found their way to Canada. He treated the deserving poor with every consideration, and each year distributed large quantities of meal among them.

The villages of Stix, Croftmoraig, Achloa, Acharn, and Stronfearnan were built about the end of the eighteenth century and the beginning of the nineteenth, as part of the fourth Earl's policy to improve the condition of the people. The occupiers of houses in these villages were provided with pendicles, or grazing for cows, in adjoining parks, and given work about the Taymouth policies and gardens. The position in 1793 was that on the Breadalbane estates in the parishes of Kenmore and Killin, there were 555 tenants or small farmers, 207 crofters, and 69 cottars. There were besides some 40 tenants and cottars on the Macnab lands. The Statistical Accounts for these parishes show that at this time there were in Kenmore, 63 weavers, 38 tailors, 36 wrights, 26 shoe-makers, 20 flax-dressers, 10 smiths, 9 masons, 8 coopers, 4 hosiers, and 1 dyer. The tradesmen in the parish of Killin were :—36 weavers, 22 tailors, 14 wrights, 19 shoe-makers, 6 smiths, 7 merchants, and 2 bakers. There were meal mills at Strathfillan, Edravinoch, Auchlyne, Killin, Finlarig, Morenish, Carwhin, Crannich (Balnahanaid), Lawers, Fearnan, Taymouth, Acharn, Ardeonaig, and Cloichran. The emoluments of the several millers varied somewhat; but in addition to an allowance of meal, or grain, from each boll that the miller ground, he received presents, or *bonnags*, of mutton yearly at Christmas from the tenants thirled to his mill. He was obliged to procure mill-stones, and to keep the machinery of his mill in proper repair. The tenants on their part had to carry home the mill-stones.

In reviewing the condition of his parish, Mr. Patrick Stuart of Killin stated in 1794, that at the beginning of the eighteenth century the people were averse to industry, owing to their love for fighting and raiding. A well-doing, diligent man was then held in contempt by his neighbours. The people were poor, and always behind with their rents. In many cases the rents were never paid at all. The proprietors had, however, encouraged the sober and industrious ; while the turbulent and irregular were expelled. The result of all the influences that were brought to bear upon them was that, by the last decade of the century, the people had become sober, industrious, and regular in their habits ; and they were in easy and affluent circumstances.

The fourth Earl spent considerable sums of money on making new lines of road, the erection of bridges, and the laying out of plantations. As an indication of his activity in these directions the following items are taken from the accounts for the years 1788-9 and 1789-90 :—" For making the new line of road above the Fort, £70 " ; " To Munro and McIsack for building the dyke on both sides of the Burn at Aberfeldy, £182 16 6 " ; " Building the dyke around the West Mailer of Lawers, £87 " ; " To Campbell and Haggart for building the two bridges at Acharn, and above Taymouth, £17 13 " ; " To Hugh Cameron for bruising mill added to lint mill at Lawers, £20 " ; " Planting Den above Aberfeldy, £30 9 " ; " Planting West Mailer of Lawers, £11 5 " ; " Enclosing oak woods in Crannich, £70 " ; " To Mr Macnab at Inschewen for bu'lding a bulwark for confining water of Dochart within its natural channel, £10." The Earl's enterprise and success in turning waste land to account was recognised by the Society of Arts in 1805, when he was awarded a gold medal for 44 acres of such land that he had successfully planted with Scots firs and larches.

The Breadalbane Fencibles.

When war broke out between Britain and France early in 1793, the fourth Earl of Breadalbane responded to the call of his country with great enthusiasm. He at once offered to raise a corps of Fencible men for the internal protection of Scotland, and his offer was immediately accepted. Lord Breadalbane was himself appointed to command the regiment, and he was granted power to nominate the officers who were to serve under him. Each man attested and enlisted was to receive three guineas on his arrival at the appointed rendezvous. While recruiting for the battalion might be carried out in any part of the British Islands, it was understood that it was Lord Breadalbane's intention to procure as many of the levies as possible from the county of Perth and its neighbourhood. The regiment was to be raised for service in any part of Scotland, and not to march out of it except in case of the invasion of the southern part

MISTS ON BEN MORE, GLENDOCHART.

of the Kingdom. The hope was expressed that the corps would be completed within three months—the period that Lord Breadalbane himself had indicated.

The response to the Earl's call for recruits was so hearty and spontaneous, that within one week of receiving authority to raise the first battalion, he offered to raise a second. The War Office wrote him on the 8th March approving of his design. The second battalion was to be enrolled upon the same terms and to be of the same strength as the first. Recruiting on the Earl's own estates for the Fencible regiments was under the charge of Lieutenant James Campbell of Glenfalloch, cousin to the Earl, and grandfather of the sixth Earl of Breadalbane. Lieutenant Campbell was later promoted to the rank of Captain. Lists were prepared of all the men in each part of the estates who were suited for service, and the terms were made widely known. The Earl gave two guineas to each officer for every man that he enlisted beyond the number allocated to him to enroll. Tenants who had no sons of their own to offer were given an opportunity of showing their loyalty by procuring a suitable recruit, and paying the bounty required on his behalf. Quite a number of persons took advantage of this opportunity.

Recruiting proceeded so briskly that by the 8th April, it was necessary to reduce the age for enrolment from 45 to 36 years of age ; and by the 23rd of the same month it was reported from the headquarters at Perth that a sufficient number of men had been procured to complete the two battalions. The Earl's own estates in Perthshire and Argyllshire answered the call splendidly, and it was estimated that of the 2,300 men enlisted, no fewer than 1,600 of them were drawn from these estates. There were, however, a few tenants who deliberately refused to send their sons, and who criticised the Earl's action in calling upon them to join up. These persons were marked as recalcitrants, and it is probable that the names of most of them were on the list of tenants warned off the estates in 1795.

The men recruited in Breadalbane were embodied in the first battalion. There were not more than twelve from that district in the second battalion, but it included 200 Perthshire men, and many from Argyllshire. It had representatives from every county in Scotland, besides 10 men from England, and 47 from Ireland. In 1794, a third battalion was embodied, and its range of service was extended so as to include Ireland, whither it was soon sent, and there kept until it was disbanded in 1802. During the five years of their existence the first and second battalions were stationed at various places in Scotland, among others, Aberdeen, Glasgow, Falkirk, Kinnaird, Musselburgh, Banff, and Fort George. Although the war still continued the authorities resolved to reduce these two battalions in April, 1797, as the restriction upon their range of service rendered them .of little further value.   When the Fencibles returned to Breadalbane, the Earl treated them with great consideration.   Many of the men were granted crofts free of rent for life, in different parts of the district.   Others were provided with employment about Taymouth and Killin.   Some were settled on holdings in the township of Cuiltrannich, Lawers, which was laid out about this time.

While they were stationed at Glasgow in 1795 a somewhat serious disturbance broke out among the Breadalbane Fencibles. Several men had been confined and threatened with corporal punishment for a military offence.   When their comrades learned of this, they rushed out and forcibly released the prisoners. No person was hurt, and no violence was offered ; but it was decided that such a breach of discipline could not be overlooked. Measures were immediately taken to secure the ringleaders. There were, however, so many involved that it was impossible to fix upon those who were primarily responsible.

When the men realised the serious character of their offence, several of them voluntarily offered themselves to stand trial, and they were accordingly marched to Edinburgh Castle.   They were there tried, and four of them were sentenced to be shot. Three of the condemned men were afterwards reprieved, while the fourth, Alexander Sutherland, was shot on Musselburgh Sands.

During the march from Glasgow to Edinburgh one of the men, named MacMartin, told the officer in charge of the party, Major Colin Campbell, that in view of his probable fate after trial, he wished to transact some important business with a friend in Glasgow, and that he felt that he could not die in peace unless this bit of business had been settled.   He therefore requested that he might be allowed to return to the city, at the same time promising on his word of honour that he would turn up and rejoin the party in time to be delivered up with them at the Castle.   Major Campbell, who knew MacMartin and his family well, had the utmost faith in his promise, and permitted him to return.   The man took a circuitous route through fields in order to avoid detection, and arrived at the city during the night.   He settled his business, and early next morning he set out.   He hurried on to overtake the party, but although they had marched slowly, they had approached within a few miles of the Castle, and yet there was no sign of MacMartin. Major Campbell moved slowly forward, but at length he felt he could delay no longer.   He entered the Castle gates, and was in the act of delivering over the prisoners, but had not given in his report, when the absent soldier, all pale and breathless with anxiety and fatigue, rushed forward and took his place beside his fellow-prisoners.   He was filled with fear at the thought that his benefactor should get into trouble on account of his non-appearance. This story, which is told by General David Stewart, has often been quoted to exemplify a characteristic quality of true Highlanders, fidelity to their word.

Some of the Fencibles who had acquired a love for soldiering during the five years of their service joined the regular army, and won fame for themselves and credit for Breadalbane. Others developed a desire to try their fortunes overseas, and when the Napoleonic wars were over, and agriculture in Breadalbane depressed, they emigrated to Canada.

When Britain was threatened with invasion in June, 1798, Lord Breadalbane issued an appeal to his Perthshire tenants for volunteers to do national service. From a census taken it was estimated that there were 1,310 men between the ages of 15 and 60 years available. The numbers in the different parts of the estates were :—183 at Aberfeldy, 646 in Kenmore and Lochtayside, 325 in Killin, 67 in Strathfillan, and 89 in Glenquaich. Out of this total of 1,310 men no fewer than 993 came forward offering their services in the national cause.

The Building of Taymouth Castle.

As the eighteenth century was drawing to a close the fourth Earl of Breadalbane proceeded to pull down the stronghold that his ancestor, Sir Colin, the sixth Laird of Glenorchy, had built. Old prints and drawings make us familiar with the external appearance of the Castle before its demolition. Originally it had consisted of a central block, three stories high, and flanked at each end by square towers of corresponding height. At the corners of the towers there were small circular turrets. The chief entrance was by a flight of steps, leading to a door that opened on to the first floor, and in the centre of the south wall of the main block. At a later period the original fortress of 1560 was modernised by the addition of two wings, which took away from its castellated appearance.

The household books and inventories of the seventeenth century give us some indication of the apartments of the old Castle of Balloch. We are told the " graith," or furniture of rooms that are termed " The Ovir Chalmer of the Wester Tour," the " Study in the head of the Wester Tour," " My Lord Lorne's Chalmer," the " Laird's Chalmer," the " Chalmer of Deace," " the Studie at the Kingis Chalmer Door," " Duntrune's Chalmer," the " Laigh Chalmer." At the " Yett " was the Prison with its " graith," which included a pair of iron fetters, and one heading-axe.

The work of demolishing the central portion and the east wing of the old Castle was begun in 1799 ; and the foundation stone of the central block of the new Castle was laid on 30th March, 1801. This portion of the castle was completed six years later from designs made by Elliot, the architect of the

Regent Bridge, Edinburgh. John Atkinson, the fashionable architect of his time, who designed Scone Palace, Rossie Priory, Roseberry, and Abbotsford, made the plan for the portion in which the Chinese rooms are situated. These rooms get their name from the fine old China paper with which they were hung. The west wing of the old Castle remained standing, and was in use until it was removed by the second Marquis in 1838, when it was replaced by the present handsome block, which was completed on the eve of Queen Victoria's visit in 1842. The architect of this part of the Castle was David Bryce, R.S.A. Since 1842 any alterations made to the structure of the Castle have been of a minor character ; and although it has been transformed into a hotel, its external appearance has remained unaltered. The bluish-grey stone of which the Castle is built was procured from a quarry situated above Bolfracks House, about three miles distant. It was from the same quarry that General Wade got the stone for the erection of the Tay Bridge at Aberfeldy. This stone is composed of chlorite-slate, and is soft when taken from the bed-rock, but it hardens with age. In Taymouth Castle it harmonises admirably with the background and the surroundings.

The Interior of the Castle.

The main doorway of Taymouth Castle admits to a vaulted corridor leading through to the central tower. The rooms on either side of the corridor are said to have been part of the old Castle. Until recent years they were used as retiring rooms. They now constitute the office and a lounge in the hotel, respectively. The great tower is occupied by the principal stairway, which has been declared to be the finest piece of plaster work in Britain. A few steps bring one up to the half-way landing, where the stair divides to the right and to the left, both sides leading to the landing on the first floor. Above this landing the stairs become invisible. On the stair and on the landing are niches, in which are set figures in armour. Brass plates on the stair commemorate visits of royal personages to the Castle. Among these were :—Prince Arthur of Connaught in 1877, The Duke of Albany in 1877, Frederick Grand Duke of Baden in 1879, Prince George, Duke of Cambridge, in 1881, and again in 1884, King Oscar of Sweden in 1884, and H.R.H. Fredrica of Hanover in 1885.

The principal rooms are arranged round the tower. A door to the right of the first landing leads to what used to be known as the Print Room, which has an oak coloured ceiling lightly relieved with gold. The walls of this room used to be covered with scarlet cloth, and adorned with fine engravings and prints. Hence the name of the room.

A short passage to the right leads from the Print Room to the Barons' Hall or ·dining room. The ceiling is vaulted in imitation of stone, and richly relieved with Gothic tracery. On the ceiling are painted the armorial bearings of the cadet families of the Campbells of Glenorchy. These all respond fittingly to the motto of the Chief, " Follow me." Campbell of Glenfalloch says, " Thus far," and his devotion is indicated by the crest which shows a dagger piercing a bleeding heart. Campbell of Auchlyne's answer to the call is, " With heart and hand " ; and that of Achallader, " With courage." From Campbell of Bar- caldine comes the ready reply, " Paratus sum " ; while Campbell of Glenlyon makes the more cautious response, which was not always observed, " Quae recta sequor." The great Gothic window of stained glass lighting this magnificent chamber from the west represents the figures of the early Lairds of Glenorchy, showing their descent from Duncan Campbell, Knight of Lochawe, the common ancestor of the great houses of Argyll and Bread- albane.

The Breakfast Room, which is now used as a second dining room, adjoins the Barons' Hall. Its walls are hung with several fine oil paintings, which were taken over when the Castle was sold. The Drawing Room occupies the greater part of the south front of the main block, and, along with the ante-room at the end, extends to over seventy feet. The doors and the dado are of unstained satin wood, while the fire-place is of pure white marble. The ceilings of these rooms took seven years to paint. They are done after the style of the illumination of manuscripts of the fourteenth century, in Gothic arabesque. The armorial bearings and figures introduced are illustrative of the history of the Breadalbane family.

From the Drawing Room a short passage leads to the Banner Hall, which is nearly fifty feet long, and twenty-six feet from floor to roof. The vaulted ceiling of this stately apartment is groined, and ornamented with richly carved oak moulding. The moulded ribs form ninety-two clear spaces, which contain shields surrounded by foliage in vellum scrolls. These shields show the arms of the numerous families with which the house of Breadalbane has been related directly, or by marriage. On the one side are the shields indicating the connection with the Royal Stewarts of Scotland. The massive fire-place is beautifully and ingeniously carved from blue chlorite-slate. The decorations of this room and of the Drawing Room were designed by Mr. Crase of Wigmore Street, London, who employed British and foreign artists in the execution of the work.

The Library Gallery adjoins the Banner Hall. Guarding the arched door are three figures carved in wood. It is said that these figures were brought from an Italian monastery, and represent Reformers in Purgatory. Carved on the bases of the figures are inscriptions in Italian, and the dates, 1415, 1554, and 1557. On the walls of this Gallery there are panels of oak

TAYMOUTH CASTLE FROM THE SOUTH.

that decorated some religious house at one time. A two-leaved Gothic door of carved oak leads from the Gallery to the Library. This apartment has a carved ceiling ornamented with carved moulding and tracery work. It presents a perfect maze of Gothic designs. With windows to the south and west it is well lit, and the decorations are most effectively shown up. The designs, and the ornamentation of the Gallery and the Library, are the work of Mr. Gillespie Graham of Orchill. A door in imitation of a bookcase opens from the Library to the apartments occupied by Queen Victoria and Prince Albert during their famous visit in 1842.

The fourth Earl and first Marquis of Breadalbane died at Taymouth on 29th March, 1834, at the age of seventy-two years. The mourning for this good and worthy Scottish nobleman was deep and genuine. He had been an enlightened and considerate landlord, having always at heart the good of his tenants, and the improvement of his vast estates. He was in a very true sense the father of his people, who were always ready to recognise his worth. On his death the Marchioness removed to Langton House, where she died on 25th September, 1845.

N

THE SECOND MARQUIS OF BREADALBANE.

CHAPTER XVIII.

The Second Marquis of Breadalbane.
(1834-1862).

JOHN Campbell, only son of the first Marquis of Breadalbane, was thirty-eight years of age when he succeeded his father. He was born in the Nethergate of Dundee, on 26th October, 1796, and had gone under the title of Lord Ormelie. He had been educated at Eton, and in 1820, at the age of twenty-four years, he entered Parliament as member for Okehampton. On 23rd November, 1821, he married Eliza, sister of George, tenth Earl of Haddington, and eldest daughter of George Baillie of Jerviswood. In 1832, he succeeded in being elected member for his own county of Perth, supporting the Liberal party. He was appointed a Knight of the Thistle in 1838 ; and the following year was made Lord Lieutenant of Argyllshire. Lord Breadalbane was elected Lord Rector of Glasgow University in 1841. He was chosen to be a Privy Councillor in 1848, and held the office of Lord Chamberlain of the Household from 1848 to 1852, and again from 1853 to 1858. In 1861 Lord Breadalbane went as Envoy Extraordinary to Prussia in order to invest King William, afterwards Emperor of Germany, with the Order of the Garter. For several years he was president of the Society of Antiquaries of Scotland.

The second Marquis was a man of austere cast of countenance and commanding presence. He was proud of his ancestry and of his exalted position. On one occasion he published a tractlet giving advice to his tenants on farming, but he left the management of his estates to others, with the result that on the advice of his factor, James F. Wyllie, he cleared the farms of Morenish, Kiltyrie, and Cloichran of crofters, in order to make room for more sheep. Glenquaich was subjected to the same fate. These wholesale evictions roused a great deal of resentment in the country, and the Marquis was severely taken to task for his actions in a pamphlet that was issued anonymously by the fearless Alexander Robertson, the " Chief " of " Dundonnachie," Dunkeld. The Marquis's pride was stung, and he resented the attack, but could not deny the charge. The only thing he could do was to buy up the pamphlets, and have them destroyed. A few have, however, survived to tell the tale of the Breadalbane clearances. The people evicted went to Canada,[1] where their

(1) Miss Mary McLennan, Stratford, Ontario, published a book in 1936, giving an account of the Perthshire pioneers in Ontario. She gifted a copy to the Sandeman Library, Perth.

descendants still cherish the traditions of Breadalbane and Glenquaich. One of those Glenquaich men, Duncan MacGregor Crerar, gave forcible expression to the feelings of many when he said :—

"Evicted thus were Albyn's sons of fame,
Their lands are teeming now with sheep and game,
How sad and lonesome this once happy glen,
Where, Oh Glenquaich, have gone thy gallant men ?
Doomed on whom falls the heartless factor's frown,
Oh, God, arise and crush such tyrants down."

The second Marquis had the belief that there was great wealth hidden in the rocks of Breadalbane. His father had closed down the lead mines at Clifton, near Tyndrum, about 1798, but the second Marquis had them re-opened in 1838, and he spent quite a fortune in keeping them going. Copper had been discovered at Tomnadason, Ardtalnaig, and here again he began to exploit the ore at considerable loss. These unprofitable concerns did not, however, dishearten him, and he might be seen anywhere among the hills between Taymouth and Tyndrum with a leathern bag over his shoulder, and a geologist's hammer in his hand, chipping away at fragments of rock, as if his very life depended upon his work. On these expeditions he was usually accompanied by one or two favourite terriers. Numerous trials were made for minerals, extending over many years, at different places on the Breadalbane estates. Chromite was found at Corry-charmaig, Glenlochay, and worked for a time there. Iron pyrites was discovered at Dalkillin in Glenquaich ; chalcopyrites, and tetrahedrite at Tomnadason, and Corrybuie ; galena at Meall na Creige, and quartz was wrought on Meall Cruadh, one of the spurs of Ben Lawers. It was from this quartz outcrop that the picturesque, milk-white Dairy at Taymouth Castle was built. These trials all ended in financial failure, although the copper mine at Tomnadason was carried on until the death of the Marquis in 1862.

The Queen's Visit to Taymouth.

Few events in the early nineteenth century aroused so much interest and enthusiasm in Scotland as the first visit of Queen Victoria and Prince Albert in September, 1842. With the exception of the visit of George the Fourth to Edinburgh in 1822, Royalty had left the Northern Kingdom severely alone from the time of Charles the Second. When it came to be known that Taymouth Castle was to be included in the "Royal Progress," there was intense excitement and joy in Breadalbane, and throughout all Perthshire. The preparations for the coming event were begun long in advance ; and no effort was spared to make the historic occasion what it proved to be, a splendid success. The arrangements were on a princely scale ; and the outburst of loyalty and patriotism was simply amazing. Floral arches were erected at the principal entrances to the grounds. The Marquis had selected upwards of two hundred of the finest looking men on his estates to act as a bodyguard to the Queen. His neighbour, Sir Neil Menzies of Weem, was there with his two stalwart sons at the head of one hundred men. There was a band of a hundred ghillies, all clad in coats and kilts of shepherd tartan, ready to join in the deer and grouse drives. In addition, there were a company of the 92nd Regiment, a detachment of the 6th Carabineers, and the Band of the 66th Regiment. They were all drawn up in front of the Castle when the Queen arrived there, on the afternoon of Wednesday, the seventh of September, having had a triumphal progress from Scone Palace through Perth and Dunkeld. The Marquis himself commanded the Breadalbane Highlanders ; and among the officers who assisted him were Campbell of Glenfalloch and his son, Campbell of Boreland (Killin), Campbell of Edinample, Gordon Campbell of Glenlyon, Campbell of Auch, Stewart Campbell of Cloichfoldich, and Campbell of Melfort. The signal indicating the approach of the Royal party along the road from Aberfeldy was given by men stationed on the Rock of Dull. All along the drive from the Principal Gate to the Castle crowds lined the way, and cheered again and again. The batteries within the grounds thundered forth the Royal salute as the Queen drew near.

The Breadalbane flags were lowered, and the Royal Standard was run up by Captain MacDougall of Dunolly. On alighting from the carriage, the Queen was welcomed by the Marquis, and conducted to the Drawing Room, where she and Prince Albert looked out upon the joyful gathering. Stepping through the window on to the balcony they graciously acknowledged the welcome they had received. The autumn darkness had fallen when the party rose from dinner, and from the windows they saw the surroundings of the Castle illuminated with thousands of little lamps. On the sloping lawn opposite the Royal apartments were the words, " WELCOME—VICTORIA-ALBERT." A giant crown shone out on an elevation in front of the Castle. It was estimated at the time that forty thousand lamps were used for the illuminations. As the night advanced the hill-tops blazed with bonfires. An observer found it impossible to count them all.

The following day (Thursday) was wet with drizzling rain, but the programme of hunting arranged was carried through. Prince Albert accompanied by the Marquis set out early with a large company of beaters for the hillside between Taymouth and Aberfeldy, known now as the Bolfracks moor. Their bag consisted of 20 roebucks, $4\frac{1}{2}$ brace of black game, 3 brace of grouse, 1 brace of capercailzie, 1 partridge, 1 woodpigeon, 12 hares and 7 rabbits. It is not surprising that the number of

The Staircase, Taymouth Castle.

grouse was small, as the noise of the guns, and the cheering of the previous day had quite unsettled the birds. In the course of the day, Her Majesty, along with the Duchess of Norfolk, walked to the Dairy, where she turned the handle of a churn, sipped a glass of milk, and tasted an oatmeal cake. When Prince Albert returned from the moor, the Queen and he, escorted by the Marquis, the Marchioness, and the Duchess of Sutherland, took a drive through the village of Kenmore, across the bridge, and along towards Comrie bridge, entering the Castle grounds by the Newhall bridge. After dinner that evening the Royal party listened to a Scottish concert. John Wilson, who was one of the best known vocalists of his time, had been brought specially to Taymouth for the occasion. Among other songs, he sang, " Farewell to Lochaber," " The Lass o' Gowrie," " The Flowers o' the Forest," " Wae's me for Prince Charlie," and " Cam ye by Atholl." To show her appreciation of his talents Her Majesty permitted Wilson to dedicate his book on Scottish Song to her.

Friday was also devoted to sport by the Prince and the noblemen ; while the Queen, with the Duchess of Norfolk,. took a quiet walk through the grounds. The afternoon was taken up with a drive to the Pass of Glenlyon, along the side of Loch Tay, past Fearnan. That evening a grand ball was given in the Banner Hall of the Castle. The company at the dance included, besides the Queen and Prince Albert, two dukes, four duchesses, three marquises, two marchionesses, five earls, and three countesses. The ball was opened by the Queen and the Marquis of Breadalbane, and by Prince Albert and the Duchess of Buccleuch. The health of the Marchioness of Breadalbane did not permit her to mingle in the dance. The scene in the Hall was brilliant in the extreme. The dances included quadrilles, country-dances, and reels. The Queen and Prince Albert entered joyously into the spirit of the scene, and appeared to charm and captivate all hearts. The enthusiasm of the company was unbounded ; and although the Queen and the Prince retired soon after midnight, the dance was continued far into the morning.

The Queen was so charmed with her visit to Taymouth, and with the magnificent scenery of its surroundings, that she would fain have prolonged her stay until the following Tuesday ; but as this would have caused a total alteration of the arrangements previously made, the Royal party had to leave on Saturday morning for Drummond Castle, Strathearn, the seat of Lord Willoughby D'Eresby. Before departure from Taymouth the Queen and Prince Albert paid a visit to the old flower garden situated to the east of th ᛫ Castle. There, each planted an oak and a fir tree to commemorate the Royal visit. Those present at this interesting little ceremony included the Duke of Buccleuch,

THE BANNER HALL, TAYMOUTH CASTLE.

the Earl of Aberdeen, the Earl of Liverpool, the Earl of Morton, Lord Kinnaird, Sir Robert Peel, and the Hon. Fox Maule, who was the intimate friend and companion of the Marquis of Breadalbane, and who gave valuable assistance in making arrangements for the visit.

The route to Drummond Castle was by Loch Tay and Glenogle, and the Queen embarked at the Bridge of Kenmore in a barge that had been specially built for this occasion. It was rowed by eight stalwart oarsmen, and commanded by Captain Mac-Dougall of Dunolly. There were other four barges in attendance, in one of which was the Marquis of Breadalbane himself. As the Queen's barge glided into Loch Tay through the central arch of the bridge the band struck up the National Anthem, in the singing of which thousands of spectators joined. The scene had all the appearance of an enchanted land. The reflections of hills, rocks, trees, and clouds on the placid surface of the loch were perfect, as the boats sped on their way to Auchmore, where arrangements had been made for lunch. On their voyage to Auchmore the Royal party were entertained with Gaelic songs by members of the crew.

This visit of the Queen and Prince Albert to Taymouth fired the imagination of Scottish people in a most remarkable way. The number of strangers who gathered into Kenmore and neighbourhood during those few days was estimated at over ten thousand. Many of them came from the remotest parts of the Empire. All available accommodation was fully taken up. Even at the Castle it was difficult to accommodate all the guests, and many a coroneted head was obliged to shelter under the humble roof of a workman's cottage.

The visit was fully described in prose and verse. Sir Thomas Dick Lauder of Fountainhall tells the story in his great volume, "The Royal Progress"; a National Record of it was prepared by James Buist, and published at Perth. Rev. Samuel Fergusson, minister of Fortingall, relates the happenings at Taymouth in verse; while Andrew Park, a Glasgow bard, published a neat little volume of poetry on "The Royal Visit," which he dedicated, with permission, to the Duchess of Kent, the Queen's mother.

The Queen herself was deeply affected by the welcome she received at Taymouth. She made several observations on her visit in "The Journal of our Life in the Highlands." After referring to the welcome on arrival, she says, "The firing of the guns, the cheering of the great crowd, the picturesqueness of the dresses, the beauty of the surrounding country, with its rich background of wooded hills, altogether formed one of the finest scenes imaginable. It seemed as if a great chieftain in old feudal times was receiving his sovereign. It was princely and romantic." Describing the illuminations at night the Queen writes, "A small fort, which is up in the woods, was

LOCH TAY, DRUMMOND HILL, AND LAWERS RANGE. TAYMOUTH CASTLE IN THE FOREGROUND.

illuminated, and bonfires were burning on the tops of the hills. I never saw anything so fairy-like. There were some pretty fire-works, and the whole ended by the Highlanders dancing reels, which they do to perfection, to the sound of the pipes, by torchlight, in front of the house. It had a wild and a very gay effect." There were nine pipers in the Castle ; sometimes one, and sometimes three played. Both the Queen and the Prince became fond of the bagpipes, and they showed a special interest in the playing of John MacKenzie, the Marquis's piper, and in the dancing of young Donald, his son. The Queen took farewell of Taymouth and its hospitable host and hostess with the words, " The kindness and attention to us of Lord and Lady Breadalbane were unbounded."

Twenty-four years passed before Queen Victoria looked upon Taymouth again. In the interval time had wrought many changes both in her own household and at the Castle. Prince Albert had passed away in 1861. The Marchioness of Breadalbane died the same year, while the Marquis himself followed her in 1862, dying a lonely death at Lausanne. He left no child to succeed him, and the succession to the peerage and his vast estates was in dispute. In the meantime the property was being managed by commissioners. The glory had truly departed from Taymouth. Referring to her visit to the locality of Taymouth on 3rd October, 1866, the Queen writes, " We passed to the right the principal lodge of Taymouth, which I so well remember going in by, but as we could not have driven through the grounds without asking permission and becoming known, we decided on not attempting it, and contented ourselves with getting out at a gate, close to a small fort, into which we were admitted by a woman from the gardener's house, close to which we stopped, and who had no idea who we were. We got out and looked down from this height upon the house below, the mist having cleared away sufficiently to show us everything, and here, unknown, and quite in private, I gazed, not without deep inward emotion, on the scene of our reception, twenty-four years ago, by dear Lord Breadalbane in a princely style, not to be equalled for grandeur and poetic effect. Albert and I were only twenty-three, young and happy. How many are gone who were with us then. I was very thankful to have seen it again. It seemed unaltered . . . . We got into the carriage again ; the Duchess of Atholl sitting near to me to prevent our appearance creating suspicion as to my being there. We drove on a short way through splendid woods with little water-falls, and then turned into the little village of Kenmore, where a tryst was being held, through the midst of which we had to drive, but the people only recognised the Duchess. There was music going on, things being sold at booths, and on the small sloping green near the church, cattle and ponies were collected—

a most picturesque scene. Immediately after this we came upon the bridge; and Loch Tay, with its wooded banks, clear and yet misty, burst into view. This again reminded me of the past—of the row up the Loch, which is sixteen miles long, in 1842, in several boats, with pibrochs playing, and the boatmen singing wild Gaelic songs.''

For several years after the Queen's visit a Highland gathering was held in Taymouth parks to commemorate the historic event. The Marquis was patron of the gathering, Sir Neil Menzies, Bart. of Weem, president, and J. Stewart Menzies of Chesthill, one of the leaders. Prizes were annually given for bag-pipe playing, dancing, throwing the stone and the hammer; for tossing the caber, running, and leaping ; and for the person most accurately equipped in the Highland garb (home spun). The gathering was opened each year with a procession from the Castle to the field, accompanied by the firing of guns, and the hoisting of the Royal Standard. In such ways as these the Highlanders of Breadalbane kept green the memory of an event that stood out above all others in the long and varied history of Taymouth.

The second Marquis was an elder of Kenmore church. In 1843 he joined the Disruption movement ; and through his own and his factor's influence, two-thirds at least of the people of Breadalbane joined the Free Church. The leaders of the Free Church rejoiced at securing the support of so well-known and distinguished a nobleman, and they gave him a prominent place in their councils. The Marquis erected churches and manses for the congregations that were formed in connection with the Free Church at Aberfeldy, Kenmore, and Killin ; and, until his death, he gave liberally to the support of the ministers placed in these charges.

The Marquis had led a busy public life, and in his later years he fell into ill-health. The Marchioness had never been strong since her marriage ; and she died in 1861 without leaving issue. In the following year, the Marquis, in the hope of regaining his health, went to Lausanne, where his father had spent a great part of his youth. He was not long away, however, when the news came to Breadalbane that he had died on 8th November, 1862, at the age of sixty-six years. His body was brought by his private secretary, Lieut.-Col. Smollett Montgomerie Eddington, to his house in Park Lane, London. The arrangements for the funeral from there to Finlarig were in the hands of Mr. Laurence Davidson, the Edinburgh agent of the Breadalbane estates. Thus passed the second Marquis of Breadalbane, a nobleman whose ability, munificence and virtues made the name of Taymouth famed throughout the Empire. His death was saddened by the fact that with him the Mochaster branch of the family of Sir Robert Campbell, the third baronet, became extinct in the male line.

CHAPTER XIX.

The Disputed Succession.

(1862-1867).

BY the death of the second Marquis without issue, the
marquisate became extinct, but the Scottish peerage and
the estates devolved upon the heir male in general of the
first Earl of Breadalbane under the patent granted him in 1677.
When the succession was thus thrown open several claimants
came forward. Donald Campbell, Fort William, who has been
already referred to, maintained that he was the great-grandson
of Duncan Lord Ormelie, eldest son of the first Earl. John
MacCallum appeared claiming descent from a daughter, Margaret
Lillias, whom the third Earl was alleged to have had by his
second marriage, and who was said to have eloped with and
married Duncan MacCallum, known as "The Fox-hunter,"
about the year 1769, or 1770. John MacCallum claimed to be
the great-grandson of this Margaret Lillias, and contended that
the titles and the estates should go to him under the designation,
"to heirs whomsoever." He stated that John, fourth Earl of
Breadalbane, was not the son of Colin Campbell, but the illegitimate son of the third Earl himself. Neither Donald Campbell
nor John MacCallum could produce documentary evidence in
support of their petitions. Both claimants depended upon the
statements of aged witnesses who related old traditions that
they had heard in their youth. The judges had no difficulty
in disposing of these claims.

The question then arose of finding the legitimate heir to the
dignities and the estates among the descendants of William
Campbell of Glenfalloch, the third surviving son of Sir Robert
Campbell, the third Baronet. This process involved the examination of many witnesses, as well as much searching among family
and other papers, and the case was not finally settled until 16
July, 1867, when the House of Lords decided in favour of John
Alexander Gavin Campbell of Glenfalloch, who then succeeded
as sixth Earl of Breadalbane, and was put in possession of the
estates.

In 1862, the Lord Ordinary of the Court of Session had found
it proved that Campbell of Glenfalloch, a fourth cousin twice

removed of the second Marquis, was the rightful heir. This decision was, however, challenged by Charles William Campbell of Boreland, second cousin to Glenfalloch, on the ground that William John Lamb Campbell, father of John Alexander Gavin Campbell, was not the legitimate son of his father, James Campbell. On a reclaiming note the majority of the judges of the Court of Session adhered to the interlocutor of the Lord Ordinary, on 26 June, 1866. This decision was confirmed by the House of Lords by a majority, the Lord Chancellor and one Lord being for, and one against the judgment.

The Breadalbane Case.

"The Breadalbane Case," as the litigation over the succession was called, created so much interest at the time that it may be well to state it in more detail. William Campbell,[1] Sir Robert's third surviving son, was born in 1621, and was given the estate of Glenfalloch by his father. He was killed at Stirling in 1648. He had married Jean, daughter of Colin Campbell of Ardkinglass, and had a son, Robert, who was born in 1647. Robert Campbell married Susanna, daughter of James Menzies of Culdares, and had a son, Colin, born in 1680, and died 1737. Colin married Agnes, daughter of Robert Campbell of Auchlyne, and had three sons—Robert, who died without issue; James, who was served heir to his grandfather, in 1740; and William, who succeeded to Glenfalloch on the death of James in 1751.

William Campbell married twice. His first wife was Effie McNicol, by whom he had one daughter. His second wife was Susanna, daughter of Duncan Campbell. By this marriage William Campbell had a family of seven sons, of whom five married, but only three left male issue. His eldest son, Colin, married first a daughter of Gregor MacGregor of Inverardran. The children of this marriage all died in infancy. Colin's second wife was a Mrs. Constable, who bore him a son, William Erskine Campbell. This William entered the Civil Service, and died at Colombo, in 1806. He had succeeded to Glenfalloch on the death of his father, but held the property for only one month. William married Susanna, daughter of Charles Campbell of Lochdochart, and left one son, John Breadalbane Campbell, born 2 October, 1801, who became laird of Glenfalloch at the tender age of four years, on his father's death. This boy died six years later, and thus the succession to the estate of Glen-falloch was opened to the heirs male of his grand-uncle, James Campbell, the second son of William Campbell. James Campbell was born in 1754, and died in 1806. He left one son, William John Lamb Campbell, who was father of John Alexander Gavin Campbell, the respondent in the case. On the death of John Breadalbane Campbell, in 1812, William John Lamb Campbell had succeeded unchallenged to the estate of Glenfalloch, and his

(1) See Genealogy, p. 114.

son, John Alexander Gavin was laird of Glenfalloch when the second Marquis died ; but now the right of Glenfalloch to succeed to the Breadalbane titles and lands was disputed by his own second-cousin, Charles William Campbell of Boreland (Killin), who was the grand-son of John Campbell, the sixth son of William Campbell of Glenfalloch.

The claim of Charles William Campbell was based upon an alleged irregularity in the marriage of James Campbell and Elizabeth Blanchard, the parents of William John Lamb Campbell. The story of this alliance carries us back to about the year 1780, when James Campbell was a gay young ensign in the Fortieth Regiment of Foot, and stationed at Chipping-Sudbury, in Gloucester. He fell in love with Elizabeth Blanchard, who was the wife of Christopher Ludlow, and had borne her husband an infant son named Daniel. Christopher Ludlow carried on business as a grocer and apothecary in the town, and also practised as a doctor. One night when Christopher returned from visiting patients he discovered that his wife had deserted him, leaving her little son in his cradle. Ludlow was so deeply affected by his wife's faithless and heartless conduct that he gave up business, and, after leaving his son to be brought up by his own parents, he sailed to America. He joined the staff of a military hospital in New York, but his health broke down, and at the end of 1783 he embarked for England. His father went to Portsmouth to await the arrival of the ship, but when it came into port, Christopher had either died the previous day, or was in a dying condition. The old man took charge of the body, and set off with it intending to bring it to Sudbury for burial. It was, however, the end of January, and being delayed by a severe snowstorm, he was compelled to lay his son's remains to rest in a cemetery at Salisbury.

In the meantime James Campbell and Mrs. Ludlow had been going about as man and wife. In 1783 they went with his regiment to Nova Scotia, and returned the following year to England. They paid frequent visits to his relatives in Perthshire, and no question with regard to their marriage was ever raised. James assisted the fourth Earl of Breadalbane with the raising of the Fencibles, and was appointed a captain and quarter-master in the first battalion. He died in 1806, leaving one son, William John Lamb Campbell, and two daughters. On his death Elizabeth Blanchard found herself in a destitute condition, and with no evidence of her ever having been married to James Campbell. She applied to the War Office for a pension on the ground that, although she could produce no documentary evidence she and James Campbell had been married in 1783. The papers, it was stated, had been lost at sea, and the witnesses were dead. The fourth Earl of Breadalbane gave a certificate to the effect that he believed her to be the wife of the deceased

OLD VIEW OF KENMORE SHOWING HOTEL AND READING ROOM.

James Campbell. This was accepted by the Pension authority as sufficient proof, and in 1807 Mrs. Campbell was granted a small pension, which was continued to her until she died in London, in 1828.

William John Lamb Campbell, only surviving son of James Campbell and Elizabeth Blanchard, was baptised at Gateshead, Durham, in January, 1788. In 1803 he matriculated at the University of Edinburgh, taking classes in Anatomy and Surgery. By the death of his father in 1806 he was reduced to poverty. He was, however, befriended by Miss Ann Butter, Braehouse, Edinburgh, a sister-in-law of his uncle, John Campbell of Boreland. Miss Butter sent a strong appeal to the Earl of Breadalbane on behalf of his kinsman. This generous lady offered to contribute £50 herself, if Lord Breadalbane would give £100 in order to pay off William's debts and place him in some post. The Earl responded immediately to Miss Butter's appeal, and soon afterwards William Campbell entered the Navy as a mid-shipman. The Earl undertook to make him an allowance of £20 a year. During his term in the Navy William Campbell served with the Walcheren Expedition. He appears to have left shortly afterwards, and to have established contact with his half-brother, Daniel Ludlow, who at this time was practising as a doctor in Hampshire, and under him he resumed his medical studies. William Campbell ultimately qualified as a doctor, and purchased a practice in London. On the death of his cousin, John Breadalbane Campbell, in 1812, he succeeded to the estate of Glenfalloch, and in the same year he was married at Paddington to Rosanna Doughty, daughter of John Doughty, Co. Salop. His mother was present at the wedding, and was one of the witnesses to sign the marriage register. Although the estate of Glenfalloch brought in a rental of over £1,000 a year, William Campbell still continued to reside in London, and to carry on his practice. He left the management of the estate to his uncle, John Campbell of Boreland, whose grandson came forward as the appellant in the case of succession in 1862.

Although the fourth Earl of Breadalbane had befriended William Campbell in 1807, he took little further interest in his subsequent career, until a son was born to him and Rosanna Doughty on 30 March, 1824. The Earl and the Countess then realised that this son would probably succeed their own son, Lord Ormelie, as Earl of Breadalbane. They themselves were becoming aged, and although Lord Ormelie had been married several years he had no family, while the condition of his lady's health made it very unlikely that she would have children. When, therefore, William Campbell's son was baptised in the parish of Paddington, on July 14th, 1824, Lord and Lady Breadalbane were represented at the ceremony by their daughter, Lady Elizabeth Pringle,

o

and by the desire of the Countess her own name (Gavin) was added to that of John Alexander. The relations between the two families of Breadalbane and Glenfalloch henceforth became very friendly. Soon after the birth of his son and heir, William Campbell decided to give up his practice in London and to come to Scotland to reside. When the Earl of Breadalbane heard of his intention, he placed the House of Moness, near Aberfeldy, at the disposal of his kinsman, and here William Campbell resided until his death in 1850. During the early years of Glenfalloch's stay at Moness he was visited by his half-brother, Daniel Ludlow, but very few were aware of the relationship between the host and his guest until long after Daniel's death, which took place in 1836.

As little John Campbell grew up the Earl and the Countess of Breadalbane took an increasing interest in his education. They secured as tutor for the boy, John Kennedy, son of the minister of the Independent Chapel at Aberfeldy, who was at that time a student at King's College, Aberdeen. The experiences of John Kennedy at Moness are told in his reminiscences published by his son, H. A. Kennedy, under the title, " Old Highland Days." After the death of the first Marquis his widow, who removed to Langton, arranged for John Campbell being sent to the Edinburgh Academy for the completion of his education ; and in 1842 the second Marquis secured a commission for him as an ensign in the 79th Regiment of Foot. During the residence

" JUDGES IN THE RING "—KILLIN SHOW, 1880.

of Queen Victoria at Taymouth William Campbell acted as Lieutenant-Colonel of the Royal Guard of Honour, while his son was principal standard-bearer to the Clan Campbell Battalion.

It will be evident from the above narrative that when the second Marquis of Breadalbane died in 1862, everyone expected that Campbell of Glenfalloch would succeed without any difficulty to the peerage and the estates. He was, however, kept out of both the titles and the lands for five years owing to the validity of his grand-parents' marriage being called in question. The courts held that according to Scottish law the marriage of James Campbell and Elizabeth Blanchard was quite legal and valid, although there was no documentary evidence to show where, or when, it took place. The couple had been recognised by their friends as man and wife, and in virtue of that recognition their son, William, had succeeded to the estate of Glenfalloch. The conclusion of the Lord Chancellor's judgment was as follows :—" After a close and careful examination of the facts of this case I am clearly of opinion that the strong presumption in favour of the marriage of the respondent's grandfather and grandmother, and of the legitimacy of his father has not been shaken by any proof adduced by the appellant which is inconsistent with the respondent's title, and the interlocutor appealed from ought to be affirmed."[1]

The Sixth Earl of Breadalbane. (1867-1871).

The long drawn-out dispute over the succession was everywhere followed with intense interest. The new Earl was hailed as a " model landlord," and as one who could retain the affection of his numerous tenantry. His career, although brief, fulfilled all these expectations. Under him the estates were administered with the utmost consideration for the tenants. He was said never to have allowed an old tenant to leave his property, if he could honourably retain him. For every tale of woe he had a sympathetic ear, and wherever he found real distress he always granted relief.

In politics the sixth Earl was a strong Conservative, and in religion he was a staunch supporter of the Established Church of Scotland. His interest in the Church was shown by his renovation of the church of Kenmore, which had been rebuilt by the third Earl in 1760. While the church was externally a handsome edifice, and its tower a pleasing object in the landscape, its interior was described as " cold, damp, and chilling in appearance, from the circumstance of the walls having never been lathed or plastered, and from its being causewayed under the seats with stone." By the Earl's direction the church was completely renewed internally with the best material and workmanship available. At the same time the tower was heightened so as to raise it above the surrounding trees.

1—See Breadalbane Succession Case. Ho. of Lords' Documents. Breadalbane Succession Case, James Paterson, 1863. All in Nat. Lib. Scot.

As a sportsman the sixth Earl had few equals in his youth, but in his latter years the only form of sport that he could engage in was salmon fishing. He spent part of almost every day during the season on Loch Tay, and was usually the most successful angler on its waters. He abolished net-fishing for salmon, and introduced trolling. He threw the greater part of Loch Tay open to anglers who resided in the hotels and shooting lodges. This privilege was never afterwards withdrawn.

The sixth Earl was married, 20 April, 1853, to Mary Theresa, daughter of John Edwards, Dublin. His surviving children were Gavin, born at Fermoy, Co. Cork, 9 April, 1851, who succeeded as seventh Earl ; Eva, born 22 July, 1855, married 2 May, 1876, John Cuthbert, second son of Rev. S. J. Heathcote, vicar of Williton, Co. Somerset, with issue ; Ivan, born 17 November, 1859, married 23 July, 1884, Lady Margaret Ellis, daughter of James, third Earl of Normanton. The Hon. Ivan Campbell was a lieutenant in the 79th Regiment ; captain in the 3rd Battalion Royal Scots ; fought at Tel-el-Kebir in 1882 ; and served in the South African War during 1899-1900. He was a Deputy Lord-Lieutenant of Argyll. He died 1917, leaving an only son, Iain Edward Herbert, born 14 June, 1885, who succeeded his uncle as eighth Earl, in October, 1922. The sixth Earl had a son, Norman, born 1866, who died in infancy. Both the sixth Earl and the Countess of Breadalbane suffered much from ill-health, and they died at a comparatively early age. She died at Nice, 27 February, 1870 ; while he survived her by little over a year. He passed away at his London house, 20 March, 1871, at the age of forty-seven years. They were both buried at Finlarig.

CHAPTER XX.

The Third Marquis—the Sale of Taymouth Castle—Eighth and Ninth Earls.

(1871-1936).

WHEN Gavin Campbell, the elder son of the sixth Earl of Breadalbane, applied to the House of Lords for legal recognition of his position as seventh Earl, he was opposed by Donald and John Campbell of Fort William, and by John MacCallum, who again came forward asserting their right to both titles and lands. The House of Lords, however, declared on 25 July, 1872, that the title was clearly and distinctly traceable to Gavin Campbell's father. There was no question that his father had formed an intimacy with his mother prior to marriage ; but a marriage had unquestionably taken place afterwards, and that subsequent marriage according to Scottish law had the effect of establishing the claim to the Earldom in the person of the claimant, Gavin Campbell.

The seventh Earl had been educated at the University of St. Andrews.[1] During his long career he played the part of a territorial magnate with great popularity. He gave much attention to the development and management of his estates. He was always kind and considerate towards his tenants, and on several occasions they recognised his genuine interest in their welfare.

Lord Breadalbane held many important offices in the State. In the House of Lords he consistently supported the Liberal party. He was (Assistant) Director and (Deputy) Chairman of the Ambulance Department, and Knight of Justice of the Order of St. John of Jerusalem ; Brigadier-General of the Royal Company of Archers ; one of the Lords-in-Waiting on Queen Victoria during 1873 and 1874 ; Treasurer of the Household, 1880-1885 ; Lord Steward of the Household, 1892-1895. He acted as Lord High Commissioner to the General Assembly of the Church of Scotland for the years 1893 to 1895, a position which he filled with great acceptance. Lord Breadalbane was created a Knight of the Garter in 1894. On 25 March, 1873, he was created Baron Breadalbane of Kenmore, Co. Perth ; and on 11 July, 1885, he was raised to the dignity of Marquis of Breadalbane. From 1907 he acted as Keeper of the Privy Seal in Scotland. During the latter part of his career he was Lord Lieutenant of the County of Argyll. He took a great interest in the Volunteer Forces, and for many years was Colonel of the 5th Battalion Black Watch. He was also A.D.C. to the King.

He was married on 27 July, 1872, at Cowes, Isle of Wight, to Alma Imogen Leonora Carlotta, youngest daughter of John

(1) See letter from Lord Breadalbane to Prof. W. Knight, in " Andreapolis, being writings in praise of St. Andrews."

GAVIN, THIRD MARQUIS OF BREADALBANE.

fourth Duke of Montrose. Lady Breadalbane was born on 7 October, 1854. There was no issue of the marriage.

The third Marquis had many and varied interests. He was a good shot, and deer stalking was his favourite recreation. He had a strong antiquarian bent, which showed itself in the valuable collection of old silver which he formed. He also made a large collection of Scottish Church tokens. He had a wide and most accurate knowledge of Highland lore and traditions. He showed a deep interest in public affairs, and frequently took part in newspaper discussions on such questions as roads and means of transport in the Highlands. He set up the Loch Tay Steamboat Company in order that his tenants on Lochtayside might be brought into contact with the Oban and Callander railway. For many years he was a director of the Caledonian Railway Company, and gave facilities for the passing of the West Highland Railway through his property from Ardluie to Achallader.

Until within a year of his death the third Marquis was one of the largest land-owners in Scotland. His possessions covered some 400,000 acres of land, extending across central Scotland from Aberfeldy to the islands of Luing and Seil on the west coast. His position as a great land-owner was humorously hit off in *Punch* of February 4, 1903, by a contributor, J. L. Robertson, in the following lines :—

IN BRAID ALBYN.

Lines from Ben Lawers.

(*To be read Scotto Voce.*)

From Kenmore
To Ben Mohr
The land is a' the Markiss's ;
The mossy howes,
The heathery knowes,
An' ilka bonnie park is his.

The bearded goats,
The toozie stots,
An' a' the braxy carcasses ;
Ilk crofter's rent,
Ilk tinker's tent,
An' ilka collie's bark is his.

The muircock's craw,
The piper's blaw,
The gillie's hard day's wark is his ;
From Kenmore
To Ben Mohr
The Warld is a' the Markiss's !

The Marchioness of Breadalbane was a keen sportswoman, and was the author of a small volume entitled, " The High

Tops of the Black Mount," in which she related her deer-stalking experiences. She took a deep interest in the nursing of the sick poor, and through her agency Nursing Associations were established at several places on her husband's estates. For over a year before his death the Marquis had been in feeble health, but he insisted on attending to his numerous duties. It was while at Glasgow for a meeting of railway directors, that he died suddenly in the Central Hotel of that city, on 19 October, 1922, in the seventy-first year of his age. After the death of the Marquis the Marchioness went to reside at Ardmaddy Castle, Nether Lorn, where she remained until she died on 10 May, 1932. By their own desire they were both buried, not in the Mausoleum at Finlarig, but in the open court-yard of the ancient Castle, where two crosses mark their graves.

The Sale of the Eastern Portion of the Estates.

Soon after the Great War was over the Marquis intimated his intention of selling Taymouth Castle and the eastern portion of his Perthshire estates. He had found it increasingly difficult to maintain the great house and to keep it adequately staffed. Wages were high, and the burden of taxation heavy. The Marquis and the Marchioness were no doubt all the more inclined to follow the example of many other land-owners in disposing of their property as they had no son to inherit either titles or lands.

The portion exposed for sale in December, 1920, extended to 57,335 acres of sporting and agricultural land, including the policies around the Castle ; the shootings of Bolfracks, Moness, Remony, Lochan, Glenquaich, Wester Shian, and Kynachan ; with house property and feu-duties at Aberfeldy, Kenmore, Fearnan, Acharn, and Amulree. These subjects were exposed for sale in five lots ; but no single purchaser came forward to offer for any one of the lots as a whole. It was therefore found necessary to hand over the property to land agents, who proceeded to break it up into lots suitable to the requirements of purchasers. Eventually the lands and the houses passed into the possession of over forty different owners, the principal of whom were the following :—Moness, Mr. W. Russell, C.B. ; the feu-duties of the burgh of Aberfeldy with the farms of Duntaylor and Dunskiag, Mr. James D. Haggart ; Bolfracks with the lands of Stix, and Braes of Taymouth, Mr. and Mrs. J. K. Hutchison ; Taymouth Castle, the policies, and the village of Kenmore, Taymouth Castle Hotel Company ; Portbane, Mr. Robert Wilson ; Remony farm-house with Balmacnaughton and Ken-more Hill, Mr Peter Macnaughton ; Remony Lodge and shooting, with the village of Acharn, Sir James Duncan Millar, K.C. ; Glenquaich, Mr. W. H. Cox ; Lochan, Mr. R. J. Rowatt ; Kynachan, Col. Charles McKinlay ; Duneaves, Mr. T. F. Stewart ; Comrie farm, Mr. William Taylor ; Mains of Tay-mouth, Mr. Duncan Menzies ; Drummond Hill, Mr. Thomas

McAinsh, who has leased it to the Government's Forestry Commission under a long lease ; Letterellan, Mr. G. Parker Ness ; the farm of Boreland, Messrs. Alexander and John Campbell, and Miss Catherine Campbell ; the Piers at Kenmore and Fearnan and houses in Kenmore, London Midland and Scottish Railway Company ; Tigh-an-loan Hotel, Fearnan, Mr. John Stewart. Several of the crofts at Stron-fearnan were acquired by the tenants, while a few others were bought by persons from outside the district for holiday residences.

Taymouth Castle and four hundred acres surrounding it were sold to a company formed by Glasgow business men, and after undergoing internal alterations costing over £100,000 it was opened in June 1923 as a hotel. The contents of the Castle were sold by auction. The six days' sale realised a sum of over £24,000. The dearest article sold was a tapestry panel, which was bought at 1,150 guineas for the Kent Gallery, London. The greater number of the articles offered at the sale remained in Scotland. Those particularly associated with the Castle found local purchasers, prominent among whom was Mr. J. D. Haggart of Aberfeldy. The Castle Hotel Company made purchases to the extent of £12,000.

The entailed portions of the Breadalbane estates had been disentailed soon after the succession of the third Marquis, and he was therefore able to dispose of all his heritable property in any way he pleased. In the exercise of his powers he arranged that after his death the estates should be administered by trustees during the life-time of the Marchioness, and that on her decease they should pass to whomsoever should then hold the titles. When the third Marquis died the peerage became vested in his nephew, Iain Edward Herbert Campbell, only child of Ivan Campbell and Lady Margaret Campbell. The eighth Earl had never enjoyed good health. He attended the funeral of his uncle at Finlarig, but survived him by barely seven months. He died at Bournemouth on 10 May, 1923, and was buried in the Mausoleum at Finlarig. By the provisions of the third Marquis's will the eighth Earl had been excluded from succession to the estates.

The Ninth Earl.

When the descendants of James Campbell, second son of William Campbell of Glenfalloch, failed in the male line by the death of the eighth Earl, the succession to the Breadalbane titles devolved upon the male descendant of John Campbell of Boreland (Glenlochay), the youngest son of William Campbell. John Campbell was born at Stuckchaple, 19 November, 1763. He became an ensign in the Western regiment of Fencibles in 1781 ; captain in the Earl of Elgin's Fencible Infantry, in 1794 ; captain in the Royal Perthshire Militia, in 1803. He married, 13 June, 1788, Janet, daughter of William Butter, Braehouse, Edinburgh. He died 12 March, 1823, leaving a son, Charles

William of Boreland, who was born at Edinburgh, 14 March, 1789. Charles William Campbell entered the Army in 1809; served in the Peninsular War with the 39th Regiment of Foot; fought in many important engagements, including Nivelle, Orthes, and Toulouse. He was awarded the War medal and four clasps. He died 18 January, 1861. He was married at Kinloch, Amulree, on 14 March, 1832, to Charlotte Olympia Cockburn, daughter of John Campbell of Kinloch. He resided at Boreland, Glenlochay, and was styled "of Boreland." The son of Charles William Campbell, also Charles William, was born at Boreland, 4 April, 1836. He entered the Army in 1854, served with distinction in the Indian Mutiny, and the China campaign of 1860. He was also engaged in the Egyptian war of 1882, and at the time of his death he was Major-General of the Bengal Staff Corps. In 1888 he married Gwynnedd, daughter of William Edward Brinckman, Esq., R.N. Major-General Campbell was the appellant when the Breadalbane succession case was decided by the House of Lords in favour of his second-cousin, John Alexander Gavin Campbell of Glenfalloch; but his son, Charles William Campbell, born 11 June, 1889, succeeded without opposition as ninth Earl.

Major-General Campbell had also three daughters; Colina Edwy, married Captain Thomas Macdonald Hussey, late Hampshire Regiment; Mary Gwynnedd, who was awarded the Military Medal for gallantry and devotion to duty during an air raid at Etaples, married Lieut.-Commander Reginald Victor Barton, R.N.; Margaret Alice, married Charles Cunradi, Esq.

The ninth Earl of Breadalbane inherits the peerage conferred upon the first Earl under the patent of 1677, and also the baronetcy of Nova Scotia, bestowed upon his ancestor, Sir Duncan Campbell of Glenorchy, in 1625. He is therefore Sir Charles William Campbell, Earl of Breadalbane and Holland; Viscount of Tay and Paintland; Lord Glenorchy, Benederaloch, Ormelie, and Weik, 1677; Baronet of Glenorchy; Baronet of Nova Scotia (cr. 1625).

The Earl adopted a military career, thus following the tradition of his family. He was educated at Shrewsbury School, and at the Royal Military Academy, Woolwich. On the outbreak of the Great War he went to France with the Second Division, August, 1914; commanded C/93 Battery and A/311 Battery in the European War. He was wounded at the Battle of the Aisne, won the Military Cross, and the 1914 Star. He took part in the following actions :—Mons, Basses Maroilles, Villers Cotteret, Marne, Aisne, Loos, Beaumont-Hamel, Vimy Ridge, and Messines. After the Armistice the Earl was A.D.C. to the F.M. Commanding-in-Chief, Rhine Army of Occupation; and since has acted as adjutant of the 94th Dorset and Somerset Yeomanry Brigade; and commanded the 8th Battalion Argyll and Sutherland

Highlanders.   He is one of H.M.'s Bodyguard (Hon. Corps of Gentlemen-at-Arms) ; a member of the Argyll Territorial Association ; and a Member of the Royal Company of Archers, His Majesty's Body Guard for Scotland.

He was elected a Scottish Representative Peer in 1924 ; and since becoming vested in the Breadalbane Estates the Earl has taken an active interest in all matters relating to his property, and the affairs of the counties of Perth and Argyll. He is President of the Scottish Salmon Angling Association : Member of the Departmental Committee on Valuation of Sheep Stocks in Scotland ; Member of Committee of Argyllshire Club ; President of Breadalbane Agricultural Association ; President of the Breadalbane Angling Club ; Patron, Breadalbane and Atholl Association (Glasgow) ; Chairman of the Awe District Board. He is also a Justice of the Peace for the County of Perth.

The Earl married, in 1918, Armorer, daughter of Romer Williams, Esq., J.P., D.L.   She was the widow of Captain Eric Nicholson of the 12th Lancers, by whom she had a son, Hugo Nicholson.   Lady Breadalbane has borne the Earl one son, John Romer Boreland, born 28 April, 1919 ; styled Lord Glenorchy.

During the interval between the death of the third Marquis and that of the Marchioness, his widow, the Breadalbane estates were administered by trustees, who found it necessary to sell portions of the estates in order to meet payments of taxation and death duties.   During that period the trustees disposed of Roro and Lochs in Glenlyon, Edinample, Lochearnhead, Armaddy, the islands of Seil, Easdale, and Luing (Argyll), the Black Mount, and Glenfalloch.   After the decease of the Marchioness of Breadalbane the Earl was assumed as a trustee of the estates ; and then on 1 January, 1935, the trustees denuded themselves of their trust in his favour.   He thus entered into the personal possession of the remaining portion of the estates, which are still of considerable extent.

The depressed condition of Agriculture has recently compelled many of the farmers on the estates to take advantage of breaks in their leases, and give up their farms.   In this way Lord Breadalbane has had to take over large stocks of sheep at acclimatised value, and sell them to the incoming tenants at market value, which has entailed him in considerable losses. In order to meet these heavy charges and to effect renovations on his property, Lord Breadalbane has parted with the estates of Ardeonaig and Auchlyne.   He has effected considerable improvements at Auchmore House, which he has adopted as his principal residence ; and has also renovated Boreland Lodge, so long associated with his own branch of the Glenfalloch Campbells.   Kinnell House, the ancient home of the Macnabs, where old relics of the clan, and weapons that once were wielded by Rob Roy may be seen, has also been greatly improved.

AUCHMORE HOUSE, KILLIN, SEAT OF THE NINTH EARL OF BREADALBANE,

CHAPTER XXI.

Cadet Families of Glenorchy Campbells in Breadalbane.

The Lairds of Lawers.[1]

FOR two hundred and twenty years the forty-merk land of Lawers, extending from Allt Phaderley on the east to the western boundary of Croftantygan, was held by the senior cadet family of the Campbells of Glenorchy. The FIRST laird of Lawers was John Campbell, son of Sir Colin Campbell, first laird of Glenorchy, by his fourth wife, Margaret Stirling, daughter of Luke Stirling of Keir. Lawers had been given to Sir Colin in 1473 by King James III. for services that he had rendered in bringing to justice the murderers of his grandfather, James I. This property had previously belonged to Thomas Chalmer, one of the regicides. Sir Colin made over Lawers to his son, John, who is styled " of Auchreoch." The first laird married for his first wife Margaret Moncrieff, daughter of Sir John Moncrieff of that Ilk, by whom he had three sons. James, the eldest son, succeeded ; John of Murthly signed a bond of manrent with Alexander Menzies of Rannoch in 1536 ; was designed in Murthly, 28 April, 1546 ; had a tack of Kiltiry in 1542, and got a charter of Auchmore from Robert Menzies of Weem in 1550 ; Archibald, the third son of John Campbell, is mentioned in charters of Lawers of 1525 and 1540. He married Elizabeth Wedderburn. The first laird of Lawers took for his second wife Christian Ogilvy. He was killed at the battle of Flodden along with his half-brother, Sir Duncan Campbell of Glenorchy.

The SECOND laird of Lawers was James Campbell. He had sasine of Lawers as heir to his father on 27 October, 1513. In 1525, King James V. erected the lands of Lawers into a free barony, and bestowed them anew upon James Campbell. Reference is made in this charter to the circumstances under which Lawers was granted by King James III. to Sir Colin Campbell of Glenorchy. The second laird's first wife was Margaret Forrester, daughter of Sir William Forrester of Torwood. She died in 1527, and was buried in the Parish church of Stirling. The second laird and Margaret Forrester, his spouse, obtained a charter of the lands of Fordew, Glentarkane, and Balmuck in Strathearn from John Drummond on 29 January, 1525-6. He also acquired the superiority of Carwhin from John Haldane of Gleneagles in 1526. His second wife was Janet Gray, daughter

(1) See article on the Loudon Peerage in Scots Peerage, Vol. V.

Loch Tay from Carwhin, showing Stron a Chlachain above Killin.

of Lord Gray. He married thirdly, Isobel Hay. They procured a charter of the lands of Auchtertyre in Strathfillan from Sir John Gray, prior of the monastery of Strathfillan, on 28 February, 1542. A commission of Justiciary was granted in 1548 to James Campbell of Lawers, his brother John, and his son Duncan, for the trial of Finlay Macmyllar, " common thief and sorner and oppressor." The second laird died at Perth on 12 February, 1561. According to the Chronicle of Fortingall it would appear that he " fell down the stair of the inn, and broke all his bones." It is further stated that at the time of his death he was living " in the Lutheran law."

James Campbell, the second laird, had several sons. Archibald, the eldest, and his wife, Agnes Ross, daughter of John Ross of Craigie, had a charter of half the lands of Lawers from his father in 1542. He predeceased his father, dying before 1546. John, the second son, was styled " of Fordew." Duncan, who was styled " of Auchreoch," died 8 June, 1554, and was buried at Finlarig. There is mention made in charters of two other sons of James Campbell, Edward and Walter.

The THIRD laird of Lawers was John Campbell, son and heir of Archibald, who was the eldest son of James Campbell, the second laird. On 30 April, 1558, he raised an action of choosing curators. In connection with this action he called his nearest of kin, James Campbell of Lawers his grandfather, and Colin Campbell of Glenorchy. He had sasine of Auchreoch on 11 September, 1558. John Campbell married Beatrix, eldest daughter of Sir Colin Campbell of Glenorchy by his first wife, Margaret Stewart, who was a daughter of Bishop Alexander Stewart. They had a joint tack of the lands of Schian, Glenquaich from the Earl of Atholl in 1582. The third laird of Lawers was knighted at the coronation of Queen Anne in 1590. He had a family of seven sons and one daughter. His first son was James, his heir and successor. His second son, Colin, had a charter of Aberuchill on 12 July, 1596. He was the founder of a family of Campbells who are now represented by the Campbells of Kilbryde. Of the third son, Duncan, there is nothing known ; but the fourth son, Archibald, was quite a notable man in his time. There are numerous references to him in the registers of the Privy Council in connection with the proceedings against the Clan Gregor. He is styled " of Glencarradale." He was commendator of Strathfillan, and granted a tack to his brother, James, of the whole kirk teinds of the monastery of Strathfillan, which had been given to him by the Crown on 19 March, 1607. Archibald Campbell had a grant of the monopoly of making red herrings on the East coast of Scotland on 18 October, 1615. He was granted a pension of £500 a year for life in 1635, and this gift was ratified by Parliament in 1644. He was knighted in 1644, and died five years later. His wife was a Bessie Napier.

Of Andrew, fifth son of Sir James Campbell, nothing is known. The sixth son, John, married Margaret Menzies. He secured a charter for himself and his spouse from John Earl of Perth of the town and lands of Clathick, on 27 November, 1628. He was styled " of Easter Ardeonaig, Innergeldie, and Clathick." Nothing is known of William, the seventh son. Marjory Campbell, who was the eighth member of the third laird's family, married Edward Tosach of Monzievaird.

The FOURTH laird of Lawers was Sir James Campbell, eldest son of the third laird. Sir James was much in favour with King James VI., and was appointed sheriff of Perthshire. He married Jean, daughter of Lord Colville of Culross. He obtained a charter of Sestill on 4 March, 1603 ; and on 21 August, 1612, he acquired the lands of Easter Ardeonaig, including Succoch, Finglen, the Haugh, and Carie, together with the tenandries of Carwhin and Carie on the north side of Loch Tay. For this property Sir James paid James Haldane of Gleneagles the sum of 8,500 marks. The Crown charter giving confirmation of the transaction is dated 21 August, 1612, but the contract was signed on 8 June, 1609. Sir James held lands also in Rannoch. He died at Lawers in 1645.

Sir James Campbell had considerable influence with King James. In 1615 he went to London, and procured the king's consent to a scheme by which the Clan Gregor were to be pacified by money payments from a fund to be raised by the Scottish

FIRS AT LAWERS.   (Planted before 1769).

land-owners. Sir Duncan Campbell of Glenorchy, uncle to Sir James, strongly opposed the scheme, and it came to nothing. Sir James next approached the Privy Counsel with a proposal to burden the landlords with the payment of 2,000 marks a month for the maintenance of sixty or eighty MacGregor orphans whom he was to maintain at Lawers. Sir Duncan again objected. He gave as his reason for so doing that "he haid gotten moir skaithe of the Clangregor nor all the subjectis of the kingdom, and that he had done moir service to his Majestie nor all the rest in oppressing of the Clangregor." Glenorchy was apparently jealous of his nephew's influence with the king, and when he found that the laird of Lawers was going to participate in the fines levied upon parties who were convicted of sheltering the MacGregors, Sir Duncan went to London, and got the king to agree that no fines should be exacted from his tenants or servants.

The quarrel between the house of Glenorchy and the house of Lawers was further aggravated by the fact that the laird of Lawers took the forest of Benmore, Glendochart, over the head of the laird of Glenorchy. This forest had been held by the lairds of Glenorchy for over one hundred and eighty years, and Sir Duncan strongly resented the act of his kinsman and vassal in taking it from him. The writer of the Black Book of Taymouth, after recounting these grievances of the laird of Glenorchy against the laird of Lawers, adds, "Sua, sen thir greate wrangis wes done be the laird of Laweris to the lairdis of Glenurchay, be deutie and all ressoun, they will enter into no love or friend-schip withe the hous of Laweris until theis wrangis be repairit."

The FIFTH laird of Lawers was Mungo Campbell, second son of the fourth laird. John Campbell, eldest son of the fourth laird, was born in 1598. He was knighted in 1620 by King James VI.; married Margaret, Baroness of Loudon in her own right, 1633; and resisted the attempt of King Charles I. to force Episcopacy upon Scotland. He was present at the famous General Assembly of the Church of Scotland in 1638, and displayed much zeal and learning as one of the assessors to the moderator; he garrisoned the castles of Strathaven, Douglas, and Tantallon for the Coven-anters. He endeavoured to open up negotiations with the King, but was committed to the Tower of London on a charge of treason. He was liberated through the influence of Hamilton, and permitted to return to Scotland in 1640. He was created High Chancellor of Scotland in 1641, and commanded the van of the Scottish army at the battle of Newburn. He again negotiated with Charles at Carisbrooke Castle, and laid the King's concessions before the Estates in February, 1648. He was president of the Scottish Parliament in March of the same year. When the Marquis of Montrose was brought to the bar to receive sentence, Lord Loudon commented with severity on his conduct, no doubt embittered by the losses that his own kinsmen had

P

suffered at the hands of the great general. After the battle of Worcester, Loudon summoned Parliament to meet at Finlarig Castle in 1651 ; but only three members attended. He supported the Glencairn rising, and after the defeat of the Royalists he had to take refuge in the Highlands. He finally submitted to General Monk, and was fined. At the Restoration Lord Loudon was deprived of his office of Chancellor.

When Sir John Campbell was created Earl of Loudon, the estate of Lawers was settled upon his younger brother Mungo, who thus became the Fifth laird upon his father's death in 1645. Sir Mungo raised a regiment for the Covenanting cause. This regiment was known as the Lawers' regiment until 1651. He supported his brother, Lord Loudon and the Marquis of Argyll against the Marquis of Montrose ; and on this account the House of Lawers was burned down, and the lands ravaged by Montrose's army when it swept through Breadalbane on its way to Inveraray in January, 1645. Sir Mungo was at the battle of Inverlochy, 2 February, 1645. In the poem celebrating the defeat of the Campbells on that disastrous field, *Iain Lom*, the Lochaber bard, who was a spectator of the battle, says of Sir Mungo,

> " On thy side, Laird of Lawers,[1]
> Though great be thy boast in thy sword,
> Many a youth of thy father's clan
> Is lying at Inverlochy."

After Inverlochy Sir Mungo was sent with his regiment to garrison the town of Inverness. He was killed at the battle of Auldearn, where he commanded the right wing of the main body of foot. His brother, Archibald, was taken prisoner. According to General Stewart[2] of Garth, Sir Mungo was seventy years of age when he fell in battle fighting with a two-handed sword. Stewart also states that four out of six sons who were present with him in the field fell on the ground on which they stood. This statement so far, at least, as regards Sir Mungo's age cannot be true, as his elder brother, Lord Loudon, was born 1598, and the battle of Auldearn was fought on 4 May, 1645. Sir Mungo Campbell married Helen, daughter of Sir Alexander Menzies of Weem. He was survived by at least two sons, Sir James Campbell, who succeeded as sixth laird of Lawers, and Colin, who was a lieutenant-colonel in the Lawers regiment, in 1648-49.

The SIXTH laird of Lawers, like his kinsman, Sir Robert Campbell of Glenorchy, was greatly embarrassed by financial difficulties owing to the part that his father had taken in the Civil War. He had an act of Parliament passed in favour of his mother and her family in connection with arrears due to his father. He claimed the sum of £96,855 Scots for losses incurred by himself and his father through the destruction of their

(1) Turner's Collection, p. 50.   (2) Sketches, Vol. II., Appendix, p. LIII.

property. He further claimed £98,000 Scots for services rendered by his father's regiment in Scotland, and £17,000 additional for services in Ireland during 1642-3. Parliament paid him the sums of £2,300 and £1,500 on account of his claims, and further orders were made later. He was colonel of his father's regiment, and was served heir to Lawers on 4 March, 1653. He was appointed by Oliver Cromwell to be Lyon King-of-Arms,[1] when in his later years the Protector surrounded himself with a House of Lords. He lost this office, however, at the Restoration. Sir James, the sixth laird of Lawers, married first Margaret, sister to Rorie MacLeod of Dunvegan, and by her he had a son, James, and a daughter, Margaret. He married as his second wife in August, 1678, Ann, daughter of Sir William Stewart of Grantully. She had a son, James, who was served heir to his half-brother, James, on 12 July, 1703. This James was murdered by Duncan Campbell of Edramuckie while asleep in his bed at Greenock, on 22 April, 1723. He was unmarried. There was also a son, Thomas, by Ann Stewart, who was baptised on 14 March, 1686. Sir James Campbell, the sixth laird, is believed to have died soon after 1689.

The sixth laird's financial difficulties compelled him to make over the barony of Lawers together with his other lands on Lochtayside, and in Strathearn, on 15 December, 1657, to George Chrystieson and James Russell, master of Cowan's Hospital, Stirling, in consideration of the sum of 4,200 marks Scots. principal, and certain annual rents and expenses due, amounting in all to £6,051, together with £200 6s. 4d. of sheriff's fees. From this time onwards there is evidence that Sir James became more and more involved in debt.

His son, James, succeeded as SEVENTH laird of Lawers, but he held the estate only in name. The barony was in the hands of the bond-holders; and the lands were sold to John, first Earl of Breadalbane, on 24 February, 1693. The Earl thus acquired in addition to Lawers, the lands of Carwhin, Auchreoch, and the superiority of the half of the lands of Ardeonaig. In 1686, James Campbell had disposed to the first Earl of Breadalbane the superiorities of his paternal lands in Glenquaich, which included Turrerich, Kinloch, Tirchardy, and Garrows. The lands of Easter Shian, Glenquaich, had been sold by the fourth laird of Lawers with the consent of his son, Mungo, to John Campbell of Edramuckie in 1637. It is said that when the Lochtayside lands were sold earth was taken from Lawers to Fordew in Strathearn, which was afterwards designated " Lawers " after the original patrimony of the family.

The Campbells of Lochdochart.

The Campbells of Lochdochart were descended from Alexander, the seventh son of Sir Robert Campbell of Glenorchy. In 1650

(1) See Scot. Notes and Queries, 3rd Ser. VII. 3.

his father granted Alexander a feu of the lands of Lochdochart which included the Port and Isle of Lochdochart, Crianlarich, Inverherive, Euich, Inverhaggernie, the sheilings of Coninish, Downish, and Leiragan. Some of these lands had formerly belonged to the Macnabs of Bovain. Alexander Campbell was twice married. His first wife was Julian, daughter of Alexander Robertson of Strowan, whom he married on 29 January, 1656. He married, secondly, Magdalene, daughter of William Menzies of Carse, 19 September, 1671. He had five sons, John who succeeded, Patrick, Archibald, Colin, and Robert.

John Campbell, the SECOND laird of Lochdochart, had sasine of the lands granted to his father, on 14 March, 1691. He married first, Susanna Campbell, daughter of his own kinsman, Robert Campbell of Glenfalloch. His second wife was Margaret Stewart, sister of Patrick Stewart, merchant in Edinburgh. John Campbell had two sons—William, who was served heir to the estate, 31 January, 1724, and Alexander, who became a doctor of medicine in Edinburgh. His daughters were Susan, who married John Macfarlane of Finart in 1720, and Anna, baptised 8 April, 1711.

William Campbell, the THIRD laird, married Katherine Cameron before 4 April, 1729. He was infeft in the lands of Lochdochart on 16 January, 1743, and obtained a Crown charter in March of the following year. His family consisted of five sons—Charles, who succeeded as FOURTH laird, James who was Sheriff-Substitute of Perth, Alexander, John, and Ewen; and one daughter, Isobel. Charles Campbell had sasine of Lochdochart in 1765. He married Anna, daughter of William Campbell of Glenfalloch ; and late in life he married as his second wife, Catherine Buchanan, daughter of Archibald Buchanan of Callander. He died in 1815. The family of Charles Campbell by his first wife, Agnes Campbell, were, William, who was baptised 21 March, 1772, lieutenant in the Rifle Brigade ; Catherine, baptised 26 November, 1774, died unmarried 9 July, 1823 ; Colin, baptised 14 July, 1776 ; Susanna, baptised 28 September, 1778, married William Erskine Campbell of Glenfalloch ; Agnes, baptised 14 August, 1780 ; James, baptised 27 October, 1782 ; Margaret, died at Edinburgh, 1813. Charles Campbell had a son, Charles Edward, by his second wife, Catherine Buchanan. He was baptised on 30 September, 1814. He became a physician and went to Montreal where he married Marjorie McGillivray, and had issue. His son, James, married Louise Phillips of Chicago, and their family claim to be the only direct descendants of the Lochdochart Campbells. In the event of the failure of the Glenfalloch line of Campbells the Breadalbane peerage would probably devolve upon the Lochdochart[1] branch of the family of

1—See Scots Peerage, Vol. II., p.p. 172-214. Genealogies in Lyon Office, Reg. House ; Guide to Crianlarich by Mrs. Place. Article by Scott Fittis in " Recreations of an Antiquary."

Sir Robert Campbell. The Lochdochart estate was sold at the beginning of the nineteenth century to Mr. Edward Place of Skelton Grange, Yorkshire, and part of the property is still held by his descendant, Mr. Gordon Place of Crianlarich. Lochdochart House with the small lodge and the bridge over the river were built by Mr. Edward Place. He also planted the fir woods around the House, which were recently cut down.

The Campbells of Auchlyne.

Sir Robert Campbell, the third baronet, granted the lands of Auchlyne, which had been acquired from the Macnabs of Bovain, to his youngest son, DUNCAN CAMPBELL. These lands included Wester Ardchyle, Auchlyne, and Blairnaskae. Duncan Campbell of Auchlyne was born in 1631, and died in 1703. He married Christiana Dalgleish, only daughter of Walter Dalgleish of the Regality of Dunfermline. Their family were— Robert, succeeded as second laird ; John, in Blairnaskae on 28 July, 1703, married Margaret White, widow of Colin Campbell ; Colin, living 16 July, 1696 ; Christiana, married Hugh Campbell in Ledcharrie ; Catherine, married John M'Intyre, son of Donald McIntyre of Letterbane ; and Duncan.

Robert Campbell SECOND of Auchlyne was born 28 March, 1676, and served heir to his father 27 July, 1703. He married Agnes or Anna Goodlate, who was stated to be his widow on 18 August, 1740. It was probably from this lady that the Auchlyne

GARBH-EILEAN, KILLIN.

family adopted the name " Goodlate Campbell." The family of
Robert Campbell and Agnes Goodlate were, Duncan, succeeded
his father as THIRD laird of Auchlyne ; Agnes, married Colin
Campbell of Glenfalloch, 22 April, 1712. Duncan Campbell, third
laird of Auchlyne, married Louisa, daughter of John Campbell
of Achallader. She was living in 1791. Their family were James,
baptised 20 March, 1731 ; Agnes, born 1734 ; John, born 1737 ;
Margaret, born 1747 ; Louisa, born 1749 ; and Arabella, born
1750.

James Campbell, FOURTH laird of Auchlyne, married Janet
Logan, sister of Hugh Logan of Logan. He died on 4 January,
1785, but she survived until 3 May, 1803. They had a family of
fifteen children, but, strange to say, the Campbells of Auchlyne
are now said to be extinct in the male line. The last survivors
of the family of James Campbell and Janet Logan were, Hugh,
baptised 8 December, 1767, a merchant in Glasgow, served heir
to his mother 1803 ; and Elizabeth, who is described as sister
and portioner of Hugh Campbell, 20 March, 1827. The lands
of Auchlyne, which were held in feu of the house of Glenorchy,
were acquired by John, fourth Earl of Breadalbane. The burial
place of the family was within the ancient chapel situated
between the House of Auchlyne and the River Dochart. This
chapel is known as *Caibeal na Fairge*. It was here that the
" Fergy," one of the relics of St. Fillan, was preserved in Pre-
Reformation times. The late Mr. Dugald Christie, farmer,
Auchlyne, who died at the age of ninety-seven years several
years ago, did not remember any burial taking place in the
chapel. He remembered, however, it being said that two
surviving members of the Auchlyne family would be brought
there on their death, but he could not say that this was ever
done.

Note.—For genealogy of Campbells of Auchlyne see Campbell genealogies, Lyon Office,
Register Ho., Edin. Also papers lodged there by the late J. H. Mayne Campbell.

CHAPTER XXII.

The Lady of Lawers.

ACCORDING to local tradition the residence of the lairds of Lawers on Lochtayside was situated close to the water's edge, a little distance to the west of the burn of Lawers, where the ruins of a double-storied, thatched house still stand. The original house of Lawers was probably a " castle " similar to the keeps that once stood on Wester Ardeonaig and Edramuckie ; but after the house of Lawers was destroyed in 1645, it would be replaced by a less pretentious building, as the family were regarding Fordew as their principal seat. The old house was occupied by the tenants of the farm of Milton of Lawers down to the latter part of last century ; but the ruins are still pointed out as *Tigh Ban-tighearna Labhuir*, "the House of the Lady of Lawers."

The Lady of Lawers, whose sayings are often quoted in the Highlands of Perthshire, is said to have been a Stewart of Appin, Argyll, and to have been the wife of one of the lairds of Lawers. This tradition, however, conflicts with the known records of these families ; and although diligent search has been made among old records and genealogies no reference so far has been found to such a person. On the other hand the traditions about the Lady of Lawers are so strong and definite that there can be no doubt as to the existence at some period in the past of a woman who was gifted with a wonderful measure of wisdom and shrewdness, and who was closely related to the lairds of Lawers. Tradition asserts that a family of Stewarts, known on Lochtayside as *Na Combaich*, " The Companions," first came to Lawers from Appin in Argyll, as an escort with the Lady ; and references to these Stewarts in the Kirk Session records of Kenmore of two hundred years ago confirm the tradition as to their district of origin being " Appin of Stewart." Some of the Lady's prophecies refer to the old church of Lawers, now a ruined building beside her house. A stone over the doorway of this church bears the date 1669, which would suggest that she lived about the middle of the seventeenth century. It is possible that she was the wife of a younger brother of Sir James Campbell, the sixth laird, and that she resided in the house rebuilt after 1645, by which time Sir James and his family had removed to Strathearn.

One or two of the prophecies ascribed to the Lady may be echoes of sayings credited to other well known Scottish seers ;

OLD CHURCH OF LAWERS—BUILT 1669.

some relate to the church of Lawers ; others to social and economic changes on Lochtayside ; and a few to happenings in the history of the Breadalbane Campbells. The sayings were uttered in Gaelic, and have been handed down in that language from one generation to another. A saying of a general nature is to the effect that the feather of the goose would drive the memory from man, which no doubt referred to the destructive influence of writing upon the power of remembrance. In olden days when people in the Highlands could neither read nor write many persons were to be found who could recite thousands of lines of poetry from memory. With the introduction of printing and of books this gift has to a great extent been lost. A prophecy about fire-coaches yet to be seen crossing Drumuachder Pass was accepted as foretelling the coming of the Highland Railway, and it may be compared to the prophecy of the Brahan Seer with regard to the " English mares with hempen bridles that would be led round the back of Tomnahurich," which was taken as forecasting the Caledonian Canal.

The Church of Lawers.

Several remarkable sayings are connected with the ruined church of Lawers, which was probably built by Sir James Campbell, the sixth laird, and the erection of which the Lady appears to have watched with special interest. When the building was nearing completion, she said that the ridging-stones would never be placed on the roof. The builders brought stones for the ridge from Kenmore by boat, and as the workmen threw them on the shore they said, " We shall prove the Lady to be a liar." That night, however, a terrific storm raged along Loch Tay, the stones were swept into the depths, and no attempt was made to recover them. The ridge of the church was covered with some other material.

She said that a tree, which probably she herself planted, would grow near the church, and at various stages of its growth certain events of importance would happen. When the tree reached the height of the gables of the church the Church of Scotland would be rent in twain. It was said that this stage corresponded with the Disruption in 1843. When the tree attained the height of the ridge the house of Balloch, Taymouth would be without an heir ; which came to pass in 1862 when the second Marquis died. The Lady further predicted with regard to this fateful tree that whoever should cut it down would be sure to come to an evil end. About sixty years ago John Campbell the tenant of the Milton farm along with a neighbour had the temerity to lay an axe to the stem of the tree. As they did so the neighbours shook their heads, feeling assured that they were courting disaster. The neighbours' fears were shortly confirmed. John Campbell was gored to death by his own Highland bull, while his assistant lost his reason, and had to be removed to the district asylum.

Even the horse that was employed in carting the tree away did not escape. It came to a sudden and unaccountable end, although quite a young, strong animal.

Social and Economic Changes.

Several of the Lady's sayings predicted changes that would take place in the social and economic conditions of Lochtayside. She first foresaw a period when the population would greatly increase, during which time the land would be intensively cultivated. She said that there would be a meal mill on every stream and a plough in the hands of every lad ; and that the two sides of Loch Tay would resemble a kail garden. These prophecies would appear to have come true about the end of the eighteenth century when there were fourteen mills on the whole lochside ; and on the south side alone there were nearly two hundred ploughs between Auchmore and Taymouth. The land was carefully, although not skilfully, cultivated on the run-rig system, under the old in-field and out-field arrangement that was brought to an end when the fourth Earl of Breadalbane formed compact farms surrounded by dry stone dykes.

Looking beyond this period, when there was a large population in the district, the Lady foretold a time when the district would first be riddled, and then sifted of its people. This prophecy was understood to predict the evictions that took place on Lochtay-side during the early years of the second Marquis, who allowed his factor to clear the people off the land and to form large sheep-runs. Before 1838, fourteen families had been removed forcibly from Rhynachuilg, twelve from Edramuckie, thirteen from Kiltyrie, nine from Cloichran, and nineteen from the farm of Acharn, all places lying at the west end of Loch Tay.

These evictions were carried out with ruthless severity. No sooner were the people turned out of their homes than men with grapes climbed to the roofs. The thatch was thrown down, and the whole set on fire to prevent the poor people from returning. A man who was very active as an agent in carrying out the dastardly work was himself evicted, and forced to emigrate. As he was leaving the township some one asked him, " Is there no more dirty work to be done in Breadalbane when they are sending you away ? "

The Lady further said that the jaw of the sheep would drive the plough out of the ground ; that many holdings would become one holding ; that the home-steads on Lochtayside would yet be so far apart that the one cock would not be able to hear his neighbour crow ; that Ben Lawers would become so cold that it would chill and waste the land around it for seven miles. The last prophecy is somewhat difficult to interpret ; but the import of these sayings taken together would appear to indicate that the Lady foresaw the conditions that now exist. Although the evictions came to an end under the pressure of public opinion,

depopulation continued, and the land has gradually gone out
of cultivation. The old primitive houses built with dry-stone
walls and thatched roofs decayed. The young people left the
district. The estate had no housing policy. Tenants had no
security of tenure, and there was no assurance that they would
be compensated for improvements that they effected. The
result was that holding was added to holding and farm to farm
until there was not sufficient man power to work and manage
the land. The country-side is rapidly reverting to the state
of nature from which generations of industrious toilers reclaimed
it by clearing away the brush-wood, gathering out the stones,
and erecting those miles and miles of boundary walls that fill
us with amazement. Fields that were not so long ago under
cultivation are now covered with briars, thorns, bracken, and
birch. In this way have the Lady's predictions been fulfilled
to the very letter.

Prophecies regarding the Campbells of Glenorchy.

It would appear from several of the Lady's sayings that she
had a very strong antipathy towards the Campbells of Glenorchy.
The two families had quarrelled during the time of Sir Duncan
Campbell of Glenorchy, and the feud still remained. With
reference to the lairds of Balloch (Taymouth) she said, " John
of the three Johns, the worst that has come, or will come ; but
nothing will be right until Duncan arrives." The third John
in the Glenorchy line of chiefs was the first Earl who bears an
unenviable reputation in history. Duncan was his eldest son,
who might have been expected to succeed as second Earl of
Breadalbane ; but he was passed over by his father in favour
of his brother John. She said that the family of Glenorchy would
attain to the height of its glory when a certain prominent rock
would be covered with trees ; and that when *Clach an Tuirc*,
the Boar's Stone at Fearnan, would topple over, a strange heir
would come to Balloch. The rock referred to is not known;
but it may be taken that the splendour of Taymouth was never
greater than when the second Marquis entertained Queen
Victoria in 1842. *Clach an Tuirc* is a mighty boulder, and it is
difficult to conceive of it ever toppling over ; but the Lady's
prophecy regarding it gives an added interest to this landmark.

The sayings that have been most frequently quoted in recent
years relate to the breaking up of the vast Breadalbane estates.
The Lady foretold that the estates of Balloch would come in
time to yield only one rent, and that ultimately they would
yield no rent at all : and that these estates, which had been put
together in hides, would be put asunder in laces. The effect
of taxation and of other economic conditions has brought about
the virtual fulfilment of these prophecies. Each successive
laird of Glenorchy from Sir Colin, the Black Knight, to the First

Marquis made it his policy to " conques and to keip thingis conquest " until the Breadalbane estates stretched for one hundred miles across Central Scotland. The process of dis-integration, begun in 1922, when the eastern portion was sold, has been continued, and it is possible that in time the Lady's prophecies in this respect may be completely fulfilled.

The only prophecy of the Lady with regard to the Macnab lands is to the effect that they would be added to the Breadalbane estates when a broken branch from a fir-tree would fall on another fir-tree, and then grow as part of the tree on which it fell. It is said that such an instance of grafting did actually take place about the second decade of the last century when the Macnab lands were acquired by the First Marquis of Breadalbane.

During the Lady's time a drowning accident happened on Loch Tay whereby a number of people lost their lives. The district was deeply affected; but the response of the Lady was that a greater loss would yet occur on Loch Tay when a ship with smoke would sink and cause the death of a great number of people. This prophecy has kept not a few persons from ever venturing for a sail on the Loch Tay steamboat.

One saying attributed to the Lady was inscribed on a peculiarly shaped stone that used to lie near the summit of Ben Lawers. The stone disappeared some fifty years ago, having probably been carried away by a collector of antiques. The saying on the stone was as follows :—

> " Caith mar a gheibh,
> Is gheibh mar a chaitheas ;
> Caomhain 's co dha ?
> Cuimhnich am bas."

Translation :
> " Spend as you get,
> And get as you spend ;
> Save, and for whom ?
> Remember death."

By her personality and her prophecies the Lady of Lawers made a strong and lasting impression upon her own generation in Breadalbane; and the succeeding generations have watched with interest, not unmixed with awe, the fulfilling of many of her remarkable predictions. It is said that at her own request she was buried beside the old church with which so many of her sayings are associated. It was here apparently that her faithful servant, *An Combach Ruadh*, had been laid, and it was her desire to rest near him who had been her friend in the land of the Campbells.

CHAPTER XXIII.

The Baron Courts of Breadalbane

THE lairds of Glenorchy possessed the right of holding courts within the bounds of their estates both for legislative and judiciary purposes right down to 1747, when Heritable Jurisdiction was abolished in Scotland. The records of the Baron Courts of Breadalbane are preserved from 1573, and they constitute a perfect mine of information with regard to the conditions prevailing in the country during the seventeenth century.

Tradition leads one to imagine that the lairds of old presided in person at their own courts, which were usually held on prominent knolls ; that the trembling prisoners were dragged before them to hear the sentence that committed them to a dungeon deep and dark, or to be hanged on the nearest tree. Indeed, at Finlarig visitors are shown the knoll on which the laird used to sit, as well as the pit where his victims were executed. They are told, however, that the gallows tree has crumbled away. When Mrs. Hughes, a friend and correspondent of Sir Walter Scott, visited Finlarig in 1824, the old Highlander who showed her round the ruins impressed her with the idea of one particularly cruel laird, probably Sir Duncan, surnamed " The Black," who chained his prisoners round the middle and hanged them by the hundred round the tower of the castle. When Mrs. Hughes remarked that the space assigned to them would scarcely admit of so many, her informer gravely assented.

The Baron Court records enable us to see that the tribunals were regularly constituted. The laird himself or his bailie presided. He was assisted by a jury of fifteen men chosen from the most respectable tenants in the district. The dempster announced the verdict of the Court, and usually carried out its sentences. An officer kept a record of the proceedings, which was afterwards engrossed in the Court book, initialled by the laird, and preserved. The proceedings were conducted with formality and every appearance of fairness. There is no doubt that when the laird or his representative was the prosecutor, the jury might be inclined to side with the strong against the weak, but this was not always the case.

The Court formulated a code of statutes and enactments for the regulation of the social and economic life of the country, and there were few aspects of the life of the rude peasantry of Breadalbane that were not touched by restriction or precept.

There were rules for the cutting of peats, which were not to be
cast, except with " Lawland peit spaudis." It was forbidden to
cut briars and thorns, " except in the waning of the moon " ;
and broom was not to be cut at any time without special permission from the laird. Regulations were made for the burning
of heather, which was to be done in the month of March ; and
then, if any " wood, or danger of wood," were near at hand,
the burning had to be carried out under the supervision " of six
honest neighbours," whose opinion was to be taken previously
as to the day and the wind convenient ; the neighbours were to
stand by as long as the fire was allowed to last, and, further,
it was their duty to help in quenching it. The amounts payable
out of " thirlages " to the smiths and millers were fixed by the
court, and the tenants were obliged to keep the smithies and
mills watertight, and to assist the millers in procuring mill-
stones. On 21st July, 1617, Allastair Andersone, miller at
the mill of Acharn, reported to the Court several men who were
convicted of refusing to take part in the " hameganging " of
the mill-stone.

The Court also fixed maximum charges for the weaving of
cloth. On 11th January, 1622, it was decreed that " no webster
take more for the weaving of a good head-plaid than one firlot
meal, or else the price thereof." The charges for weaving of a
grey plaid of half hues was two pecks meal and two shillings
silver ; for a plaid that had only one sprang (stripe) of hues, one
peck, two lippies meal and two shillings silver ; for grey cloth,
twopence and one peck meal the ell ; and for tartan, fourpence
the ell and one peck, two lippies meal. It was further ordained
that every webster who should contravene these statutes would
be compelled to pay ten pounds for each offence. In 1618, an
order of Court was made to the effect that every tenant and
cottar within the parish of Inchaddin (Kenmore) keep the Nine
Virgins Day next at Kenmore, and yearly thereafter ; and also
that they repair every Sunday to the said parish kirk with
their " bowis and baggis, or ellis with swordis and targis
under paine of XX. lbs. for disobedience."

Licensing Laws.

The bylaws relating to brewing and the sale of ale were
peculiarly quaint and interesting. In those days the man who
sold ale had to do his own brewing, and no one could carry on
the trade without permission from the laird. On 18th March,
1618, Callum Mcoleane (M'Lean) in Ledchroisk (Glenquaich)
was convicted " for brewing and selling of aill without the
lairdis leave," and fined five pounds, " or alse ane good swyne
at Pesche " (Easter). All ale brewed had to conform to a certain
standard in quality, and in order to ensure this, " cunstaris "
or inspectors visited the ale-houses every Sunday. To guarantee
that the beverage was " worthy " and fit for use on Sunday

it had to be brewed the Thursday previous.   A bylaw enacted
that no ale could be sold before preaching on Sundays ; and
it was probably for an offence under this statute that John
Dow, brewster, was ordained by the Kenmore kirk session, in
1652, " to compear at the foot of the pillar the next and the
following Sabbath, to declare the real truth as demanded, and
to give satisfaction for his scandalous offence."   The landlord
of an ale-house was bound to sell his ale, and must not withhold
it from any person wanting to buy it, even although the purchaser could only make a token payment.   At a court held at
Finlarig in August, 1622, the following remarkable licensing
law was passed :—" It is statued and ordained that no brewster
refuse ale to honest old country men, either by day or by night,
when they please to send for it ; and if the ale be in the house,
and the brewsters refusing, they shall pay four pounds fine,
because they refused the same ; and it shall be lawful for them
(the honest old country men) to come with the officer to break
up the house door, and take out the ale and give it to the poor."
Drunkenness was a punishable offence, and drinking " on the
premises " was forbidden.   A person convicted of drunkenness
was liable to a fine of five pounds, and had to make " public
repentance on the stuill."   For a second offence a man was
sent to Dunkeld.   Frequent fines were imposed upon persons
for " troublance and extraordinar drinking."   Wives who were
found in any brewster's house unaccompanied by their husbands
were fined twenty shillings, and, as an additional penalty,
they were sent to sit in the " lang gadde," probably a kind of
stocks, for a period of twenty-four hours for each choppin of ale
that they drank.   The manufacture and sale of whisky was prohibited, and the laird prosecuted men for the drinking of
" aquavitae."   One such man admitted that he had " the
aquavitae man " in his house for one night, but he stated as an
excuse for his offence that he only drank " one *boddach* thereof
in his own house."

Afforestation and Agriculture.

Sir Duncan Campbell, seventh laird of Glenorchy, was a great
lover of trees.   He formed plantations in his own parks, and
he also endeavoured to get all his tenants and even the cottars
to plant young trees every year in proportion to the area of their
holdings.   The laird's gardener supplied the saplings of oak,
ash, and plane at the rate of " two pennies a piece."   The saplings
were to be planted first in the " kailyards," and as soon as they
were ready to be taken up they were to be planted in the most
suitable part of the holding.   These young trees were protected
by statute.   Any one found wantonly cutting or destroying them
was liable to a fine of £20, and a reward of £10 was offered for
information that would lead to the conviction of an offender.
At the Court of the Lordship of Discher and Toyer, held at

Finlarig on December 5, 1615, the following were accused by the Rt. Hon. Sir Duncan Campbell of Glenorchy and convicted by the assize for cutting and destroying of woods :—John Rioch M'Ewen and Donald McKeich for VII. posts of ash cut and taken away by them out of Camuschurich. John Dow Mcillerioch in Cloichran for ane ash. Malcolm M'Eanvoyle in Auchmore for cutting of hazel and XVII. flakes.

In the same year Duncan M'Inowcater, forester of the wood of Letterellan, pursued Ewen M'Ewen, Calowm Dow McOleane, and Donald McMichie for " halding of their goat in Letterallan all last winter to the great hurt of the wood." They were all convicted on their own confession, and fined. Donald Roy Ferguson was fined 40s. " for suffering of swyne to be in the wode of Stix."

Provision was made for the sowing of a certain quantity of what was called " uncouth " (foreign) oats, in place of the common black oats grown in the Highlands at that time. The maintenance of houses and farm steadings was not left to the discretion of the tenants. The buildings were regularly inspected by the officers to see that all defects were made good. All head dikes and fold dikes had to be repaired yearly " with divot, earth, and stane " ; and they were to be kept at such a height that " neither horse, mare, nor cow, nor sheep, nor goat could get within the same." Kailyards were to be planted with " sufficient kail and other necessaries." The protection of river banks was necessary in a district where floods were common,

GREY STREET, KILLIN.

and it was therefore enacted that no cultivation of the soil was to be made within certain distances of the sides of burns and rivers. Legislation extended even to the protection of animals. One man was prosecuted for " taking of ane sore horse of his to Rannoch in the summer of 1629, and putting on him ane great burden of timber, and letting him go through the wood where he stuck between two trees all night and the timber on his back." The man was, however, able to prove that after the occasion for which he was charged another man had gone with the same horse to Edinburgh, and he was therefore dismissed. John Spedie and John Dow McDonchie Tailleor were fined twenty pounds " for ane oxe that diet in the Waird in their defaultis." The latter was also fined " for ane other oxe that diet in the byre of Balloch in his default." Rather a strange decree was to the effect that any one who came across an unattended " scabbit " horse was empowered " to cast him over ane craig and break his neck."

In olden times dues payable by a meal mill to the laird were an important source of revenue ; and we find that the lairds of Glenorchy were very careful to see that every person who lived within the " sucken " of the mill, that is the territory legally attached to it, sent all their grain to be ground there. Any evasion of this law was severely punished ; and hand-mills or querns used for grinding corn at home, were confiscated and destroyed. At a court held in 1641 it was ordained that " all quarnes be brokine, and ilk tenent and cottar to goe with their grindable cornes to the milnes whereto they are thirled, under the paine of ten pounds." The only concession under this law was the " knocking " or hulling of barley by tenants and cottars for making broth. The former were allowed to " knock " a firlot each and the latter two pecks each. The importing of grain from other districts, except in times of scarcity, was prohibited. In 1618 Andro Dow in Wester Balloch was fined three pounds " for bying of bear outwith the country."

The Court fixed the dates for the moving of stock from the low ground to the hill pastures, and later in the season to the shielings. The tenants had to send all their cows, horses, " nolt," and sheep outwith their head dikes from the first of May each year, where they remained until the eighth of June, when they were transferred to the shielings. Cattle were grazed at the shielings until the fifteenth of July, and it was laid down by law that no beast be brought back until they all returned together, the only exceptions being in the case of a cow that was " lifting " (sick) and one required at home to supply a sick man or woman with milk.

In 1622 the bridge over the Dochart at Killin was stated to be decayed, and all the " cadgers " were ordained to bring four dozen boards for its repair. Two years later a tax of eightpence was imposed on every load of salt brought across the bridge.

Q

At Achanich—Looking to Glenlyon Hills.

Game Laws.

As might be expected, game was strictly protected, and severe penalties were imposed on any persons discovered poaching either on the moor or on the water. On 6th December, 1632, John Campbell, elder, in Portbane, who was a cousin of the laird, had to find caution for his son, Duncan, " that he shall not burne a blase, schuit a wasp (three-pronged spear), nor put out a wand on any pairt of the water of Tay heirefter, under the paine of one hundred pound for ilk fault." No one was allowed to give meat, drink, house-room, or any kind of bield (shelter) to any manner of man that shot at deer, roe, blackcocks, etc., without the laird's own license, and under the pain of a fine of twenty pounds. It was, however, enacted that every tenant should co-operate with his neighbours in destroying rooks, hooded-crows, magpies, etc., and any one refusing to harry their nests,when called upon to do so was liable to a fine of forty shillings.

We find occasional references to wolves at the end of the sixteenth century and the beginning of the seventeenth, which seem to indicate that they had to be reckoned with as a menace to cattle. In 1594 a two-year-old quey was " slane be the wolf " at the foot of Ben Doran ; and as late as 1621 every tenant within the bounds of the laird of Glenorchy's lands was ordained to make " four croscattis " of iron for slaying of the wolf yearly in all time coming, under pain of four pounds money for each failure. On 20th February, 1622, John Dow McInstalker in Cloichran sued Patrick McNab of Suie for taking away his own hired herd, and for the loss of three cows which were slain by the wolf. The assize ordained the said Patrick to pay two merks money and one pair of shoes in contention of the claim.

Punishments.

Cases of murder and theft were brought before the Court, which had power to inflict the penalty of death. The sentence upon a convicted thief was that he " be instantly hangit " ; but, strangely enough, a murderer was given the privilege of having his head stricken from his body, which was regarded as less disgraceful. Prisons were not made much use of, probably because such accommodation was limited, and the persons confined would have to be fed at the laird's expense. Fines constituted an important source of revenue, and although they were assessed in money, they were often paid in kind, or partly in money and in kind. In those days currency was scarce, but the laird's requirements in goods were enormous. The equivalent of a fine of 25 merks was a " mart," that is a cow or ox fattened and salted for winter use. Sometimes we find " a pair of schone " included as part payment of a fine. The kirk branks were in frequent use, not only for scolding women, but also for outrageous and unruly men. The miller at Balloch was sentenced to remain in the branks for half-an-hour after sermon for troubling of John Menzies' wife at the mill, "offering to strike her, and giving her ill tongue, and to her daughter." The old law of compurgation had not become obsolete in 1622, when Donald Taillour in Morenish was accused of theft. Donald was permitted to "cleanse" himself by the oaths of six persons out of twelve, or four out of eight chosen by the Assize. On getting the necessary number to vouch for his honesty he was dismissed.

The Court dealt with cases of gambling with cards and dice. It punished guardians of orphan children for the neglecting and starving of their wards while they had the deceased parents' goods with which to maintain them. In times of extreme scarcity of food people were sometimes driven to bleeding even the laird's cattle to procure a little blood to mix with their meal, but the Court imposed penalties upon such offenders. A woman who had been for years the accomplice of a notorious thief who was convicted and hanged, was sentenced to be scourged and banished the country, and whoever should give her meat or drink was to be fined ten pounds.

The Baron Courts were held at different centres in Breadalbane, chiefly at Balloch, at Kenmore, at Finlarig, and at Tom nan Aingeil (the knoll of the Angels), Killin. This last spot may have been the artificial hillock immediately behind the school in the village. It is evident from the following case which the Court dealt with at Finlarig on 20th February, 1622, that the earth of Tom nan Aingeil was supposed to possess some magical virtues. Donald Taillour McGillechrist in Morenish, who appeared in connection with another case, sued a woman named McVane, also in Morenish, for a pock of earth that she took from Tom nan Aingeil and brought to McOlean's house, and thereafter to his, "whereby since then the pursuer's gear had not luckit with him, and his corn grew not." The Court absolved the defender at that time, and discharged all persons from using of the said pock of earth in all time coming, seeing it inclined to no good but to an evil custom. In this judgment the tribunal gave proof of its wisdom, as it did in most of its laws and decisions for the government of Breadalbane and the ordering of the affairs of its people.

When Heritable Jurisdiction was abolished and the administration of justice was transferred to the Sheriff Courts, the lairds in whom such jurisdiction had been vested were allowed to lodge claims for compensation with the Court of Session. The second Earl of Breadalbane claimed £6,000 for being deprived of the Lordship of Discher and Toyer (North and South side of Loch Tay), Glendochart, and Glenlyon, which he and his predecessors had held for over two centuries. It is not, however, known whether the Court granted the whole, or only part, of the amount claimed.

CHAPTER XXIV.

THE CHURCH.

IN pre-Reformation times Breadalbane lay within the diocese of Dunkeld, and the district included the parishes of Inchadney or Kenmore, Killin, Ardeonaig, and Strathfillan. Within the area there were also several detached portions of the parish of Weem, which at one time or another had been in possession of the Menzieses. After the Reformation, when ministers were scarce and stipends small, Ardeonaig and Strathfillan were united to Killin, and placed under one minister ; while for all practical purposes the parts of Weem within the bounds of Breadalbane, being far removed from the church of the parish, were under the supervision of the minister of Kenmore or of Killin.

The Parish of Kenmore.

Inchadney, or Kenmore, was a vicarage held of the Dean of Dunkeld Cathedral. In the Cathedral rentals[1] of 1505-17, it is shown that the living paid annually thirteen score merks into the exchequer, besides paying the stipend of the vicar. The names of the following pre-Reformation vicars of Inchadney have been preserved for us in deeds and charters[2] which they drew up, or witnessed as attorneys :—1468, Robert McNair ; 1501, Mauris Macnaughton ; 1523, Duncan Macnaughton ; 1547, Alexander McGillespie ; 1556, William Lumisdaine. All these clergy were knighted by the Pope.

The first minister of the Reformed Church at Kenmore was Mr. WILLIAM RAMSAY, who was settled at Inchadney on 28 May, 1561. He was chaplain at Finlarig in 1555. His name is mentioned in an order that was issued by Robert Crichton, Bishop of Dunkeld, on 19 May, 1557, for the summoning of the parishioners of Killin to pay their dues to the parish clerk, William Ruthven. Ramsay was then curate at Killin. The contract[3] between him and Colin Campbell of Glenorchy drawn up at Balloch at his admission is an interesting document, and is as follows :—
" At Balloch, the xxviij day of May in the yeir of God ane thousand vc threscoir & ane yeir, It is apointit, agreit, and concordat betuixt ane honorable man, Collyne Campbell of Glenurchquay, one that ane part and Maister William Ramsay,

(1) Rentale Dunkeldense, Scot. Hist. Soc.   (2) B.Ps.   (3) B.Ps.

KENMORE CHURCH AND VILLAGE FROM THE MANSE.

mynister in the kirk of God, one that uther part, in maner, forme, and effect as followis ; that is to say that the said Maister William sall mak dew mynistratione in the paris kirk and house of prayeris of Inchekadyn, and all uther partis necessar within the paris of the samyn, in teching and preching synceirly the Word of God, and mynistering of the sacramentis to the glory of God and instructione of the pepill, in sa far as God will withschaiff his giftis and grace to hym, according to the vocatione and·dewte of ane trew pastour and mynister. And sall enter to the said office within ten dais nixt efter the dait heirof, and thairefter remane still in the said office of mynister for the haill space and dais of ane yeir :

" For the quhilkis the said Collyne sall at the entre of the said Maister William to the said office put hym in peciabill possession of the manse and gleib lyand besyd the said kirk, with the tenement and yaird perteining thairto, occupyit in tymis past be the vicaris of the said kirk, and sall warrand hym the samyn unto the ische and compleit furthrynnyng of the said yeir ; and also for the uphalding of hymself, his wif, and children, that he be nocht onerit with caris of the warld, the said Collyne sall content and pay, and thankfully delyver to the said Maister William fourty bollis victuall, viz. : — xxvj bollis meill and xiiij bollis beir, or malt, gude and sufficient stuff ; twenty stanis cheis, & fifty merkis gude and usuall money as followis :— that is to say, sevin bollis meill, and thre bollis beir or malt at his entre to the said office, and ten merkis money, with ten stanis cheis, the last part of the cheis to be pait afoir Lammes, and uther ten stanis cheis in hale pament of the haill cheis to be pait afoir Hallowmes ; the remnant xix bollis mele and xj bollis beir or malt to be delyverit hym of the new crop upon the ground ay as he requiris, sua that the last part thairof in haill pament of the said fourty bollis sall be payit afoir Zule, and the remnant fourty merkis money to be completely pait betuixt this and the feist of Mertymes nixt to cum completeand in the haill the sowme of fyfty merkis ; Providing alwise that the said victuall, cheis and money be pait and delyverit fre to the said Maister William at his dwelling place upon he said manse and glebe ; And heirto bayth the saidis parteis bindis & oblysis thame by the fayth and trewyth in thair bodeis but fraud & gyle to fulfill, observe, and keip the premissis to uttheris in forme as efferis : In witness of the quhilk thing thai hef subscrivit this present contract with thair handis, day, yeir, & place forsaidis, Befoir thir witnes, Johne Campbell of Laweris, James Ruthwen, Johne McEwyr, and Andro Qhuyt, noter publyct, with uderis diverse."

William Ramsay took the degree of M.A. at the University of St. Andrews in 1537, and he afterwards taught for several years on the Continent. In Calderwood's History his name appears

in the list of " learned men " who were thought by the General
Assembly of 1560 best qualified for the ministry. He remained
at Kenmore until 1564, when he was translated to Kilmany,
Fife. He attended the General Assembly of 1566 ; and as one
of the masters of St. Salvator's College, St. Andrews, he prepared
an answer to Henry Bullinger, " touching the apparel of preachers
in England." In the following year William Ramsay returned
to the Perthshire Highlands[1] as minister of Fortingall, with
Weem and Grantully also in charge, being presented by James
VI. on 5 July, 1568. Two years later he was translated to
Kemback, Fife, and held the mastership in St. Salvator's College
jointly with that charge. He appears, however, to have died
soon after his admission, at the age of fifty-three years.

Owing to the scarcity of ministers and the inadequacy of the
stipends after the Reformation, the Church found it necessary
in many cases to place two or even more parishes under the
charge of one minister. In order to relieve the difficulty of
ministering to the people, readers were appointed to parishes
for which no regular ministers were available. The situation
in the Highlands was rendered more difficult by the fact that
the people knew only Gaelic.

In 1572, Duncan McLagan was reader at Kenmore with a
stipend of twenty pounds. Two years later DUNCAN McAULAY
was appointed minister of the parish, with Fortingall, Dull,
Grantully, Foss, and Weem also in charge. His stipend was
£96 13s. 4d. He was chosen a visitor within the bounds of the
presbytery of Dunkeld by the General Assembly of 1581. By
1589 he had removed to Blair Atholl, and was succeeded by
JOHN BURDOUN, who came from Fowlis Wester. It is probable
that Burdoun had no Gaelic, and, finding his duties impossible
to overtake, he returned to his former parish within a year.
The next minister was JOHN McLAGAN, who was translated
from Kirkmichael in 1593. He had Killin, Strathfillan, Ardeonaig,
and Moulin also in charge. GEORGE GRAHAM,[2] Dean of
Dunkeld, and afterwards Bishop of Orkney, understanding that
the parishioners of Kenmore were " destitute of the ministration
of God's Word," took up the charge, and was duly presented to
the vicarage ; but he discovered to his " great grief " that he could
not minister to the people owing to his ignorance of their language.
He therefore resigned the charge and teinds in favour of JOHN
McLAGAN, who continued until he was translated to Logierait
in 1607.

The parish appears to have been vacant until 1611, when
Duncan McAulay was readmitted to Kenmore from Blair Atholl.
It was forty-four years since McAulay had begun his first ministry
at Kenmore, and by 1611 he must have been an old man and very
unfit for the task of ministering to the four parishes within
the bounds of Breadalbane. In 1613 he granted a receipt for

(1) Calderwood's Hist., Ch. of Scot.   (2) B.Ps.

stipend in which he describes himself as minister "at the kirk of the Candmoir, and supporter of the kirkis of Killin, Strathfillan, and Ardeonaig." It is not surprising to find him on 16 March of that year stating that he is " lying bedfast and sicklie unto death."[1]

The next minister of Kenmore was NEIL MALCOLM or McCALLUM, son of John Malcolm, vicar of Kilchrenan. He was admitted some time prior to 16 May, 1627, when the parish was reported upon by the Commissioners appointed by the king for " the Plantation of Kirks." Neil Malcolm was educated at St. Andrews, where he graduated 26 July, 1613. His stipend was five hundred and twenty merks, besides the manse and glebe. The number of communicants in the parish was returned as six hundred. Neil Malcolm was still minister at Kenmore on 29 April, 1629 ; but by 21 December of the same year he had been translated to Kilchrenan, and had been succeeded at Kenmore by JOHN MALCOLM, probably a brother. John Malcolm had also been educated at St. Andrews, where he took the degree of M.A. on 16 July, 1620. Neil Malcolm appears to have died, or to have removed from Kilchrenan, and to have been succeeded by John, for on 20 November, 1632, the latter granted a receipt[2] for stipend to Sir Colin Campbell of Glenorchy, in which he describes himself as " parsone of Lochow and minister of Candmoir."

It was impossible for ministers under the conditions that prevailed in those days to supply ordinances over such a wide area, and to instruct the people in the doctrines of the Reformed Church. The Commissioners[3] who visited the district in 1627 reported with regard to Dull—" The inhabitants never, or seldom repair to the parish kirk, except on necessity of receiving the Lord's Supper, and baptism, and marriage ; and great ignorance abounds in the land, and neglect of discipline, to the great grief of many of the inhabitants, and to the ministers' great grief and trouble." This description of the religious state of a neighbouring parish would, no doubt, be true also of the Breadalbane district ; but the next minister, WILLIAM MENZIES, set himself with courage and marked ability to improve the religious and moral condition of the people.

William Menzies had been minister at Killin before 17 June, 1618. He was laird of Wester Shian, Glenquaich, and was descended from the Menzieses of Comrie.[4] The baptismal register which he began to keep on 2 March, 1636, when he was admitted to Kenmore, is preserved in the Register House, Edinburgh. Besides containing the names of infants baptised and persons proclaimed, the register also includes minutes of kirk session meetings, which shed light upon the steps taken by the minister and elders to improve the religious and social condition of the people. The parish was divided into districts, each of which was

(1) B.Ps.   (2) B.Ps.   (3) Report of Commission on Plantation of Kirks.
(4) John MacGregor's papers, Reg. Ho., Edin.

placed under the oversight of an elder, who had to report to the session any matter demanding attention. Attendance at Communion and at the minister's round of examination was made compulsory, and fines were imposed upon persons who were absent without cause. Those who were ignorant of the Creed and the Ten Commandments were also punished. Regulations were enforced for the limiting of the number of people attending Penny Weddings which were then a cause of serious scandals. Profaners of the Sabbath, drunkards, and other scandalous persons were severely dealt with. During the autumn the elders were required to go out on the Sabbath to prevent people from going to the woods to gather nuts. They were also exhorted to be diligent themselves in the observance of family worship, and to encourage others to follow their example. The collections taken in the church and fines imposed upon delinquents were applied to the relief of the poor. The kirk session granted loans to persons requiring temporary financial help, but always upon the security of some man of good standing. The following entry dated 22 June, 1648, is an example of such transactions :—" This day six pounds money lent out of the box[1] to Patrick Beg McKercher to be payit before the last of August next 1648, under the paine of doubling. Cautioner for him, Patrick Campbell."

The Civil War and the devastation of the Breadalbane country by the wild host that followed Montrose caused much distress among the people, and rendered the task of the minister and his elders more difficult than ever. The raiders broke into the kirk of Kenmore, and stole the baptismal basin. The old poor's box somehow escaped being pillaged, for on 12 January, 1645, the minister and elders were able to distribute three pounds out of it among " poore people who had been spoyled and burned, and had nothing to live on." The country continued in a lawless condition for some time after these troubles, and it was extremely difficult to enforce discipline and maintain order. The heritors were so impoverished that they could not pay the ministers' stipends ; and Mr. William Menzies had to think of removing to another sphere. Sir Robert Campbell appealed by petition to the Commission of the General Assembly, with the result that the following letter was sent to the presbytery of Dunkeld with regard to the position of Mr. Menzies :—

" Right Reverend,—Having received a petition from the lairds of Glenorquhy representing to us the lamentable condition of themselves and their tenents, disabling them to give that maintainance and provision which is due to Mr. William Menzies, their minister ; Therefor our desire to yow is that the vaking fruits and stipends of any kirks within your boundis, which

(1) The Poor's Box of Kenmore Church is still preserved. The earliest reference to it is in a Kirk Session Minute of January 12th, 1645. It is strongly made of oak and iron, with two locks and two keys in use.

by act of Parliament printed (the cope quhairof we have sent unto yow under our Clerks hand, least ye have not the printed acts of Parliament there), are appoynted to be employed upon pious uses, may be given to him, or some competent proportion therof, for his present subsistence, and that the patron, titulars, heretors, and others adebtit in payment therof, be dealt with for that purpose, and that notwithstanding of the destination of the Act in favours of youths that have the Irish toung for their breeding at schooles and universities ; wheranent these presents shall sufficiently warrand yow, which we do seriously recommend to your care : And in the mean tyme that yow delay his transportation (which we heare is intended) for some time, being resolved also at our next meeting to think upon some farther mean for our brothers maintainance there : And that discipline in the mean tyme may be better exerced and execute in the said Mr. William his parish of Kendmoir, and the people may be more awed when they see the same countenanced and authorized by yourselves, we think it very convenient that yow send tuo or three of your number to joyne with the minister for nominating and appoynting a session in that congreagtion and fitting elders and deacons to regulat and order the same, and to crave accompt of their diligence in censuring of vyce and the discharging of other duties. Yow will also be pleased to have a care that the kirk of Killin be provyded and all ministerial duties done there in the absence of the minister, who is now at the army in England. Commending these things to your care, we remaine,

Your loving brethren,
THE COMMISSIONERS
OF THE GENERAL ASSEMBLY.[1]

Edinburgh, 20 January, 1647."

The kirk session records show that the presbytery duly carried out its instructions. The parish was visited ; new elders were added to the session ; and Mr. Menzies continued his good work in Breadalbane.

Mr. Menzies took a prominent part in the work of the provincial synod,[2] as well as in that of the General Assembly of the Church. He was moderator of the presbytery of Dunkeld in 1651 when the unhappy dispute took place between the Resolutioners and the Protestors, by which the presbytery was divided into two separate bodies. He was a member of the General Assemblies of 1638 and 1639 ; and also attended the meetings of the Commission of the General Assembly of 1647-48. He died on 23 July, 1657, at the age of sixty-two years. He married Agnes Burd, who survived him and became the second wife of Thomas Ireland, minister at Weem. Ireland, who appears to have settled down at Inchadney manse during the vacancy in Kenmore parish, proceeded to administer the affairs of the deceased minister as

(1) Assy. Com. Records, vol. II., pp. 179-180.   (2) Eccles. Fasti., Scot.

if he were his executor. James Menzies, son and heir of Mr. William Menzies, found it necessary to raise an action against Ireland on his own behalf and that of his two sisters, Grizel and Christian, in order to inhibit Ireland from selling, or letting, or putting away his lands to the prejudice of his father's creditors.

The parish of Kenmore was vacant from the death of William Menzies in 1657 until 22 May, 1660, when PATRICK CAMPBELL[1] was admitted by the Protestors. Patrick Campbell was a son of Duncan Campbell of Lagvinsheach, who, on the death of his father, Archibald Campbell, fifth son of Sir Duncan Campbell of Glenorchy, succeeded to the estates of Ibert and Monzie. His mother was Agnes, daughter of Patrick Murray of Ochtertyre. Patrick Campbell's close relationship to the family of Glenorchy would account for the presence at his admission of a large representation of kinsmen. The sermon was preached by his uncle, Mr. Colin Campbell of Blair Atholl. There were also present Alexander Campbell of Lochdochart, Duncan Campbell of Auchlyne, Patrick Campbell of Easter Shian, John Campbell of Kinloch, John Campbell in Portbane, and James Campbell in Achianich. Patrick Campbell took the degree of M.A. at the University of St. Andrews, 9 July, 1655. Because he had been admitted to Kenmore by the Protestors he was termed " an intruder " by the synod on 12 April, 1661. He married Marjorie Menzies, and at his death, which occurred some time before 21 July, 1675, he left a family of two sons and a daughter. Duncan was a student of Divinity in 1685, and afterwards became governor to Alexander Gibsone of Durie; Colin, who was baptised 17 October, 1669, was a lieutenant in Col. McGill's regiment, went to Darien, and died at Jamaica, 1699 ; Anna married Duncan Campbell, son of Colin Campbell of Edramuckie. Judging from frequent references in the kirk session records to the minister's absence from the church on Sundays owing to sickness, it would appear that Patrick Campbell was in feeble health for the greater part of his ministry. It was during his ministry that the old church at Lawers was built, but there is no reference to its erection in the session minutes of 1669—the date on the lintel above the door.

The next minister of Kenmore was ALEXANDER COMRIE, who had been settled at Killin in 1673. He was translated on 7 March, 1676. He was the son of Patrick Comrie of Ross and Anna Murray; and had been educated at St. Andrews. He matriculated at the University on 25 February, 1663, and took the degree of M.A., 26 January, 1666. Comrie married Jean Campbell and had a son, John, baptised 18 December, 1677.

Before his admission he gave an undertaking to the first Earl of Breadalbane, patron of the parish, that he would rest satisfied with the condition and situation of the manse and glebe, and

(1) See Hunter's " Diocese and Presbytery of Dunkeld " for Patrick Campbell and Alexander Comrie.

would seek no change so long as he served the cure of Kenmore. He seems to have prejudiced the interests of the Church also by granting to the Earl a tack of the teinds.

Comrie was an ardent Episcopalian, and at the Revolution he refused to conform to Presbyterianism. In 1693, and again in 1695, he ceased to preach for several Sundays on account of the oaths imposed and of the act of Parliament demanding submission to the Revolution Settlement. He was, however, a diligent minister, and until he was finally expelled from the church and manse in 1723 he attended most faithfully to his duties. He went on prolonged rounds of examination to the remote parts of his parish, and, supported by his elders, he maintained strict discipline. He was no sooner installed at Kenmore than " the session taking to their consideration the great abuse of the Sabbath by many, especially in time of divine service, lying about without the church, and will not come in to hear sermon, they ordain two of their number to go out each day in time of sermon, and to take notice of every transgressor of that nature that they may be accordingly punished." Steps were also taken to put a stop to the practice of frequenting the woods during Autumn for the gathering of hazel nuts on the Sabbath day. Comrie observed Easter as a festival of the Church, and on the Monday after each celebration of the sacrament of the Lord's Supper the people were " exhorted to thankfulness, obedience, and faithfulness in performing of their vows and promises made at the Lord's table." The collections taken at the several services connected with the celebration of Communion, after extraordinary expenses had been paid, were forthwith distributed among the poor. It was, however, enacted that " the poor shall every Lord's day attend sermon and catechising, otherwise their names are to be cancelled out of the roll of the poor." In 1699 the people of Lawers had not been attending church as regularly as they were expected to do. The minister, therefore, with the aid of the Earl of Breadalbane, proceeded to impress them with a sense of their religious duties, as the following minute shows :—" 1699, September 24— This day the Earle of Breadalbane sitting in the session with the minister and elders, the people of Lawers being summoned from the pulpit Sunday last were convened, and, being accused for not waiting on the ordinances, were sharply rebuked, threatened, and exhorted to better and more frequent attendance."

Comrie and the Earl of Breadalbane were on very intimate terms. Both were strong Jacobites. When the Earl was summoned to Edinburgh on the suspicion that he was conspiring with the Earl of Mar in the rising of 1715, Comrie* along with John Murray, a doctor in Perth, upon " their soul and conscience " testified that the Earl, who was eighty years of age, was " much

* Original Letters relating to the Rebellion, p. 21.

troubled with Coughs, Rheums, Defluctions, and other Maladies and Infirmities," so that he could not travel. Notwithstanding the many and serious infirmities under which, according to Comrie and Murray, the Earl suffered, he was seen on the following day coming out of a boat at Logierait to wait upon Mar.

It is stated that Comrie advanced 400 merks to Lord Breadalbane for the expenses of Captain Robert Campbell of Glenlyon (of Glencoe notoriety) in order to enable him to join his regiment in Flanders. During the rebellion of 1715 Comrie was active on the Jacobite side which had the support of the Earl and of the majority of his people. He prayed for king James, and read proclamations from him and from the Earl of Mar in the church. He employed James and George Robertson, sons of Alexander Robertson, minister of Fortingall, both of whom had acted as chaplains and combatants at Sheriffmuir, to preach for him at Kenmore. On May 23, 1716 the presbytery of Dunkeld proceeded to libel Comrie, and cited him to appear before them on 12 June. He, however, failed to put in an appearance, but sent the following letter :—" Reverend Sirs, By bearers hereof, they can declair that I am not in capacity to compear and answer your calamnatious letter. I am hardly able to walk my room. My church is like to be soon vaccant."

Although Comrie was cited several times to answer to the charges brought against him, he persistently declined to appear at the presbytery ; and at length on 26 October, 1716, the presbytery passed sentence of deposition upon him. James Stewart, minister at Moulin, was appointed to intimate the sentence of deposition in the church of Kenmore, and to declare the parish vacant. Comrie, however, retained possession of the church and manse, and when members of the presbytery went to preach at Kenmore they could only get access to the church by his goodwill and pleasure. Mr. Duncan McLea of Dull reported to the presbytery that he failed to obtain entrance to the church, but nevertheless he preached, " but he and his congregation were stoned." The presbytery thereupon resolved to complain to the Earl of Breadalbane, and to make application to the proper authorities that Comrie should be placed in the " Porteous Rolls " for retaining possession of the church after his deposition.

The sympathies of the people were entirely with Comrie. When a committee of presbytery visited Kenmore on 26 September, 1721, no one attended the church although three bells had been rung, and no service was held. The presbytery at length decided to exercise their right of *jus devolutum,* and to translate John Hamilton from Blair Atholl to Kenmore. He was accordingly admitted on 4 June, 1723. Comrie then gave up the keys of the church, and a few months later he handed over to a committee of the kirk session, who waited upon him at his house at Taymouth, the following articles of property belonging to the church :—

the poor's box, 280 communion tokens, a pewter communion plate,[1] two silver communion cups, and the mortcloth.   He continued to go about the Breadalbane district ministering to persons who refused to accept the services of the Presbyterian clergy.   Several persons who acknowledged that they had been married by him were fined.   He was still residing at Taymouth on 11 October, 1730 ; but had died before 8 July, 1733, on which day Alexander Forister, who was married to Margaret Comrie, daughter of John Comrie, his son, delivered to the kirk session of Kenmore an Irish Bible and an Irish New Testament in Irish character.   At the same time Mr. Hamilton intimated that he had received from Mr. Comrie before he died a large English Bible which had formerly belonged to the church of Kenmore.

JOHN HAMILTON had been minister at Blair Atholl from 25 February, 1718.   He began his ministry at Kenmore among a disaffected people.   The only member of kirk session who attended his admission service was John Graham, parish schoolmaster ; and for several months the rest of the elders and the majority of the congregation absented themselves from his services. Hamilton was not a man to be easily discouraged ; and by his earnestness and sincerity he gradually won the respect and affection of the people.   In co-operation with his neighbours, the ministers of Killin, Weem, and Dull, he applied himself to the problem of providing schools for places remote from the parish schools.   In this he was very successful.   Hamilton laboured at Kenmore under many disadvantages.   His stipend was only £526 8s. 4d. (Scots).   In an application for augmen- tation of stipend he stated, " My stipend is paid in very small fractions by the Tennants, a great many of whom are residing in the parish of Killin, in Glendochart and Glenlochay, 17 miles from my dwelling-house, which is very great drudgery for me to uplift it, and some of which are owing for 2 years ; nor have I any title but use and wont to pursue the deficients."   The old manse at Inchadney was inconveniently situated, and in a bad state of repair.   On one occasion he and his family were greatly alarmed by stones falling from the inside of the chimney, which nearly killed his wife and the infant in her arms.   He proposed that a new manse be erected on the same side of the river as the church, and suggested a suitable site at the village of Balnatibert, on the farm of Portbane.   After much trouble a small increase[2] of stipend was granted, but the building of a new manse had to wait for over thirty years.   John Hamilton died at Kenmore in January, 1742 ; and was survived by his widow, who was a member of the family of Stewarts of Urrard, Pit- lochry.   She was still residing at the manse on April 3, 1743, when she handed over to the kirk session minute books, tokens, Bibles, and communion vessels belonging to the church.

(1) This pewter plate, dated 1685, is preserved.   (2) Teind papers.

JOHN DOUGLAS, who was licensed by the presbytery of
Perth, 25 June, 1740, was ordained at Kenmore, 23 March,
1743.   His name appears in the kirk session records of Kenmore
as presbytery bursar on 19 November, 1738. He married Beatrix
Ainslie, 26 April, 1750. Douglas supported the third Earl of
Breadalbane in his efforts to restrain the people from joining
in the Jacobite rebellion of 1745. In 1754 he made application[1]
to the Commissioners for the Forfeited Estates for a grant with
which to repair the church at Lawers, which, he stated, was
then roofless. He represented that the church served the west
end of the Fearnan district, for which the Commissioners were
responsible ; that he went to preach at Lawers once in six or
seven weeks, and was compelled to conduct his services in the
open air for want of a suitable building. The Commissioners
gave a grant, and also timber from the Black Wood of Rannoch.

The presentation in favour of John Douglas to the church of
Jedburgh, secured for him from the Crown by the third Earl
of Breadalbane, raised a storm in the Church courts, and caused
Douglas no little trouble and expense.[2] When the parish of
Jedburgh fell vacant in 1755, the elders entered into a pact
by which they bound themselves to stand or fall together in the
election and choice of a minister against all intrusions that might
be attempted ; and at the same time they set their hearts on
securing as their minister Thomas Boston of Oxnam. The Crown,
however, granted a presentation in favour of John Bonar,
minister at Cockpen ; whereupon the elders and some of the
congregation so intimidated the presbytery that that court
delayed taking steps towards his translation until the case came
before the General Assembly of 1756. Bonar was induced to
decline the presentation ; but the Assembly declared that it
was still open to the Crown to make a new presentation.
Accordingly, on 2 June, 1756, George II. granted a presentation
in favour of John Douglas, which he accepted. The presbytery
of Jedburgh delayed consideration of the call for two months ;
and when they proceeded to deal with the matter, the elders
again raised various objections. They maintained that the right
of presentation, owing to the lapse of time, had passed into the
hands of the presbytery ; and further that Douglas, being settled
in a Highland charge, could not accept of a presentation elsewhere.
The majority of the heritors petitioned the presbytery asking
them to proceed with the translation of Douglas ; but the
presbytery put off consideration of the call from time to time.
At length the presbytery by a majority decreed that the right
of appointment had devolved upon that court, which decision
was contrary to the judgment of the previous General Assembly.
An appeal was then taken to the synod ; but the synod referred
the affair to the Commission of the General Assembly which
met in November, 1756. The Commission appointed the pres-

(1) Forfeited Estates Papers, p. 233.   (2) Gen. Assemy. Minutes and B.Ps.

bytery to proceed with the translation of John Douglas with all convenient speed ; but the presbytery persisted in its dilatory tactics until the General Assembly of 1757, to which the case was carried by the Lord Advocate.

By their methods of obstruction the elders and the presbytery managed to hold up the translation of Douglas from Kenmore to Jedburgh for another year ; and the issue developed into a contest between an inferior court and the supreme court of the Church. The General Assembly of 1758 finally agreed without a vote that the sentence of the presbytery of Dunkeld transporting John Douglas to Jedburgh should be carried into execution, and that Douglas should be admitted to Jedburgh before the end of July. The Assembly further declared that every member of the presbytery must attend the service of admission, and anyone of their number who absented himself must be reported to the meeting of the Commission in August, when he would be dealt with. The presbytery this time carried out its instructions to the letter, and every member was present when John Douglas was inducted to his new charge on 28 July, 1758.

When the call to Douglas came before the presbytery of Dunkeld, he made a statement[1] in which he set forth his reasons for seeking the change to Jedburgh. He said that he loved the people of Kenmore, and that he was on good terms with the Earl of Breadalbane who had done much to promote the religious interests of the congregation. His income, however, was less than £45 a year with a small glebe, and he found it impossible on that stipend to maintain and educate his family. The parish was large, and contained 2,300 examinable persons whom he had to visit and catechise during winter, as most of them went to the shealings in summer. When visiting the parish he was often away from home for ten and twelve days at a time, and had to sleep at night on a little straw in smoky and disagreeable houses. The manse was at a distance from the church at Kenmore, and he had to cross the river every Sunday in a boat, which in winter was often dangerous.

Throughout his prolonged struggle Douglas had the support of the Earl of Breadalbane.[2] He was also aided by John Campbell of the Royal Bank, Edinburgh, who advanced the money to meet his expenses. Before Douglas got himself and his family settled in the manse at Jedburgh the case had cost him £310, which was reduced by vacant stipend due to him to £195. Even this amount was a large burden under which to begin his ministry among a people who were largely hostile to him. The opposition had built a meeting house and called Thomas Boston to be their minister. The Relief congregation thus formed continued until a few years ago, when it entered the re-united Church of Scotland.

(1) See Perthshire Scrap-book, Sandeman Lib., Perth, article by Rev. John Sinclair, Rannoch.
(2) B.Ps.

R

In a letter that Douglas sent to his friend, John Campbell of the
Bank, on 31 July, 1758, three days after his induction to the
charge of Jedburgh, he thanked John Campbell for his " sub-
stantial favours," and stated :—" I and my company arrived
here on Thursday, and were wett to the skin by the time we
reached Ginklekirk.   On Friday the presbytery mett, not one
of the ministers being absent, and I was admitted peaceably
according to the usual custom on such occasions.   Many came
from all quarters of the church to take me by the hand, as an
evidence of their heartily accepting me as their minister. After
sermon we had a numerous company of the highest and best
people in the town at dinner with us, but none of the magistrates,
though invited.   In the evening I walked to the head of the
town, and mett with many marks of respect, but not with the
least rudeness, or indecency.   Yesterday Mr. Main, my friend,
preached in the forenoon, and I in the afternoon to a decent
audience, at least 500, and as I came through the church severals
that I did not know took me by the hand.   In short, everything
succeeded beyond expectation, and great reason have I to be
thankful to kind over-ruling Providence that matters are brought
to so happy a conclusion."[1]

John Douglas died at Jedburgh 16 November, 1768.   He
left two sons, and at least one daughter.   Robert Douglas,[2] born
at the old manse of Kenmore, 19 July, 1747, was educated at
the University of Aberdeen, and became minister of Galashiels.
He was made a D.D. of King's College, 1797, and died in 1820.
By his efforts the manufacturing industry of Galashiels was
developed, and he was called " The Father of Galashiels."
It was from him that Sir Walter Scott purchased the small
estate of Abbotsford ; and he was the minister to whom Sir
Walter addressed the thirteenth of " Paul's Letters to his
Kinsfolk."   John Douglas's other son was Walter, who was a
Deputy-adjutant General in the Army, and died in India.

JAMES CAMPBELL, who succeeded John Douglas as minister
at Kenmore, was admitted to the parish from Carnwath, Lanark-
shire, on 8 November, 1736.   He was licensed by the presbytery
of Dalkeith, 27 July, 1746.   Before going to Carnwath, Campbell
had been minister at Dull.   He married Janet Cross, and was
survived by a son, Duncan.   He and his wife died within a few
days of one another in February, 1780, and a headstone marks
their grave in the churchyard of Kenmore.

Soon after James Campbell was admitted to Kenmore the
third Earl of Breadalbane proceeded to transfer the manse and
glebe of the parish from Inchadney to Croftnacaber overlooking
Loch Tay.   The Earl also reconstructed the Kenmore church,[3]
adding the transepts and the tower.   The old church and manse

(1) B.Ps.   (2) Eccles. Fasti Scot.
(3) The bell still in use was cast by Thomas Janaway, London, in 1759.

at Inchadney were allowed to crumble, but the latter was still occupied at the end of the eighteenth century. About the beginning of the last century both church and manse were completely demolished, and the stones removed. The church green, at Kenmore, on which a few burials had taken place before 1760, was laid out about that year as the parish church-yard, and the pre-Reformation churchyard at Inchadney was closed. The walls were demolished, and the ancient and hallowed spot was planted with trees before 1769. It is still possible to trace the foundations of the enclosing walls. Some of the head-stones were removed to Kenmore ; but those remaining are said to have been taken to cover drains at Taymouth Castle.

In 1763 John Campbell of Achallader, chamberlain to Lord Breadalbane, wrote to the factor for the Forfeited Estates, which included Fearnan, stating that the new manse of Kenmore was nearly finished, and that the church was nearing completion ; that the cost of the former was about £450, and of the latter double that sum. Lord Breadalbane had borne the entire expense ; but Campbell suggested that the Commissioners might wish to make a contribution towards the cost of erecting the manse and church in respect of their interest in the parish.*

James Campbell was followed at Kenmore by THOMAS FLEMING, who was translated from Kirkmichael, Perthshire, of which parish he was a native, on 24 August, 1780. Fleming was brought to Kenmore through the influence of the pious Lady Glenorchy, with whose evangelical principles he had much sympathy. He removed to Kirkcaldy on 10 July, 1788 ; and from there he went to Lady Yester's church, Edinburgh, where he had a successful ministry. He died in 1824. Thomas Fleming married Anne Robertson, who died in 1829. They had two sons and three daughters. It was during Fleming's ministry at Kenmore that the remarkable agitation of the waters of Loch Tay took place, and although not at home at the time, Sunday, 12 September, 1784, he afterwards wrote a report of the occurrence for the Royal Society of Edinburgh, which was reproduced in the Statistical Account of the parish written by Colin McVean in 1794.

The ministry of Fleming's successor, PATRICK McVEAN, at Kenmore was brief. He was admitted from Dull on 30 April, 1789. He was the son of John McVean, minister of Glenorchy, who was a native of Glenlochay, Breadalbane ; was educated at St. Andrews ; and licensed by the presbytery of Lorn, 23 March, 1770. He died at Edinburgh, 24 March, 1793. He married a second time, in 1791, Mary Lockhart of Ayr, who died in 1823. He left a son, Archibald, who went to Grenada and died before 1825 ; and a daughter, Christian.

COLIN McVEAN was admitted minister at Kenmore on 13

* Forfeited Estates Papers.

Rev. J. B. MacKenzie, Kenmore. 1872-1912.

March, 1794. He was a native of Glenlochay, Breadalbane, and was probably a relation of his predecessor. He was educated at St. Andrews, and licensed by the presbytery of that town on 7 May, 1788. He was ordained to the newly-created mission station of Lawers and Ardeonaig on 3 May, 1791. This mission was financed from funds bequeathed by Lady Glenorchy, and ultimately led to the formation of two separate charges, one on each side of Loch Tay. Colin McVean married Ann McArthur, 26 June, 1799. She died at Strontian, 22 February, 1849. They had two sons and three daughters. Donald was minister of Iona at the time of the Disruption, and joined the Free Church ; Colin Archibald became minister of Strontian, and was afterwards translated to Killin. Colin McVean died at the Manse of Kenmore on 20 August, 1830, in his sixty-seventh year ; a headstone marks his grave in Kenmore churchyard. He wrote the report of the parish of Kenmore for Sinclair's Statistical Account.

DAVID DUFF had a ministry of twenty-five years in his native parish of Moulin before he was translated to Kenmore on 14 April, 1831. He was educated at Moulin school, Dundee Grammar school, and St. Andrews Univeristy. He was given the degree of D.D. by his University, in 1843. He married Grace McLagan on 10 September, 1810. She died, 17 October, 1846. They had a family of three sons, and one daughter, Elspeth, who died at Kenmore, 23 July, 1838, at the age of eighteen years. Dr. Duff wrote the description of the parish for the New Statistical Account. At the Disruption a large section of his congregation, under the influence of the Second Marquis of Breadalbane, left him and joined the Free Church. The six elders who seceded from the kirk session at the meeting held on 12 June, 1843, expressed themselves with regard to Dr. Duff and the other members of session in the following terms :— " The seceding elders were desirous of having an opportunity of expressing and recording the sincere regard they have always had, and still have for the Moderator and remnant members of the kirk session ; but as they distrusted their ability to do it to the satisfaction of their own minds on the spur of the moment, they stated that in the course of two or three days they would send to the kirk session a document to that effect." Dr. Duff continued his active ministry until 1862, when owing to age and infirmity he installed Ewen McEwen, who had been ordained minister at Amulree, as his assistant. He himself retired to Birnam, leaving the work at Kenmore to be carried on by a succession of assistants (licensed) until his death on 14 April, 1872, in the ninety-second year of his age. For three years before his death he was Father of the Church of Scotland. Dr. Duff was buried at Kenmore churchyard beside his wife and daughter.

JAMES BANNATYNE MACKENZIE was translated from Colonsay, and admitted to Kenmore 26 August, 1872. He was the son of Rev. Neil Mackenzie, minister of Kilchrenan, and was born 6 December, 1833, in St. Kilda, where his father was then minister. He was educated at Glasgow University, and was ordained to the Mission church at Kingairloch, in 1858. He married Catherine Campbell, daughter of Donald Campbell, minister of North Knapdale. Mrs. Mackenzie died at the manse of Kenmore in 1910. Mr. Mackenzie retired from the active ministry of the Church in November, 1911, and went to reside

REV. WILLIAM A. GILLIES, B.D., KENMORE.

in Edinburgh, where he died, 25 December, 1920. He was buried at Kenmore. He was survived by his son, Duncan Campbell Mackenzie, a solicitor, who was for some years in business in Edinburgh. On retiring he went to reside at Silloth. Rev. J. B. Mackenzie wrote an account of the island of St. Kilda from notes kept by his father while resident there. Mr. Mackenzie was greatly interested in antiquarian subjects and also in photography.

WILLIAM ALEXANDER GILLIES, the present incumbent of the parish, was born at Isleornsay, Sleat, Skye, 2 September,

1873 ; the son of John Gillies and Agnes Orr. He was educated
at Kingussie school, and Glasgow University, graduating M.A.
1900, and B.D. 1903 ; assistant to Rev. C. M. Grant, D.D.,
St. Mark's Church, Dundee, 1903-6 ; ordained to Tiree, 14 May,
1906 ; translated to Duncansburgh Church, Fort William,
July, 1909 ; admitted to Kenmore 10 January, 1912 ; served as
a chaplain with the Forces in Macedonia during 1917-18. The
two congregations at Kenmore were united under him in May,
1931. During his ministry in Tiree he promoted the pier which
was built by the Government for the islanders. He had the
church of Kenmore improved and renovated, 1923. He married,
18 September, 1906, Margaret Macdonald, daughter of Alexander
Macdonald and Margaret Mackenzie, Edinburgh. Their children
are, Barbara Sinclair,* born 4 August, 1907; Margaret Mackenzie
St. Clair, born 25 July, 1911 ; Kenneth Alastair Mackenzie,
born 30 March, 1919.

Free Church of Kenmore.

The Free Church of Kenmore was built by the second Marquis
of Breadalbane and the foundation stone of the building was
laid on 8 November, 1844, by the Marchioness. The first minister
of the congregation was the Rev. ALLAN SINCLAIR, who
was born, April, 1821, at Livisy, Glenmoriston, eldest son of
Robert Sinclair and Mary Macdonald—later of Borlum in Glen
Urquhart.

He was educated at Elgin Academy, graduated in Arts
at Aberdeen University, and took Divinity at Edinburgh. He
was ordained Minister of the Free Church of Scotland in the
Parish of Kenmore on March 19th, 1846, where he continued
his ministry till his death on June 8th, 1888.

He was married in Edinburgh on 5th February, 1852, to
Sarah Fraser, second daughter of the Rev. Alexander Garden
Fraser of New Jersey, New York, a son of James Fraser of
Charleston, South Carolina, who was the eldest son of John
Fraser by his wife, a member of the family of Hogarth the
painter. John Fraser was the younger brother of Simon Lord
Lovat.

Mr. Sinclair was the author of " The Life of Dougal Buchanan,"
and published in Gaelic the Life of the Rev. Robert Murray
McCheyne. He prepared the revised edition of the Shorter
Catechism in Gaelic ; wrote and published " Reminiscences—
Historical and Traditional—of the Grants of Glenmoriston " ;
and contributed numerous articles on Celtic subjects to Magazines,
etc. He was a Fellow of the Celtic Society of Montreal.

Mr. Sinclair possessed a remarkable knowledge of Highland
history and tradition, and had great eloquence and freedom in
the Gaelic language, which was his mother tongue.

* She married Rev. Thomas Calvert, Waterside, Ayr, 18th October, 1933.

Rev. Allan Sinclair, M.A., Free Church, Kenmore, 1846-1888.

During the earlier part of Mr. Sinclair's ministry at Kenmore the district was thickly populated by a Gaelic-speaking community. The Sabbath morning service was conducted in Gaelic, followed by a shorter service in English. The afternoon services were held at Bridge of Lyon and elsewhere, and in the evening, until the death of the second Marquis of Breadalbane, he conducted household worship at Taymouth Castle.

Mr. Sinclair's eldest son, Robert Hamilton, M.A. (Aberdeen) entered the Ceylon Civil Service in 1874. He was accidentally drowned in the Lake of Kandy in 1886. Alexander Garden, A.R.S.A., was an artist resident in Edinburgh; he died in 1930. The photograph of the Rev. Allan Sinclair shown here was taken from the portrait painted by his son. One of his daughters, Mary Macdonell, studied Medicine in Edinburgh, and after qualifying practised in London. The youngest son, Arthur Henry Havens, M.D., F.R.C.S.Ed., became an Ophthalmic Surgeon in Edinburgh. He was appointed in 1927, Surgeon Oculist to H.M. the King in Scotland. He was President of the Royal College of Surgeons of Edinburgh, and President of the Ophthalmological Society of the United Kingdom.

The Rev. Allan Sinclair's memory is still fresh and greatly revered in the district. He was buried in Kenmore churchyard, where a beautiful Celtic cross marks his grave. A mural tablet erected by his congregation to his memory in the Kenmore Free Church was removed to the Parish Church after the congregations were united.

JAMES MACMILLAN, M.A., son of John Macmillan, farmer, Glenbarr, Kintyre; educated at Killean School, Glasgow University, and Trinity College, Glasgow; licensed at Campbeltown, May, 1887; ordained at Kenmore 24 October, 1888; resigned his charge at Kenmore 1906, and in December, 1910, was admitted to Aberuthven; translated to North Knapdale, May, 1924; now retired and resides at Crieff; married Mabel S. Gill, May, 1896; she died 25 November, 1911; issue, two sons, John C. G. Macmillan, M.A., solicitor, Rothesay, and Harry H. G. Macmillan, M.A., of the Church of Scotland Mission, Gold Coast.

JOHN BONAR ATHOL GORDON, M.A., born 1868, only son of Patrick Gordon, Doctor of Medicine, Colinton, Midlothian, and Margaret Bonar, daughter of Dr. John Bonar, minister of Larbert; educated at Collegiate School, Edinburgh, the University, and Free Church College of Edinburgh; assistant at Largs, and St. Andrews Free Church, Edinburgh; ordained at Borgue, Kirkcudbrightshire, December, 1898; translated to Kenmore, July, 1906; retired for health reasons 1931, when the two congregations at Kenmore were united.

CHAPTER XXV.

THE CHURCH.

The Parish of Killin.

THE church of Killin was a vicarage in the diocese of Dunkeld. In 1317, king Robert the Bruce granted the patronage of the church, with its fruits and revenues, to the Abbot and Convent of Inchaffray,[1] on condition that they should provide a canon to officiate in the church of Strathfillan. The right of instituting the vicar and the dues payable to the bishop and the archdeacon were reserved to Dunkeld. The pre-Reformation church was situated within the churchyard beside the river Lochay, and part of the ruins were still standing in 1842 when the New Statistical Account of Scotland was written. This church was apparently in use until the present church was built in 1744. Its measurements[2] were recorded when the accommodation was allocated among the heritors in 1732.

The lands in the vicinity of Killin had been granted by king James I. to the Carthusian monastery in Perth, which was founded by him in 1429. In 1488, we find the prior of the monastery granting a " croft of land in Killin to Donald M'Cause, with houses and garden, with pasturage of four cows and two horses, with power to bake, brew, and sell flesh, and to buy and sell within the Lordship of Glendochart, according to the assize of the country, paying yearly to the parish church of Killin, three pounds of wax in honour of the blessed Virgin and St. Fillan, and all Saints, and for the increase of St. Fillan's lights before his image, one pound whereof at the feast of St. Fillan in summer, and another at the feast of St. Fillan in winter."[3] In 1510, the vicar of Killin was Sir Robert McNair. On 19 May, 1557, an order was issued by Robert Crichton, Bishop of Dunkeld, to the curate of Killin to summon the parishioners to pay their dues to the parish clerk, William Ruthven.

The earliest minister of the Reformed Church to whom any reference has been found as serving at Killin is JOHN McCORCA-DILL, who was exhorter and notary public there in 1567. He was still at Killin in 1583, when he made a statement with regard to the teinds, which at that time were held by Lady Glenorchy, the widow of Colin Campbell, sixth laird. By 1585 he was parson and minister of Logy. For some years after his departure Killin was served by the ministers of Kenmore, but in 1606 we find GEORGE MCGILLECHALLUM settled in the parish. Again

(1) Charters of Inchaffray, Scot. Hist. Soc., intro. p. XLIV.   (2) B.Ps.
(3) Christie, Lands and Lairds, p. 63.

for several years there appears to have been no resident minister, but in 1618 WILLIAM MENZIES was admitted. He remained at Killin until 1636, when he was translated to Kenmore. In 1621 a glebe was laid out for him by Sir Duncan Campbell on the latter's lands of Killin known as " Croit-chandich." He also received an augmentation of stipend from the laird of Glenorchy in 1632, " for the love and favour " that he had for him. In the same year Sir Colin Campbell of Glenorchy gifted the bell,[1] which is still in use, to the kirk of Killin. There is no doubt that William Menzies was the first minister to organise the congregation. In 1627, when the Commissioners for the Plantation of Kirks visited Killin, they reported that there were 460 communicants in Killin and Strathfillan, and at Ardeonaig 70 communicants. The stipend of the minister was 520 merks out of the teinds of the three united parishes.

After William Menzies removed to Kenmore the three churches were served by COLIN MCLAUCHLAN for a few years. He, however, was translated to Lochgoilhead in 1640, and we find him petitioning the presbytery of Dunkeld for help in recovering stipend due to him from Killin which " the patron, teind-masters, takismen, and parishoners " owed him.

COLIN CAMPBELL, son of Archibald Campbell of Lagvinsheach, was admitted minister of Killin before 6 May, 1645. He was educated at St. Andrews, and took the degree of M.A. there, 6 June, 1640. He acted as chaplain with the Scottish army in England during the Civil War,[2] and on his return home was translated to Blair Atholl. He married Jean, daughter of James Stewart of Fincastle. At Blair Atholl he was beside his brother, Robert, who was minister of Moulin.

JOHN CUNISON, who was admitted to Killin prior to 8 October, 1650, was the son of John Cunison, minister of Dull, and Elspethe Crychtoun of Polcak. He was educated at St. Andrews. He removed to Kilbride in Arran, and from there he went to Saddell.

PATRICK CAMPBELL was admitted to Killin by the Protesting presbytery of Dunkeld on November 11, 1656. He refused to conform to Episcopacy in 1662, and declined to seek a presentation to his charge from the bishop. He was therefore deprived of his benefice, and ordered to remove from the bounds of the presbytery, under the operation of the Act of Glasgow. He appears to have been a diligent minister and to have preached regularly in the three churches under his care both in Irish and in English. The heritors had failed to pay him the stipend for 1662, and he raised an action against them which the Lords of Council allowed. He married Nicolas Somerbell.

(1) The Church Bell of Killin bears the inscription, " Sir*Coline*Campbel*of*Glenurchy* Knygth*Barronet*causid*cast*yis*Bel*1632*R H*"   The bell was probably made by Robert Hog, Potterraw, Edinburgh. The space between the maker's initials bears a hammer surmounted by a crown. The bell cracked in 1931, but was successfully welded and rehung.
(2) Assy. Com. Records, vol. II., p. 199.

KILLIN CHURCH BELL (Cast 1632).

ALEXANDER COMRIE was admitted to Killin before 5 June, 1673, and was translated to Kenmore 7 March, 1676.

ALEXANDER REDDOCH,[1] minister at Killin, signed a certificate along with Alexander Comrie of Kenmore and others on 26 February, 1677. Reddoch had previously been schoolmaster at Inverkeithing.

ROBERT STEWART was long remembered by the Gaelic nickname, " *Curam an t-saoghail*," " Care of the World," because he was always preaching on this subject, while gathering all the wealth he could lay his hands upon. Stewart was admitted to Killin before January 6, 1680. He was a student of Divinity on 18 September, 1678, when he signed an obligation to John Campbell, then Earl of Caithness. He married Agnes Campbell.

Shortly after his admission to Killin Robert Stewart had a glebe laid out for him, which he afterwards exchanged for another piece of land. He also contracted with the heritors to build and to leave a manse worth 800 merks. He does not appear to have been implicated in the Rising of 1715, although he was an Episcopalian. In 1727 the presbytery discovered that the parish of Killin was religiously much neglected, and a visitation was ordered. This visitation[2] was carried out on 6 September, 1727, and a deplorable state of matters was revealed.

(1) See Rev. W. Stephen, D.D., Hist. of Inverkeithing.
(2) See Hunter's Diocese and Pres. of Dunkeld.

For some years Stewart had been laid aside with infirmity and old age, but even when he was younger and stronger he had not attended to his duties. He had ceased to preach, and for over twenty years the sacrament of the Lord's Supper had not been administered in any part of the parish. He never visited, and except for seven or eight years, he had not resided in his parish. There were no vessels for Communion ; and for several years the school had been closed. Stewart admitted that the evidence submitted by the heritors and the parishioners was substantially correct ; but he does not appear to have been in any way concerned. His only trouble was that a bit of grazing on which he had kept sixty sheep had been taken from him. He asked the deputation of presbytery to take steps to recover it from the Earl of Breadalbane. It was represented to him that the spiritual interests of the parish were suffering, and that he must agree to the appointment of an assistant and successor. This he reluctantly did, and Adam Fergusson was ordained at Killin. When, however, Fergusson proceeded to inquire about property belonging to the church, friction began between the old minister and the assistant over the poor's box, which the former refused to give up. The trouble ended on 4 March, 1729, when Stewart died. By his hoarding methods he managed to leave his four sons in estates—James had Kilchassie ; Duncan, Blackhall ; Alexander, Cloichfoldich ; and Robert, Derculich.

Alexander Comrie of Kenmore installed Stewart as his vicar at Lawers in 1714, with power to hold session, and to baptise and to marry. Stewart was to keep a register of all that he did, and send a scroll to Kenmore, so as not to wrong the clerk, the beadle, or the box. He, however, " neither kept register nor scrolls, and monopolised all the dues payable to the Clerk, Bedal, and Box."

ADAM FERGUSSON was ordained at Killin, 11 September, 1728. He was translated to Moulin 3 February, 1736, and was moderator of the General Assembly of the Church in 1772. During his ministry at Killin he maintained regular services in the three churches, and promoted schools in outlying districts.

JAMES STUART was born at Glenfinlas in 1701, and was educated at St. Andrews University. He was licensed by the presbytery of Dunblane, 3 July, 1733, and was for a short time assistant to the minister of Weem. He was ordained at Killin, 23 March, 1737, and died 30 June, 1796. He married Elizabeth Drummond who died 22 February, 1789. His family consisted of four sons and two daughters. John, who was born 31 July, 1743, was minister of Luss ; Thomas, born 5 April, 1745 ; Patrick, born 2 April, 1747, succeeded his father as minister of Killin ; Elizabeth, born 28 April, 1748 ; Donald, born 13 January, 1754 ; and Catherine, born 29 April, 1756.

New Churches Built.

Soon after James Stuart was admitted to Killin steps were taken to have new churches built at Killin, Ardeonaig, and Strathfillan. The builder was Thomas Clark, mason, Dunkeld. The accounts show that Clark contracted to build the Killin church for £3120 Scots ; Ardeonaig chapel for £540 Scots ; and Strathfillan chapel for £600 Scots. There were, however, additional outlays for which he was paid extra. In the case of the Killin church the following items appear in the accounts :—

Six men six days clearing the rubbish out of the church	£9	0	0
By seasoned deals bought by Thomas Clark for sashes to windows	56	14	0
By sclaters board wages the days they could not work	4	4	0
By drink money to Thomas Clark and his men when the kirk was finished	3	0	0
By cash to Alexander Gentle, wright, for stocking the bell, and setting up the same	4	16	0
By the smith at Killin his account for iron work to bell and pulpit	11	8	6
By glob for the cupola as follows :—			
James Graham, plumber	£37	16	0
James Norrie, painter, for gilding	25	4	0
William Richardson, smith, for a spire	19	4	0
James Runcyman, his account for a box	7	4	0
By express to Alloa to know if the glob was come there	2	10	0
By cellar rent for glob while at Alloa	2	0	0
By cartage of ditto from Alloa to Glenalmond	7	4	0
By cash to clerk Cameron and Alexr. Gentle for measuring and dividing area of the church	6	0	0
By setting of the Laird's loft in the church	80	10	6
For setting up of the south side of east loft	69	10	6

The amount of £3159 Scot. was levied upon the tenants of the Earl of Breadalbane in the parish of Killin and adjacent parts of the parishes of Kenmore and Weem. The Duke of Perth, Campbell of Glenfalloch, Campbell of Lochdochart, Campbell of Auchlyne, and the Laird of Macnab had to find the balance of £1480 Scots. A stone on the north gable of Killin church bears the following inscription :—

THOS. CLARK
THE BUILDER
OF THIS
CHURCH
1744.

CHURCH OF KILLIN AND STUART MEMORIAL.

The Gaelic Scriptures.

James Stuart did a valuable work for the Highlanders of Scotland by translating the New Testament into Scottish Gaelic. It was published at Edinburgh in 1767. Prior to the appearance of Stuart's translation the Highlanders did not have any part of the Scriptures in their own language ; and ministers had to translate from the English version to the people, or use Irish translations, which were rather difficult to read and to understand. The policy of the Church towards Gaelic had for a long time been one of suppression and extirpation. Whenever a proposal for the translation of the Bible into Gaelic was brought forward it was met with bitter opposition. Leading Churchmen sympathised with the Highlanders in their troubles ; but their remedy was to destroy the language root and branch—if only the barbarous Irish tongue could be stamped out, and the people made to speak English, all the evils that existed in the Highlands would disappear.

This stupid attitude was challenged in an anonymous pamphlet that appeared about 1699. The writer, in a well reasoned statement, brought forward arguments to show the absurdity of thinking that a language that was spoken by over 200,000 persons could be extirpated. He stated that it could not be done in that age, and it was doubtful if it could be done in any age. Various proposals had been made with a view to destroying the language, such as the introduction of English speaking colonists into the Highlands, and of sending the Highland children into the Lowlands. The writer examined these schemes with care, and showed that they were utterly impracticable. He then proceeded to indicate that the better way was to educate the Highlanders in their own language, and to give them the Scriptures in it. This pamphlet was widely broadcasted throughout the country, and it had the effect of winning a certain amount of support for the writer's suggestion that the Bible should be translated into Gaelic ; but nothing was done in this direction until over sixty years later.

The writer of this remarkable pamphlet entitled, " An answer to the objection against Printing the Bible in Irish, as being prejudicial to the design of Extirpating the Irish Language out of the Highlands of Scotland," proved to be James Kirkwood,[1] who had at one time been resident at Taymouth as chaplain to the first Earl of Breadalbane. Here was a man who proved himself a veritable *Caraid nan Gaidheal*," a " Friend of the Highlanders." Kirkwood was born at Dunbar about 1650, and was educated at Edinburgh University. He was recommended for trials for license on 13 July, 1676 ; and soon afterwards he went to Taymouth. He was inducted to the parish of Minto in 1679 ; but after two years he was " outed " for refusing to take the Test. He then went to England, where be obtained the small rectory of Astwick, Bedfordshire. He was ejected from his living in 1702 for refusing to conform to statutes passed in king William's reign. He died in 1708.

Kirkwood never forgot his residence in the Highlands, and the painful impression that the ignorance and illiterate condition of the people made upon him. When he went to England he came to know the Hon. Robert Boyle, whose attention had been directed to a similar state of matters in Ireland. Kirkwood explains how he got Boyle to procure Irish Bibles in Irish character for the Scottish Highlands. " It was soon after our acquaintance was begun that I had the opportunity of talking to him of the sad state of religion in the Highlands of Scotland, where they had neither Bibles nor Catechisms in their own language." Boyle informed him that he had five hundred Bibles in Irish character for the use of Irish people who did not understand English ; and he offered a few of these Bibles to be sent into Scotland to see how they would be received. At first some twelve copies were dispatched, and afterwards two hundred, which allowed one for each Highland parish. Only copies of the Old Testament were sent, as all the New Testaments had been

(1) Papers relating to Gaelic Bibles, in Church of Scotland Library, Edinburgh, presented to the library by the Very Rev. James Curdie Russell, D.D.

given to Ireland. Kirkwood entered into correspondence with Robert Kirk, at that time minister of Balquhidder, and told him of Boyle's gift. The Bibles were shipped to Leith from London, and consigned to Colin Campbell of Carwhin, W.S., Edinburgh, who was to distribute them through Robert Kirk. Nine copies were sent to Alexander Comrie of Kenmore for the presbytery of Dunkeld, accompanied with the following instructions, " Rev. Brother, Cause deliver, and keep the books carefully and clean after you have received them, and see that they are never alienated to privat use. Get receipts from the ministers, and send them to Carwhin." Of the nine copies given to the ministers of the presbytery of Dunkeld five are still preserved These are in the churches of Killin, Kenmore, Weem, Moulin, and Blair Atholl. They each bear an inscription indicating that they are " The Donation of the Honourable, Pious, and Learned, Robert Boyle, Esq., a Principal member of the Royal Society, bestowed on the Church of———— to continue there as a Church Bible for the use of the present minister, and his successors, ministers of the parish." The inscriptions on those five Bibles are in the handwriting of Robert Kirk himself, and dated 1688. Boyle also gave 3,000 Catechisms and Prayer-books for the Highlanders.

Boyle's donation of Bibles and Catechisms was well received in the Highlands, as the following contemporary statement bears out, " In all these places where the Bibles have been sent, the people express a wonderful joy, and a great desire to know the Word of God, so that they who can read are at some pains to teach others to read also. And such is their zeal that they send for the Bible, sometimes to one part of the parish, and sometimes to another, that they may read on the week-days, and then they return it to the Church on the Lord's Day, that all may hear it publicly."

When ministers in the Highlands discovered the benefit of the Irish pulpit Bibles they expressed a desire for a small Bible in Roman character. Encouraged by Kirkwood and with financial help from Boyle, Robert Kirk produced such a Bible in 1690. It included the Old Testament according to Bishop Beddell and the New Testament after O'Donnell. Three thousand copies of Kirk's Bible were circulated in the Highlands along with a thousand copies of the New Testament and three thousand Catechisms. All this work was carried through in the face of opposition from the party in the Church who maintained that the circulation of the Scriptures was prejudicial to the design of extirpating the Irish language out of the Highlands. It was in answer to those unreasonable people, among whom was the Bishop of Ross, that Kirkwood issued his famous pamphlet. At first the Society for the Propagation of Christian Knowledge supported the opponents of the Gaelic language, and although

8

the directors did most valuable work in the Highlands by setting up schools in places remote from parish schools, they gave positive injunctions to their schoolmasters to teach scholars to read only English books. The unwisdom of such a course was pointed out in strong terms by Dr. Samuel Johnson in a letter which he wrote to James Stuart of Killin ; and ultimately the directors of the S.P.C.K. resolved to have the New Testament translated into Gaelic, and asked Stuart* to undertake the work. For such an important task Stuart was well qualified. He had an extensive knowledge of Divinity and of general literature. He had a most retentive memory, and was so well acquainted with every passage in the Bible that he was called by his friends, " The Living Concordance." When Stuart had completed his translation the manuscript was revised by Fraser of Alness, who made many useful suggestions. The publication of the New Testament created an increasing devotion to religion, which led up to the great revivals that moved many parts of the Highlands at the end of the eighteenth century. It had the further effect of stimulating an interest in the Gaelic language itself. A second and improved edition of the New Testament in Gaelic was prepared by James Stuart's eldest son, Dr. John Stuart, minister of Luss, who also carried through part of the translation of the Old Testament, the last section of which was completed in 1801.

In a letter which Dr. Samuel Johnson wrote on August 13,

* See notes in Highland Monthly, vol. I., p. 494, by Dr. Donald Mason.

St. Fillan's Mill, Killin.

1766, to Mr. William Drummond[1] he referred in the following terms to James Stuart, who was at that time engaged upon his work of translation :—" You will be pleased, Sir, to assure the worthy man who is employed in the new translation, that he has my wishes for his success ; and if here, or at Oxford, I can be of any use, that I shall think it more than honour to promote his undertaking." In a subsequent letter to the same gentleman Dr. Johnson further says with regard to James Stuart :— " I hope the worthy translator goes diligently forward. He has a higher reward in prospect than any honours which this world can bestow. I wish I could be useful to him."[2]

During his tours in Scotland, Thomas Pennant, the English naturalist and traveller, became acquainted with James Stuart, and from him obtained a great deal of information relating to the Highlands, its people, and their language. In the preface to the first volume describing his tour to Scotland and the Hebrides in 1772, Pennant couples the name of James Stuart with that of the Rev. Mr. John Lightfoot, lecturer of Uxbridge, who was a noted botanist in his time, and who supplied him with all the botanical remarks in his book. Pennant's words are these, " To Mr. Lightfoot, I must join in my acknowledgments, the Rev. Mr. James Stuart of Killin, for a variety of hints, relating to customs of the natives of the Highlands and of the Islands, which by reason of my ignorance of the Erse or Gaelic language, must have escaped my notice. To both I am indebted for all the comforts that arise from the society of agreeable and worthy companions."

Mr. Stuart was blessed with good health throughout his long life, and to the end had the use of all his faculties almost unimpaired. In 1779, Patrick, his son, was ordained as his assistant and successor ; but he himself continued to discharge some of the parochial work until within a few months of his death, which took place on 30 June, 1789, in the eighty-ninth year of his age, and the fifty-second of his ministry. He was buried in the churchyard of Killin, but, strange to say, his grave is unmarked and unknown. It was evidently intended to erect a stone at the grave, and an epitaph[3] was prepared by his friend, Mr. Ramsay of Ochtertyre, but this pious project was never carried out, and to-day no one can point out the spot in the churchyard where this minister, so eminent for his piety, learning, and the simplicity of his life, lies buried. Fifty years ago the Gaelic Society of Perth, acting on a suggestion made by Mr. Charles Stewart of Tigh an Duin, Killin, erected a monument to James Stuart's memory in front of the church which had been built during the early years of his remarkable ministry.

PATRICK STUART was licensed 6 October, 1778, and was ordained assistant and successor to his father 27 October, 1779.

(1) Drummond was a bookseller in Edinburgh. (2) Boswell's Life of Johnson. (3) Dr. Mason's notes.

Throughout his ministry he suffered from poor health. He wrote the report of the parish of Killin for Sinclair's Statistical Account of Scotland.

HUGH MACDOUGALL, a native of Lochtayside, and a member of the family of the Macdougalls of Achomer, Ardtalnaig, was educated at St. Andrews University, and licensed at St. Andrews, 25 March, 1795. He was ordained at Killin 24 December, 1795. He married Janet, daughter of Patrick Campbell, minister of Kilninver. His son, Patrick, was professor of Moral Philosophy at the University of Edinburgh. Another son, James Ewen, was minister of Ladyloan, Arbroath. The present manse of Killin was built for Hugh MacDougall in 1806, at a cost of £700. The only part remaining of the previous house is the kitchen at the back. Hugh MacDougall died 29 July, 1827, at the age of fifty-eight years.

HUGH MACKENZIE was born at Pulrossie, Sutherland, in 1786 ; educated at the University of Aberdeen ; licensed by the presbytery of Tongue, 25 July, 1815 ; ordained missionary at Eribol, 1816 ; and translated to Assynt, 24 September, 1817. He took a medical course at Aberdeen, and graduated M.D. in 1819. He became a Member of the Royal College of Surgeons, Edinburgh. He was translated to Clyne, 3 August, 1825, and was admitted to Killin, 26 June, 1828. He was an evangelical preacher, and was always ready to give the benefit of his Medical knowledge to the poor of the parish. Hugh MacKenzie's ministry was cut short by a gig accident, from the effects of which he died 24 April, 1833. He married first, Helen, daughter of William Mackenzie, minister of Tongue. She died 7 May, 1820 ; and he married as his second wife Sophia Jane, daughter of William Mackenzie, chaplain to the 74th Regiment of Foot.

ROBERT ELDER, M.A., was translated from Kilbrandon, and admitted to Killin 18 December, 1834. From Killin he went to be minister of St. Paul's Church, Edinburgh.

ALEXANDER STEWART, born at Lochearnhead in 1811, was educated at the University of Glasgow, where he graduated M.A. in 1832. He was licensed by the presbytery of Skye, and acted for some time as missionary to the Highlanders within the presbytery of Paisley. He was ordained at Killin 24 July, 1839. At the Disruption Alexander Stewart joined the Free Church, and a church and manse were built for him by the second Marquis of Breadalbane. He married Rose Robertson. Mr. Stewart wrote the report of Killin for the New Statistical Account of Scotland.

DONALD MACNAUGHTON was born in 1782, and licensed by the presbytery of Mull, 5 May, 1828. He was ordained as missionary at Glencoe 29 March, 1813; admitted to Duror in 1828; translated to Killin 5 April, 1844. He died 31 March, 1850.

JOHN CAMPBELL was born in 1820 ; educated at Glasgow University ; and ordained at Kilchrenan 29 November, 1843. He was admitted to Killin 19 December, 1850, and died at Rothesay 3 June, 1867.

COLIN McVEAN, son of Colin McVean, minister of Kenmore, was born at Kenmore 27 July, 1813. He was educated at the University of St. Andrews, and ordained at Strontian 13 April, 1844 ; removed to Kilninver in 1849 ; and translated to Killin 16 July, 1869. He married Elizabeth, daughter of Neil Macken- zie, minister of Kilchrenan, and had a family of four sons and six daughters. Colin entered the Church, and was minister of the parish of Brydekirk, Annan ; Patrick, educated at High School and the University of Edinburgh, qualified as a doctor. He entered the Royal Navy, and on leaving the service took up a Medical practice in Bradford. He married Phyllis Yeoman who is a well known authoress, and writes under the name of " Phyllis Hambledon."

GEORGE WILLIAM MACKAY was born at Stoer, Suther- land, 23 November, 1863. He was the son of Donald Mackay, minister of Stoer, and afterwards of St. Columba's Church, Paisley, and later of a church in Canada. Mr. Mackay was educated at Stoer, at Pictou Academy, Nova Scotia, and at the University of St. Andrews. He was licensed by the presbytery of Kintyre in May, 1885 ; was assistant at Beauly and at the High Church, Inverness. He was ordained at Killin 6 June, 1888. He died at Cairnhill, Dunblane, 18 March, 1931, after a long illness. The University of St. Andrews conferred the degree of D.D. upon him in consideration of his services to the Church and his efforts to promote the Gaelic language and Highland music through the Comunn Gaidhealach, of which he was for a time president. His ministrations in the parish were singularily acceptable and he was much beloved. He worked zealously for the cause of the Union of the Churches, and was a member of the Union Committee of the Church of Scotland. After his death the congregations of the Church of Scotland and of the former United Free Church were harmoniously united.

DONALD THOMSON, born at Aird of Tong, Stornoway, 7 August, 1891 ; son of Donald Thomson and Mary Campbell ; educated at Nicolson Institute, Stornoway, and Aberdeen University, of which he is a graduate in Arts and Divinity ; trained at the United Free Church College at Aberdeen, and licensed by the presbytery of Lewis ; ordained at Avoch, June, 1918 ; translated to Brora, February, 1921 ; removed to Glasgow, Wellpark Church, September, 1924 ; admitted to the Highlanders' Memorial Church, Glasgow, May, 1927 ; became the first minister of the united congregation of Killin, 30 March, 1931 ; married Isobel Murray, who was born at Soay, Skye,

Rev. George W. Mackay, D.D., Killin (1888-1931).

12 July, 1892 ; their children are, Donald Murray, born 31 May, 1920 ; and Marie Campbell, born 9 November, 1923.

Killin Free Church.

The great majority of the congregation of Killin followed their minister, Rev. Alexander Stewart, into the Free Church at the Disruption. The Marquis of Breadalbane built a church in the village for the congregation, and until a manse was erected he placed the farmhouse of Finlarig at the disposal of the minister. The membership of the congregation in 1848 was 271, but by 1900 it had fallen to 180. Mr. Stewart retired in 1881, and was succeeded by

WILLIAM JOHN MACDONALD, M.A., eldest son of Murdo John Macdonald and Jane MacRae ; born at Barvas, Lewis, 27 September, 1854 ; educated in Lewis, and at the University and Free Church College of Aberdeen ; translated to St. Brycedale's Church, Kirkcaldy, 1887 ; died 25 May, 1902, and was buried at Cupar, Fife ; married 5 April, 1887, Alexis, daughter of the Rev. Hugh Macmillan, D.D., LL.D. of Greenock, who died in Edinburgh, 12 April, 1934. Issue—Aline Jean, born 31 August, 1891, who married (1) Cecil Blake, who died from the effects of War service, (2) Alexander Burn-Murdoch, W.S. ; Somerled, born 5 August, 1893, died November, 1919 from disease contracted while on Army service in Macedonia ; Ronald Annandale, born 23 May, 1899, a consultant psychologist in Harley Street, London, married Alison Paton Brown.

JOHN MACBEAN, son of Alexander MacBean, headmaster of Bowmore School, Islay ; was married with no issue ; translated to Tobermory in 1912.

DUNCAN MACGREGOR, a native of Taynuilt, educated at the University and Free Church College of Glasgow ; ordained 1902, and admitted to Killin 1912 ; translated to Tighnabruaich 1928, and retired to enable the two congregations there to unite ; appointed to Glencoe 1930 ; married with no issue.

GRAHAM F. ADAMSON, M.A., son of Rev. R. M. Adamson, D.D., Ardrossan ; ordained at Killin, 1928 ; retired for the sake of union, 1931 ; appointed to West Church, Grangemouth, 1932.

CHAPTER XXVI.

THE CHURCH.

Strathfillan, Ardeonaig, Lawers.

Strathfillan.

THE names of the following clergymen connected with St. Fillan's Priory, Strathfillan, appear in pre-Reformation documents :—

1414, John Mortimer, canon of Inchaffray, resigned.
1414, Clestine Johnston, canon of Inchaffray, appointed.
1486 and 1498, Dean John Murray.
1542-3, Dean John Gray, canon regular.
1547, Sir Malcolm McGillequhonill, curate.
1550, Sir Hew Curre, prior.
1555, Sir John Patersone, prior.

For many years after the Reformation Strathfillan was served by the ministers of Killin or of Kenmore. On 18 April, 1569, John McCorcadill, exhorter in Killin, was presented by king James VI. to the priory and vicarage of Strathfillan. Donald McVicar was minister there in 1585. The parish was united to Killin in 1617. This remote district, which included Glenfalloch, must have been grossly neglected by the Church until the pious Lady Glenorchy gave £1,200 to the S.P.C.K. for the purpose of building a manse and establishing a missionary in the parish who was also to serve the Braes of Glenorchy. A chapel had been built in the parish in 1744 by Thomas Clark, the builder of Killin church, at a cost of £600 Scots. The new chapel was set up where the old chapel or kirk of Strathfillan stood. This was at Kirkton. In 1772 a glebe was laid out for the minister by the third Earl of Breadalbane. A statement relating to this grant is in the following terms, " Lady Glenorchy moved with the destitute situation of these poor people, and in order to their comfort and relief has signified an intention to settle or mortify a yearly sum for the maintenance of a chaplain.

" Lord Breadalbane is to allot a portion of ground for a glebe of 6 acres 1 rood 14 falls, to include the Miller's croft, Croftvrachnish, and Ellichivulin, parts of the farm of Kirkton of

Strathfillan, with liberty of pasturing 4 cows, and a horse, and
20 sheep on the pasture of, and with the cattle of the possessors
of that farm, with liberty of casting peats, feal, or divot on the
moor of the said farm of Kirkton."*

The first minister of the restored charge was DAVID
McCULLOCH, who was presented to the parish, 3 October, 1774.

ALEXANDER MACDOUGALL was minister in 1789.

DONALD McGILLIVRAY was minister in 1813, and afterwards removed to Kilmallie.

JOHN MACDOUGALL was ordained June 20, 1822. He
was translated to Campbelltown, 22 November, 1826.

JAMES McLAURIN, a native of Callander, was educated
at the University of Edinburgh, and licensed by the presbytery
of Dunblane, 1 September, 1818. He was ordained at Glenlyon,
11 May, 1820, and admitted to Strathfillan, 10 February, 1835.
He was deposed for drunkenness and fighting in 1840, and went
to America, where he recovered himself, and had charge of a
congregation. He married Lilias Menzies of Chesthill.

ALEXANDER MACKINNON was born in Arran in 1802,
and educated at Glasgow University. He was ordained at
Strathfillan in 1840. At the Disruption he joined the Free
Church, and continued as minister of the congregation of the
Free Church in the parish until his death, 23 May, 1884. He
married, in 1845, Catherine Boston Simpson. In 1843 the church
was held by the minister and the congregation of the Free Church,
and very few of the people adhered to the Church of Scotland.
The S.P.C.K. maintained services in a small wooden erection
near Crianlarich until 1882, when the parish was disjoined
from Killin and erected into a parish *quoad sacra*. A church and
manse were built on a site granted by the third Marquis of
Breadalbane, and WILLIAM DUFF, M.A., B.D., was admitted
minister of the parish, 9 May, 1882. He was translated to
Kilninver, 14 March, 1888, and was succeeded by JOHN DOW,
who was admitted 30 September, 1888. He was translated to
Knockbain 7 December, 1892.

JAMES MACKINNON was translated from the chapel of
Kilbride, Cowal, to Strathfillan, 1 June, 1893, and removed to
Kildalton, 2 January, 1894.

GEORGE CALDER, a native of Kincardineshire, was educated
at Stonehaven, Aberdeen Grammar School, and University of
Aberdeen, where he graduated M.A. 1881. He was licensed by
the presbytery of Fordoun in 1884. He was assistant at Aber-
lour, and missionary at Struan, at Ardgour, and at Connel
Ferry. He applied himself to the study of Gaelic during his
residence at these Highland stations, and gained ability to
preach in that language. He was ordained to Strathfillan,

* B.Ps.

15 November, 1894, and after a successful ministry there of eighteen years he was appointed lecturer on Celtic at the University of Glasgow. He retired from his lectureship in 1935, and the University bestowed the degree of D.D. upon him in the following year. He married Edith, daughter of William Campbell, merchant, Leith.

NEIL DUNCAN MACKINNON was born in Tiree ; the son of Donald Mackinnon, schoolmaster, Cornaigmore school. He was educated at Glasgow University, where he graduated M.A. in 1907 and B.D. in 1911. He was ordained at Strathfillan 5 March, 1913. On the outbreak of the Great War he joined the R.A.M.C. and resigned his charge in 1920. He entered the Medical profession.

JAMES GOURLAY was ordained at Strathfillan on 21 December, 1920 ; and resigned his charge 30 September, 1929. The Rev. Alexander McColl of the United Free Church of Strathfillan resigned at the same time, and the two congregations were united, 28 January, 1930. The parish church and manse underwent complete renovation, while the church and manse of the former United Free Church were sold.

The present minister of Strathfillan, CHRISTOPHER MACKINNON, was ordained and admitted as first minister of the united charge 22 January, 1931. He is a native of Broadford, Skye ; was educated at Kingussie school, and at St. Andrews University, where he graduated M.A. in 1927. After completing his Divinity course he was assistant in Holburn Central Church, Aberdeen.

Strathfillan Free Church.

ALEXANDER MACKINNON, minister of Strathfillan at the Disruption, joined the Free Church, and continued until his death in 1884. His successors in the charge were, D. F. MACKAY (1876-1888), HUGH FRASER (1889-1911), ALEXANDER McCOLL (1911-1929). Mr. McColl retired for the sake of union.

Ardeonaig.

Before the Reformation Ardeonaig was a small parish under the charge of a resident priest. In 1474 the rector was Patrick Scott.* After the Reformation the parish was placed under the charge of the minister of Kenmore or of Killin. The parish church was at Cill-ma-charmaig, and within the existing churchyard. It was rebuilt in 1744 at a cost of £646 Scots. By 1807 the church had fallen into disrepair, and we find the minister of the time drawing the attention of the fourth Earl of Breadalbane to its condition. Soon afterwards the condition of the church became so bad that the congregation had to worship in the open air. In 1820 a church was erected on the east side of Alltvine, beside the manse which was built in 1791. At Alltvine

* Christie's Lands and Lairds, p. 68.

the church was midway between Ardtalnaig and Ardeonaig. The old Boat croft was given to the minister as a glebe.

In 1791 the S.P.C.K. established a mission on Lochtayside in order to serve the districts of Ardeonaig and Lawers. The funds for the purpose were procured from bequests left by the pious Lady Glenorchy. The first minister to be appointed to the station was COLIN McVEAN, who was ordained at Ardeonaig 3 May, 1791. He became minister of Kenmore, 13 March, 1793. At Ardeonaig his salary was £50 per annum. After a vacancy of two years he was succeeded by JOHN CAMPBELL, a native of Killin, where his family had a holding. He had a brother a surgeon who was abroad, probably with the Army, in 1807.

The next minister of Ardeonaig and Lawers was ROBERT FINDLATER, the memory of whose devoted ministry still lives on Lochtayside, where he turned many to righteousness. He was settled there by the presbytery of Dunkeld in April, 1810, and continued until he was translated to the Chapel of Ease at Inverness in May, 1821, where he died of Cholera, 7 September, 1832, in the forty-sixth year of his age. Findlater was a native of Kiltearn, Ross-shire. The story of his life and of the religious movements on Lochtayside and elsewhere in the Highlands with which his remarkable ministry was associated is told in a memoir of him written by his brother, Rev. William Findlater of Durness, and published in 1840.

The following ministers served the charge of Ardeonaig in succession to Robert Findlater :—

ALEXANDER MACKENZIE, 1821-1824.

COLIN HUNTER, 1824-1827.

DONALD MACKENZIE, who was a nephew of the Rev. Lauchlan Mackenzie of Lochcarron, was ordained at Ardeonaig, 21 December, 1827. He continued until his death, 10 October, 1873, and was buried in the Ardeonaig churchyard.

Donald Mackenzie joined the Free Church at the Disruption, and the majority of the congregation followed him. The Church of Scotland left the minister and congregation in possession of the buildings. In 1834, when a new church was erected at Lawers, that district was separated from Ardeonaig, and an ordained minister was appointed to serve there.

JOHN McCALLUM, 1874-1907, retired ; and died at Edinburgh, 21 November, 1909.

DONALD MACKINTOSH, 1907-1912.

JOHN SOUTER, 1912-1918.

ARCHIBALD McCALL, 1918-22, now minister of Glenmoriston. After Mr. McCall's departure the status of the congregation was reduced owing to the decrease in the population, and since then the charge has been served by ordained missionaries.

Lawers.

At the beginning of last century the old church of Lawers fell into disrepair, and as the population of the district at that time numbered over 1,500 souls, it was decided to set up a separate mission for that part of Lochtayside, and to erect a new church close to the public road, on the lands of Tomb. A manse for the minister was built beside the church. The foundation stone of the new church was laid on 16 May, 1833.

The first minister of the mission at Lawers was DUNCAN CAMPBELL, a native of Glenlyon, where he was born, 21 August, 1796. He was educated at the University of Edinburgh, and licensed by the presbytery of Dunkeld. For two years before coming to Lawers he worked under the Perth City Mission. From Lawers he removed to Glenlyon in 1837, where he became minister of the Parliamentary and *Quoad Sacra* parish. In 1835 he married Margaret, daughter of Dr. John Macdonald of Ferintosh who was a frequent visitor to Lawers, Ardeonaig, and Glenlyon during the revivals of the early decades of the eighteenth century. Duncan Campbell and his brother David— who had preceded him in the Perth City Mission and was at a later date also minister at Lawers—had come under the influence of Robert Findlater during his ministry on Lochtayside, and both were notable evangelical preachers, especially in the Gaelic language. People went long distances across hills, lochs, and rivers to attend their services. In 1842 Duncan Campbell was translated to Kiltearn, Ross-shire, where he died in 1873. The story of his ministry on Lochtayside is told in a little book written by the Rev. Duncan MacGregor, minister in Dundee, who was himself a native of Breadalbane, and intimately acquainted with the Campbells.

DUGALD CAMPBELL, a native of the island of Lismore, was minister at Lawers from 1837 to 1842.

At the Disruption the congregation joined the Free Church, and retained possession of both church and manse. In 1843 JOHN LOGAN was settled at Lawers, and continued there until 1854, when he removed to Dundee. He was succeeded by DAVID CAMPBELL, brother of Duncan, the first minister of the mission. David Campbell died at Lawers in 1877, and was buried at Kerromore, Glenlyon.

MURDOCH MORRISON came to Lawers in 1878, and continued there until 1888, when he was called to Bernera, Harris. His son, Rev. A. J. Morrison, M.A., is at present (1937) one of the ministers in the city of Aberdeen.

ALLAN MACKENZIE was ordained at Lawers in November, 1889, and continued until his death which took place while he was on holiday at Stornoway, in May, 1910.

WALTER CALDER came to Lawers from Stornoway in 1911, and continued there until he retired from the ministry in 1929. Mr. Calder was born at Swordale, Bonar Bridge, 15 April, 1851 ; was educated at Aberdeen University and Free Church College ; married Annie Lawrence Black, who died at Lawers, April, 1927. Their family are—Walter J. R. Calder, minister of Strichen, Aberdeenshire ; James B. Calder, schoolmaster, Monquhitter ; and Alexander Calder, medical doctor, Hornsea, Yorkshire. Before going to Stornoway Mr. Calder had been minister at Bourtreebush (Kincardine), and at Strathy. He died at the Manse of Strichen, 26 March, 1937, and was buried at Machuim, Lawers. He was a man of gracious personality. All through his long ministry he advocated the union of the Free Church and the Church of Scotland, and on his retirement the congregation connected with the former Church of Scotland at Carwhin united with that of Lawers. Mr. Calder published a brochure on Lawers and its ministers. The united congregation called KENNETH MACLENNAN from Mallaig to be their minister. Although he was a native of Harris, Kenneth MacLennan's ministry, except for the few years at Mallaig, had been passed in China and in Canada in connection with the Canadian Presbyterian Church. His wife, Elizabeth MacLeod, a native of Tarbert, Harris, died at Lawers, and shortly after her death he returned to Canada, where his family had settled.

ALEXANDER ANDERSON STRATHEARN, M.A., born at Kirriemuir, Angus, 12 July, 1879 ; son of Alexander Anderson Strathearn and Mary Rodger ; educated at Webster's Seminary, Kirriemuir, United College, St. Andrews, and New College, Edinburgh ; licensed at Newton Stewart, 10 September, 1907 ; ordained to Cargill United Free Church, 6 January, 1909 ; inducted to Liff, 29 April, 1915 ; Blair Atholl, 20 October, 1920 ; translated to Lawers, 8 November, 1933 ; joint-clerk to the Presbytery of Dunkeld since the Union of the Churches in 1929, and prior to that had been clerk to the United Free Church Presbytery of Breadalbane. He is now sole clerk to the Presbytery.

CHAPTER XXVII.

THE CHURCH.

Kirk Session Records.

THE records of the Kirk Session of Kenmore begin with the ministry of Mr. William Menzies in 1636 ; and although there are several blank periods, these records constitute a most valuable source of information with regard to the religious and social condition of the people. During the first hundred years entries of baptisms and proclamations are intermixed with entries of acts of discipline, collections, fines received from delinquents, and disbursements from the box to the poor.

The earliest baptimal register of the Killin Church dates from 1689, and with the exception of two blank periods—1698 to 1709, and 1717 to 1727—it is complete until 1854. The register of proclamations was begun in 1687, and is blank from 1698 to 1709, and again from 1717 to 1782. The Session minutes of Killin Church have been lost, and the earliest record of finance is a cash book which was begun on 6 January, 1774. From that date it gives a complete account of the Session's financial transactions until 1806.

Extracts from Kenmore Kirk Session Minutes.

2 March, 1636—The names of the infantes Baptised at Candmoir.

Number of baptisms in 1638—35, in 1639—34.

2 February, 1639—Given out the said day to Andro Scott, wright, for putting up a new Bell house the soume of 12 lbs. money, and the 22s and 8d to be given to the wright's boyes for rests. Nothing in the box of balance before this day.

27 September, 1640—Thomas Whyt, John Menzies, Patrick Campbell, and John Campbell ar appointed to go thro the paroch to collect the voluntar contribution, as likewise to tak notice of all kloth that is to sell, and that warning be given to the sellers to bring it for to be sold to the sojours.

17 October, 1641—A dollar taken out of the box and given to Mr. Thomas Glass, bursar.

7 March, 1641—The Laird, minister and elders being present, they renewed the old act that ilk person wanting the Belief and the Ten Commandments shall pay 40s.

22 May, 1643—The said day the minister and elders did ordaine such as came not to the Communion to be summoned

before the Session that they protest against such as had not a Bible and Belief according to the order of the Kirk.

23 January, 1643—Duncan, John, Alexander, Mary, and Elspet NcKillop compeared upon the stole of repentance for not taking Communion this year.

8 August, 1643—Donald McIanduglass and Alester Mcalester made their publick repentance for not communicating.

7 January, 1645—The minister and elders being convened, it was regrated that ther wer many poore people who wer burnd and spoyled and had nothing to live on, and ther was taken out of the box III lbs qlk was distribut the said day.

The said day it was shown that the Kirk bason was taken away be the enemies, and the Kirk lock broken, and the smyth is desyred to mak a lock therfor.

4 May, 1645—The minister and elders being convened there was ane admonition given to the brewsters to be at the Kirk everie Sabbath, and to sell no drink in time of divine service under paine of V lbs.

30 May, 1647—The said day John McPhail, elder, was ordained to bring the box to the house of Balloch, and to bring it furth everie Sabbath, and at all occasions being required.

The names of the defunct elders since the last visitation (of Presbytery) :—Sir Mungo Campbell, John Campbell (elder), Donald Dow, Alistar Gald, James Campbell, John Campbell (younger), James Mcilichear, Patrick Bane, Ewen McEwen, The names of the elders and members of the Session at this present :—John Campbell fiar of Glenurchay, Alexander Menzies of Comrie, Patrick Campbell in Portbane, Thomas Whyt, Gilchryst Roy McArthir, Donald McCommie, John McPhail (elder), John Menzies, Patrick McPhatrick Roy, Malcolm Mclean, George Lumsdane in Lawers, Alexander Crearar, Duncan McPhatrick Vic Robert.

6 July, 1647—The Laird, Minister, and elders being present, and they taking to hart the manifold abuses at young brydles in the country have ordained herafter that all young brydles in the paroch shall not extend ls. the man, and the number shall not exceed VIII persons the syde ; and attour the bryde and brydegroome and their parties shall pledge a dollar the syde for obedience to the Act.

22 June, 1648—This day six pounds money lent out of the box to Patrick Beg McKercher to be payit before the last of August next 1648 under the paine of dubbling. Cautioner for him, Patrick Campbell.

21 October, 1649—This day the paroch was distributed among the elders.

26 May, 1650—This day intimation of a publick thanksgiving· was made to be keepit on Wednesday the 29th. of this instanto.

11 August, 1650—This day ane publick fast was observit for the pnt calamities on the Kingdom be the incoming of the English. This day a deliverance of the Universall Assembly was read against the declaration of the English Parliament.

22 June, 1651—This day the publick Fast was observit and publick intimation made anent a voluntarie contribution to the armie.

3 August, 1651—This day Patrick Campbell, Thomas Whyt, siclik Donald McOrthir, and Donald McVane declared that they sought among their bounds the voluntarie contribution, but could get nothing.

28 March, 1652—The said day the elders wer exhorted to continue in their familie worship.

2 May, 1652—The said day ther was given out of the box for ane bason for the baptisms 02—02—00.

27 June, 1652—The said day John——, sevant to Donald McCome in Ardrednike for the tyme, is cited for libbing of lambs on the sabbath day.

1 August, 1652—The said day the Act anent the breaking of the Sabbath was announced because of persons that went to the woods to gather nuts.

15 August, 1652—This day the supply for Glasgow was intimate.

5 September, 1652—This day a publick fast is intimated to be keepit the 12 and 19 September, and the reasons therefor publickly read.

7 November, 1652—This day the contribution for Glasgow is sent be Donald McChercher to Mr. Boreland, minister at——to be sent to Glasgow.

1 May, 1653—This day the elders wer exhorted to go among their quarters to urge familie worship, and to see if ther be Swearers, Drunkards, and Sabbath breakers.

27 January, 1656—This day a publick intimation is made be the Session and the Justices of Peace against any manner of buying and selling on the Lord's day privately or publickly.

11 May, 1656—This day Mr. William Anderson, assistant, preached, the minister himself ye said day at Lawers to a number of people, Ther was collected for the poore Vs—4d.

1 June, 1656—Intimation is made of a support to be given to the distressed in Edinburgh which were impoverished be fyre, and to be prepared before the end of June.

22 June, 1656—This day Thomas Whyt was ordained be the Session to present their supplication to Colonel Daniel for reparation of the losses done be the armie to the Kirk, and 31s. Scots allowed him thairfor.

19 October, 1656—Being the Sabbath after the Synod the minister preached in the Chappel of Shian within the paroch.

22 May, 1660—Qlk day preached Mr. Coline Campbell, minister at Blair in Atholl, at the admissione of Mr. Patrick Campbell to the Church.

....

The Kirk box being brought present and opened ther was found in it eight lbs. eleven shillings and eight pence gross. Ther was ordained to be given to Eyen Smith for making of glass bands to the church windows 4 merks 5s. Given to Patrick Wright for making weir casements 4 merks. Resting in the box of old collections and penalties 4 merks 6s. 8d. Qlk day it was enquired if ther wer any fornicators or adulterers who had not satisfied in the paroch, and if ther wer, their names should be brought in the next day.

3 June, 1660—Qlk day no Session in regard the minister was speedlie called to the Ladie Glenurchie who was then seeke.

10 June, 1660—Qlk day ther was 3 lbs. ordained to be given to Patrick Dewar for making up a stoole of repentance.

17 June, 1660—Qlk day it was ordained that no testimonial should be given by any of the elders, but at the Session.

22 July, 1660—Qlk day the Session taking to their consideration the great abuse of the Sabbath by many, especialie in tyme of divine service that many lie about without the Church, and will not come in to hear sermon, ordain two of their number to go out each day in tyme of sermon and take notice of the transgressors of that nature that they may be accordinglie punished.

Qlk day the Session considering the great abuses there has been committed these years bygone on the Sabbath days by a number of people frequenting the woods for gathering of nuts on the Sabbath ; therfor for preventing of the evil in tyme coming they ordain that non shall frequent the woods for that end on the Sabbath day, and if any be found by the surveyors therin, everie man that hes a familie by and attour his satisfaction as a scandalous person shall pay 3 lbs. *toties quoties* ; everie man or woman servant 30s. ; and everie man for his children, if they be found ther 20s ; and the Act ordained to be intimate by the Bedal to the people next day.

13 December, 1668—No sermon in regard of the tempestousness of the weather, no boat crossing so as the minister could not get to the church.

10 October, 1669—Qlk day given to Neill McArthur out of the box for taking down the bell and mending the bell and bell house 3 lbs.

5 June, 1670—Qlk day was intimate to the congregation that ther was appointed a collection for the towns of Dundee and Kilmarnock, and they wer exhorted to bring in the same against the next Sunday. Qlk day Catherine NcGrigor ordered to the stoole.

T

19 March, 1671—Qlk day given to Thomas Williamson, slater, as two years' pension for mending the Kirk—8 lbs.

23 March, 1673—Qlk day Wm. Rutherford, John McGrigor, and Maryt King all in Shian in this paroch ar ordained to be summoned against the next day for drinking and playing on the Sabbath night.

29 May, 1673—Collected 9s. qlk together with 12s. out of the box given to Duncane McGrigor, supplicant, who was going to London to be cured of the King's Evil.

7 March, 1676—On which day Master Alexander Comrey was entroduced to the Kirk of Kenmore. The same day Mr. William Nairne, moderator, with severall others of the brethren present got a sight off what money was in the box which in all extended to seven pounds ten shillings Scots.

12 March, 1676—There was nothing done, but only the minister sought for the Session book to which the elders answer was that a gentleman in the paroch called Robert Stirling had it in his custody.

30 January, 1687—At the Church of Kendmore, this day Mr. Duncane McGrigor was received by the minister to be reader and precentor.

6 March, 1687—Donald McEnoig, having grossly miscarried to the minister this by-past week by reason of his beastly drunkenness before the people that were gathered for the examination, is ordered by the Session to give signs of repentance, and make satisfaction this next Thursday at the publick examination at the Church.

12 July, 1687—Taken out of the box to be lent to Robert Stirling in Lawers the sum of forty pounds Scots money, which sum was delivered and his bond for payment of the same was taken, and it being payable at the terme of Martinmas next.

7 August, 1687—This day was collected for the poor twenty-four shillings. Given for helping to build the Bridge of Anstruther, or harbour I suppose it was.

20 June, 1693—No more sermons till the 22 July, the ministers forbearing because of the oaths proposed; but since by Providence and the goodness of God they were indulged.

25 August, 1695—There was no sermon at Kenmore from Sabbath 25th. till September 15th, because of the Act of Parliament against ministers.

10 May, 1696—This day the Earl of Breadalbane sitting with the Minister and his Lordship's chamberlain, Mungo Campbell of Kinloch, sitting in the Session, it was enacted with the consent of all pnt that the schoolmaster of Kenmore henceforward should have an hundred merks of salary payable yearly at Whitsunday.

3 July, 1697—Saturday there was a sermon preached in Irish by Mr. Robert Stewart, another in English by Mr. Alexr. Robson,

and preparatory to serving the Sacrament of the Lord's Supper on the morrow. Collected 5 lb. 1s. Sunday—The sacrament was celebrated, coll. 24 lb. 6s. 8d. Munday coll. 3 lb. 2s. The poore of the paroch were convened and according to their exigencies every one got part of the collections.

18 July, 1697—It was enacted this day that the poor should attend sermon and catechising, otherwise their names where absent their-selves are to be cancelled out of the Roll of the Poor.

9 May, 1698—Munday, this day both in English and Irish there was sermon and the people exhorted to thankfulness, obediance and faithfulness in performing their vows and promises made at the Lord's Table yesterday. Coll. 9 lbs. 6s. 8d. Given to the poor fourty lb. 10s. Poor's list of 66 names.

22 July, 1699—Given out to buy white iron to be badges for the poor 02—19—00.

24 September, 1699—This day the Earle of Breadalbane sitting in Session with the Minister and elders, the people of Lawers etc. being summoned from the pulpit Sunday last were convened, and being accused for not waiting on the ordinances were sharply rebuked, threatened, and exhorted to better and more frequent attendance.

14 April, 1700—Given out to buy a large coat for the beddle which he is to wear only when in office 4—0—0.

15 September, 1700—It was enacted this day that because the Session was troubled with people suggested to use enchantments, any who were found to use any charms should be reported guilty of witchcraft.

1 June, 1701—People were exhorted several Sundays to prepare themselves for receiving the Holy Eucharist against Sunday next, and to stay and get their tockens this day, and who would not take them this day to wait upon the Minister on Saturday next after the Irish and English sermons were over.

8 June, 1701—Whitsunday—Mr. Mungo Murray, minister of Logierait, preached the Irish sermon, and Mr. Alexander Comrie, minister of Kenmore, the English sermon in the forenoon and afternoon, and after the latter had excommunicated and invited, as use is, then the Elements were blessed and distributed devoutly to eight tables. Colln. for 3 days 62s.—12d. Scots.

16 August, 1702—Sunday, the Minister was detained by rains and rivers on his road from Stratherne.

20 June, 1703—Lent to Patrick Taylor, elder in Lawers, six pounds Scots out of the Box, payable on demand. Given out of the Box, towards the repairing the Leonardine Colledge twelve pounds Scots.

21 November, 1703—Given to Finlay McThomie to buy his son a winding-sheet 16s. 6.

16 January, 1704—Lent to Quentine Ross out of the Box on bond, Dond McIntyre in Kenmore Cautioner, three pounds

LOCH TAY AND BEN MORE FROM ARDTALNAIG.

sterling to buy a stell which is pawn for it. Given to Mrs. Robson, a minister's relict, 40s. Scots.

17 September, 1704—Given to a man who had a living creature in his stomach one shilling.

25 August, 1706—Compeared John McNeill late McGregour. Stix, and confessed that on the —— day of June last he took physick from John Drummond for an exquisit paine he had in his stomach for 5 years or thereby, and by it and a plaister applied outwardly within 24 hours he void at the fundament two big stones produced there, and immediately after he found ease of his pain.—A prodigy.

31 March, 1708—Mr. Coline Campbell of Ardmaddy, the Ear of Breadalbane's 3rd son dyed at London.

27 March, 1710—Letter from the Earl of Breadalbane to the Minister and Kirk Session of Kenmore :—" Whereas it pleased God to remove my son Master Coline at London, the last day of March, 1708, He did by his latter will Mortifie and bequaeth an Hundred pounds sterling in money Chargeable upon His Estate in Nether Lorne : and the annual rent thereof To be yearly paid by Our order and Our successors Direction and the Minister and Kirk Session of Kenmore to the said Minister and Kirk Session of that parish . . . . . . to be distribute by the said Minister and Session To Six indigent persones condescended upon by him . . . .

The interest was accordingly distributed to the following :— Margaret McGregor, Mill of Acharn, Donald Fisher in Acharn, John McDerack, Mill of Cloichran, Finlay Mciliwie in Tullich, of Glenlochie, Mary McKimie in Edramuckie.

14 June, 1713—Tuesday being a day of thanksgiving for the peace with France. Coll. 5s. 10d.

8 November, 1721—Being the Lord's day, quhilk day John Grahame, schoolmaster, was received by the Minr. and Session to be reader and precentor.

4 June, 1723—Mr. John Hamilton, Late minister of Blair in Atholl, where he was ordained minister, February 25, 1718, And being transported therefrom to Kenmure was Admitted there June 4, 1723, Mr. Robert Bissett, present minister at Blair, but at my Admission was minister at Kirkmichaell in Strath Ardle, preached the Admission Sermon In the Kirk of Kenmure.

9 June, 1723—This day the minister did ask at John Graham (schoolmaster) He being Clark to the Session in Mr. Alexander Comrie Late Incumbent his time, Whither or not The Session in his time had any utensiles belonging to the Kirk and In whose Custody they were, Answered that to his knowledge, they had, silver cups for the Communion, a Kirk Box, bible, mort-cloath, and, as he thinks, a plate for the Communion Elements, and that, as he supposed were in Mr. Comrie's Custody, and David

Walker's box-master, to the Session, and that they had left the Laver for Baptism within the Church, it being for daily use.

8 September, 1723—Donald and Neil McGrigors in Fernan who formerly sate with Mr. Comrie, late Incumbent here, in his Session, appear this day.

21 October, 1723—Hugh (Ewen) McDugall in Glentallanaig and Donald Mcgorrive in Ardtallanaig, who two used to sit with Mr. Comrie in his Session. The minister to wryt to David Walker, Box-master to Mr. Comrie's Session, anent the Kirk Box, and the keys thereof, that he deliver up the same to this Meeting, and that the Minister should wryt a letter to Mr. Campbell of Auchaulader, anent a year's arent of one hundred pounds sterling money, sometime agoe Mortifyed by the Deceased Mr. Coline Campbell, Late of Ardmaddy, to the Poor of the Paroch of Kenmure.

26 December, 1723—At Taymouth, Present, Mr. Alexander Comrie, Mr. John Hamilton, David Walker, John Barrow. Patrick Campbell at Kenmure, Duncan Forrister Gardiner at Taymouth. The sd Committee received from Mr. Comrie, These following utensils ; The Poor's box having two locks and two Keys, wherein was of money not distribute the sume of thirteen pounds twelve shillings and two pennies Scots Money. Together with the Receipts and Discharges thereto belonging for what was disbursed in Mr. Comrie's time, with two hundred and eighty Communion tokens and a large peuter plate to hold the Sacramental bread, with two Communion Cupps of silver having the following Inscription Ingraven on them, For the Kirk of Kenmure, Anno 1685 ; Received also the Mort Cloath

(Blank in Records until 1728).

15 December, 1728—The Session not Constitute by reason of the coldness and badness of the day, which was far spent, and that Mr. Mcleish absolutely refused to give a sight of the minutes in his Custody, alleadging for his Refusal that he would only give them to the Powers from whom he had Received them.

22 December, 1728—Compeared Patrick Campbell, Vintner at Kenmure, and sat with the Elders, whereupon the Modr. in name of the Session, Asked him whether or not he had any affair to lay before them, Answered, That by virtue of an order from the Earl of Breadalbane's Commissioners to attend the Session according to Custom formerly, He took place therein, that according to the Power granted him He might oblidge any who might hereafter prove contumacious to the Session in the Exercise of their discipline to be obseqious.

23 February, 1729—Janet Nelmichael rebuked in sackcloth before the Congregation for the first time, she having been remitted to the Session by the Committee of the Presbyterie, which sat a long time ago at Inchaiden to take in delinquents.

16 March, 1729—All other affairs are superseded this day because the persons foresaid were not summoned because the Minister should have gone to Glenqueach this day, but could not for the Storm of frost and snow in the hill and The Beddell Lying Sick.

John Barrow appointed to speak to Mr. Mcleish to take account of his schollars for breaking the glass and weir of the Kirk.

30 March, 1729—The Session Appoints to Alexr. Mciandui in Ballynaskaig, a poor man with a numerous family, one shilling sterling money—Given to David Walker, elder, to give him.

20 April, 1729—The minister having laid before the Session the necessity of keeping Privy censures from time to time forward, in obedience to the Acts of the Assembly of this National Church, are satisfied the same begin Wednesday next, the Fast day, after Sermon.

23 April, 1729—Fast day appointed by the Synod of Stirling for their bad season and prevailing sickness thro year—Prayers said.

The Session went about Privy censures this day according to their resolution taken last dyet, And all the elders being removed one by one, and the usuall Questions proposed to them, they Answered them satisfyingly & their Life and Conversation being Inquired into, nothing was found in them but what was savory, and so were Encouraged in the Lord. The Beddel also was removed & his Life and Conversation as a Christian and his behaviours as Beddel being Inquired into, nothing was found but what was savory, and so Encouraged Likewise.

8 June, 1729—The Session being informed that Patrick McVurich, Lunatic, asks for a Testimonial, Its referred to this dyet that so Inquiry may be duly made of what the Design by it, whether his friends intend to convey him to a Popish priest or not, and if that be not, what use a Madman can make of it, if he leave the Country alone.

13 July, 1729—The Session appoints two shillings sterling to be given to ——— Campbell, daughter to Mr. James Campbell late minister of the Gospel at Killinver and Melford in Nether Lorn, who is reduced to great straits by the death of her cattell.

23 November, 1729—The Session appoints one pound eight shillings and four pennies Scots money to the Smith for shakels mending, & a new one making for John McNicol, a madman.

28 December, 1729—The Minister went to the ferry, but could not get crossing for the storminess of the day, and so no sermon at Kenmure—but at Inchaidon there was both lecture and sermon to all that came thither, and on that side of the water.

8 March, 1730—Patrick Campbell reports he received a Letter from John Tait, Glazier in Crieff, craving paymt for glazing the Kirk, Wherefore the Session appoints the Minr to write a letter

to Ardeonaig to pay up his bill with Certification that if He do it not They are to hand it to Edr for a horning.

11 October, 1730—The Minister reporting to the Session that he wanted a seat That Alexander Forrister, son to Duncan Forrister, Gardiner to My Lord Breadalbane, having taken possession of the room and seat in the name of the Laird of Strowan Robertson in which the Minr used to sit formerly, and to avouch Strowan's right thereto in whose name he possesses the same, said that the Division of the Kirk was registrate in the records of the Session In Mr. William Menzies' time.

September 4, 1653.

This day the Elders and most of the Heritors being present, Alexander Menzies of Comrie Craved that a part should desyned to him to set up a seat within the Kirk which was unanimously granted viz :—That He should have the liberty to set up an seat 6 foot in Length on the north side of the Kirk Contiguous with the Laird of Glenurchay's seat upon the west hand ; And it is also ordained that all the seats already set up stand unmoved in all time coming to the present owners and to their successors, heritors within the paroch ; And therefor desyred that their   designation should be registrate in the Kirk book *ad futuram rei memoriam* after this manner :—That is to say, 2 dasks appertaining to the Lairds of Glenurchay on the North side, bewest the partition wall ; one side appertaining to the Laird of Laurs on the south side close to the partition wall forsaid. A seat set up by Mr. William Menzies as Heritor of Wester Shian betwixt the Laird of Laurs & the pulpit ; An dask appertaining to the Laird of Strowan Robertson on the south side of the Kirk bewest the pulpit ; An dask to be set up by the said Alexr. Menzies of Comrie as above mentioned.

15 November, 1730—This day Compeared Donald McGrigor one of the elders at Fernan And Angus Mcdonald, officer to the Laird of Strowan there, and Entered a Complaint that they had no room in the Kirk to accomodate the people, Tennants in the 20 pound Lands of Fernan, and were constrained to stand at the Time of Divine service, particularly such of them as could not purchase seats for themselves for that dyet, and that the ground allotted in the Church for the Lands of Fernan was occupied by others, and that they had planted seats thereon to the exclusion of the people of Fernan, the rightful owners, from their possession, and that they had suffered this treatment for a long time etc.

The Session taking the above affair into Consideration with them as to the present disadvantage they laboured under, and being straitened how to direct them for a speedy remedy thereof, resolved That all that the Session could take upon themselves to do was to lay the matter before the Earle of Breadalbane, undoubted patron, or before His Honourable Commissioners, with the rest of the Heritors concerned.

28 February, 1731—The Session appoints four shillings Scots to David Waker boxmr. for making a Little box to go within the prill one and to keep the white money.

21 March, 1731—One pound three shillings Scots to be given to Hugh McGrigor, son to Grigar McGrigar in Dualan, a poor boy at the school of Lawrs to buy a bible to the sd boy.

13 June, 1731—This day Professor Crauford preached at Kenmure being Sabbath, and collected after sermon fourteen shillings Scots money.

4 July, 1731—Six shillings Scots to Mary Stewart, a poor object Labouring under a Cancer in her face wt five small children, well Attested from the paroch of Magera, in Ireland, dated Febr. 2, 1731.

18 July, 1731—Preaching at Glenqueach. After sermon which was at Turrerich. Collected one pound fifteen shillings and four pennies Scots. Dundas and his Lady at the Goat whey.

12 August, 1731—Fast day before the Sacrament. Collected ten pounds eight shillings and eight pennies Scots.

Hugh Mcdougall for the Bread, Mr. Mungo and James Waker for the cupps. John Barrow and Dold Mclgorrive for the Tockens. David Waker and Duncan McMihi for the stops (stoups) ; Donald and Neil McGrigar for the Collections ; Andrew Waker and William Stewart also for the same ; Doors, John Lumsdane and Donald Mclean in Lawrs for the east door. West door, John Ferguson and William Anderson in Ballynasium.

14 August, 1731—Saturday before the Sacrament. Coll. eight pounds & eight shillings Scots.

15 August, 1731—Communion day. Collected fifty pd. seventeen shill. & six pennies.

16 August, 1731—Munday after Sacrament. Coll. eight pounds eight shilling Scots.

22 August, 1731—Sum of Collections at Sacrament 78 pds. 2 shill. 2d. This day distribute of above, To Mary Mcdonald, Corsmichael, well attested by the Minr., Mr. Andrew Dick & the Justices of the peace that she & her husband being going to New England suffered shipwrack & Lost about 100 pd. sterling Money. Given one shilling sterling. To Duncan Menzies, old Beddel of Weem, a poor man, given also one shilling sterling.

24 August, 1731—The collections taken at the Sacrament season were distributed to 53 poor people in the parish.

To Mr. Mcleish, schoolmr. and precentor, six pounds Scots.

John Macintyre, in Lawrs, schoolmr. for precenting in Irish three pounds Scots.

John Campbell in Glenqueach, schoolmr. a poor boy, half a crown stg.

John Ban, Kirk officer, for his service, three pounds Scots.

William Anderson for fixing the Communion Table and Keeping the door during the serving of the Tables, six pence Scots.

John Ferguson, Weaver, for keeping the other door, six shill. Scots.

The Sess., finding that John Pawtown now in Kenmure did come into the Kirk This morning and set up his seat, and took asunder the communion table and did several other things, appoints him to be sumd to Tuesday.

2 January, 1732—Archibald Campbell delinquent & Kathren McPhaul payed four pounds Scots mulct betwixt them, This given to John Mcintyre, schoomr. in Lawrs to help to pay his board.

9 January, 1732—The Session appoints three shillings Scots to the Beddel to buy a Creel of peets for firing in the Schoolhouse when the Session sitts during this cold season there

27 February, 1732—The Session appoints one shilling sterling to one John Ferguson, a poor schollar at Lawrs school.

10 September, 1732—The Session appoints one shilling sterling money To James, Mary, and Anna Hamilton, Three children belonging to one Capt. Hamilton & his spouse Elizabeth Hamilton who were lost at sea coming from Philadelphia in Pensilvania to set up in Scotland, but their children above named were saved by the good providence of God from the shipwracke, and the said Capt. Lost with himself the sume of 900 lb. sterling as their certificate dated at Somersershire shews, dated the 9 day of February, 1731, more fully bears.

29 October, 1732—Mortcloath given out to the funeral of Mr. George Robertson his mother who was interred November 1, 1732, and given in to the Session therefor half a crown, the price being now lessened, In regard that the Session of Weem have got a fine velvet one better than this which is only of plush, and the said half crown put in the box.

26 November, 1732—John Mcintyre, schoolmr. in Lawres, applyed the Session for help to pay the wryting Table in his school.

John Campbell, schoolmr. at Auchianich, applyed the Session for payment of wages for some poor schollars.

17 June, 1733—The Assistants wryton to for the Sacrament designed the 5 Sabbath of July viz :—the 29th day thereof are as follows :—
Fast day Irish, myself.
                English—Mr. Adam at Killin.
Saturday, English—Mr. Archibald Campbell at Weem.
                Irish—Mr. Duncan Mclea at Dull.
Communion Sabb. Action Sermon—English, myself.
                        Irish—Mr. Duncan Mclea.
(After serving of English tables Mr. John Logan in English).

Sabbath night, English—Mr. Fergus Ferguson.
Irish—Mr. Mclea.
All to take their respective turns at the tent
during the time of serving the tables.
Munday, English—Mr. Adam Ferguson at Killin.
Irish—Mr. John Logan, preacher.

1 July, 1733—Mr. John Mcleish craved a Testimonial from the Session declaring that since He came to Kenmure he taught a considerable number of schollars gratis.

25 August, 1734—The Minister reports that He saw a Printed Recommendation in favour of one Christian Handy, a Turk born at Smyrna, and taken by the Spaniards, was robbed and came to Britain, turned Christian & was baptised, dated Aug. 10, 1733, recommending him as an object of Charity to all the presbyteries and sessions in the Kingdom. The Session therefor appointed him five shillings sterling money.

27 April, 1735—Collected this day five pound three shilling & eight pennies Scots money, My Lord Minto and My Lord Monzie being at sermon occasioned the collection this day to be 05 03 08.

The Session appoints one shilling sterling to Margaret Ncintyre alias Nclnoive, a poor old woman in Port Lochtay.

They appoint two shilling sterling To Kathren Stalker in Peet croft Lying in the Dropsie.

David Waker, Treasurer, reports that He & Mr. Mungo Campbell according to the Session's appointment sold to John Mcilontic, Tinkard in the west end, nine pound and a half-penny of bad sanded copper babies which were of no manner of use & got for them one pound seven shillings Scots of currant money, which is of loss seven pound thirteen shilling & six pennies Scots.

The Session appoints Hector Mclean, a poor supplicant from Tirii in Crosigar who had his House & Plenishing & Cattel & one of his children burned, as Attested by Archibald Campbell, Bailiff the 3d day of February 1735 & Mr. William Morison, Minister, Sixpence.

11 May, 1735—The Afternoon sermon at Taymouth. The Earle having a sore Leg & could not come to Church & My Lord Monzie Likewise being there. Collected one pound six shilling Scots.

1 February, 1736—The Mortcloath was given out last Lord's day to the funerals of Mr. Alexander Campbell, sometime a preacher, commonly called by the nick name Padua, and he being but poor and Living mostly upon charity, The Session Thought fit to Exact no more from his Exottrs for it than what a Tennant within their own parish is to pay, which is eighteen shillings Scots, which his Cousin Duncan Campbell in Tomintegill has promised to pay.

11 April, 1736—There being a complaint given in by the people of the sucken of the Mill of Aucharn against Isobel NcCorkadale

& Helen Criarar, her daughter in Tomgarrive, for raising nick-
names upon all her neighbours about were appointed to be sumd
to their next dyet.

9 May, 1736—The Session This day have found that sometime
since their Last meeting here which was upon the 25 of Aprile
last the Poor's box was broken & the Poor's (money) stolen out
of it, particularly a Guinea & a half of Gold, a Crown & three
or four shillings of White money in specie & besides a Great
dale of Copper currant, the sume of which the Session knows
not as yet. The Session have appointed the Box to be lodged
in John Haggart's untill it be mended & find out a fitt place
for keeping it for Time to come.

18 September, 1737—The Last Lord's Day an act of the General
Assembly was read for a collection to the Chirurgeons at Edinburgh, and this being the Day appointed for the said Collection
& the Session considering the smallness of the above Collection,
they thought it proper to appoint fortey six shilling & 6 pennies
to be added to it.

18 December, 1737—The Session appoints a shilling sterling
to be sent to Perth to buy a Tow for the Bell.

18 March, 1739—This day compeared James Fraser alias
McKimi, son to the Late Patrick McKimi Late in Rumuky, and
Craved a Certificate, He being to go to the Lowlands to Herd.
The Session knowing nothing why he may not get one Appointed
a Certificate to be given him.

23 March, 1743—Which day Mr. John Douglass was ordained
Minister of the Gospel in the Parish of Kenmore by the Reverend
Presbytery of Dunkeld, Mr. Thomas Man, Minister of Dunkeld,
having preached the Ordination sermon. After sermon the
Presbytery kept Session and admitted the said Mr. Douglass
Member of the Kirk Session of Kenmore.

24 June, 1744—The Minister produced a receipt for the four
pounds Scots which were Collected for the Relief of John
Anderson in Slavery at Tangiers, as also He shewed the Receipts
he had from the Treasurer of the Royal Infirmary at Edinburgh
for Eleven pounds fifteen shillings sterling which was Collected
by the Minister from house to house in this Parish for the said
Infirmary.

26 January, 1746—Mr. McLeish did not produce the minutes
of the Session as he was appointed, but said he was busy writting
them out and would have them ready soon.

11 May, 1746—The Committee appointed to demand the
minutes of Session reported that in obedience to the Session's
orders they waited on Mr. McLeish Friday last and demanded
the Session minutes from him, and that he delivered to them a
Bundle of loose disjointed papers as the Session Minutes in so
great confusion that they could not take a note of them, but
that they laid them up tyed in a Cloath, as he delivered them,

in a Closet in the Schoolhouse, locked the door of the said Closet, and took the key with them, and that they are now ready to give them to the Session. The Session approved of their Committee's conduct, and received the Minutes from them which were in great disorder, and begd of the Minister he would take them and put them in the best order he could, which he agreeing to, the Minutes as received from Mr. McLeish and delivered to him, he was desired to officiate as Clerk till the affair anent Mr. McLeish was ended.

24 August, 1746—This day the Minister produced Mr. Porteous his' receipt for the twenty-two Pounds eight Shillings collected Sunday August the Third for the Kirk of Amulrie and the seven Pounds four Shillings more which the Minister collected at Taymouth the Evening of that Day.

11 June, 1747—After stating of accounts there was Disbursed this day nine Pound fourteen Shilling Scots and there was added to the money in the Boxmaster's hands the Remaining Eighty-one Pounds of Mr. Coline's money, so that the whole money in their hands Just now is One Hundred and Ninty-nine Pounds Eighteen shillings and two Pennies Scots. Considering which the Session judge they may Lend out Two Hundred Merks, and as it may be dangerous to have so much money Lying in the Box they agree that the said Two Hundred merks be lodged with the Minister, Mr. Douglass, till a proper hand cast up that will take it and give sufficient security for it, and accordingly the Two Hundred Merks were given to Mr. Douglass.

27 December, 1747—John Robertson in Fernan having Borrowed the other Hundred Merks that was in the Minister's hands of the Poor's Money, he gave his Accepted Bill Payable at Martinmas next, which Bill this day by appointment of Session given to Donald McCallum, Pitmacky, to be kept by him for the Session, and of the said Hundred Merks the Minister is Discharged. The Session having modified Donald McAndrew's fine to Twelve Pounds Scots upon his paying his Crown of fine for Sabbath Breaking.

9 April, 1749—The Session considering that it was proper to regulate their Officer's dues they did ordain as follows :—For every summonds given on the East side of Ardtallanaig on the South side of Loch Tay and for every Summonds be east Lawers on the North side, forty Pennies Scots ; for each Summonds to any being in Ardtallanaig, Lawers, or Glenqueach a half merk ; for every one that Mounts the Pilliory for single fornication twenty Pennies ; for a Relapse in fornication half a merk ; for a Trilapse or Adultery ten shillings Scots. And they appoint him of yearly Salary for his attendance on and service to the Session four Pounds Scots ; And that over and above Allowance be given at time of Sacraments or other extraordinary services ;

and the Regulations to continue in force till the Session finds cause to alter all or any of them as they see cause.

19 July, 1749—The Minister reported that having got Good Information that all or most of the People in the Officiary of Taymouth were guilty of Prophaning the Lord's Day by setting out with their horses and creels for Coal Carriages in fair Daylight, Sunday was a fortnight he laid this before a great number of the Elders met at Lawers, who all expressing their detestation of such open and daring Prophanation of the Lord's Day thought a Session should be held here this day and the said persons alledged guilty should be called before them ; that therefore he did cause the Kirk Officer Summond the Tennants of the said Officiary this day, at least such as he heard were concerned in the Transgression, and that this is the Reason of his Calling the Elders together.   The Session having heard this report Approve of the Minister's Conduct, and resolve to Proceed to enquire into the Scandal to know who was guilty and therefore they agree to call in the people.   The Tennants of Comrie, Dalmartaig, Inchadney, Balnasuim, Portbane, Forty Shilling Land, Revan, Aleckich, Tomgharve, Ballinlaggans, Auchianich, and Callelochan compeared, and acknowledged that they sent off their servants and horses that Sunday before the sun set. They confessed themselves guilty of sin, and professed their sorrow and repentance.   The Session considering this Affair, and remembering that they all expressed their sorrow in a

THE STREET, KILLIN.

penitent way, so far as they can judge, and that all promised
to walk more Christianly and circumspectly, Unanimously
agree that they be Sessionally rebuked, and this rebuke to be
intimated to the Congregation the next Lord's Day, The
Session reserving to their after Consideration whether they shall
be fined or not. The said Tennants being called in, this was
intimated to them, and they acquiesced, were sharply rebuked
and seriously Exhorted.

3 March, 1751—Mr. Stewart, Minister of Kilbrandon, paid the
seven merks interest due upon his Bill to the Poor & Renewed
his Bill for Two Hundred and Ten merks payable against
Candlemass next.

5 May, 1751—The Session appoint their Officer to summond
Dod Crerar in Tomflower, Ardtallanaig, for causing to open a
grave upon the Lord's Day, also Patrick Crerar in Callelochan,
John McEwan at the Milltown of Ardtallanaig, Alexr Crerar at
Creitdow, and Alexr Mcnacaird in Lurgin for attending upon the
Burial & immediately drinking thereafter in time of Divine
Service this day was a fortnight.

3 July, 1752—The Session in order to prevent Sturdy Beggars
belonging to this paroch from imposing on the Country, have
resolved that none be allowed to begg through the Country save
such as have Badges or testificates to certify their being in
Indigent Circumstances ; and further resolve that none get
Charity out of the Box but such as will dispone to the Kirk
box a right to all their goods and effects of everie kind at the
hour of their Death, unless they fall to some Considerable Legacie
after being supplied out of the Box, or after making the said
Disposition ; and Desire the Minister to intimate this their
resolution to the Congregation Sabbath first. The Chamberlain
of Breadalbane was present and concurred with both the said
Resolutions.

19 January, 1757—The Kirk Session considering they had
frequent complaints from the Elders in the west end of the
Parish, That the Kirk Session of Killin do not take care of the
poor, particularly of the Invalids, or the poor objects that are
confined to beds and unable to travel, in that west end of this
Parish, tho' that Kirk Session ought, According to the Agreement & paction that subsists between the two Kirk Sessions,
to take the same care of our poor in that end as they do of their
own, Therefore resolve to lay a memorial before them for that
purpose.

8 November, 1759—Mr. James Campbell was duly admitted
by the Presbytery of Dunkeld to be minister of this parish.
The admission sermon was preached by Mr. Stewart Minr. of
Killin.

28 December, 1760—It was reported to the Session That
Peter Haggart in Acharn was in harvest last guilty of a breach

of the Sabbath by working among his Corns to the great Scandal and offence of all who saw him, and that when he was found fault with by one of his neighbours, he did not seem to think that he had done wrong. The said Peter being called compeared, and this report being intimate to him, & he being told how heinous a sin this was & how scandalous & offensive in the sight of men, he acknowledged his guilt, alledged nothing in his own vindication, and declared his sin was provoking in the sight of God, and offensive to all Christians around him. He expressed his sorrow and grief for it, and pray'd that God through Christ would forgive him. The Session delayed sentence this day, but referr the whole till this day eight days, and appoint the Elders in Peter Haggart's neighbourhood to enquire into the particulars of this affair. The said Peter was summonded *apud acta* against that day.

30 August, 1761—Duncan McPhail, Donald Campbell, & Duncan McIchuaish, tenents in Carie of Coirewhin, compeared before the Session and alledged several things against the moral character of Malcolm McGibbon, designed Elder in Carie, but the said Malcolm not being present this day, the Session desired them to have their proof in Readiness and to attend here Sabbath next in the forenoon, in order to have their affair examined into before sermon.

27 September, 1761—Compeared the above designed objectors and being asked what they had to say that might hinder Malcolm McGibbon from being an Elder, They affirmed he was a bad neighbour who showed not only covetous disposition, but had actually defrauded some of his neighbours by seducing and bribing their servants to connive with him in his villany. They were desired to prove what they had alledged, but they could give no manner of evidence for it but their bare assertion. Said Malcolm being called and told what was said of him, made it evidently appear to the Session that the whole preceeded from the malice of his accusers. He produced a certificate signed by all the Tennents of Coirewhin testifying his good moral character & declaring their ignorance of everything alledged against him, and that in their opinion he was fit to be an Elder. There were several honest and Creditable persons present from the neighbourhood of Coirewhin who all declared in terms of the foresiad Certificate. . . . The accusers begged God might forgive them, and asked Malcolm's pardon for the injury they intended. Malcolm very readily forgave them, and they all promised before the Session to live as good neighbours.

23 September, 1781—It was represented that Donald Stewart, Ewen McDougall, Willm McGrigor, Christian Cameron, & Janet Cameron in Fearnan, art or part of a breach of the Sabbath by grinding corn at the Miln of Fearnan on the Lord's Day. In consequence of an intimation they all appeared, acknowledged

what they had done, and professed their sorrow for it. The
Session satisfied with the sincerity of their profession & promises
of a stricter observance of the Lord's Day in time to come after
rebuking, dismissed them.

9 March, 1783—The Moderator represented that John Anderson
in Brae of Taymouth had applied to him for baptism of a child
of his whom he had about four years ago presented for Baptism
to Mr. Campbell then Minr. of Kenmore ; but that while Mr.
Campbell was pouring the water on the face of the child a woman
unexpectedly fainted, by which circumstance all present were
thrown into such discomposure that Mr. Campbell omitted to
baptise the child in the name of the Father, Son, and Holy
Ghost. Considering this circumstance as indispensibly necessary
to the right celebration of the Ordinance the Minr. agreed to
baptise the child, providing the father would bring sufficient
evidence that the words of the institution had been omitted,
which he promised to adduce before the Session. Compeared
James McNaughton, Brae of Taymouth, & being interrogated
declared that about four years ago he was present when Mr.
Campbell was baptising John Anderson's child, that as he was
sprinkling the water Catherine Walker, spouse to Angus
McNaughton now in Cloan-lawer, fainted ; that Mr. Campbell
desired the water remaining in the bason might be given her,
that in the confusion naturally following, Mr. Campbell did not
pronounce the words, " I baptise thee in the name of the Father,
Son, and Holy Ghost," and concluded the service without it.

10 October, 1784—The Moderator laid before the Session a
copy of a Summons with which he had been served at the instance
of Jean McTavish, some time in Cloan, Lawers, to compear before
the Lords of Council & Session to answer to the points of a libel
prefixed, in which she sets forth that the Moderator had refused
to admit her to the Lord's Supper, and afterwards to grant her
a certificate of her moral character, and craves that he may
be decerned to make forthcoming to the pursuer a Sufficient
Certificate of her moral character and to call a meeting of the
Kirk Session for that effect, and to make payment of twenty
pounds sterling in name of damages and expenses. The Session
considering the matter, find that the refusing Jean McTavish
token for admission to the Lord's Table, and a certificate of her
character was their act, founded upon what appeared to them
to be good grounds, and that Mr. Fleming whom she pursues,
acted in that matter officially as their Moderator ; On this
account they consider him pursued in their name to answer for
their act ; and therefore unanimously resolve to join with him
in defending against this persecution, and also in any expense
that may be incurred in making that defence.

After this period there is very little of general interest in the
Kirk Session records. In connection with the discipline imposed

U

by the Kirk Session of Kenmore upon delinquents an amusing story of retaliation is told. The minister of Kenmore and his neighbour, the minister of Killin, being in Edinburgh, decided to pay a visit to the theatre, which in those days was regarded as out of bounds to members of the Cloth. At the door they asked the usher to show them to a seat where they would not be seen ; but instead of doing so he led them forward to the very front, and pointing them to their places, shouted in his loudest voice, " Make way there for the minister of Kenmore." The usher happened to be a Kenmore man who at some time had been under the censure of the minister and his session.

The following figures give some indication of the numbers that used to gather to the Communion services at Kenmore a hundred years ago :—

1815	12 tables	919 communicants.
1820	11 ,,	813 ,,
1825	9 ,,	686 ,,
1830	9 ,,	648 ,,
1835	7 ,,	412 ,,
1840	6 ,,	408 ,,
1842	5 ,,	323 ,,
1843	3 ,,	107 ,,
1844	3 ,,	159 ,,

From 1800 to 1840 the population of the district was greatly reduced by emigration. In 1843 half of the congregation entered the Free Church of Scotland largely under the influence of the second Marquis of Breadalbane.

The following beautiful description of an open-air Communion service at Kenmore was written by a Bishop of Sodor and Man some time about the end of the eighteenth century.

The reference to the Bridge which was erected in 1774 proves that the bishop's visit took place after that date. The passage was found in some book by the late Marchioness of Breadalbane. who had a copy printed in large type and set up in the porch of Kenmore Church.

" The Communion in Scotland has oftern been celebrated out of doors. Doubtless the Sacrament of the Supper, when solemnly administered, is an imposing ordinance, even in a crowded church ; but, in summer, during fine weather, when all nature blooms around, the ceremony, to my mind, acquires additional excitement: On the edge of a venerable wood, in the midst of a flower-studded lawn, how delectable to receive the Bread of Life. But when river, wood, and lawn combine—above all, if a lovely lake sweep among the mountains, and the church and churchyard are on the banks of the lake, can fancy devise a scene more fitted for the blessed purpose ?

" In the summer of—— an English bishop and some travellers happened to attend a Communion service in Breadalbane.

The travellers wished to view the scenery round the lake ; the prelate, along with the excitement of a tourist, wanted to witness a Caledonian Communion. Although the church at Kenmore is capacious, they can sometimes celebrate the Sacrament thus, and in dry weather the option is agreeable.

" The tables and forms were placed in the field, and, after an excellent action-sermon, the service began. The rows of communicants rose and retired, and still they were succeeded by another band. Ever and anon the breathing anthem was answered by the echoes of the lake. The hanging woods waved verdant around, and the infant Tay seemed to murmur a solemn melody. Many an aged Celt took the Cup of Salvation. Many a tartaned maid ate the Bread of the Saviour. Health, harmony, and solemnity pervaded the meeting. The birds carolled above their heads, the waves of the lake died softly at their feet, the blue sky on Ben Lawers shed a richer hue, and superior spirits seemed to look down on the hallowed scene.

" When the more solemn service was ended, ' Let us,' said the bishop to his friend,—' Let us take a walk by the lake, I want to relieve the swelling of my soul.'

" They crossed the beautiful bridge, they moved a little up the wood-skirted road to Killin ; ' And what do you think of this scene,' said the bishop ; ' I mean this Scottish Sacramental scene ? '

" 'I have been,' said the stranger, 'in the fine churches of Italy. I have seen all the solemnities of the Popish worship : but *never, never,* did I witness a scene like this.'

" 'What with this lake and mountain scenery around, what with the simple seriousness of those poor Highlanders, and what with the simplicity, the power, and eloquence of this plain Presbyter,' said the bishop, ' I never witnessed a more solemn scene. We have, to be sure, our instrumental music ; but here the birds of heaven sing chorus to communicants. A hundred times during the service did I look up that sweet lake and fancy to myself that I was on the Lake of Genesareth. I shall never again despise the simplicity of Presbyterian worship.'

" 'And I,' said his friend, 'never witnessed a more cordial Communion, all here is from the heart and soul. The solemnity of the sacred scene and the sublimity of the natural scene shall never be effaced from my mind.'

" They returned to witness the close of the solemnity. The benediction was pronounced, the assembly began to separate, and long did the English tourists stand at the foot of Loch Tay, viewing the lake, the wood, and the mountain ; but most of all they delighted to mark the happy Highlanders swarming up each side of the lake to finish the Sabbath in their respective habitations."

CHAPTER XXVIII.

Schools and Schoolmasters.

THERE can be no doubt that learning and the knowledge of letters were first brought into Breadalbane by the early missionaries of the Celtic Church. Columba and his brethren had not been long settled on Iona when they began to make expeditions across Druim Alban into our district. The great saint and statesman had resolved to effect a reconciliation between the pagan Picts of Alban and his own kinsmen from Ireland, who had colonised Argyll ; and he hoped to secure his aim by spreading the Gospel in Pictland and bringing the people of this region under its civilizing influences. Columba himself is said to have founded an abbey at Dunkeld ; while the names of such missionaries as Eonan (Adamnan), Branu, Gunna, Coede, Carmac, Dobee, and Ciaran, are still attached to the sites of ancient churches, graveyards, fields, fords, and mountain passes in Glenlyon and the district of Breadalbane. Eonan, the biographer of Columba, set up a monastery at Dull ; while his contemporary, Fillan, founded a similar institution near the head waters of the Dochart. The monks who gathered into these primitive monasteries taught the people how to clear and cultivate the land. They set up mills driven by water, and introduced other arts and crafts connected with agriculture. Hitherto these rude people had lived mostly by hunting.

Young men who were attracted to the monasteries gave themselves up to religious studies. They learned to read the Bible and to study books of Theology ; and in order to be able to take part in the services of the Church they were instructed in Music. Those of them who were most proficient in writing passed a great part of each day transcribing books. In this way many of these students qualified as missionaries, and went forth to evangelise other regions. There were, besides, at every monastery of this type a number of part-time students, who were taught the elements of education, and in return worked on the abbey farm. They were called *sgolagan*, a Gaelic term that is still applied to farm servants in the Highlands.

These ancient abbeys continued to shed their light with more or less success until the twelfth century, when they came under the richer and broader culture of the Church of Rome. According to a well confirmed tradition the abbey of Dull developed into an important seat of learning, the endowments of which were ultimately transferred to the University of St. Andrews. Evidence of this tradition is found in the fact that eighteen bolls of black oats are still payable from the Priory of St. Andrews to the stipend of the minister of Dull. The abbey at Dunkeld had ceased to exist when the bishopric was erected in 1127; but it is probable that a school was maintained in connection with the Cathedral until the time of the Reformation. Glendochart retained its priory, at least in name, throughout the Roman Catholic period ; but it is doubtful whether education received any attention. Most of the lands belonging to the abbey had passed into the hands of a powerful layman who was known as the Abbot (*Aba*) ; while the Prior was left with a mere remnant of the revenue to which he was entitled. From the *Aba* are descended the Clan Macnab, who for centuries held most of the lands in Glendochart.

There was no parochial system of education during the Roman Catholic period ; but here and there priests would voluntarily take lads in hand and teach them to read and write. The condition of the Highlands with regard to education is set forth in the Bull addressed by Pope Alexander III. to king James IV. authorising the erection of Aberdeen University, in 1484. In that document the following statement is made, " In the northern or north-eastern parts of the Kingdom there are certain places separated from the rest of the Kingdom by arms of the sea and very high mountains in which dwell men rude and ignorant of letters, and almost barbarous, so ignorant of letters that not only for preaching the Word, but also for administering the Sacraments of the Church proper men cannot be found." At this period we find that such notable chiefs as MacDougall of Dunolloe, MacNaughton of Dunderave, MacDonell of Keppoch, Campbell of Barbreck, and Menzies of Roro, required to have their hands led at the pen when they subscribed their names to documents. When such a state of illiteracy existed among the chiefs, there could be no trace of education among the common people.

The Reformation.

The condition of the Highlands did not improve much with the Reformation. Religious agitation and disorder reigned everywhere. The nobles and chiefs seized Church lands, and secured them for themselves and their descendants by Crown charters. It was with extreme difficulty that even a pittance from the teinds could be procured for the maintenance of ministers and readers. The few schools, Dunkeld among them, that had been kept going before the Reformation, were closed for want of funds. John Knox and his supporters might advocate a school for every parish in Scotland, but it was only in the latter part of the seventeenth century that this ideal was realised in Breadalbane ; and in 1758 there were still no fewer than 175 parishes north of the Grampians without a school or schoolmaster. The illiterate condition of even important persons after the Reformation is shown by the fact that out of forty persons who gave their support to a petition at Kenmore in January, 1579, asking for permission to erect a new church, only four could write their names, and these four were lairds. The names of the others were adhibited by the notary. Even a person of such consequence as Alexander Menzies of Comrie Castle was among those who could not write.

In 1567, James VI. made a grant for the erection of a grammar school at Dunkeld. This school was designated in the charter as " The Royal School of Dunkeld." The right of presentation to the school was conferred upon the Earl of Atholl and his successors ; but the examination and admission to the office of the person presented was vested in " the superintendent of the Church of God within the bounds of Perthshire." The ideal of a school for every parish was not entirely lost sight of ; and in 1616, the Scottish Privy Council decreed " that all His Majesty's subjects, especially the youth, be exercised and trayned up in civilitie, godliness, knowledge and learning ; that the vulgar Ingleeshe tongue be universalie planted ; and the Irish language, which is one of the chief and principall causes of the continuance of barbaritie and incivilitie among the inhabitants of the Isles and Hylandis, may be abolishit and removit." This edict produced no effect whatever in the Highlands of Perthshire. The commissioners who visited this district in 1627 in connection with the planting of churches, the state of the teinds, hospitals, and schools took evidence in each parish from the minister and heritors. The reports for Dull, Weem, Kenmore, and Killin reveal the fact that there were no schools in any of these parishes. It was, however, indicated that the people wanted schools ; and there is a pathetic ring about the statements made by the witnesses. At Dull it was stated, " There is no schoole in the paroche, nor foundatioune for a skool, but requisit, if ane provisioun mycht be haid for ane " ; at Kenmore, " Thair is no schoole nor reider thair ; nether hes thair bein any provisioune here-to-foir for thame " ; at Weem, " Thair is no schoole nor reider thair, nether hes thair bein any provisoune heir-to-foir for thame " ; at Killin, " We had ane schoole, bot for laik of meanes it dissolved. It is necessarye."

Parish Schools.

In 1646, the Scottish Parliament passed a law enacting that a school be set up in every parish under the superintendence of the presbytery of the bounds. The terms of this act were less offensive to the Highlanders than the decree of 1616, which described the Gaelic language as the principal cause of their barbarity. The presbytery of Dunkeld was now better organised and equipped with ministers, and the heritors were more sympathetic towards education. The result was that steps were soon taken to give effect to the requirements of the Act by providing a salary for a schoolmaster of not less than one hundred merks money. He was, besides, to receive fees from parents, and all dues payable to the session clerk for baptisms and marriages. A school was established at Moulin in 1649 ; at Blair Atholl in 1650 ; at Kenmore in 1651 ; at Logierait, and at Dull in 1654 ; at Roro (Glenlyon) in 1665 ; and at Dowally in 1684. There is no reference in the records to any school at Fortingall until 1700, or at Killin until after this date ; but it is unlikely that the requirements of these two important parishes. were overlooked when the needs of the others within the bounds of the presbytery were supplied.

The following extracts from the Kenmore Session records show the steps taken in that parish to provide a school :—

" June 23, 1650.—This day it is condescendit be the heritors present that thair be a bond drawn up of ane hundred merks at least to be a stock to a schooll in all tyme coming yearly ; and the said bond to be sent abroad to the rest of the heritors to be subscrybit." It would appear, however, that no progress was made with the school for another year. On 14 September, 1651, it was minuted, " This day the Laird of Glenorchy, the Laird of Laweris, the Laird of Strowan, and the rest of the heritors within the paroch condescendit to give the schoolmaster five shillings out of every markland yearly, to begin at Martinmas next."

John Hepburne, the schoolmaster, had evidently arrived at Kenmore ; and until the heritors' assessment was available, the Kirk Session made an advance of money to him. On the same day as the above entry was made in the records it was also minuted that a loan of ten pounds (Scots) was given to Hepburne, which the elders were under obligation to put into the box again. The Session was meantime proceeding with the erection of a schoolhouse, which would be built with dry-stone walls, roofed with cabers, and covered with thatch. Payments were made to John McKerchar for " bigging the schoolhouse," and afterwards small outlays were incurred " for dore and bands." There is no reference to the setting up of seats, as the pupils would probably be expected to provide their own stools.

John Hepburne was still at Kenmore in 1653 ; but we find him at Logierait in the following year, where his position appears to have been none too happy. On 19 February, 1654, he was appointed schoolmaster, precentor, and session clerk in that parish, at a salary of forty marks for the half year, which was to be uplifted from the interest of the stipends for 1648 and 1649 still lying in the hands of the heritors. It was provided, however, that " in regarde the tymes are troublesome and the country not in quyetness, it is ordained that the said John Hepburne

be payed monthly out of the penalties, if the said annual rent
cannot be gotten in."

The following schoolmasters served the school of Kenmore in
succession to John Hepburne during the two centuries of its
existence :—1660, William Martine ; 1687, Duncan MacGregor,
reader in the church ; 1693, Thomas Gilbert, who married
Margaret, daughter of Mr. John Alexander, minister of Durrisdeer;
1721, John Grahame, reader in the church; 1729, John McLeish,
still in office in 1751 ; 1758, Archibald McArthur ; 1783, Joseph
McGibbon ; 1788, Robert Armstrong ; 1828-1873, William
Armstrong.

The Armstrongs, father and son, deserve something more than
mere passing mention. Between them they carried on Kenmore
school for the long period of eighty-five years, during which
time   many lads were educated who distinguished themselves
in several walks of life. Of the two, Robert was the greater
scholar, and probably the more successful teacher. The Latin
inscription on his tombstone in Kenmore churchyard, which
was composed by his son, Robert, the author of the Gaelic
dictionary, describes him as " a man of singular purity of mind,
and equally remarkable for the charming simplicity of his
manners. The love which he so well merited in his relations
with his pupils and others of his fellows, he received from all
alike. Finally weighed down with a very serious sickness in his
73rd year of his age—from which he emerged the purer, like
gold tried in the fire—he departed this life on August 9th, 1828."*
William Armstrong retired at the passing of the Scottish
Education Act in 1873, when the Free Church school at Acharn
was adopted as the school for the district of Kenmore. He
survived until 1879, and was buried in the family lairs in the
churchyard.

The public school at Acharn was conducted for over forty
years by the late Mr. Dugald McEwen, who was described by
a former inspector of schools as " a splendid specimen of the
old type of schoolmaster." On a very modest salary and with
the assistance of only one teacher Mr. McEwen produced
marvellous results, and worthily maintained the traditions of
the old parish school. On his retirement he was succeeded by
Mr. Joseph J. Coull, M.A., who carried on the school with marked
success until, owing to the diminishing number of pupils in
attendance, he was transferred to Deanston, in 1933. The school
has now been reduced to a one-teacher school with some twenty
pupils.

Owing to the absence of Session records it has not been possible
to secure anything like a complete list of the parish schoolmasters
of Killin. The school was situated on the crofts of Ballechroisk, a
little distance to the south of the village. The building has been
converted into a private house. The first schoolmaster of whom

* Translation by Donald Macnaughton, Esq., H.M.I.S. (Remony).

any trace can be obtained was Mungo Malcolm, who was appointed in 1727, when a deputation from the presbytery of Dunkeld visited the parish, and ascertained that although there was a salary available for a schoolmaster, the school had been closed for some time. In 1771, James McGibbon taught the parish school of Killin. He was succeeded by a person of his own name, who was probably a son. The two McGibbons carried on the school for over sixty years between them. The second of them made meteorological observations, which were continued by his family after his death. From these records the Rev. Alexander Stewart, who wrote the New Statistical Account of the parish, was able to give the average readings of the barometer and thermometer for the year 1820.

At the passing of the Education Act of 1873, the parish school was taught by Robert Cameron, who retired in 1874, and died in 1879. Since 1874 the Public School of Killin has been taught by the following masters :—1874, Alexander Hodges, M.A. ; 1875, Archibald W. Borthwick ; 1888, James Stevens, M.A. ; 1909, A. J. Ross, M.A., B.Sc., now headmaster of Dunoon Grammar School ; 1915, James McGraw, M.A., educated at Aberdeen University, still in office, 1937.

S.P.C.K. and Church Schools.

The increasing demand for education during the early decades of the eighteenth century in Breadalbane could not be adequately met by the schools at Kenmore and Killin. There were many children in the district who resided over ten miles from either of these schools ; and no provision whatever was made for them until the Honourable Society for Propagating Christian Knowledge came to the assistance of local effort. This beneficent Society, which was founded in 1709, set up schools at Glenlednock, Glenartney, and Rosearne, in the following year. On 4 September, 1716, the presbytery of Dunkeld drew up a memorial for submission to the Society, setting forth the educational requirements of the Highland portion of their bounds. With regard to the needs of the district of Breadalbane the memorial states :—

" Strathfillan annexed to the parish of Killin, and twelve miles from any legal school, requires one to be settled opposite to Lochdochart above the Suie, for serving Glendochart, Glenfalloch, and the said country, in which places there are, as is computed, about six or seven hundred examinable persons. Fifteen pounds sterling of a salary is needed for the schoolmaster's encouragement.

" Ardeonaig in the parish of Killin, upon the south side of Loch Tay, and Lawers in the parish of Kenmore, on the north side of the same loch, about each of which places there is a populous country, and most of the inhabitants four or five miles from any settled school, do require an itinerant school settled in them per vices, and fifteen pounds sterling of salary for the schoolmaster's encouragement.

" There is need of a school at Glenlochay, which lies in the parishes of Kenmore, Killin, and Weem, and several of the inhabitants six miles distant from any school, and consisting of four hundred examinable persons, to be settled at Innis-chaorach, with fifteen pounds of salary for the encouragement to the schoolmaster."*

The needs of Glenquaich, part of which lay in the parish of Kenmore, were specially emphasised. The memorial was sent not only to the Society, but also to the Commissioners appointed under Act of Parliament " for the more effectual securing the peace of the Highlands." The modest income of the Society was not, however, equal to the many requests for help that were coming in from every part of the Highlands, and it was not until 1720 that a grant could be given to a parish in the bounds of the Dunkeld presbytery. The minister of Blair Atholl at this time was Mr. John Hamilton, who was translated to Kenmore in 1723. Mr. Hamilton and his session secured a grant for a school at Struan ; and the parish records reveal the difficulties they had in erecting a schoolhouse, and procuring trees to form a bridge over the Erochtie, by which the children might safely cross. The Duke of Atholl offered to give fir trees in Rannoch, but the transport of them to Struan could not be arranged. The Kirk Session of Blair Atholl undertook to give a shilling

* Hunter's Diocese and Presbytery of Dunkeld, Vol. II.

OLD SCHOOL AT MORENISH.

sterling for each tree that could be dug out of the peat-bogs ;
and in this way the necessary number to construct a bridge
was procured.*

As soon as Mr. Hamilton was settled in Kenmore he took up
the question of procuring schools for the outlying parts of his
wide-spread parish. He found the people clamouring for education
for their children. Many of them united in procuring for a
portion of the year a person who could teach their children to
read and write ; and the minister and his elders gave them every
encouragement. In the records of this period we find such
entries as the following :—" The Session appoints three shillings
Scots. to John Anderson in Milltown of Ardtalnaig for three ells
of kloth to Patrick Forbes who taught a school, and who was
poor." " Testimonial to be given to Daniel McNaughton, soldier,
and Margaret Campbell, his spouse, who keeped school at
Ballynatibert." " This day (20 June, 1731) the people of the
Forty-shilling Land compeared and applied the session for
setting a school there, and promised a house for the master and
scholars, and obliged to send sixteen there to-morrow. The
Session allowed the school to be taken up to-morrow at the
Forty-shilling Land, and to remain there until the Session find
out a convenient place to transport it to Aucharn, which is to
be done with all conveniency." " Two pounds ten shillings
given to John McIntyre, schoolmaster, in Lawers, to help to
pay his boarding." " John McGrigor's mulct, four pounds
Scots., given to John Campbell in Muttonhole to help to pay
Duncan Mcnab's board, a poor scholar, and for his precenting
in Irish." " The Session appoints two shillings sterling money
to John Campbell, son to John Campbell in Forty-shilling Land,
a poor scholar at the school, to buy a Bible to learn to read,
and which he is to return to the Session after he is done, nor is
he to sell it, nor dispose of it, or any for him."

On 21 October, 1729, Ewen MacDougall, elder in Ardtalnaig,
and his brother John, applied to the Session for help to settle
an itinerant schoolmaster in that district ; 'and the Session,
taking the circumstances of that place into their serious consideration, and finding that there were a great number of children
there, and the people willing to have them educated, and they
being poor, " appointed the first and the readiest mulct that
shall be got to be given them for their encouragement in so good
and pious a design." A similar application was received from
Lawers where the people had already made an agreement with
John Wright to be schoolmaster. They undertook the burden
of the wages upon themselves, providing the Session would grant
them " some help out of the pecunial mulcts," and that some
measure might be found by which those who had children fit
for school, and able to pay for them, would send them to it, or
pay their quarter's wages whether they sent them or not. The

* Blair Atholl Kirk Ses. records.

Session agreed that the minister should write to Lord Breadalbane's chamberlain requesting him to compel all parents in the Lawers district who had children to send them to the school.

The educational requirements of the south side of Loch Tay and of Lawers had been pressed upon the Society for several years ; but owing to the lack of funds the Society was unable to assist with a grant. Mr. Hamilton of Kenmore along with the ministers of Dull and Weem made strong representations to the Society for a schoolmaster who should be settled in Glenquaich, where there was a large population far removed from any school. On 16 November, 1729, Mr. Hamilton intimated to the Session that he had received a letter from Mr. Nicol Spence, secretary to the Society, stating that its funds were nearly exhausted, but that a grant of 50 marks Scots. had been voted for a schoolmaster to be placed at Alltvin, half-way between Ardeonaig and Ardtalnaig. A grant for the school at Lawers was obtained shortly afterwards ; and in 1731, provision was made for setting up a school in Glenquaich. The Session had to erect the schoolhouse and the bridges over the burns by which the children crossed to school. On September 5, 1731, " the Session appoints David Walker, treasurer, to buy upon Tuesday next, the fair at Kenmore, six backs to the doors for the schoolhouse at Glenquaich. The Session is to refund him out of the collections, as also they appoint William Stewart, elder in Shian, to buy two dozen and a half of cabers out of the Wood of Moness, with a sole tree and top tree, also to make up a partition in the said schoolhouse, and the same to be rebursed to him out of the collections." Trees for a bridge were supplied by the lairds of Wester Shian and of Turrerich, while the Kirk Session of Kenmore paid for the cost of its construction. By 1738, the thatch required renewing, and on 10 September of that year, when a service was held in the glen, it was recorded that the collection amounted to " a groat which was given to one to go through the glen to gather thatch for the schoolhouse."

In remote places where the Society was unable to give a grant, the Kirk Session encouraged the people themselves to start schools. In 1739, the tenants of Carwhin and Crannich attended the meeting of Session at Kenmore, "and being interrogated if they had agreed for this year as yet with Alexander Irvine to be their schoolmaster and catechist, said that they had promised him 3 bolls meal and 20 merks money, but they were desired to give him 24 merks and three bolls of meal, which the said Alexander alleges they had promised him, and the Session left it on that footing until Whitsunday." Such entries as these reveal the poverty of the people, but also their strong desire to have their children educated.

The teachers of those " Charity " schools were young lads who had been educated at parish schools, and who had been recommended to the directors of the Society as suitable. Some of them turned out notable successes, and ultimately qualiied as parish schoolmasters. The first schoolmaster of Glenquaich was Charles McHardy,[1] a native of Glenmuick, Aberdeenshire. He was sent by the Society to take charge of a school that had been started in the island of Lismore ; but after walking across Scotland to take up his post, McHardy found that the Kirk Session had appointed another man. All he could do was to walk another hundred miles back to Glenmuick. The minister of the parish intimated McHardy's disappointment to the Society, whereupon the directors withdrew the grant voted for Lismore, and transferred it to Glenquaich, whither McHardy was instructed to repair. After several years' service in the glen, he was appointed to the Society's school at Portree, Skye; and from there he went to be parish schoolmaster of Laggan. His widow is mentioned by Mrs. Grant in "Letters from the Mountains."

Books were both scarce and dear ; but the Society did its utmost to keep the schools supplied with Bibles and other religious books from which the children could learn to read. On 16 November, 1731, while a meeting of the directors was being held in Edinburgh, Duncan Wright,[2] schoolmaster at Ardeonaig, was waiting outside to receive a parcel of books for his school. There were 14 Bibles, 14 New Testaments, 12 Small Confessions of Faith, 12 Vincent's Catechisms, 12 Guthrey's Trial, three dozen copies of the Book of Proverbs, 4 Copy-books, and two dozen Syllabising Catechisms. With this precious burden of books, a register in which to record the observations of visitors to the school, and some writing paper, Duncan Wright set off on his ninety mile journey to Ardeonaig. Mr. Adam Fergusson, minister of Killin, reporting upon a visit paid to Wright's school in 1731, stated that, " he with some elders and honest men in that corner did visit the school, and found thereat 36 scholars who attend well and make progress, of whom 28 begun in the Catechism within these two years, do now read the Bible pretty distinctly ; the success of the school has been very considerable, as has been that of catechising, the people being wonderfully advanced in the knowledge of the principles of Religion, and expressed great inclination to be instructed, some of whom did lately partake of the Sacrament of the Lord's Supper, with no small devotion, and these never did it before, under a Presbyterian ministry."

John McIntyre, another of the Society's schoolmasters, was a man of good standing in Breadalbane. He began his career as schoolmaster and catechist at Lawers, and when that school became self-supporting he was removed to Morenish, and later on from there to Glendochart. McIntyre was simply adored by the people both for his own sake and for the services he rendered.

(1) Minutes of S.P.C.K., Reg. Ho., Edin. (2) Minutes of S.P.C.K., Reg. Ho., Edin.

During the week he taught their children, and on Sundays he conducted religious services for them. He was their comforter in trouble, and their guide in temporal matters. When he was transferred to Glendochart his praise was sung in a song that was composed by John Campbell (MacGlasserig), the bard of Morenish.

According to the regulations* laid down by the Society the school day began early. During the summer months the school opened at seven o'clock and went on until eleven, when there was a break of two hours. Lessons were again resumed at one o'clock and continued till five. In the winter the school hours were from nine o'clock to twelve, and from one o'clock to three in the afternoon. Education was free ; where the children of well-to-do people attended, the parents were, however, expected to compensate the master. The schoolmaster of a Charity school was forbidden to teach Latin or Gaelic, or to engage in any business that might prevent him from giving his whole time to his work. If he were musical he was expected to teach the people to sing Psalm tunes ; and on Sundays, in places remote from the Church, he conducted worship. Duncan Wright at Ardeonaig was reported to the Society as " being desirous to have a sermon book to read to the poor people these Lord's Days when the minister preaches in another corner of the parish." In addition to all these duties the schoolmaster had to assemble the children on Sundays, and spend some hours with them in reading and explaining the Scriptures. His was certainly a strenuous life.

From such beginnings the Society continued, as its funds increased, to extend its activities. By the end of the eighteenth century there were Society schools at Amulree, Shian, Morenish, Lawers, Ardeonaig, Glendochart, and Strathfillan. When the schools were first started, the number of girls attending did not exceed five per cent. of the total pupils ; but as time went on parents came to realise that the education that was good for boys was good for the girls also. The following statement shows the position of the Society's schools in the Breadalbane district in the year 1787 :—

Lawers—John Ferguson, salary £5, boys attending 31, girls 29.

Morenish—Patrick McPherson, salary £8, boys 63, girls 22.

Ardeonaig—John Campbell, salary £5, boys 46, girls 17.

Shian (Glenquaich)—Duncan McGibbon, salary £10, boys 60, girls 24.

Strathfillan—William Rose (no statistics).

In 1790 there were 40 pupils in Strathfillan school and the same number in the school at Glendochart, which was then taught by James McIntyre. In 1796-7, the Society was making provision in the Highland district of Perthshire for the education

* Minutes S.P.C.K.

of 1,600 children at the modest cost of £250 a year. In the Breadalbane area, the salaries given by the Society were augmented by the Earl of Breadalbane and the Kirk Sessions of Kenmore and Killin, so that no master received less than ten pounds sterling a year.

As time went on, the Kirk Sessions of Kenmore and Killin, with the help of Lord Breadalbane, were able to supply schools for corners of the district that were still unprovided, such as Cloichran situated between Ardeonaig and Killin, Glenlochay, and Fearnan. In 1786, the tenants of Fearnan petitioned Lord Breadalbane asking for assistance to maintain a school. They stated that since 1761 they had provided a teacher for their children to whom they paid £1 6s. 8d. sterling for the half-year from Martinmas to Whitsunday yearly, without any other payment, " except his chance at Handsel Monday and cock-fighting, together with his maintenance, which he got by going from house to house regularly with the scholars, which was an advantage, because he teached their children at night in every house he came to."[1] The school in Glenlochay was upheld from the income of a sum of 6,000 marks Scots. which had been bequeathed in 1740 by the Rev. Archibald Campbell, minister of Weem, for the purpose of maintaining schools in detached portions of that parish.[2]

By the end of the eighteenth century there were at least ten schools in Breadalbane, as against the nine that exist at the present time. There is no doubt that many of the teachers employed were poorly qualified for their work, and that they were miserably paid. They taught in houses that had been hastily and roughly built ; the conditions both for themselves and the children were extremely trying, and compared very unfavourably with modern standards of comfort. It will, however, be recognised that the educational position in this district was rather remarkable, when one considers that in 1822 half the children in the Highlands[3] were not attending any recognised school, and that thousands were living more than five miles from the nearest school. The happy conditions in Breadalbane were achieved through the co-operation of the Church, the local Kirk Sessions and a succession of generous and progressive landlords, whose efforts were splendidly supported by the Society for Propagating Christian Knowledge. The provisions thus made for education bore rich fruit. From the middle of the eighteenth century a constant and increasing stream of lads, and not a few girls, passed out of the schools equipped with a sound elementary education. Many of the lads who studied higher subjects at the two Parish schools went on to the Universities and there qualified for the learned professions ; others made their way to the expanding cities of the South, or went overseas to play their part in laying the foundations of our Colonial Empire.

(1) B.Ps.   (2) B.Ps.   (3) Result of Unofficial Inquiry.

CHAPTER XXIX.

Folklore.

THE folklore of Breadalbane would require a volume to itself. All that can be attempted here is to give a brief account of some ancient beliefs that existed among the people, and to relate a few stories that have been handed down from the past. The late Mr. James Macdiarmid, whose family had long been connected with Breadalbane, and who with his brother, Dr. John Macdiarmid, at one time occupied the farm of Morenish, collected several tales which he contributed in papers to the Gaelic Society* of Inverness. These papers, some of them in Gaelic, have been published in the Society's "Transactions," and are thus available for any one interested in the old customs and superstitions of the district.

The old Highland peasantry were as sure of the existence of fairies, urisks, and witches as they were of the fact that they were alive themselves. Green conical hills, called in Gaelic *sitheanan*, burns, waterfalls, and islands were the dwelling places of mysterious beings who had to be considered in arranging the affairs of ordinary life. At some places in the countryside strange sounds were heard, and at others fearful lights were seen whenever events of special importance were going to happen. It is almost impossible to over-estimate the influence that such beliefs, which appear to us absurd and extremely foolish, exerted upon the minds and imaginations of a credulous people who lived close to Nature in her wildest moods.

Fairy Tales.

The people of long ago explained the origin of Loch Tay in the following way :—Once upon a time the large spring which rises in the Corrie of Carie, on the south-west side of Ben Lawers, was kept secure by a strong door, and under lock and key. Near this fountain, on the hillocks, were tethered a great herd of polled, dun cows which a dairy-maid supplied with water every evening. One evening after watering the cows she was late in finishing her work, and forgot to lock the door of the fountain. The result was that it flowed all night, and when the people looked out next morning the whole valley was filled with water, and they called out "*Loch Tatha*," "It is a loch." An old rhyme gives the number of cows tethered on the hillocks thus, "Three nines of hillocks, on every hillock three nines of stakes, and to every stake three nines of polled, dun cows tied."

According to another ancient tale Fionn, the hero of Celtic mythology, used to stand with one foot on Cioch na Maighdean

* Vols. XXV., XXVI., XXVII., XXVIII.

and the other placed on Ciste buille a Chlaidheimh, two hills about a mile apart, above Ardtalnaig. Standing in this position the giant was able to stoop towards Glenlednock, wash his hands in Lochan nan Lamh, and then turn and take a drink from Loch Tay.

Lochdochart was associated with the death of Fionn, if the following tale is true :—Long ago a certain man named Taileachd lived on Eilean Iubhar, the isle on Lochdochart, and he had a fairy sweetheart. Fionn got to know the lady, went to the island to see her, and took much pleasure in her company. At last Taileachd came to know that Fionn was visiting his sweetheart, and when he had examined them both concerning the matter, he and Fionn grew so jealous of each other that they were like to fall to blows.

" Nay," said the lady, " I will make order for you, and be not angry with each other. The man who wins the victory in a leap, it is he that I will follow with pleasure."

The warriors then went out to leap. Taileachd leaped from the island on to the shore, and Fionn leaped nimbly after him. Then said Taileachd, " I would leap the channel backwards, and unless you do the same, I shall have the fame by right." They both leaped backwards, but Taileachd leaped first, and landed on dry land. But when Fionn leaped after him he sank down to the head. Then Taileachd seized the advantage at Fionn's back and swept the head off Fionn ere he could turn round. Taileachd fled for fear of the Fiann (Fionn's band of warriors), bearing Fionn's head with him till he reached the head of Loch Laidon. There, being weary of carrying the head, he put it up on a pole on a black knoll, at a ford of the river, and that ford was afterwards called Ath Chinn. Now, when the Fiann found Fionn's headless body beside the loch, they raised up their king and their lord, and they buried him behind a knoll, in a grave which has ever since been called Cill Fhinn (Killin). The story then relates how the Fiann, being wroth at the wrong and the insult that had been done to them, went on the track of the head till they found it. By putting a finger under Fionn's tooth of knowledge, it was revealed to them that Taileachd was hiding in a cave on Ben Alder. There they found him, and put to him the question, " Do you repent of slaying Fionn ? " To this Taileachd replied, " I do not repent unless Goll repents of his persecution of the Clan Chuilgeadan." Thereupon the Fiann struck off Taileachd's right hand and then his left in requital of the great evil he had wrought. Taileachd was further pressed to repent, but he persistently refused. The Fiann then drove their spears through Taileachd's heart, and thus he died.*

It is evident that while these tales are very old they appear to have been invented in order to explain the meaning of such place names as *Lochan nan Lamh*, the Little Loch of the Hands, *Ath Chinn*, the Ford of the Head, *Cill Fhinn*, the Cell of Fionn.

* See Paper on Breadalbane Placenames by Prof. W. J. Watson, Trans. G. Soc. Inverness, Vol. XXXIV.

v

The Fairies.

According to Armstrong,* the fairies or *sithichean* were the most active sprites of Highland mythology. They were inveterate child-stealers, and many cunning ceremonies were practised to baffle the fairy power, otherwise the new-born infant might be taken off to Fairy-land, and a withered brat laid in the cradle in its stead.

Most of the tales of the Breadalbane fairies are associated with the *Sithean* beside the old lint mill at Lawers, *Sith a Bruaich* a short distance to the east of the House of Bovain, and *Sithean Dubh* about half a mile to the west of the same house. Fifty years ago, there was living at Killin, a man who was in the habit of relating his wonderful adventures with the white horse of the fairies of Lawers. Once when returning at night from Kenmore market he heard the most enchanting music coming from the *Sithean*. Unable to resist the temptation, he gradually went nearer and nearer the fairies' place of abode, until at last he found himself right in their midst. They received him most kindly, and on parting gave him one of their white steeds to carry him home. The steed flew through the air at the speed of lightning, and in less time than it takes to tell the tale the man found himself right above Tyndrum. He shouted " Woa," and immediately the fairy horse threw him off its back. He dropped through a chimney into a house in which wedding festivities were going on. The assembly were much surprised and alarmed at his sudden appearance ; but they kept him with them until morning, when he made his way slowly back to Killin.

Tradition says that the fairies of *Sith a Bruaich* had a treasure hidden near their knoll ; but that it was impossible for any mortal to find it. An old Gaelic rhyme about this treasure is translated as follows :—

" There is a treasure in *Sith a Bruaich*,
Whichever time it comes out.
It will never be found :
It is in the place of the trout."

The last line of the rhyme would seem to suggest that the treasure is concealed in the river Dochart which flows near the fairy knoll.

There is a tale which is too long to relate describing the experiences of an Auchlyne man who spent a year and a day in the *Sithean Dubh*. He had gone with a neighbour to procure a keg of whisky from Killin in order to celebrate the birth of a son. On the way home they were both lured into the *Sithean*; but after listening to the music for a short time the neighbour made for home. The other man, however, refused to leave, and it was a year and a day from the night he entered that his friend was able to break the spell that had been cast over him, and get him away to his home and his family.

* Dictionary, p. 495.

The following is a translation of a fairy tale taken from Mr. James Macdiarmid's collection :—In the days of old there was a man in Breadalbane who had a great wish to see the fairies. He had heard from old people that they dwelt in a *sithean* on the slopes of Schiehallion, and he resolved to go there in order to gratify his long cherished desire. His name was *Gleusda*, which indicates that he was a wise and shrewd man ; and before setting out, he prepared his plans well. He started away on a fine summer evening when the cows were returning home for the milking ; and he arrived at the knoll about midnight. As he approached the place in the stillness, he listened for any sounds that might suggest the presence of the fairies. He even held his breath ; and very soon he heard music and the patter of the fairies' feet, for they were singing and dancing in the hall within the hill. His heart was greatly lifted ; and he felt that he must sing himself. With a tuneful voice he began his song to the air of " Alastair Macalastair." His song was simply a repeating of the days of the week in Gaelic, and ran as follows :—

> " Monday and Tuesday,
> Monday and Tuesday,
> Monday and Tuesday,
> And Wednesday."

His song pleased the fairies and out they came trooping from the hill in hundreds, and started singing his song with him, and dancing in a ring. They led him into their hall which was lit with scores of tiny lamps, and there he stayed with them quite a long time dancing and singing merrily. At last he took farewell of the merry company ; and returned to his home to tell all his neighbours of the joyous time he had passed with the fairies of *Cnoc an Tiobart*.

One of his neighbours decided that he, too, must go and see the fairies. He was, however, an ungenial, ill-natured man, and there was no music in his soul or in his voice. He went to *Gleusda*, and asked him what song he should sing, and he suggested the words :—

> " Tuesday and Wednesday,
> " Tuesday and Wednesday,
> " Tuesday and Wednesday,
> And Thursday."

When *Buamasdair*, for that was the man's name, reached the *sithean*, the fairies were still singing with great glee the song they had learned from *Gleusda*, and gaily dancing to the tune. After listening for a short time *Buamasdair* began shouting his own tuneless song ; but as soon as the fairies heard him they ceased their merrymaking, and trooped out of the hall in crowds. They seized him, and dragged him before their queen. Some of them pushed him about, others pinched him in the ribs. They threw him on the ground, and jumped upon his back. At length they drove him away from the *sithean*, and when, sore and weary, he got home, there was a great hump on his back.

Strange to tell, the fate of *Buamasdair* did not prevent another man from going to see the fairies. He was warned by his neighbours, but he would not be advised. He thought that if he introduced the word, " Sunday," into his song the fairies would be pleased with him. He arrived at *Cnoc an Tiobairt*, and after listening for a while to the music and dancing of the little folk, he began to sing :—

> " Friday and Saturday,
> Friday and Saturday,
> Friday and Saturday,
> And Sunday."

At the mention of Sunday the fairies became terribly enraged, and dragging him into their hall they gave him such a rough handling that he lost one of his eyes. He found his way back to Lochtay-side, but got little sympathy from his neighbours, whose advice he had refused to take. After that no one ever sought to go near the fairies, although many a person listened to the music that came from their knolls.

The Urisks.

Of all the supernatural beings in whom the old people of Breadalbane believed, the *uruisg* held the foremost place in their imagination. As the name suggests, he was associated with water (*uisge*), and haunted deep ravines, waterfalls, and lonely moorland lochs. Unlike the fairies, who were regarded as being of both sexes, the urisk was always looked upon as a being in whom the qualities of a man and a spirit were curiously mingled together. He was a lover of solitude, but about the end of harvest he became sociable, and hovered about the meal-mills, farm-yards, and cattle-houses. Robert Armstrong, the author of the Gaelic Dictionary, who in his boyhood was familiar with stories of the Breadalbane urisks, gives the following account of them :—" The urisk had a particular fondness for the products of the dairy, and was a fearful intruder on milk-maids, who made regular libations of milk or cream to charm him off, or to procure his favour. He could be seen only by those who had the second-sight ; yet I have heard of instances where he made himself visible to persons who were not so gifted. He is said to have been a jolly personable being, with a broad blue bonnet, flowing yellow hair, and a long walking-staff. Every manor-house had its *uruisg* ; and in the kitchen, close by the fire, was a seat which was left unoccupied for him. The house of a proprietor on the banks of the Tay is, even at this day, believed to have been haunted by this sprite, and a particular apartment therein has been for centuries called *Seomair Bhrunaidh*,

'Brownie's Room.' When irritated through neglect or disrespectful treatment, he would not hesitate to become wantonly mischievous. He was, notwithstanding, rather gainly than formidable. Though, on the whole, a lazy, lounging hobgoblin, he would often bestir himself on behalf of those who understood his humours and suited themselves thereto. When in this mood he was known to perform many arduous exploits in the kitchen, barn, and stable with marvellous precision and rapidity. These kind deeds were done without bribe, fee, or reward ; for the offer of any one of these would banish him for ever. Kind treatment was all that he wished for ; and it never failed to procure his favour. . . . The urisks seldom discoursed with men, but they held frequent and affectionate converse with one another. They had their general assemblies too ; and on these occasions they commonly selected for their rendezvous the rocky recesses of some remote torrent, whence their loud voices, mingling with the water's roar, carried to the ears of wondering superstition detached parts of their unearthly colloquies." Armstrong gives the names of several urisks which were well known in Breadalbane, and adds, " They still live in legends which continue to amuse old age and infancy." The following Gaelic rhyme gives a list of the principal urisks of Breadalbane :—

" Peallaidh an Spuit
Is Brunaidh an Easain,
Babaidh an Lochain
Is Brunaidh an Eilein ;
Paderlan a Fearnan,
Peadragan, Patragan.
Triubhas-dubh a Fartairchill,
Fuath Coire Ghamhnain,
Cas-Luath Leitir,
Amhlagan-dubh
Is Catan Ceann-liath,
Is Uruisg dubh more Eas-amhlagan."

Peallaidh of the Spout had his abode near the Upper Falls of Moness ; and gives his name to the town of Aberfeldy which is *Aberpheallaidh*, the Confluence of Peallaidh's burn. Aberfeldy has no connection whatever with Saint Palladius, as has been supposed by some writers. Peallaidh's name is also attached to the slope of a hill in Glenlyon. Brunaidh an Easain frequented the Lower Falls of Moness. These two urisks used to enter the houses of Aberfeldy at night, and play tricks upon the inmates. Brunaidh an Eilein dwelt in the Isle of Loch Tay ; while Paderlan had his home in the deep ravines of the burn to the west of Fearnan, which still bears his name, " Allt Phaderleigh." He frequented another burn about half a mile to the east of Crianlarich, which used to be known as " Allt na Paderlan." Triubhas

WATERFALL ON LAWERS BURN.

Dubh (Black Breeks) dwelt somewhere near Fortingall ; while Cas Luath (Fleet Foot) used to meet people about the old wood of Letterellan. Fuath (the Spectre) had his haunt in Coire Ghamhnan at the foot of Ben Doran. Bruanaidh an Eilean, Cas Luath an Leitir, and Paderlan commanded the road leading to Lawers from Kenmore, where, in olden times, the markets for the district were held. It has not been possible to find the localities of the other urisks mentioned in the rhyme.

Mr. James Macdiarmid relates several stories about the Breadalbane urisks ; and the following are translations of a few tales taken from the " Transactions " :—

The Ardeonaig Urisk.

On the evening of a certain day, when the good wife in one of the houses of Bealach, Ardeonaig, was busy baking oat-cakes, a young urisk came to the door. He walked in without being invited, and silently took his seat by the side of the fire. He kept his eyes steadily fixed on the cake that was baking, and no sooner was it ready then he seized it and quickly devoured it. This went on for a while, but the goodwife said never a word. At length she could not stand such conduct on the part of the urisk any longer ; because it was evident that the creature could never be satisfied. She decided to put a stop to the thing, and in order to do so, she swept a hot bannock from the brander, and laid it on the bare knees of the urisk. He jumped up at once, and bolting out at the door screamed his loudest, running away towards the waterfall. The woman knew that the old urisk would be sure to come to the house. She therefore barred the door tightly, and placed some heavy furniture behind it. The windows were so narrow that the urisk could not possibly come through them. It was well that the door was barred ; for the old urisk came to it with a great noise, and by knocking and kicking he tried to break it. Thanks to the good, sound wood of which the door was made he was unable to open or break it, and before the men-folk returned home he had given up the effort and had retired to his den. As long as she lived that woman was not without a tale to tell about the urisk.

The Blairmore (Carwhin) Urisk.

There is a deep pool in the Carwhin burn called *Linne na slige*, the Pool of the shell ; and many years ago an urisk, whose name was *Sligeachan*, dwelt there. Sligeachan had a young urisk, who, according to the tale, was continually annoying the good-wife of Blairmore, and asking her name. Wisely and cunningly she answered, " My name is Myself ; and nobody but Myself." As often as the little urisk put the question he got the same answer, " Myself, Myself." At length, an end came to the patience of the good woman, and she could stand the bare legs and the mischievous fingers of the urisk no longer. She lifted a dish of hot water and threw it over his legs. When Sligeachan heard his young one screaming and crying he went hurriedly to see what was wrong. " What has happened to you, my child ? " he asked. " My ankles have been scalded," was the reply. " Who did that ?" the old one inquired. The answer came, " Myself, Myself, and nobody but Myself." " Well," said Sligeachan, " it is a good thing it was no one else did it, or I would punish him." In that way the wife of Blairmore got rid of the urisk that troubled her ; and Sligeachan never discovered that it was she who threw the hot water at his son.

The urisk of Carwhin is said to have been a splendid weaver, and at that work he was equal to any six men.

Adaidh of the Lochan.

Adaidh was an urisk who dwelt in Glenlochan, the short pass that connects Glenquaich with Glenalmond. He was famed for his kindliness and obliging nature ; and is said to have been the first to introduce sheep into these parts, which must have been long, long ago. He was very good at managing sheep, and attending to them when they were sick. He was also sympathetic towards human beings. Once when a Glenalmond woman required the aid of a mid-wife (*bean-ghluin*) Adaidh went in the dead of night, took a horse from the stable, saddled it, and rode off to Glenquaich. He placed the mid-wife behind him on the horse, and when they were passing the loch where Adaidh was said to have his haunt, the woman became afraid and said, " What if Adaidh of the Lochan comes out and catches us ? " To this the urisk replied, " You need not fear for Adaidh. He will not be nearer to you tonight than he is at the present moment." Adaidh's cave is at the foot of a rock near *Loch a mhuilionn*.

Caobarlan of Drummond Hill.

An amusing story is told of *Caobarlan*, the urisk who had his den in the Deep Burn on Drummond Hill. He got his name from his mischievous habit of throwing *caoban* (sods and stones) at belated pedestrians, some of whom were unsteady on their feet, as they passed from Kenmore to Fearnan. Once upon a time there was a woman in Fearnan who was thrifty, diligent, and well-doing, but she was cursed with a lazy lout of a husband who insisted on eating, and yet would do no manner of work. The woman had a cow that grazed on Drummond, and that usually found its own way home in the evening. One evening, however, the darkness was fast falling, but the cow did not return. The woman asked her husband to go with her to look for the wandered beast ; but he sullenly refused. With that she set out herself in the dark ; and as she passed Caobarlan's den she was trembling with fear, and began to say aloud, " Blessing on thy name, Fellow that lives in the burn ; early or late from thee I take no fear." On hearing this, who appeared from his hollow but the urisk ; and he gave her great praise for her words. " Do you know," he said, " it is a blessing from one of the children of Adam that I have been waiting for all through my life."   He asked her if he could do anything to help her. She explained her errand at that time of night on the hill ; and off he went with her to seek the cow. They found it in a hollow, and beside it was a fine bull-calf. Caobarlan helped the woman home to Stron-fearnan with the cow and calf ; and when he had got them safely into the byre, he went into the house and gave to the lazy husband a trouncing that he remembered to the end of his life. Having performed that good deed, and received the blessing of a human being, Caobarlan removed from Drummond ; but the hollow where the cow and calf were found is still called *Lag an tairbh Dhuibh* (the Hollow of the Black Bull).

Paderlan's Removal.

Many stories used to be told of *Paderlan's* pranks ; but his sojourn in the burn that has retained his name for centuries came at last to an end, and in the following way :—One late autumn evening an old farmer from Balnasume, Lawers, was making his way home from the Kenmore market. He hurried on as fast as he could so that he might get past Allt Phaderleigh before it was too late ; but hard as he trotted his horse past the burn, he felt some creature lithely and lightly jumping up on the horse behind him. He guessed that it must be a young urisk, but the old farmer was not afraid, and he wrapped his plaid round the creature, and strapped it tightly to himself. He then drove home as fast as his horse could carry him. On getting into the house he unfolded his queer burden, and showed the little urisk to his sons. He told one of them to bar the door, and ordered another to put on a large fire of peats, and place the end of the old coulter of the plough in the fire. Then they all waited breathlessly for the arrival of Paderlan ; for the old man was certain he would come for his son without delay. They had not long to wait. Paderlan made a great din at the door, and demanded back his child. At first those within did not answer ; and then Paderlan put his head in at the window, and said with a fearful voice, " Give me my son." The farmer said, " I will do what you want, but you must first promise me that you will leave this country, and never again return." " To please you I will go, then, to the Carn-dearg, above Ardeonaig," answered the urisk. " That will not do," replied the farmer, " You must leave Breadalbane, or you will not get your son." Paderlan at last said, " I yield to you, and shall do what you wish." The old farmer then handed the little urisk out by the window, and as he did so, Paderlan said, " Old man, in the parting I should like to get a shake of your hand." " That you will have," said the farmer, and with that he took the coulter from the fire, and pushed the hot end through the window.

Paderlan took hold of it, and his hand twisted like a cork-screw. " Good-bye, old man," said Paderlan, " hard and dry is your grasp." And from that day Paderlan was never seen in the country of Breadalbane. This story about Paderlan was related to me almost word for word in the Gaelic of the above narrative by the late Peter Macdonald, Achianich. Besides the urisks already mentioned the names of the following have survived, but their several haunts cannot be identified :— Cleitean, Cludarlan, Uisdean, Martain, and Slochdail a chuirt.

The disappearance of the urisks from Breadalbane is said to have been due to the curiosity of a shepherd on the farm of Callelochan who discovered their place of assembly, and went to pry upon them. This shepherd had noticed from time to time a mysterious light late at night in an old sheep-house on the farm. He had heard much about the urisks, and believed that it was they who gathered there. Wishing to see the creatures, the shepherd concealed himself in a corner of the house one evening when he expected an assembly of the urisks to be due. He was not disappointed, for after waiting some time he saw Peallaidh from the Moness Falls arriving. Peallaidh took his place at the door, and welcomed each of his friends as he turned up, giving him a hearty hand-shake and mentioning his name. The shepherd was much interested in the proceedings ; but the language in which the urisks spoke was very different from his, and he could not understand much of what they said to one another. Anxious to get a better view of the creatures, the shepherd made a move-ment forward, and, in doing so, upset a smearing-stool. This completely startled the urisks. They blew out the fir torch that gave them light, and bolted out at the door. From that night they deserted Breadalbane in a body ; and it is believed that they took their departure to some region farther north, where they might be free from interference by human beings, and where they could keep their secrets to themselves.

Witchcraft.

Belief in witchcraft and in the power of magical processes was at one time as general and deep-rooted in Breadalbane as it was in other parts of the Highlands : but these superstitious ideas and practices gradually faded away before the growing light of education, and by the middle of the nineteenth century very few traces of them survived. During the eighteenth century the Kirk Session of Kenmore investigated and dealt with several disputes that had been caused by persons being accused of using charms and enchantments. The recorded evidence of witnesses before the Session reveals some of the methods adopted by parties who wished to hurt their neighbours and secure advantages for themselves.

In 1730, a woman residing at the Port of Loch Tay appeared before the Session complaining that a neighbour and his wife had charged her with witchcraft. The Session summoned the parties, and after hearing their statements dismissed them with " a sessional rebuke." In the same year a widow at Lawers was reported to have accused John Lumsdane, an elder of the congregation, with having caused the death of her children. When she appeared at Kenmore, she denied that she had ever raised such a slander against Lumsdane, and the case was thereupon departed from.

In the summer of 1747, Margaret Robertson, residing at Rhevucky, appeared before the Session complaining that she was unjustly charged with witchcraft and enchantments ; and particularly that Archibald Cameron and his wife in Rhevucky, accused her of these diabolical arts. Margaret craved that the Session should enquire into the scandal, by which her character was suffering in the eyes of her neighbours. The Kirk Session summoned her accusers and other witnesses, and devoted several meetings to the investigation of the affair. It transpired that Margaret Robertson had a neighbour, Patrick Tosach, who was being evicted for some reason from his house and holding, by which she was greatly enraged. She was heard to call down curses upon the head of Archibald Cameron, or any other who should dispossess Patrick Tosach. She prayed that he might have " ill meeting and ill flitting, that ill might he thrive, and that he might be drowned by sea or water." A neighbour woman alleged that very early on the morning of the day that Archibald Cameron came down the loch to enter upon occupation of Tosach's house and croft, Margaret was seen to go to the shore with her rock and spindle, and bending down she began to tie or untie the thread about the " busses." The witness added, " What could she be doing there with her rock, spindle, and thread, if she was not about some bad design."

When Margaret was faced with the statements of the witnesses, she admitted that she had gone to the shore on the morning in question, but only for the purpose of gathering a few sticks to kindle the fire, and make breakfast for her step-son who was going from home ; she strongly denied that she had any evil designs in her actions. She acknowledged, however, that one day when she and others were in Patrick Tosach's garden, she had said in wrath, " the devil take them in the air that are the instruments of Patrick Tosach's removal."

The Session, after considering the evidence of the witnesses and Margaret's own admissions, unanimously found her guilty of praying curses and imprecations, " and appointed her to stand three several Lord's days before the congregation, and there to be rebuked for her sin and scandal." They did not, however, find her guilty of witchcraft, and therefore they appointed her accuser to be rebuked by the Session for raising such a scandal, " and the rebuke to be publicly intimated to the congregation on the Lord's day."

In the same year that Margaret Robertson's case was dealt with, two young girls, Janet and Margaret McIntaggart, were charged with using charms and enchantments against Alexander Fisher in Wester Acharn. Janet confessed before the Session that, observing that the substance of their milk was taken away, she was advised by certain women to milk three drops from their neighbour's sheep as a charm to recover the substance of their own milk, and that after this was done, the substance of their milk did actually return. Margaret, her sister, acknowledged that on a recent Sabbath morning she had gone to the house of Alexander Fisher and to all the houses in the town with an egg shell having a little milk in it, because she had been informed that the milk in the shell would " earn," and the substance of their own milk would return. Alexander Fisher's wife in giving evidence stated that having been warned by neighbours she regarded the visit of Margaret McIntaggart to her house early on the Sabbath morning with some suspicion. She told the girl that if she came in God's name she was welcome to stay, but if she came in the Devil's name with the egg-shell and the milk she had better get away at once. Margaret replied that she had simply come to enquire whether her maid was going to the church that day. Mrs. Fisher, not being satisfied with Margaret's explanation, declared that she followed her quietly to the door, and saw her open her breast, and take out the egg shell with the milk in it. She thereupon went and immediately told her neighbours about the matter. When parties had been removed, the Session considered the affair, and " being difficulted how to behave in it," they desired the minister (Mr. John Douglas) to consult his brethren about it. Three weeks later Mr. Douglas reported that he had talked to some of his brethren about the McIntaggarts, and they were of the opinion " that they should be rebuked on some several Sabbaths." The girls were accordingly summoned to appear on the following Sabbath, and were ordered to stand before the congregation to be rebuked " for their base practices." They were afterwards " examined, exhorted, and dismissed."

In 1753 it was reported to the minister and elders by Tawish McCawish, the elder of the church in Glenquaich, that there was an affair in Shian that had occasioned great disturbance in the neighbourhood. He stated that three years previously the wife of Donald Thomson had been accused of using charms. On that occasion he had inquired into the matter, and finding it to be of a trifling nature he put an end to it without troubling the Session. That summer, however, Donald Thomson's servant, Janet McNicol, had been seen carrying out some unusual and unbecoming practices very early on Beltane morning (first day of May, Old Style). She had been observed by several neighbours crossing a stripe or burn back and fore three times, going down the burn, and bowing herself, as if she were putting something in the ground, or taking something hence. When she came to an ash bush she had a few sticks in her hand, and there went down on her feet and hands. After that she proceeded towards her master's house. Another woman alleged that she had been at the fold milking the cows with Donald Thomson's wife, and had seen her cut some hairs from her cow's tail, put them up carefully in a napkin round her neck, and tie a knot about it. The neighbours all concluded that such practices carried out by mistress and maid were intended to secure for themselves the produce of other people's milk, and they accused them of having it concealed in their shealing.

The Session dismissed Donald Thomson's wife with an exhortation " to beware of using anything like charms in all time coming " ; but they ordered Janet McNicol to stand before the congregations at Kenmore and Amulree, and to be rebuked in both churches for her offences, which were aggravated by the fact that she " prayed that God would inflict vengeance upon them who had brought so much trouble and shame upon her."

In 1757 Donald Macnab, Lawers, complained to the Session that he and his grandmother, Anne McInucatar, had been charged " with using charms and enchantments to the detriment of Duncan McInucatar." From statements made by several witnesses who were examined by the Session it appears that Anne had a bad reputation in the district, and was generally feared by the people. One man declared that " he would rather incur the displeasure of any other woman in the neighbourhood than that of Anne McInucatar, as he feared she might do him hurt."

Duncan McInucatar and the other witnesses related their reasons for suspecting Anne of engaging in magical practices. One man told that several years previously a number of milk coggies had been burnt because they had been made and used for enchantments, and that one of these dishes belonged to Anne. Another witness related how Anne and her daughter Elspeth used to go out in the night time when the people were at the shealings, and visit the calf bothies. Their conduct was regarded as intended for no good purpose, and gave great offence to the neighbours. Duncan McInucatar and other two men declared that they saw Anne go down on the evening of the first day of May to the shore of Loch Tay in a most suspicious manner. She had a coat over her head, as if she wished to conceal her identity. When she returned she went out of her way to a little cairn of stones, and there deposited something, which the men discovered afterwards to be a bottle of muddy water. They replaced the bottle just as they had found it, and one of them watched to see who would come for it. In a short time Anne's daughter, Elspeth Dewar, came to fetch the bottle. All such practices had led the neighbours to suspect Anne of using charms and enchantments for the purpose of doing harm to others.

Duncan McInucatar stated that Anne had strongly disapproved of the wife he had married, and he firmly believed that on his wedding day she employed Donald Macnab to do him an injury. Duncan did not think that Donald himself was capable of doing it, but he " suspected that through the arts of his said grandmother he was the instrument of doing him harm." Anne in her statement declared she wished to explain that when she went to the loch she had no evil designs against any one. Her purpose in going was to procure a little water with which to wash a sickly child, and seeing some persons working in a field and not wishing to raise their suspicions, she placed the bottle in the cairn. Anne made no reference to the other incidents mentioned by the witnesses, or to the charge which Duncan McInucatar had brought against her. Beyond hearing parties the Session did nothing further in this case, which was the last of its kind to be brought before them.

The ill fame of Anne probably accounts for the following story of a noted Lawers witch related by Mr. James Macdiarmid :— Previous to, and some time after the year 1760, there lived at Lawers a notable witch who was known as *Cailleach Dhomhnuill Bhric*, Donald Breac's Old Wife. She kept the whole countryside in fear, and was believed to be in league with his Satanic Majesty. She was an adept at the black art. Many an innocent person is said to have suffered at her hands, and all the neighbours shunned her as much as possible. She was reputed to have had the power of causing abortion in cows, and of depriving them of their milk-giving powers in a single day. She was also accused of bewitching young children, so that they fell into a decline. At other times she mesmerised or cast a spell over horses, and they would neither eat, drink, nor work, until she had been called in to undo the spell. She assumed many guises in order to accomplish her wicked designs, but according to good authority, that of a hare was her favourite guise. It was masquerading in the form of a hare that led to her detection, and enabled the *Gobhain Mor Macmartain*, the Big Blacksmith Macmartain, to put an end to her wicked and mischievous career as a witch. Some time about the fore-mentioned date, on the first day of May (Beltane), the Big Smith was making his way to the smithy, when, casting an eye in the direction of his croft, he saw a large brown hare performing many curious antics. His suspicions were aroused, and getting as near the hare as possible he was surprised to hear a well-known voice invoking the Beltane deity, and saying, " Transfer the summer's growth, and the harvest's crop from the smith's croft to the adjoining one." The adjoining croft was none other than that of the Cailleach, and so the smith's suspicions were confirmed.

Hastening with all speed to the smithy, the smith told his apprentice that there was a hare on the croft which would afford them an opportunity of testing a flint gun which the latter had been repairing. The gun was duly loaded and presented at the hare, which was immediately transformed into a woman. The apprentice took a steady aim and fired, but though his hand was steady, and his eye unerring in its aim, his shot had no effect; and the woman again turned into a hare. The smith and his assistant were confounded, but, reloading with a silver sixpence instead of lead, the smith fired in God's name at the hare and wounded it. The hare made straight for Donald Breac's house, which it entered by the cat-hole in the door. Donald Breac and his wife were the smith's nearest neighbours, and as they were not seen by him on that day, nor yet on the following forenoon, he resolved to call on them to see if anything was wrong. Accompanied by his apprentice he proceeded to do so, but was refused admittance. Thereupon he ordered his apprentice to hold the door while he was setting fire to the house. On hearing that threat the terrified inmates soon opened the door, but shame and confusion were depicted on their countenances, for the Cailleach was limping on one leg, owing to the sixpence having penetrated one of her thighs to the bone; and all around her were scattered in wild disorder the magic implements of her craft. These included charms, urns, hair tethers, stone balls, wooden cups, dried kail stocks, and a bladder full of cow's hair and raven's feathers. The contents of the bladder, when properly dried, she pounded into a fine powder, which she used for blinding people. Being at last caught, to save herself from an untimely end, she made a full confession of all her misdeeds. The smith, who knew something of veterinary science, attended to the woman's wound, and extracted the sixpence. The wound soon healed, but the Cailleach remained a cripple to the end of her life. She destroyed all the implements of her devilish art, and repented of all the evil she had done. It is believed she died a good Christian, and at peace with all men. She was buried in the gateway of Lawers graveyard; and at the beginning of last century her name was well known on the shores of Loch Tay.

Some greedy persons who were not content with their own milk supply imagined that by performing a certain ceremony they could appropriate that of a neighbour. These silly creatures would go out early on Beltane morning, and draw a hair rope over the dewy grass, saying as they did so, " *Bainne an te so shios, bainne an te so shuas 'na mo ghogan fhein.*" (The milk of that cow down, the milk of that cow up, in my own great coggie). This ceremony was known as " gathering the dew." A man who came unexpectedly upon two women on a croft at Morenish going through strange performances with a long rope of hair, cut the rope, and gave the women a scolding. About fifty years ago a young man who had never heard of such superstitious practices saw a woman dragging a rope after her early on a May morning across a field on the south side of Loch Tay. When he hailed the woman she was greatly surprised, and appeared agitated. She said to him, " Don't tell John Crerar what you saw me doing in his field." When the man mentioned the matter shortly afterwards to a neighbour, the reply he received was, " The witch ! why, she was trying to take the milk from John Crerar's cattle."

Until recently an odd person might be found in Breadalbane who firmly believed that cattle and horses could be affected by the malign influences of the " evil eye." The cure for animals so influenced was to take water in God's name from a stream over which the living passed and the dead were carried, put it in a pail along with a silver coin, and then sprinkle the water in the ears and over the backs of the ailing animals. The residue of the water was given to the animals to drink, and if the coin was found to adhere to the bottom of the pail, the cure was supposed to be complete. Cows were protected from the influences of the " evil eye " by tying a pin of rowan wood to their tails. People also believed that evil spells could be cast upon the cream in the churns so that the butter would not come, however long it was churned. They never suspected for a moment that the trouble was due probably to the cream being below the churning temperature ; and in order to counteract the spell they put silver in the form of a coin, or an ornament, into the churn.

With the decline in the population of the district and the gradual disappearance of the race that inhabited Breadalbane for centuries the old traditions and legends have been forgotten, and much interesting lore has been irrevocably lost.

> " And gone are the green-coated fairies
> That brightened the hillside of old,
> The witches that rode on the tempest,
> The urisk that haunted the fold.

> " The life of the days that have fleeted,
> Comes back not with vision or spell ;
> So rest ye, dim shadows of cloudland—
> Ye fairies, for ever fare-well ! "

ALEXANDER NICOLSON.

CHAPTER XXX.

Surnames.

A S elsewhere in the Highlands, surnames did not come into general use in Breadalbane until the seventeenth and eighteenth centuries. Prior to this period men and women were distinguished by their patronymics, with the result that it is often difficult to determine which clan or sept of a clan a person may have belonged to. Callum McNeill VcConnochie in Fearnan may have been a MacGregor ; but another Callum at Killin who was similarly styled may have been a Macnab.

An examination of old Breadalbane surnames shows that the majority of them were derived from Christian names. Among this class we find some of the most ancient names in Scotland, such as *McNaughton, McAlpin, McDiarmid, and McCairbre* (extinct). The Gaelic word *gille*, signifying lad or servant, coupled with a term expressing a personal quality or colour, or the name of a saint provides us with a large number of surnames. In this way we get such surnames as *McIllechruim,* Son of the Crooked-lad, *McIlleghorrive,* Son of the Thick-set lad. Then from *bane* white or fair, *buidhe* yellow, *ciar* dusky, *donn* brown, *dubh* black, *gorm* blue, *riach* brindled, come such surnames as *McIllebhain, McIllebhuide, McIllechiar, McIlledhuinn, McIlle-dhuibh, McIlleghuirm,* and *McIlleriach.* Sometimes the personal quality is used alone, as in *Maildheach* (Malloch), heavy eyebrowed ; or a colour may be coupled with a Christian name, as with Iain, in *McInvane* and *McInduy.* From *gille* and *Iosa* (Jesus) come the names *Gillies* and *McLeish* ; and from the same word with *Criosda* (Christ) we get *Gilchrist* and *McGilchrist. Gille* in combination with such saints' names as *Fillan, Patrick, Callum, Paul, Martin,* and *Michael,* provided another numerous class of surnames. The Church establishment originated such names as *Clerk, Haggart* (from Gaelic *sagart* priest), *Dewar, Macnab,* and *McVicar.* The Gaelic terms for trades and occupations have given us such names as *Crerar* (Sifter), *Caird* (Artificer), *Iasgair* (Fisher), *Greasaich* (Shoemaker), *Fucadair* (Walker), *Bracadair* (Maltman), *Portair* (Ferryman). When men bearing such surnames went to the lowlands long ago they often retained them in their Gaelic forms ; while those who remained in Breadalbane changed their names into English equivalents. In this way we get *Cairds* and *Nucators* in Dundee ; but in Breadalbane we have *Tinkler* (changed to *Sinclair*), and *Walker.*

w

Several small septs adopted the surname *Campbell* by agreement with the lairds of Glenorchy, among them the *McKerlichs*, *McGlasserigs*, *McNucators*, and the *McIlleghorrives*. The following surnames derived from places existed in Breadalbane, *Puderach* (Buttar), probably from *Bothchuider* (Balquhidder), *McKester* from Yester, and *Kippen*.

The following list of Surnames has been made up from old documents, muster rolls, rentals, and Kirk Session records. Notes have been added about certain families and individuals connected with them. So far as possible the year and locality of persons bearing the surnames are given.

Breadalbane Surnames.

ANDERSON. Some Breadalbane Andersons were locally called McComie. 1617, Alaster Anderson, Stronfearnan ; 1698, Alexander, Donald, Tomgarrow ; 1769, John, Morenish ; John, Duncan, Cloan, Lawers ; Alexander, Tullichcan ; John, Achianich ; Alexander, Croftmartaig ; Patrick, Portbane. John Anderson of the " Polytechnic," Glasgow, was a McComie Anderson from Tomgarrow.

ARMSTRONG. Robert, schoolmaster, Kenmore (1788-1828) ; previously at Dull ; married Mary Mckerchar ; had a family of twelve children : Robert, eldest, educated St. Andrews University, trained for the ministry, but never took a charge ; went to London, where he started a boarding-school for noblemen's sons ; published Gaelic Dictionary, 1825 ; LLD., St. Andrews ; married Anna Dungate, and had three daughters ; died 1867. William, younger son of Robert, succeeded as schoolmaster at Kenmore ; retired 1873 ; died 1879. James, son of Robert, minister at Foss.

BARRON. Agnes, wife of John Roy Campbell, Kenmore ; fined 1627, for ringing kirk bell " out of her ambitious humouris, which is appoyntit for the glory of God." 1735, John, Inchadney.

BISHOP. 1580, Duncan, alias Campbell, Glenlochay, natural son of John Campbell, bishop of the Isles, who was second son of Duncan Campbell, second Laird of Glenorchy. Duncan's name appears in Gaelic as *Mcinespic*.

BROWN. G. Mcilledhuinn. 1769, Gilbert, Kiltyrie ; Duncan, Tirarthur ; Duncan, Morenish. 1834, Archibald, Malcolm, John, Morenish.

BUCHANAN. 1769, John, Tomnadashan ; 1834, Alexander, Smith, Acharn (Kenmore).

CAMERON. Some members of this clan in Breadalbane were known as McPhail. 1698, John, Duncan, Lawers ; 1769, Donald, Balnasuim (Lawers) ; Malcolm, Camuschurich ; Duncan, Tullich ; Archibald, Acharn (Kenmore). Ewen Cameron, Lawers (1705-1817), mill-wright, first to introduce spinning-wheels and jack-reels into the Highlands ; built lint-mills all over the North ; and constructed the first mills north of the Forth for shelling barley. Robert Cameron from Lawers was Member of Parliament for Sunderland. John, his brother, wrote a book on the Gaelic names of Plants. Their father was schoolmaster at Lawers in early decades of last century.

CAMPBELL. There were very few members of this clan in Breadalbane prior to the coming of the first Laird of Glenorchy to the district. Ewen Campbell (1570), of Lix and Craignavie, was probably of the Strachur Campbells. In 1769 there were eighteen Campbells paying rent on the south side of Loch Tay, and ten on the north side.

The only members of this clan, other than the Earl of Breadalbane, now owning lands in Breadalbane, are Mr. John Campbell and Miss Catherine Campbell of Boreland, Fearnan. Their grandfather and father had been tenants of Boreland during last century, and the family gradually took over the tenancy of Balnearn to the west of Fearnan. When the eastern portion of the Breadalbane estates was sold in 1923, Messrs. Alexander and John Campbell and their sister, Miss Catherine Campbell, purchased the lands of Croftnallin, Boreland, Corrie-cherrow, Balnairn, Ballemenach, Tomintyvoir, and Lagfearn. Mr. Alexander Campbell died in January, 1930. He had a profound love for Breadalbane and an extensive and accurate knowledge of its history and traditions. He made a valuable collection of Gaelic books. Another member of this family, Christina, married Mr. William Angus, Builder and Contractor. Their son, Mr. William Angus, is at present Keeper of Registers, Register House, Edinburgh. On their mother's side this family of Campbells is descended from the Campbells of Ardeonaig. The charm stone of the Ardeonaig Campbells is preserved at Boreland. This property, including the farm of Boreland and the west side of Fearnan, is for sale (1937).

CHRISTIE. This surname was confined to Glendochart and Killin. The family may be descended from Harry Christie who was chamberlain to Sir Robert Campbell of Glenorchy, 1655 ; 1698, James, Waulk mill of Killin ; 1800, Donald, Mid-lix ; John, Gilbert, Ledcharrie. A silver brooch of Celtic design made at Killin, was presented to a nursemaid of the name of Christie by Campbell of Auchlyne at the beginning of the eighteenth century. It is still in possession of a descendant, Mr. Duncan Ferguson, Carie. Dr. Dugald Christie, the famous missionary of the Church of Scotland in Manchuria, belonged to the Christies of Glendochart. He died in 1936. The family is still represented in Glendochart by Mr. James Christie, tenant of Auchlyne farm, and his sisters, the Misses Christie, Crianlarich.

CHRISTISON. A family of this name held Ledcharrie in the fifteenth century ; 1456, sasine to Thome Cristin de Laidquerne

(Exchequer Rolls) ; 1484, sasine to Donald Crystesoun ; 1494, charter to Donald Cristisone.

CLARK. G. *Clerach*, Mcillechlerich. 1480, a tenant of this name in Eddergoll ; 1541, Duncan, Kiltyrie ; 1769, Duncan, Craig ; Donald, Croftmartaig ; Finlay, Edramuckie ; Duncan, Drumnaferoch. Peter Clark from Kiltyrie became minister of Free Church of Scotland, went to Canada, died there, 1885.

COMBACH, alias Stewart. G. *McCombich*. This family claims to have come to Lawers with the " Lady of Lawers " from Appin of Stewart, Argyll. 1734, Donald, Milton of Lawers ; 1769, Duncan, Morenish ;   Duncan, Lawernacroy ;   Archibald, Lurginbuy.

COMRIE. 1698, John, tenant, Port of Lochtay, probably son of Alexander Comrie, minister of Kenmore ; John's daughter, Margaret, married Duncan Forester, gardener, Taymouth.

CRERAR, alias McIntosh. G. *Mcachrerar*. Rev. Allan Sinclair of Kenmore tells that the Crerars, who were numerous around Kenmore and Acharn, were descended from a McIntosh of Monivaird who came over the hills to escape from justice. He took refuge from his pursuers in the mill of Acharn. In order to conceal him the miller shook meal over him, and placed the sieve in his hands, and told him to carry on sifting the meal. The pursuers arrived, entered the mill, but failed to identify the fugitive. He settled down at Acharn, and was ever after known as *An Criathrear*, " The Sifter." 1541, John McAchrerar had half of Balinlagan ; 1579, Donald, Remony ; 1644, Patrick, Carnbane ; Gillechreist, Ardtalnaig ; John Dow, Ten-Shilling Land ; Donald, Tullich (Ardtalnaig). The last named was the only man to possess a gun on Muster Roll of 1644. 1769, John, Morenish ; Donald, Edramuckie ; Donald, Balnasuim (Lawers) ; John, Ardeonaig ; Alexander, Claggan ; Donald, Tomflower ; Patrick, Callelochan ; Patrick, Balnasuim (Kenmore).

DEWAR. G. *Deor, Mcindeor*. Name derived from *Deor*, " Custodier " of a relic of St. Fillan. There were at one time five such custodiers in Glendochart, and the name was therefore common in the glen and around Killin. At the east end of Loch Tay, John Mcindeor in Portbane was a prominent man in 1597. A son of the Laird of Glenorchy was fostered in his family, and John entered into an agreement with Sir Duncan Campbell " for the benevolence received by him from the deceased Colin Campbell of Glenorchy." 1834, Donald, Balinlagan ; John, Croftmartaig ; Donald, Portbane ; Alexander, Stronfearnan. Duncan Dewar, minister of Dull (1839-1861) was a native of Acharn (Kenmore). His accounts as a student at St. Andrews University were published with a commentary by the late Sir Peter Scott Lang, in 1926. Four of his nephews, sons of John Dewar, clerk of works, Taymouth, were ministers of the Church of Scotland :—Duncan, Applecross ; John, Kilmartin ; Peter, North Bute ; Alexander, Amulree.

DOUGLAS. 1698, John, Taymouth ; 1769, Andrew, Croftmartaig ; 1834, Andrew, Lurgloman.

DOW, alias McCalman. Patrick Dow's heirs had wadset of Corrycharmaig in 1699.

DUFF. 1699, Alexander had wadset of Camuschurich.

FERGUSON. 1585, Donald Roy McFergis, Balloch ; 1769, John, Morenish ; Patrick, Rhynchuilg ; Duncan, Duallen.

FISHER. G. Iesker, Mcinesker. Numerous around Loch Tay. The Fishers claim to have been fishers to the Scottish kings. 1624, John McConochie V'Nesker in Achessan ; Duncan, Bovain ; 1698, John, Acharn (Kenmore) ; Donald, Croftmartaig ; 1769, Duncan, Patrick, John, Donald, tenants in Ardeonaig ; John, Portbane ; Donald, Fearnan ; descendants of John Fisher, Portbane, now at Culdamore, Fortingall.

FLEMING. John ; tenant in Port of Loch Tay, 1579 ; signed petition for new church at Kenmore.

FLETCHER. 1698, William, Croftmartaig.

FRASER, alias Mckimi. 1585, James Mcfinlay Mckemy ; 1698, Robert, Croftintygan ; 1834, Hugh, Tomb (Lawers). Some families of this name are descended from Simon Fraser, who was well known around Taymouth and Kenmore at the end of the eighteenth century. He is belived to have been connected with the Frasers of Lovat. John Fraser Graham, D.D., Glasgow, came from Lawers.

GORDON. 1644, William, cottar, Tullich (Ardtalnaig) ; may have been a MacGregor.

GRAHAME. 1834, Duncan, Miller at Lawers and elder.

GRESICH. G. McGresiche, McaGresich. 1624, Donald, Balloch; McGressiche, Tirarthur ; 1644, Donald, Skiag ; 1763, Donald Mor Gresich alias McDougall.

HAGGART. G. Sagart, Mcintaggart. Name common around Acharn and Kenmore ; 1582, Mcintaggart ; 1698, Christian, Balnaskiag; 1736, John, Kenmore (poor's box of church placed for safe custody in his house after being burgled) ; 1769, John, Lurgloman ; Donald senior, and Donald junior, Acharn ; Margaret, Rhevucky ; John, Balnasuim, Kenmore. In 1834, there were seven heads of families of this name connected with Kenmore Kirk, all in the Acharn district. James Haggart, Acharn, became woollen manufacturer, and sons founded the business of Messrs. P. & J. Haggart, Aberfeldy, now carried on by Mr. J. D. Haggart, son of Peter, and grandson of James. Another son of James Haggart was minister of Lochcarron, Dr. John Haggart. From Acharn came also John Haggart, doctor in Aberfeldy ; educated at Edinburgh University ; senior prizeman for year in surgery and Materia Medica ; M.B. ; C.M. (1873) ; skilful practitioner, keen antiquarian, lover of Breadalbane and its traditions ; buried at Kenmore, April, 1913.

HAY, alias Mckester. A tenant of the name of Makester appears in the Exchequer Rolls of 1480. The Hays of Kenmore district are said to have come originally from the parish of Yester, and were therefore called " MacYester " locally. 1572, Hugh Hay, first tenant of hostelry at Kenmore ; 1698, Duncan Mceister, Portbane ; 1702, Thomas Hay, Balinlagan ; 1769, Finlay, Donald, Croftmartaig ; Dr. Hay Hunter, minister of St. Andrew's Church, Edinburgh, was related to the Hays of Croftmartaig.

IRVINE. The Irvines may have come into Breadalbane about 1621, when Elizabeth, daughter of Sir Duncan Campbell of Glenorchy, was married in the kirk of Kenmore to the second son of Irvine of Drum. The following entry is found in the Kenmore Kirk Session records :—Jan. 16, 1647—John Irvin presented ane lawful dochter of umquhill Duncan Irvin, his sone, who wes killed be the enemies, the 4th. Jun, at Stronchlachan, and his spouse Margaret Ferguson, and wes callit Marione. In the last century descendants of the Breadalbane Irvines were notable ministers and doctors in Perthshire.

KENNEDY, alias Mcalister. Bard Mcalister mentioned in Household books of Balloch ; 1622, John Dow, Balnasuim (Kenmore) ; 1702, John, Remony ; 1763, John, Skiag ; 1769, John, Ardeonaig ; 1834, Peter, Acharn.

KIPPEN. The Kippens of Kenmore and Acharn district were descended from Andro Kippen, gardener to Sir Duncan Campbell of Glenorchy, 1622. The agreement between the laird and the gardener is printed in B.B.T. 1698, John, Stix ; 1769, Duncan senior, Duncan junior, Acharn ; Isabel, Rhevucky ; Duncan, Remony ; Robert, Kinghallen ; 1835, Andrew, Kenmore. Last members of this family removed to Aberfeldy.

KYNOCH, alias McKenzie. 1769, William, Kindrochit ; John, Rhevucky.

LEITCH. Patrick Leitch, an Irishman, was surgeon to Kings James III. and James IV. He was granted the life-rent of Kiltyrie and part of Ardtalnaig, which was renewed to his son, George Leitch in 1523, by King James V. In the Crown charter it is stated that Patrick was a good servant to the King's most noble grandfather and father and " George is expert in the same art." 1480, Finlay Leitch had part of Tirarthur ; 1623, Duncan, Dunophuill near Coshieville.

LIVINGSTONE, alias Gorm. This surname confined chiefly to Glenquaich ; 1823, Donald, W. Shian ; 1834, Donald, John, W. Shian. Colin Livingstone, the last parish schoolmaster of Fort William, belonged to this family. He was born at Balinreich, Strathbran, died at Fort William, and was buried in Glen Nevis.

He used to say that the first Livingstone in Glenquaich came there to hide after Culloden, and hailed from Lismore. Colin claimed relationship with the great missionary and explorer, and was invited to attend the celebration of his centenary at Edinburgh, in 1913. He was a good Gaelic scholar, and was well acquainted with the traditions of Glenquaich.

LUMSDANE. This family, long resident in the Lawers district, was descended from Robert Lumsdane, assistant to George Leitch, surgeon to King James V. Robert succeeded George Leitch as surgeon, and continued the tenancy of Kiltyrie and part of Ardtalnaig. Charter under Great Seal granted to Robert, 8 April, 1550. 1627, George, Lawers ; 1698, John, Duallen ; 1731, John, elder of the church, Lawers ; 1834, Archibald, Shenlarich (Lawers) ; 1836, Archibald, Stronfearnan. The last members of the family went to Edinburgh.

MCALISTER, see Kennedy.

MCALPIN. 1774, Katherine, Monomore, Killin.

MCANDREW. 1622, Duncan, Leiragan ; 1702, Lawrence, Druimnamuick, Stix ; Kate, Lurgloman ; 1769, John, Balinlagan ; John, Balmacnaughton. The late Colin McAndrew, Builder, Edinburgh, was a native of Ardeonaig. His son, Mr. Gordon McAndrew, Edinburgh, resides for part of the year at Fearnan where he owns a house and land.

MCARTHUR. Surname common on both sides of Loch Tay ; some McArthurs were locally known as *Mcachruim* and *Mcillechruim*. 1763, Donald Mor, Skiag ; 1769, Arthur, Braeintrine ; Duncan, Licknie ; Daniel, Skiag ; John, Callelochan ; Janet, Drumglas ; Gilbert, Croftanalin ; Duncan, Kinghallen ; 1834, Donald, Aleckich ; Arthur, Acharn ; Alexander, Lurgloman ; John, Croftmartaig ; Alexander, Acharn ; Neil, Achianich ; John, Tomgarrow ; John, Croftintygan ; Dougal, Ardvoil. John and James McArthur from Croftintygan (brothers) were doctors. Donald, Acharn, died 1855 ; known as " *An Drobhair Macartar* " ; well known throughout the Highlands as a cattle dealer ; came from Aleckich. Once, coming from Crieff with money, he was pursued by robbers on horse-back, and was saved only by the fleetness of his pony.

MCAUISH. McTavish, McCawis. Some members of this family were styled Campbell. 1480, Donald, son of Duncan, and his mother had a third of Eddergoll ; 1550, McCawis ; 1618, Donald, Ledchroisk ; 1702, John, Druimnamuick ; 1729, Tais Mcavish was made an elder of Kenmore Kirk. He came regularly summer and winter over the hill from Glenquaich to attend session meetings at Kenmore for many years. 1769, John, Portbane ; 1834, Peter, Lurgloman ; Charles, Shian (Glenquaich).

MCAULAY. This name appears in Glenquaich as McCully. 1638, John, Crannich.

MCCALL, alias Mcdonald. 1582, Malcolm ; 1624, Donald, Tirarthur ; 1769, Donald, Alexander, Donald, Kiltyrie ; Rev. Archibald McCall of Glenmoriston, a native of Glendochart, is descended from the McCalls of Kiltyrie. In 1762 Malcolm and Janet McCall, his wife, gave two hundred merks Scots. to the Kirk Session of Kenmore for poor persons " betwixt the Burn of Morenish and the east end of Carwhin," reserving to themselves the interest of the capital for their life.

MCCALLUM. 1579, —— McCallum, Ardtalnaig ; 1735, Duncan Roy, Pitmackie ; 1769, Duncan, Callelochan ; Duncan, Morenish. Mrs. Janet Anderson, Guelph, Ontario, whose maiden name was McCallum, a native of Fearnan, left one hundred pounds to the Kirk Session of Kenmore in 1905 for the benefit of poor persons in Fearnan and Lawers.

MCCALVANE. 1541, John, Glenlochay.

MCCARBRE, MCARBRIE, MCCARBY. There were several wadsetters of this name in Glenlochay and the west end of Loch Tay during the sixteenth century. The name disappears after 1600. The families either left the district, or changed their name. 1480, Duncan, tenant of Morenish and Tirai ; 1541, Duncan, Tullich ; Duncan, Dalgirdie ; Finlay, Tirai ; 1594, John, Ledour.

MCCHAPMAN. 1579, Gilfillan Mcchapman Buy, Kenmore.

MCCOMIE, see Anderson. 1579, Alexander, Balloch ; 1621, Katherine, Tullichglas ; 1698, Duncan, Croftmartaig. Alaster Buidhe McComie in the Braes of Balloch was locally known as *Alaster Buidhe nan Taibhsean,* " Yellow Alexander of the Ghosts." He met a ghost who told him that he could not rest because in life he had stolen plough irons from the smithy of Kenmore. He requested Alaster to take the irons out of a cairn where they had been hidden, and restore them to the smith. Alaster obeyed, and the ghost was never seen again.

MCCORKADALE. 1698, Archibald, Rhevucky ; Janet, Peatcroft, Taymouth.

MCCROSTIE. 1587, Alaster, Corriecharmaig.

MCDIARMID. There were three branches of this clan in Perthshire :—1. The Royal McDiarmids, who had the exclusive right to burial in Cladh Dobhi, Morenish. 2. The Dubh-bhusach (Black-lipped) McDiarmids. 3. The Craigianie McDiarmids, who were known as the Baron McDiarmids. James McDiarmid and his brother, Dr. John McDiarmid, tenants of Morenish farm, and later at Dunraochan, Muthil, belonged to the Craigianie branch. Their collections of Breadalbane folklore are published in the Transactions of the Gaelic Society of Inverness. 1638, Callum McEwen VcKermit, tenant in Crannich ; 1763, James, Ledour (grandfather of the folk-lorists) ; 1769, Hugh, John, Morenish ; Angus, Finlay, John, Kiltyrie ; Finlay, Carwhin ; Hugh,

Craggantoll; Malcolm, Cragganester. The late Duncan McDiarmid, Camusericht, Rannoch, and his brothers, Hugh (Tiree), Robert (Cassels), Donald (Aberfeldy), and John (Edinburgh), were of the Baron McDiarmids.

Rev. Alexander McDiarmid of Morvern was a native of Carie.

MCDONALD. 1579, Duncan Mcillechonyle, Ardtalnaig; John Dow McIllechonyle, Ardtalnaig; 1638, The Baron Duncan Mcillechonell. The west portion of Ardtalnaig is still known as *A Bharranachd*, "The Barony." 1698, Duncan McOil, Machuim.

MCDOUGALL. In 1763, there were nine tenants of this name in the Ardtalnaig district. These were Donald Mor Greasaich, Shenlarich; Donald, Skiag; Ewen, Skiag; John, Lickbuie; John, Milton; Patrick, Milton; Patrick, Revain; Ewen, Achomer; John, Tullich.

The family name of the McDougalls of Achomer and Milton was McEwen. They have farmed lands in the Ardtalnaig and Ardeonaig districts since the middle of the seventeenth century. Several members of the family acted as officials on the Breadalbane estate, and one member, Hugh or Ewen McDougall, was minister of Killin (1795-1827). According to a legend the first of the Achomer family was John Dubh Mor, brother to Duncan McDougall, Lord of Lorn. He had killed the heir of McLean of Duart in a quarrel, and fled to Lochtayside. He heard that a wild beast, said to have been a dragon, was such a terror to the people in the Ardradnaig district that they removed from their homes. John Dubh Mor killed the dragon, and in consideration of the services he thus rendered, the Crown, to whom the lands belonged in those days, gave him a grant of land. He invited other members of his clan to join him, which accounts for the colony of McDougalls on the south side of Loch Tay.

A John McDougall of Achomer married Barbara Campbell, daughter of Colin of Mochaster, son of Sir Robert Campbell of Glenorchy. A silver mounted powder horn in the family bears the inscription, "From the First Earl of Breadalbane to John McDougall, 1683." This John's son, Ewen, fought at the battle of Sheriffmuir. Besides Achomer, Ewen held the lands of Margnadallach and Margchraggan at Ardeonaig. He and his brother, John, who occupied Milton, were elders of the Kirk of Kenmore. The representative of this family in the last generation was Archibald who farmed Milton, and latterly Claggan as well. Donald, his eldest son, succeeded him in the tenancy of Claggan, while his widow and daughters, Jean and Isabella, continued in the farm of Milton. Jean, who was deeply versed in the lore and family traditions of the district, died in 1933; and Isabella left Milton at Whitsunday, 1937. Donald moved some years ago to Dall, Ardeonaig, which his ancestors had at one time farmed, and his lease expires in 1938. He has been the leading Black-faced Sheep breeder in the North of

Scotland. Three other sons of the family of Archibald McDougall survive—Archibald, in South Africa ; Duncan, in Canada ; and Alexander Patrick, in Oxfordshire.

Ewen McDougall, a grandson of Ewen who fought at Sheriffmuir, was clerk of works on the Taymouth estate, and clerk to the Baron Bailie Court. He was the first secretary of the Lodge of Free Masons formed at Kenmore in 1818, under the name of Lodge Tay and Lyon (276). After retiring he resided with his nephew at Milton, and for the instruction of his grand-nephews, Ewen wrote a long description of the river Tay, the houses and lands in the valley, and the traditions of this region. He died in 1832, at the age of seventy-three years.

John and Isabella McDougall of Perth, who founded the McDougall bursaries for Perthshire students, were descendants of John McDougall, who was in Tullich of Ardtalnaig in 1763.

MCEWEN. Some of those who bore this surname were McDougalls, while a few were McLarens. 1579, Finlay McEwen Mor, Ardtalnaig ; Ewen McEwen, Croftmartaig ; 1623, Donald Glas, Acharn ; 1624, Finlay, Cloichran ; 1644, three McEwens from Ardradnaig on Muster Roll, three from Lickbuie, two from Revain, one from Claggan, and three from Craig, in the Ardtalnaig district ; 1769, seventeen tenants of this name on south side of Loch Tay, and three on the north side. In the last generation, John McEwen, headmaster of Kirkwall Academy, and his brother Dugald, headmaster of Acharn school, were natives of Killin. Both were very successful teachers. Descendants of the Ardradnaig McEwens are prominent citizens of Edinburgh.

MCFARLANE. 1638, Donald Roy, Suie; John Dòw, Kenknock; 1769, no member of clan on north or south side of Loch Tay.

MCGIBBON (probably Macnab). 1624, Callum, Creitchosh ; 1638, Duncan, Auchlyne ; 1769, Donald, Shenlarich, Lawers ; Malcolm, Carie.

MCGILCHRIST. G. *Mcillechreist.* 1579, Patrick, Balinlagan ; 1616, Gillmuire, Acharn ; 1624, Callum, Ewich ; 1638, John Edramuckie ; Iver McEan Vcillechreist, Ardchyle ; Iver, Killin ; 1644, Donald, Carnbane.

MCGLASSERIG, alias Campbell. 1778, Isabel, Tirarthur. John McGlasserig, alias Campbell, Morenish, published a book of Gaelic songs and poems about 1780. James McDiarmid relates a tale about a man of this name who encountered a witch in the form of a hen in a shieling on Ben Lawers. McGlasserig allowed his dogs to worry the witch who died from her wounds. She pronounced a curse upon the family with the result that they died out on Lochtayside.

MCGILLIWIE. G. *Mcillebhuie.*

MACGREGOR. Before the advent of the Campbells to Breadalbane there were numerous members of this clan settled at Balloch, Eddergoll, Fearnan, Morenish, and Ardeonaig. They lived as peaceably as their neighbours, as tenants of the Crown and of the Church. The relations between the MacGregors and the early lairds of Glenorchy were quite good ; but Colin, the sixth laird, tried to alienate them from their chief by bands of manrent. This policy led to the revolt of the clan, and their shameless persecution. After the MacGregors were outlawed and the use of the name forbidden, the name disappears until the eighteenth century. The Fearnan MacGregors became Drummonds. The only tenant of the clan on the south side of Loch Tay in 1769 was Katherine MacGregor, at Tomflower. The following were on the north side in the same year :—John, Morenish ; Duncan, Carwhin ; Donald, Lawernacroy ; Duncan, Duallen; John, Lurginbuie; Alexander, Duncan, Cloan, Lawers; Duncan, Boreland; John senior, and John junior, Stronfearnan.

During the early decades of the nineteenth century John MacGregor, who was connected with the Culdderbeg family of that name, was the miller at Fearnan. He married Christian Campbell, whose brother was farmer at the Boreland of Fearnan. Five of their six sons (the sixth died in infancy) graduated at Edinburgh University ; and their three daughters were trained for the Teaching profession at the Normal School of that city.

Malcolm, the eldest son, succeeded Dr. John McDonald, " The Apostle of the North," as minister at Ferintosh. His grandson is the Rev. G. H. C. MacGregor, D.D., professor of Biblical Criticism at Glasgow University. The second son of the miller, Duncan, was minister of the Free Church at Stornoway, and afterwards at St. Peter's, Dundee, and Augustine Church, Glasgow. His sons are the Rev. Duncan C. MacGregor, D.D., late of Wimbledon, moderator of the Presbyterian Church of England in 1920 ; and the Very Rev. William Malcolm MacGregor, D.D., Principal of Trinity College, Glasgow. Principal MacGregor's son, Mr. D. C. MacGregor, is Fellow and Tutor in Baliol College, Oxford.

The miller's third son, Alexander, lived and died Rector of Stranraer Academy ; the fourth son, Angus, went to Australia as a preacher, but turned to teaching, and ended a useful career as Librarian to the Parliament of New Zealand. The fifth graduate of the family was John, who was minister of the Free Church at Peebles, and afterwards at Stockwell Church, Glasgow. The scholastic record of this family, brought up on a Fearnan croft with the meagre income of the little meal mill, is truly remarkable. The father had little learning, but he appreciated the value of learning. His wife was a woman of great faith and strength of character.

Another member of the clan to enter the Church from Breadalbane was Peter MacGregor, minister of Duthil, who died in 1935. He was a native of Lawers.

MCHUSTON. 1638, Donald, Balnaskiag.

MCILANDIG. McLintock, alias McDougall. 1769, Patrick, Croftintygan. James Mcillandaig, who had the holding of Tomvorair, Kiltyrie, was the last of the Breadalbane smugglers. Malcolm Ferguson in his " Rambles in Breadalbane " gives stories about him. James' son, John, was innkeeper at Kingshouse, Balquhidder. He left religious and charitable bequests to the parishes of Kenmore, Killin, Balquhidder, and Callander.

MCILLECHEIR. 1622, John Dow, Suie ; 1638, Gilleroy, Balmacnaughton.

MCILLECHOAN. MCCOWAN. 1698, Catherine, Lawers.

MCILLECHUINE. MCQUEANE. MCQUEON. 1480, Donald Mcgillequhinye, Mill of Eddergoll ; 1579, Callum McQueon, Acharn ; 1638, John Dow Baine McQuaine, Balinlagan. The McQueens were probably MacGregors. Patrick McQueen, minister of Rothesay, who brought an action against Sir Duncan Campbell of Glenorchy before the Privy Council, was a MacGregor, and held Duneaves.

MCILLEGHORIVE, alias Campbell. 1621, John, Blarnaskea ; 1644, Donald, Ardtalnaig ; 1723, Donald, Ardtalnaig, an elder of Kenmore Kirk ; the last members of this family left the Ardtalnaig district at the beginning of this century.

MCILLEGHUIRM. See Livingstone.

MCILLEHUAISH. 1769, Finlay, Morenish ; John, Rhynchuilg; Patrick, Kiltyrie ; Duncan, Carie.

MCILLENOIVE, alias Mcintyre. 1698, James, Balmacnaughton ; 1687, James, Remony.

MCILLERIOCH, alias McPherson. 1624, Muroch, Kenknock ; 1615, John Dow, Cloichran ; 1793, Mcillereach, Clifton.

MCILLEVORIE. 1775, Patrick.

MCIANDUI. 1698, Alexander, Taymouth.

MCINLAROY (probably Macnabs). 1769, Finlay, Tirarthur ; Duncan, Tirarthur ; Duncan, Morenish ; John, Carwhin. The name appears to represent *Mac Fhionnlaidh Ruaidh*, " Son of Red Finlay."

MCINTOSH. 1744, Patrick, Rhevucky.

MCINTOURINE. 1638, Patrick, Daldravaig ; 1638, John, Morenish.

MCINTYRE, alias Wright. 1624, John, Leiragan ; 1638, Callum, Port of Loch Tay ; 1644, Donald, Craig, Ardtalnaig ; 1702, Donald Roy, Kenmore Inn. He provided " straw for my Lord's horses while at church, and kept my Lord's boat in the harbour, or paid the damage." 1769, six tenants on south side Loch Tay, and six on north side. A Mcintyre was smith at Kenmore in 1784. Captain James Mcintyre, late 13th Royal

Veterans, and formerly of 71st Highland Light Infantry, buried at Kenmore, 1814. 1825, Captain John, Kenmore.

MCINVANE, alias Macnab. 1698, Finlay, Duallen.

MCISAAC. 1624, Finlay, Duneaves.

MCIVER. Some of the McDiarmids were locally known as Mcivers. 1624, Duncan, Auchmore ; John Dow, Licks ; 1638, John, Cloichran ; Callum, Port of Loch Tay ; Lawran, Crannich ; John, Kenmore.

MACKAY, alias Mcnaughton. 1638, Duncan, and Donald on Muster Roll ; 1644, John Dow, Keprannich ; Duncan, Claggan ; 1702, Duncan, Callelochan ; 1769, John, Achomer ; Katherine, Achianich. Rev. Duncan Mackay, who founded the Mackay bursary at St. Andrews University, was a native of " Tuathair," south side of Loch Tay, and was probably the son of Duncan who was in Callelochan in 1702. He died at Edinburgh in 1808, and was buried in the Calton cemetery. His origin was traced by Mr. Kemp, Edinburgh, a member of the Clan Mackay Society, and a stone was erected at his grave. A brother of the Rev. Duncan Mackay was a merchant in Bristol.

MCKENDRICK. 1621, Archibald, Blarchaorin ; Callum, Drissaig.

MCKENZIE, alias Kynoch. 1615, Callum, Finlarig ; 1763, William, Ardtalnaig ; 1769, John, Rhevucky.

MCKERACHER. 1638, Donald, Gillechreist, Port of Loch Tay ; 1769, Malcolm, Stronfearnan ; Donald and Duncan, Comrie ; Alexander, Portbane ; Donald, Aleckich ; John, Rhevucky. Alexander and William Mckercher of the Breadalbane Garage, Aberfeldy, are descended from the Comrie McKerachers. John, Rhevucky, was a merchant. He was succeeded by his son, John, who later removed to Acharn village, and whose sons were John, minister of the Free Church, Fortrose ; James, Bank of Scotland, Aberfeldy ; Alexander, merchant, Aberfeldy, and afterwards at Lincoln ; Peter, merchant, Aberfeldy ; Donald, minister of the Free Church, Kilmun ; Duncan, merchant, Killin, and Arbroath ; Robert, Doctor of Medicine, Dalbeattie.

MCKERLICH, alias Campbell. 1606, John, Finlarig ; John Dow McInnes, Ardeonaig ; 1621, John, Morenish ; Duncan, Crannich ; 1638, Callum, Dalgirdie ; John, Remony ; Archibald, Finlarig ; 1644, John, Achomer.

MCKERRAS, alias Ferguson. 1585, John Roy Mcfergis, Balloch; 1624, Duncan Mckerras, Ledchroisk ; 1769, John, Morenish ; Patrick, Rhynchuilg. Malcolm Ferguson, a native of Morenish, died at Callander, 1912, at the age of ninety-seven years ; a successful business man in Glasgow. He was devoted to the country of Breadalbane, and wrote a book describing its scenery and people, entitled " Rambles in Breadalbane." He erected a cairn on the summit of Ben Lawers to bring its height up to four thousand feet. He created charitable trusts for the benefit of poor people in the parishes of Kenmore and Killin.

MCKILLOP. 1627, Finlay Bane, Balloch; 1643, Elspet NcKillop.

MCKINLAY. 1644, Donald.

MCKIOCH, alias Mcdonald. 1480, Donald McKethe, Eddergoll; 1579, Donald, Ardtalnaig; 1644, Duncan, Tullich.

MCLAREN. 1618, Callum Dow, Balloch; 1621, Patrick, Crannich; 1638, Patrick, Crannich; 1644, Donald Bane, Tullich; 1763, ten McLarens in Ardtalnaig district; 1769, fourteen McLarens tenants on south side of Loch Tay, and three on north side. Archibald McLaren, farmer at Dall, Ardeonaig, and latterly of " Dall Lodge," Killin, who left funds for the erection of a hall at Killin, and several bequests for charitable and religious purposes, was a grandson of John McLaren, tenant at Acharn, Kenmore.

MCLEAN. 1561, Patrick Mcoleane; 1595, John, Tirarthur; Malcolm, Craig, Glenlochay; 1623, Callum, Ledchroisk; 1638, John, Kiltyrie; 1769, Charles, Cloan, Lawers; Alexander, Corriecherrow; John, Stronfearnan; 1834, Lachlan, Claon, Lawers; John, Carwhin. In 1640, Tirai was let to Mulikyn McGillane. Rev. John McLean, minister of Grantully, belonged to the Breadalbane family of McLeans. He was intimately acquainted with the Natural History and the traditions of Breadalbane. Mr. Duncan McLean, Fearnan, represents this old Breadalbane family.

MCLEISH. G. *Mciliosa*. 1624, Duncan, Murlagan; 1638, Duncan Mcoleis; 1644, John, Ardtalnaig.

MCLELLAN. 1769, Hugh, Maragbeg.

MCLUKE. 1644, Donald, Shenlarich, Ardtalnaig.

MCMARTIN, MCILLEMHARTAIN. 1621, John Mcillemhartain; 1624, Gillemartain McFinlay McMartain, Cloichran; 1769, Duncan and Malcolm, Drumnaferoch, Lawers; 1798, Malcolm, smith, Lawers.; 1834, John, Tirai; 1835, Robert, Craggan, Lawers. The grandmother of Sir Donald Currie, Bart., of Garth was an Elizabeth McMartain from Glenlochay. Rev. Archibald McMartain, Nigg, Ross-shire, belonged to Balinluig, Lawers. He died at Aberfeldy in 1917.

MCMILLAN. G. *Mcillemhaoil, Mcmhaoiligan*. Tradition states that the Mcmillans were anciently numerous on Lochtayside, and that they moved from there to Argyllshire. The fact that there were six tenants of this name in the Ardtalnaig district in 1644 seems to bear out the tradition. Only one is found on the list of tenants in the same area in 1763, and none at all in 1769. In the latter year there were on the north side of Loch Tay, Donald, Carwhin; and Alexander, Balimeanoch, Fearnan. Alexander Mcmillan, merchant, Aberfeldy, died 1860, buried at Kenmore; father of Rev. Dr. Hugh Mcmillan of Greenock, and grandfather of Lord Macmillan of Aberfeldy, belonged to the Fortingall district.

The Gaelic song, " *Failte Bhraid-Albann*," " Hail to Breadalbane," at one time very popular in the district and at Glasgow Highland gatherings, was composed by a Breadalbane man, named McMillan, who, for poaching, had to leave the country. Campbell* of Achallader, then factor, hearing the song, pleaded with the author to return to Breadalbane, but in vain. The song is printed in full in Ferguson's " Rambles in Breadalbane."

MACNAB. Besides the Macnabs of Bovain, two junior branches of this clan possessed lands in Glendochart. They were the Macnabs of Acharn, and the Macnabs of Innishewan.

The following references are found to the Macnabs of Acharn:— 28 July, 1553, Donald Macnab, son of Archibald Macnab of Acharn ; 18 April, 1568, John Bane McGillespic Macnab, who married Issobel Macfarlane. 15 April, 1605, Gilbert Macnab of Acharn ; 1649, Archibald Macnab of Acharn is entered in Killin rental for £45 ; 1655, Archibald Macnab, succeeded by John Macnab of Acharn ; 23 April, 1672, Archibald Macnab, whose bowl is in Museum of Antiquities of Scotland, Edinburgh. (Note by Mr. John MacGregor, W.S. in Proc. Soc. Antiq., Vol. LXVII., pp. 314-5). 15 July, 1731, Patrick Macnab of Acharn was prosecuted for a clandestine marriage performed by Mr. Alexander Comrie, who had been deposed from Kenmore.

The earliest Macnab that has been traced to Innishewan is Finlay McEan Macnab, who was tenant there in 1599. Finlay appears to have been succeeded by his son, Alexander, for in 1611 Alaster McFinlay VcEan VcNab and his brothers, Duncan and John Dow in Ardchyle, gave their bond to Sir Duncan Campbell of Glenorchy. This Alexander was a member of the jury of a Baron's Court held at Killin in 1615. He was fined by the Privy Council in 1618 for the illegal carrying of arms. In 1638, his name appears on a muster roll. The farm of Innishewan was not returned as a separate property in the rental for the parish of Killin in 1649.

Alexander Macnab was succeeded by his son, Finlay, who married the eldest daughter of Finlay Macnab of Bovain, by whom he had three sons and a daughter. In 1661, Alexander's name appears on a list of landlords and chiefs who had failed to report to the Privy Council, and eight years later he and his sons were called upon to give their bonds to the Privy Council.

Finlay Macnab's successor was his son, John, who married Catherine Macfarlane, daughter of George Macfarlane of Rose-neath, in 1658. He died in 1676, and his widow married, as her second husband, James, fourth son of John Macnab, fiar of

* This was John 6th of Achallader. He was a great classical scholar, and gets the credit of being the first man to introduce turnips into Scotland.

Bovain. John Macnab was succeeded by his son, Finlay. On the 28th March, 1683, Finlay made over the lands of Innishewan and Bothuachdar to his brother, Alexander, who was infeft in these lands two days later. This Alexander married a Macfarlane. A bond had been granted by the first Earl of Breadalbane for two thousand merks to Catherine Macfarlane, relict of John Macnab of Innishewan, on 2nd March, 1676. This bond was assigned by Alexander Macnab to John, his eldest son, and failing him, to Duncan, his second son, and failing Duncan to Robert, Alexander's third sin, on 26th April, 1703. Both John and Duncan died without issue, and in October, 1724, we find Robert Macnab applying to the second Earl of Breadalbane for precept of *clare constat* as the heir of his brother, John. This John Macnab of Innishewan was married to Jean Campbell, in December, 1711. On 20th December, 1732, an action was raised against Robert Macnab of Innishewan for marrying Jean Campbell, his spouse, irregularly and without proclamation of banns. He acknowledged his irregular marriage, and was fined 500 merks Scots.

At the '45 Alexander Macnab in Innishewan was a captain in Keppoch's regiment, and fought with skill and courage at the battle of Falkirk. In 1759, the name of Alexander Macnab younger of Innishewan appears on a list of men fit for service. In the same year John Macnab, " Possessor of Inchoane," built the burial enclosure in the graveyard of Suie in Glendochart. On 22nd November, 1767, it was recorded that John Macnab, late of Innishewan, had bequeathed four guineas for behoof of the poor of the parish of Killin. The following obituary notice appeared in the Scots Magazine (Vol. LXXII., p. 639), " 2 July, 1810—At Borrodale, Alexander McNab, late of Inschewan, aged 91 years ; the last of that family residence who have been proprietors, wadsetters and leaseholders of it for upwards of 400 years."

A member of the family of the Macnabs of Innishewan who fought for Prince Charles Edward in 1745 went with the Prince to France, where he married a lady of fortune, and settled at Saucerre, Tours. He befriended many Scottish Jacobites in exile, among them Lord Nairne. The father of the late J. A. Macdonald of Glenaladale paid a visit to a descendant of this Macnab during the early decades of last century, and obtained from him a portrait of the Prince and also his watch. This old Macnab was thoroughly French.

(From information regarding Prince Charlie's watch in document in possession of Miss Nicholson of Arisaig House.)

MCNACEARD, alias Sinclair. The Gaelic word *ceard* means artificer. *Macaceard* is the Son of the Artificer, or of the Tinkler. As time went on the association of the name with " Tinker " became offensive, and " Tinkler " was changed to " Sinkler " and then " Sinclair." The Sinclairs latterly claimed a Caithness origin through the connection of the First Earl of Breadalbane with that county. This claim is not, however, confirmed by the tracing of the history of the name in Breadalbane. 1622, Donald Dow Mcnakerd, Camuschurich ; 1698, Duncan, Mill of Finlarig ; 1769, Donald, Rhynchuilg ; John, Stroncomrie ; Hugh, Tomgarrow ; 1834, four house-holders in Kenmore district of the name Sinclair.

One of these was Peter Sinclair, Mains of Kenmore, whose son, John, born 1817, settled in Dundee. He had been educated at Kenmore school, and his exercise books, preserved by his grandson, show the high standard of the education and training given there. John started in the office of " The Dundee Chronicle." He was successively connected with the publishing of the " Dundee Herald " and " Dundee Warder." In 1856 he started " The Weekly News," the pioneer weekly paper of Scotland. This was followed by the " Argus," which was the first penny daily north of the Forth. The latter was ultimately amalgamated with the " Courier," and Mr. Sinclair then retired from journalism. He died in 1897. His grandson is Mr. Peter Sinclair, architect, Buckhaven.

MCNAUGHTON. This is one of the oldest, if not the very oldest Breadalbane surname. There were four branches of the clan on Lochtayside, namely, the McVicars, the Mackays, the Mcintaylors, and the Urchy McNaughtons. The McVicars appear to have been descended from Maurice McNaughton and Duncan McNaughton, who were vicars of Inchadney from 1480 to 1523. In 1585 a Maureis McNauchtane was at Inchadney. 1644, Donald, Lurg ; William, Ardtalnaig ; 1698, John Lurgloman ; 1769, Patrick, Portbane. At the beginning of last century James McNaughton or McVicar, tenant in the Braes of Taymouth, and his wife, Elizabeth McLaren, gave one hundred pounds to the Kirk Session of Kenmore, the interest to be paid to poor persons of the name of McNaughton, McVicar, or McLaren. The Mackay branch of the McNaughtons has been already dealt with.

The Mcintaylor* McNaughtons have occupied lands in the district of Eddergoll for many centuries. Their names appear in the earliest Crown rentals. 1480, Donald McNachtan occupied the Forty-shilling Land, or Balnacnaughton ; 1541, Laggan and Mill of Eddergoll let to John Tailyemoir, alias McNachtane ; 1582, Mill of Eddergoll let to Malcolm McNachtane and Donald Mcintailyemoir's wife ; 1597, Duncan McOnill VcEan, Balmacnaughton ; 1623, Duncan McDonald, Balmacnaughton ; 1627, John McEntailyeour, Balnaskiag ; 1769, John, Portbane ; Daniel, Tomgarrow.

Alexander McNaughton, son of John, tenant in Portbane, took over the Waulkmill at Remony in succession to William Murray

* From Chron. of Fortingall—" 1556, John Challar Moyr died at Eddergooyllyt on 27th of September, and was buried at Inchaden, on the eve of St. Michael the Archangel."

X

about 1780.   He also began the dyeing of cloth, and thus he and
his descendants came to be styled locally as " *An Dathadair*,"
" The Dyer."   Alexander had a large family :—1. Donald was
father of Rev.   Allan McNaughton of Kirkhill, and of William,
who became a Cloth Manufacturer at Pitlochry, a business now
being carried on by his grandsons.   2. John carried on the mill
at Remony and also the farm, in both of which his eldest son,
Alexander, succeeded him.   His other three sons, Peter, John,
and James went to Canada.   3. Alexander became a doctor of
Medicine, entered the Navy, and died young.   4. James became
a Doctor of Medicine ;   went to Albany, N.Y. ;   an eminent
surgeon, and Professor of Anatomy in the College of Physicians
and Surgeons, New York ; died at Paris, June, 1874.   5. Allan,
minister of Kilbride, Arran ; afterwards of Lesmahagow ; D.D.,
St. Andrews ;   sons, Alexander, S.S.C., Edinburgh ;   and Neil,
minister of Kinclaven.   6. Peter, Doctor of Medicine ;   went to
Albany, N.Y., where he practised.

Alexander, eldest son of John McNaughton, carried on the
mill and the farm, extending the latter as smaller tenants
adjoining removed.   He married a daughter of John McKeracher,
merchant, Acharn.   Their family were :—1. John, minister of
the Church of Scotland, Lairg ; Professor of Classics, Kingston,
Canada; Divinity, McGill, Montreal; Classics, Toronto; now retired
(1937) ;   residing at St. Leonards, Sussex.   2. James, Merchant,
Aberfeldy.   3. Peter, succeeded to the farm (The Cloth Mill and
the Dyeing business gradually ceased).   4. Alexander, a merchant
in London.   5. Duncan, a merchant in London.   6. Donald,
H.M. Inspector of Schools (Secondary Branch) ; Staff-Inspector
for Classics under the Board of Education ; now retired.   When
the eastern portion of the Breadalbane estate was sold in 1923,
Mr. Peter McNaughton bought Kenmore Hill and a portion of
Balmacnaughton, together with the farm-house and steadings at
Remony.   He died in December, 1930 ; and his widow is in
possession of the lands and houses.

The Urchy McNaughtons were in Balinlagan in 1703, when
Duncan Urchy McNaughton and Janet NcaGhuirm had a child
baptised named Donald.   This Duncan's name appears also in
the rent roll of the period.   The family probably came to the
Acharn district from Glenorchy, which fact accounts for the
alias " Urchy."   Mr. John McNaughton, son of the late Mr.
Alexander McNaughton, tailor, is the only representative of this
old family left in the district.

MCNEE.   1772, Mary, Innishewan.

MCNICOL.   1769, John, Auchmore.

MCNUCATOR.   G. *MacanFhucadair*.   Son of the Fuller, or
Waulker ; alias Campbell.   1560, Donald McYnnocator ;   1579,
Gillechreist Dow Fucator, Port of Loch Tay ;   1769, Duncan,
Croftintygan ;   John, Tomb, Lawers.   Members of this family

who remained in Breadalbane gradually changed their name to Walker. Some of those who went to the cities during the early eighteenth century retained the name " McNucator." Their descendants in Dundee have now dropped the " Mac."

MCPHAIL, alias Cameron. 1510, Tailor Makfele ; 1579, John Dow McPaule, Skiag (Kenmore) ; 1769, Archibald, Carie ; Duncan, Carie ; Patrick, Balnasuim (Lawers). Mr. Peter McPhail, born at Balnasuim, Lawers, a prosperous merchant in Edinburgh, gave the sum of £2,000 in 1919 to the Kenmore Nursing Association to form a memorial of his only son, Lieutenant P. J. Stewart McPhail, R.G.A., who died in hospital at Winchester, 26th November, 1918. The Marquis of Breadalbane at the same time intimated his intention to grant a perpetual title to the Association for the cottage occupied by the nurse in the village of Kenmore ; and the Association has since been called " The Stewart McPhail Memorial Nursing Association." Mr. Peter McPhail died at Craigmillar Park, Edinburgh, 11th September, 1921. His widow, Catherine McEwen, who was born at Ardradnaig, survives (1937).

MCPHATRICK, alias Macnab. 1624, Donald, Achessan ; 1698, Duncan, Lurinbuy.

MCPHERSON. 1834, Peter, Edramuckie ; John, Morenish ; William, Cloichran ; Malcolm, Donald, Stronfearnan.

MCQUARRIE. 1698, Donald, Drumglas ; 1769, John, Tullich.

MCROB, alias Macdonald. 1644, Duncan, Ten-shilling Land, Ardtalnaig ; Laren McPhatrick VcRob, Tomnadashan ; 1698, Donald, Morenish. Descendants of McRobs at one time in Ardeonaig, who assumed the name Macdonald, are in Aberfeldy.

MCTHOMAS. Thomson. 1615, Finlay McThomas, Killin ; 1621, John, Crannich ; 1624, John, Craignavie ; 1735, John Roy Thomson, Portbane ; 1834, Andrew, Lurgloman ; Donald, Rhevucky ; Alexander, Stronfearnan. Mr. John Thomson, Kenmore, so long and well known as a keen angler and Free Mason, is descended from the last named.

MCVEAN. The McVeans were connected chiefly with Glen-lochay. 1619, Donald, Tirai ; 1624, Donald Og, Dalgirdie ; Donald Dow McDonald Roy, Tirai ; 1638, Patrick, Tullich ; John, Tirai ; Duncan Roy, Boturney ; 1763, Duncan, Tullichglas. Rev. John McVean of Glenorchy, whose son, Patrick, was minister at Kenmore, was a native of Glenlochay. The father of the Rev. Colin McVean, who succeeded the Rev. Patrick McVean at Kenmore, in 1794, was miller at Tirai.

MCVICAR, alias MCNAUGHTON. See McNaughton.

MCVICHIE, alias McDonald. 1616, Donald, Fearnan ; 1618, William, Aleckich ; 1729, Duncan, an elder of Kenmore Church, resided near Acharn ; 1763, Donald, Ardradnaig. The last of this family to reside in the district was Donald McVichie, alias McDonald, who died at the village of Acharn about fifty years ago. The descendants of Donald, who was in Ardradnaig in 1763, emigrated to Canada about the beginning of last century, and settled at Bainsville, Ontario. John D. McVichie, who died in 1929, at Curry Hill, Ontario, a member of one of the oldest families in Glengarry, Canada, was a son of Donald, who went from Ardtalnaig district to Canada in the 'thirties of last century.

MCVRACADAIR, alias Maltman.   1698, John Maltman, Balnasuim (Kenmore). 1770, Finlay McVrachadair, Auchlyne.

MCVURRICH, alias McPherson. 1624, John Dow, Tirai ; 1644, Duncan, Keprannich ; 1698, Duncan, Finlarig ; 1769, Donald, Tirarthur.

MCWALSTOUN. 1579, John Dow, Acharn.

MALLOCH. 1763, John, Lurg ; 1769, John, Carwhin ; John, Balnahanaid ; 1834, Neil, Cuiltrannich ; Donald, Carie.

MANN. 1698, John, Kiln Lands, Killin ; John, Tomb, Lawers ; 1769, Robert, Tomb ; 1798, James, Cloan, Lawers ; 1834, Duncan, Craggan, Lawers. Members of this family are still in the Killin district.

MENTEITH. 1579, Donald, Baron of Carwhin.

MENZIES. Although several parts of Breadalbane were at one time owned by the Menzieses of Weem, there were not many members of the clan in the district at any period within the past four hundred years. 1621, William, Morenish ; 1623, John, Stix.

MORISON. G. *Mcillemhoire.* 1585, Donald McIllivory, Acharn; 1769, Duncan, Morenish.

MURRAY. 1835, Peter, Kingharrie.

NISH. 1787, Duncan, Kenknock.

PUDERACH, alias Buttar. 1638, John, Crannich ; 1772, Margaret, Killin.

ROBERTSON. There were many families of this clan on the north side of Loch Tay, especially in the Fearnan district which belonged to Strowan Robertson until the property was annexed to the Crown after the Fifteen and Forty-five Rebellions.

RUTHERFORD. The first of this family was a weaver, named George, settled, 1698, at the Cooper's Croft, Taymouth. 1723, John, Brae, Balloch ; 1767, James, Ardtalnaig ; 1769, William, Rhevucky.

STALKER. G. *Mac-a'-stalcair.* 1565, James, Ardeonaig ; 1621, Finlay Dow, Crannich ; 1638, John Dow, Crannich ; 1644, John Dow, Kindrochit ; 1763, Finlay, Keprannich.

James McInstalker, known as *An Stalcair Rioch* (The Brindled Stalker), was an agent of Colin Campbell, sixth laird of Glenorchy. He murdered Gregor MacGregor, son of James

MacGregor, Dean of Lismore, in 1565. Soon afterwards he himself was slain by Gregor MacGregor of Glenstrae, at Ardeonaig.

STEWART. 1638, Walter, Ledcharrie ; 1727, Duncan, Taynaluib (Luib Inn).

WALKER. Some of the McInucators changed their name to Walker. 1698, John, Taymouth ; Donald, Peat Croft, Taymouth; 1723, John, and David, Milton of Taymouth, elders of Kenmore Church ; 1769, Gilbert, Lurgloman ; Donald, Balinlagan ; 1834, John, Rhevucky. There are Walkers still in the Kenmore district. On 6th January, 1765, Catherine Walker, daughter of Gilbert Walker, who was known in his time as " Gilbert Mor Kingharrie," was married in Kenmore Church to Benjamin Dawson. When the bridal party was crossing the ferry behind the Kenmore Inn, the boat capsized, and the bride was drowned. She was buried in Kenmore churchyard. A stone which marked her grave crumbled away. The inscription referred to her tragic and untimely death.

WHYTE. A family of this name resided in the Kenmore district from the middle of the sixteenth century. They continued for nearly a hundred years. Andrew Quhit was a notary at Taymouth in 1551. His name often appears on documents along with that of Gavin Hamilton, who was a secretary and notary in the employment of Sir Colin Campbell and of his son, Sir Duncan. Anthony, Portbane, 1618 ; Thomas, Tomgarrow, 1638.

In view of frequent inquiries received from descendants of Glenquaich emigrants in Canada regarding their ancestors, the following list of tenants on the Breadalbane lands in that glen in the year 1822-23, is given. Easter Shian was a separate property ; and no list of its tenants is available. Most of the emigrants left the glen after 1830, and many of them settled at North Easthope, County of Perth, Ontario. The story of the pioneers has been compiled and published in a handsome volume by Miss Mary Louise McLennan, of Stratford, Ontario, who also promoted the erection of a cairn to their memory. This memorial cairn was unveiled in 1936 by Lord Tweedsmuir (John Buchan), Governor-General of Canada.

AMULREE.—John McLaren.

SCHOOL CROFT.—Paterick Dewar.

LYNMORE.—Alexr. Stewart, Duncan Stewart.

CROFTNALD.—James McTavish, Peter Dow.

ACHNAFAUD.—Donald Menzies, James Cameron, Peter McVichie, James McDonald (smith), Duncan McNaughton, Wm. McGregor, John McNaughton, Donald McNaughton, John McArthur, Widow Menzies, Donald Stewart, Robert McNaughton, Duncan Robertson, Donald Cameron, Andrew Menzies, Widow McGregor, Peter McTavish, Duncan Stewart,

John Menzies, Alexr. Anderson, Duncan McLaren, Duncan McVichie, Widow Menzies, Peter McTavish, Wm. Menzies, Donald McVichie, John McVichie.

CROFTVOULIN.—Alexr. Dow, Donald McTavish.

BALNALECKINE.—James Anderson, James McTavish, John Crerar.

DALKILLIN.—John McFarlane, John Kippen, Widow Campbell.

CROFTEANAIG.—Charles McGlashan.

ACHNACLOICH.—Archd. Menzies.

CAOLVELLICH.—Geo. McCallum, Alexr. McTavish, Alexr. McGregor, Duncan McTavish (senior), John McGregor, Wm. McFarlane, Wm. Crerar, Duncan McTavish (junior), Donald McTavish, A. Crerar, John McTavish, Donald Fisher.

LEDCHROISK.—McTavish and Crerar.

WEST SHIAN.—John Stewart, Dn McLaren, Duncan Anderson, Alexr. Fisher, James McDonald, Christian Stewart, Peter McNaughton, Janet McIntyre, Donald Cameron, Donald Livingstone.

WESTER TURRERICH.—Peter Crerar (junior), Widow Crerar, Peter Crerar (senior), Robert Fraser, Peter McTavish, Donald McTavish, Katherine Hay.

CROFTMAJOCK.—James Crerar.

EASTER TURRERICH.—Alexr. McTavish, John Dow (miller), Peter Hay, Duncan McLaren, John McTavish, Robert McLaren, James Stewart, D. McNaughton.

THE POOR'S BOX OF KENMORE KIRK.

CHAPTER XXXI.

Places and Place-Names.

A N examination of the place-names of Breadalbane goes to show that except for a few modern English names, they are all of Celtic origin. Of the four hundred names recorded in this chapter, ninety-seven per cent. can be definitely traced to a Gaelic source. Of the remainder the following names are derived from the British language that was spoken in this region before the Gaelic-speaking people came from Ireland, and which was akin to Old Welsh :—Aberfeldy, Pitilie, Tay, Lochay, and Paderley. To this small list may probably be added such names as the following which present difficulty :—*Radnaig*, in Ardradnaig ; *Talnaig*, in Ardtalnaig ; and *Cailtnigh*, in Innischailtnigh (Inchadney).

The names have been taken in their geographical order, beginning at Aberfeldy, travelling west by the south side of the river Tay, Loch Tay, and the river Dochart to Tyndrum, and returning by the north side of the water, taking in Glenlochay, to the Point of Lyon, and Comrie. Many of the names submitted do not appear on the Ordnance Survey maps. Some have been gleaned from old rent rolls, and from plans made during the surveys carried out by the third Earl of Breadalbane in 1769 : not a few were obtained from old natives of the countryside who have now passed from our midst.

For several of the explanations here given I am indebted to my friend Professor W. J. Watson, who has a thorough knowledge of the Breadalbane district, and whose article on its place-names was published in Volume XXXIV. of the Transactions of the Gaelic Society of Inverness. Brief notes have been added, giving information with regard to the history of several of the places dealt with in this chapter.

ABERFELDY. G. *Obar Pheallaidh—Aber*, a confluence, and *Peallaidh*, the name of an urisk that inhabited the Den of Moness. This urisk was also associated with places in Glenlyon.

The lands now covered by the town of Aberfeldy* formerly lay on three different estates. For generations the burn of Moness formed the boundary between the Menzieses of Weem, who owned Aberfeldybeg on the west side, and the Flemyngs of Moness and the Steuarts of Grantully, both of whom held lands on the east side of the burn. The Steuarts sold their lands to

* See booklet, " The Antiquity of Aberfeldy," by John Christie, pub. 1906.

the Menzieses, who in turn disposed of all their lands south of the Tay to the third Earl of Breadalbane in 1771. After holding the lands of Moness for nearly three centuries, the Flemyngs died out in the male line, and their lands were purchased by the fourth Earl of Breadalbane in 1787. All that remains to indicate the long connection of the Flemyngs with the district is the mural sculpture of their coat-of-arms at Moness House, minus their motto, " Lat the deid schaw."

The earliest reference to Aberfeldybeg is found in a charter of 1301, by which the Earl of Atholl conveyed the lands of Croftinglass, Duness, Duntaylor, Succoth, Milntown, and the boat-lands attached to the ferry, to Sir Alexander Menzies of that ilk. These lands are described as a *davate*, that is, as much land as two ploughs could till in a year. The fact that Aberfeldybeg had been owned by the Earl of Atholl explains why it was included in the old parish of Logierait. When parish boundaries were rearranged it was transferred to Dull.

Aberfeldy proper, on the east side of the burn of Moness, was granted by the Earl of Douglas in 1414 to Alexander, fourth son of Sir John Steuart of Innermeath. This Alexander was the founder of the family of Steuarts of Grantully. The lands included in this charter were Errichel, Croftdow, the Strades (Streets), Dundai, and Brucecroft.

About 1770 there were some fifty houses on the east side of the burn of Moness. Most of these were gathered round the foot of the Tullich, an eminence that rises directly above the Square, and which prevented the town from extending to the south in that direction. The old Wade road passed through this village, crossed the burn by the bridge, and led on to the Tay Bridge in a more direct line than that now in use. This old road on the west side of the burn formed the division between the Over and the Nether Miltons of Aberfeldybeg. The meal mill occupied a site not far from the present one, while a short distance away was a lint mill driven by the same water supply. This lint mill was one of many erected by Ewen Cameron, the mill-wright of Lawers.

The acquisition of the whole of Aberfeldy by the Breadalbane family proved a great benefit to the inhabitants, among whom were many craftsmen, such as weavers, wrights, coopers, flax-dressers, and shoemakers. The fourth Earl encouraged the people to grow flax, develop the spinning industry, and make stockings. In Easter Aberfeldy some Glasgow merchants, under the name of the Moness Manufacturing Company, started a cotton factory, where muslins and similar fabrics were made. The Earl granted long leases to the villagers at nominal rents, and thus encouraged them to rebuild their houses. The bottom of the burn was laid with stones, and its banks were built up. In this way flooding was prevented, and the houses protected. The estate framed rules and regulations for the management of the village, and the officer saw that these regulations were observed. With unity of ownership and control the three old villages became one. The result was immediately apparent in the prosperity of the growing town. A visitor to the town in 1800 said of it, " The village is daily increasing in size, and the decent appearance of the new houses that are being built gives the place an air of business and even of consequence."*

The third Marquis of Breadalbane feued land to parties who built villas on the slopes above the town, and to the west. In 1887 the town was raised to the status of a Police Burgh with a provost, two bailies, and six commissioners. The seal of the burgh bears the motto, " 'S Dluth Tric Bat Abairpheallaidh "— " Swift and often goes the boat of Aberfeldy." This motto carries us back to the days before the Tay bridge was erected, when the ferryboat of Aberfeldy was kept busily crossing and recrossing the river.

When the eastern portion of the Breadalbane estates was sold in 1923, Mr. James D. Haggart, the sole partner of the firm of Messrs. P. & J. Haggart, Woollen Manufacturers, purchased the superiority of the burgh, together with the farms of Duntaylor and Duntuim. At the same time the late Mr. W. Russell acquired the House and estate of Moness.

The Forts of Aberfeldy.

Several place-names beginning with the Gaelic term *dùn* (fort) in the immediate neighbourhood of Aberfeldy suggest the existence here of round forts similar to those in Glenlyon. There are hardly any traces of these ancient structures now remaining, but the names are still attached to farms. *Dùn Dàidh*, " David's Fort," and *Dùn an t-sagairt*, " Priest's Fort," are on the east side of the burn of Moness. *Dùn eas*, " Waterfall Fort," has been identified with *Tom-ghiubhais*, " Fir Knoll," above the Breadalbane Academy, which bears distinct traces of having been at one time fortified. *Dùn an tailear*, "Tailor's Fort," *Dùn-tuim*, "Fort of the Mound," *Dùn-sgitheag*, " Fort of the Thorn," and *Dùn na craoibhe*, " The Tree Fort," are all situated within two miles of the town on the west side. On a prominent hill directly to the south of the town is " The Dun," one of a chain of hill-forts that extended right across Central Scotland from Killin to Stonehaven. This great *dùn* encloses a plateau some sixty yards in diameter. Behind its rude walls a large number of people could find shelter and defend themselves. The hill is now densely wooded, and access to it is somewhat difficult.

The following are a few well known place-names in the neighbourhood of Aberfeldy :—

MONESS—In Bleau's Atlas this place is given as " Buness " which means *Waterfall-foot*. Compare " Bunessan," in Mull. The *m* is due to ellipses in the phrase *i mbun easa.*

* Campbell's Tour, vol. I.

CROFTNESS—*Waterfall-croft.*

TYNESS—*Waterfall-house.* This was the former name of Moness House.

PITILIE—*Ilidh's portion,* name of British origin ; obscure.

ERRICHEL—*Wood* ; may have been " on-wood." G. *air choille.* A family of Mactavishes occupied this farm for over two hundred years ; the last of them died recently. Stories are told of the dexterity shown by one of this family as an archer. He is credited with having slain the last wolf in this quarter.

FARROCHIL—*The Wood on the horizon's edge.* The first part of the name appears to be *fàire,* a ridge, or viewpoint.

BOLFRACKS—*Spotted Hut.* The barony of Bolfracks belonged at one time to the Stewarts of Garth. This explains the fact that it was formerly included in the old parish of Fortingall. It was owned by the Earl of Atholl in 1635, and in 1707 passed into the possession of Alexander Menzies, who belonged to the Weem family. One hundred years later the barony was acquired by the fourth Earl of Breadalbane. It was purchased in 1923 by Mr. J. K. Hutchison and Mrs. Hutchison, Largo House, Fife. The Menzieses of Bolfracks were buried in a small enclosure behind the house.

In 1794 Sir John Menzies of that Ilk raised an action of Declarator against his kinsman, Alexander Menzies of Bolfracks, seeking to have it determined that the Baron of Bolfracks and the public had no right of way along the west side of Camserney burn from and to the ferry at Bolfracks. The Court granted a Commission which visited the Kirktown of Weem, and there took evidence from a large number of persons. The evidence was printed along with a map of the river Tay, extending from the Point of Lyon to Aberfeldy, and reveals many interesting facts regarding customs and conditions prevailing in the district at and before that time. The names and the positions of the fords on the river are also given.

To the west of Bolfracks lay the lands of STIX. This name, which is now usually spelt " Styx," is in Gaelic *Na Stuicean,* and means " The Stocks." It probably refers to the standing stones of the great circle at Croftmoraig, and to other circles that have been removed. The lands of Stix formerly consisted of the Cuill of Stix, Easter Stix, Middle Stix, and Wester Stix.

The *Cùil,* or Nook of Stix, now known as Tullichuil, *the Hillock of Cuil,* was purchased by the third Earl of Breadalbane from Sir Robert Menzies, Baronet of Weem, along with the lands of Aberfeldybeg in 1771. About the same time the third Earl acquired the lands of Easter Stix from James Menzies of Culdares in exchange for Kenknock and Eastermore in Glenlyon. Stix House, which was tenanted until recent years, is situated on Easter Stix. Middle Stix had been one of the possessions of the

Cardneys of that Ilk until they sold it in 1486 to Sir John Stewart, a natural son of King James II. His descendants, the Stewarts of Ballechin, sold it to Sir Duncan Campbell of Glenorchy, the first Baronet. Wester Stix belonged to the Atholl family, and was acquired from them about the year 1600 by Sir Duncan Campbell. Included in Wester Stix was the Inn of Muttonhole, situated opposite the church, manse, and graveyard of Inchadney. There was an important ford on the river at this point, and also a ferryboat. Not a vestige of the inn remains, but the site and the road leading up the Brae of Muttonhole behind it are still discernible. In Gaelic the inn was called *Tigh an Tuill*, " The House of the Hole." It continued until the end of the eighteenth century.

A house was built at Newhall at the end of the eighteenth century for John Kennedy, who was then factor to the fourth Earl of Breadalbane. A few years later stables for Taymouth Castle were erected at this place. These buildings are still there. The following place-names were found on Stix :—

CROFTMORAIG, sometimes spelt CROFTMORRY—*Mórag's or Mary's Croft*. There was a meal mill at one time on the Croftmoraig burn. Immediately below the Stone Circle, on the north side of the highway, there is a green eminence on which there once stood a summer-house, which was known in 1753 as " Mary Temple," and later as " The Octagon." The island on the river to the west of Stix House was called *Mininnis*, which means " Smooth Island."

DRUMCROY—*Hard Ridge*, and DRUIMNAMUICK, *The Pig's Ridge*, were names of crofts in Middle Stix, and long since forgotten.

Tradition says that there was a burial-place on Stix called *Cill Da-Bhi*, but no one living in the district within the past thirty years could give any information whatever about it.

FUARAN NAN DILEAG—*Dripping Well*, above Croftmoraig ; cured whooping-cough.

CROMALLTAN, *The Little Crooked Burn*, forms the boundary between the lands of Wester Stix and Balloch. It runs into the Tay a hundred yards to the west of the site of Muttonhole. This burn is also the eastern boundary of the parish of Kenmore. Before the parishes were rearranged in 1893, a person travelling from Kenmore to Aberfeldy passed at Cromalltan into the parish of Weem. At Easter Stix he came to Dull, and after leaving the lands of Tullichuil he passed into Fortingall parish at Bolfracks. He entered next into the parish of Logierait, and after crossing the Moness Burn at Aberfeldy, he came again to the parish of Dull. This arrangement led to much confusion, especially when proclamations of marriage had to be made.

The ruins of a brick-work in use during the time of the second
Marquis of Breadalbane may be seen on the west side of Tullichuil
burn.

BALLOCH. G. *Bealach* ; full name, *Bealach nan Laogh*, "The
Pass of the Calves." "The Pass" was probably the dip in the
ridge south of the knoll on which Taymouth Dairy stands. A
branch of the MacGregors had their house here for many
generations, and this gave rise to the expression, *Bealach nan
Laogh aig deagh MhacGriogair*, "The Pass of the Calves in
possession of the worthy MacGregor.

ALDIVALLOCH. G. *Allt a' Bhealaich*, The Burn of Balloch.
An attempt was at one time made to connect the song, "Roy's
Wife of Aldivalloch," with the village of *Balivoulin*, "Milltown"
of Taymouth, at the side of this burn ; but there is no foundation
for the claim.

CROSG MHIC DHUGHAILL—*MacDougall's Crossing*, was the
name of the ford on the Tay below Kenmore. See legend about
this ford in "Argyll Records" by Lord Archibald Campbell.

ATHNACARRIE—*The ford of the Weir*, was the name of another
ford on the river.

LOCHAN NAM BROG—*Loch of the Shoes*, was the name of a
pond within the Taymouth park near the river. It was drained,
but the hollow remains. Before wading the river travellers put
their shoes off at this loch.

TOM MOR—*The Big Mound* ; the knoll on which the Dairy
is situated ; at an earlier time known as *An Dùn*, The Fort.
The hollow below it is called *Lag an Dùin*, The Hollow of the Fort.

TOM BUIDHE—*Yellow Mound*, on the Braes of Balloch.

DRUIMINTUIRK—*The Ridge of the Boar* ; the Tower is
situated on Druimintuirk.

A' CHROIS—*The Cross* ; name given to the moor above Tombuie;
probably derived from the stone cross that used to stand on the
summit of this pass. The cross was renewed by Dougald Johnson
MacGregor in October, 1529, and given the name *Clach ur*, The
New Stone. (Chron. Fortingall).

LAIRIG MONADH MARCAICH—*Pass of the Riding Moor* ;
also *Lairig Mìle Marcaich*, Pass of the Riding Mile ; the pass
leading over the hill from Kenmore to Glenquaich.

LAG NAN CLADHAIREAN—*Hollow of the Cowards* ; a hollow
on the Glenquaich side of the *Lairig*. It got its name from the
fact that a party of men from the North "lifted" a creach in
Glenquaich, while the men folk of the glen were from home.
The thieves settled for the night in this hollow, but after dark
a few old men and some women raised shouts and showed lights
around them. The thieves fled in haste, leaving the cattle

Note.—In 1816 a number of human bones and skulls were found near Tom na Croiche.
Gen. Stewart (vol. I., p. 31) says they were the remains of men slain in a fierce fight above
Acharn, in the time of Charles II., when a quarrel arose between Argyll and Atholl.

behind them, and the women gathered the cattle together and drove them home.

BALNASUIM—*The town of the souming* ; situated to the west of Aldivalloch.

BALNASKIAG—*The town of the thorns* ; west of Balnasuim ; *Tom na Croiche*, the Gallow's knoll, is on Balnaskiag.

KENMORE—*The big-headed place* ; G. *An Ceannmhor* ; *Tigh Mor a' Cheannmhoir*, the Big House of Kenmore, is Kenmore Hotel. A tack of the five-shilling land of Candmoir, the ten-shilling land of Wester Skiag, and the forty-penny land of Coble Croft, with the tenancy of the new hostelry, was granted to Hew Hay and his spouse by Sir Colin Campbell in 1572. It was over the chimney-piece in the parlour of this old inn that Robert Burns wrote his famous poem :—

" Admiring Nature in her wildest grace,
    These northern scenes with weary feet I trace ;
    O'er many a winding dale and painful steep,
    Th' abodes of covey'd grouse and timid sheep,
    My savage journey, curious, I pursue,
    Till fam'd Breadalbane opens to my view.
    The meeting cliffs each deep-sunk glen divides,
    The woods, wild-scatter'd, clothe their ample sides ;
    Th' out-stretching lake, imbosomed 'mong the hills,
    The eye with wonder and amazement fills ;
    The Tay meand'ring sweet in infant pride,
    The palace rising on his verdant side,
    The lawns wood-fring'd in Nature's native taste,
    The hillocks dropt in Nature's careless haste,
    The arches striding o'er the new-born stream,
    The village glittering in the noontide beam—
    ....

    Poetic ardours in my bosom swell,
    Lone wandering by the hermit's mossy cell ;
    The sweeping theatre of hanging woods,
    The incessant roar of headlong tumbling floods—
    ....

    Here Poesy might wake her heav'n-taught lyre,
    And look through Nature with creative fire ;
    Here, to the wrongs of Fate half reconcil'd,
    Misfortune's lighten'd steps might wander wild ;
    And Disappointment, in these lonely bounds,
    Find balm to soothe her bitter rankling wounds ;
    Here heart-struck Grief might heav'n-ward stretch
        her scan,
    And injur'd Worth forget and pardon man."
    ....

The six annual markets at Kenmore were held on the village green. The green is now vested in and cared for by the County Council. The Reading Room at Kenmore was built in 1884 by the Third Marchioness of Breadalbane. It is now vested in the County Council.

CORRIEVROLAN—*The corrie of the manyplies*; G. *Coire bhroilean*; situated above Balnaskiag. The dry grass of this hollow caused indigestion in cattle.

CREAGANDUDAIR—*The rock of the trumpeter*; G. *Creag an dùdair*; the summit of Kenmore Hill, from which people around were summoned in olden times.

CROFTNACABER—*The croft of the rafters*; G. *Croit nan cabar*; got its name from the fact that rafters for the roofing of houses were obtained from the birch and hazel trees of *Coille Tom nan ceap*, the Wood of the sod mound, on this farm. The Manse and Glebe of Kenmore are on Croftnacaber.

ISLE OF SPRY OR SPRIES ; below Croftnacaber ; derivation obscure : perhaps from G. *spiris*, a rickety erection. This island was originally a lake dwelling, and may have got its name from the stakes on which the ancient dwellings were built. It was enlarged by the second Marquis of Breadalbane after 1842.

LOCH TAY STEAMBOAT, LEAVING KENMORE.

PORTBANE—*Fair haven*; anciently a four mark land; foundations of a house between the public road and Loch Tay may have been the site of the residence of John Campbell of Portbane, who held these lands in seventeenth century. There used to be a ferry from Portbane to *Ceann a' Ghàraidh*, Garden-end, on opposite shore.

BALNATIBERT—*Town of the Well*; village on Portbane farm; the *Tiobairt*, which is said to have had healing qualities, is close to public road.

BALMACNAUGHTON—*MacNaughton's Town*; known locally as *An Da-fhichead Sgillinn*, The Forty-shilling land.

CROFTNAMUICK—*The Pig Croft*; below Remony farm-house.

TOM CHORPAIDH—May be *Cairbre's Mound*; behind Remony farmhouse.

ALLTMHUCKY—*The Swine Burn*; now usually called Remony Burn.

RHEVUCKY—*The Swine Point*; name of a row of cottages which stood at entrance gate to Remony Lodge.

REMONY—*Level Moor*; may be from *réidh*, smooth, or level, and *monadh*, moor; name originally attached to the farm on east of burn; now applies to the estate of which Remony Lodge is the house. The Remony estate extends from Alltmhucky to Alltreich, between Callelochan and Ardradnaig. In the Exchequer Rolls of 1480 the lands included in the estate are entered under the name of Eddergoll, now entirely forgotten. These lands were acquired in 1924 by the late Sir James Duncan Millar, K.C., M.P. for East Fife, from the trustees of the third Marquis of Breadalbane. Sir James died in 1932, and is survived by his widow, Lady Duncan Millar; a daughter, Sheina Paton; and a son, Ian Alastair, who came of age in 1935.

SOCACH—*Snouted Place*; spit of land between two streams on which Remony Lodge stands.

ATHLECKICH—*Paved Ford*; G. *Ath*, ford, and *leacach*, flagged.

TOMGARROW—*Rough Mound*; G. *tom*, mound, and *garbh*, rough.

BALINLAGAN—*Town in the Hollow*; east of Acharn Burn; village of Acharn partly on this farm.

LONNAGUY—*Windy Meadow*; the marshy meadow below Holly Cottage.

ACHARN—*Field of the Cairn*; farm on west of Burn. The pretty Falls on the Acharn Burn were visited by Robert Burns; also by William Wordsworth and his sister, Dorothy, who described the view from here in her " Journal."

PIERCOUL—*The Jaw*; in Bleau's Atlas; now forgotten.

WAIRD—*The Chest* ; in Bleau's Atlas ; probably for *Bràghad,* upper part. The bridge above the Acharn Falls is called *Drochaid Bhragaid,* The Bridge of the Brae. A spring on the west side of the Burn above the bridge is called *Fuaran Barain,* Barane's Spring ; a wishing well.

TOMVULIN—*The Mound of the Mill* ; above *Drochaid Bhragaid.* It was on this knoll that Sir Colin Campbell of Glenorchy first proposed to build his castle.

FAIRE NAM BAN—*The Nun's Watch* ; a hillock on Acharn farm from which the nuns, expelled from Isle of Loch Tay, *Eilean nam Ban,* took their last look of their former home. See legend, " Argyll Records," Lord Archibald Campbell.

CROFTMARTAIG, or CROFTMARTIN—*Martin's Croft.*

LURGLOMAN—*The bare Shank.*

ACHIANICH—*Field of Fowling.*

CREAGIANICH—*Rock of Fowling.*

RHUIANICH—*Point of Fowling* ; this point juts into the loch.

ALLTIANICH—*The Fowling Burn* ; between Achianich and Callelochan.

TON RI GAOITH—*Back to the wind* ; a field on Achianich. G. *Tòn ri Gaoith.*

CALLELOCHAN—*The Meadow of the little lade* ; from G. *Cail,* a meadow, and *eileachan,* a little mill lade.

ALLT AN DUIN—*Burn of the Fort* ; the steep burn on Wester Callelochan.

LEOD A' CHAISTEIL—*Slope of the Castle* ; on west of Allt an Duin, above the bridge.

ALLT NA CRICHE—*Burn of the March,* the " march " being between the districts of Eddergoll and Ardtalnaig.

ARDRADNAIG—*Height of the Gradnaig,* the " Gradnaig " being the burn here ; may come from *grad,* swift, or speedy. This name is obscure.

CEAP RAINNICH—*The tillage plot of the brackens* ; now written " Keprannich."

SHEANLARICH—*The old site* ; on this farm is *Seana Phort,* the Old Port, from which a ferry plied to Fearnan.

SKEACH, SKIAG—*The thorns.*

LEACHDBUIDHE—*The yellow-flagged slope* ; the burn on west side is *Allt an airm,* Burn of the army, where part of Montrose's force halted on its way up Lochtayside in 1645.

ARDTALNAIG,   ARDTALLONAIG,   ARDTOLLONIE, ARDINTOLLANIE—*Height of the lonain* (the cattle pass?). This district extends from Ardradnaig to *Allt a' Mhinn,* the burn on the west of the church. It includes Glentalnaig, and the pass leading to the head waters of the river Almond. The name is difficult to explain.

AM BAILIDH—*The Bailie* ; name applied to a meadow on east of Ardtalnaig Burn, near the loch, on which the king's bailie in olden time used to graze his horses, when he visited the district for judicial purposes.

CARNBANE—*The Fair cairn* ; a field beside the Bronze Age cairn had this name.

REVAIN—*Level brake or copse* ; above Milton of Ardtalnaig ; lead was mined at one time on this farm.

LURG—*The Shank.* The following place-names are on this farm :—*Radhar Mhichidh*, Michie's outfield ; *Radhar nan damh*, Out-field of the oxen ; *Croit Ghoblach*, the Forked croft. A witch was burned long ago at Lurg.

TOMFLOUR, TOMNAFOURA (1644)—*Mound of the pasture* ; *Radhar na Lairig*, Outfield of the Pass, is on this farm. The " Pass " leads behind Ben Bhreac to the Acharn Burn.

TULLICHGLAS—*The grey knoll.*

A' CHAIL FHINN—*The white meadow* ; the glen leading to Dunan, at the source of the Almond river. Ailing infants used to be taken to a well in this glen, and dipped in the water at sunrise. The well is situated on north side of the stream.

DUNAN, NA DUNAN—*The knolls* ; a shepherd's house here is the highest habitation in Breadalbane.

LEDOUR-LEATHAD ODHAR—*The dun slope* ; used to be the highest cultivated land on Lochtayside ; on west side of Calline.

CLAGGAN, AN CLAIGIONN—*The skull.*

ACHOMER—*Field of the confluence* ; G. *Ach' Chomair* ; where the Cloy burn joins the Ardtalnaig burn.

GLEN CLOY—GLEANN GLAOIDH—Glen of the shouting (burn).?

SITH—*The conical hill* ; lies between Calline and Glen Cloy.

KINDROCHAID—*Bridge-end* ; the ruin of the old inn is still standing on north side of public road. The graveyard of Ardtalnaig on *Tom na Smeathach* was laid out in 1760, and the lairs were allocated to the sixty-three tenants in the district. There is a tradition that, once upon a time, when a pestilence raged among the cattle on the south side of Loch Tay, the people seized a poor wandering man who happened to come the way, bound him hand and foot, and placed him in the ford of Ardtalnaig burn. They made all the cattle pass over his body until his life was crushed out. It is said that he was buried on the knoll now occupied by the graveyard. This tale carries us back to the time of human sacrifices. The name is obscure.

Y

AN DEICH SGILLINN—*The ten-shilling (land)* ; west of Kindrochit.

A' CHREAG—*The rock* ; the steep slope at the top of Ardtalnaig brae.

EASTER TULLICH—*The easter knoll.*

TOMNADASON—*The mound of the ricks* (hay or corn) : the copper mines are on Tomnadason. G. *Tom nan Daisean.*

WESTER TULLICH—*Wester knoll* : church and manse on this farm ; a ferry plied from here to Balnahanaid on opposite shore ; the boat croft was near the loch.

ALLT MHINN—*The kid's burn.* There are several pretty waterfalls on this burn. It forms the eastern boundary of the Pre-Reformation parish of Ardeonaig, which was united to Killin in 1617.

LICKNIÉ—*The washing flagstone* ; G. *leac,* and *nigheadh* washing.

MARGBEG—*The little merk* (land).

MARGMORE—*The great merk (land).*

CRANNAG—*The pulpit* ; near the houses of Margbeg.

CROFT DUNARD—*The Croft of the high fort.*

LEDCHRAGGAN—*Slope of the rocky knoll.*

AN FHICHEAD SGILLINN—*The twenty shilling (land).*

DALL—*The plain* ; G. *an Dail.*

MARG NA DALACH—*The merk land of the plain.*

FINNGLEN—*The white glen* ; probably from the white appearance of the withered grass in autumn and winter ; might be " Holy Glen."

CARN DEARG—*The red cairn* ; pass leading from Ardeonaig to Glenlednock A weird story is told of a ghost that frequented this glen. See Trans. Gaelic Soc. Inverness, Vol. XXVII., p. 126.

MAINS—Name of a croft where the old castle ruins are situated. We have no account of the builder of this small castle. The last occupant was probably Colin Campbell, the second and last laird of his family. The garden and orchard lay between the castle and the burn.

ARDEONAIG ; old spelling, Ardewnane, and Ardewnan ; Gaelic *Aird-Eodhnain*—the Height of Eodhnan ; " Eodhnan " is supposed to have been St. Adamnan, the biographer of St. Columba, who founded a monastery at Dull.

TIGH NA LINNE—*House of the pool*; the name of Ardeonaig Inn.

LINNE PHIOBAIRE—*The piper's pool* ; on the Ardeonaig Burn. It is said that this pool got its name in the following way :—At Ardeonaig there once lived an archer named Donald

McKendrick, a famous *stalcar*. He had six sons whom he trained to be nearly as expert in the use of the bow as himself. One day a band of cattle thieves, numbering twelve fighting men and a piper, came down from Argyllshire on a farm house at the west end of Loch Tay, and among other misdeeds they killed for supper a calf that belonged to a poor cottar widow. The woman expressed the wish that their captain might not eat another morsel until he had seen Donald McKendrick. She was informed that her wish would be gratified, and the captain sent a message to the archer requesting him to have breakfast ready for the band next morning. McKendrick replied that he would be prepared to receive the visitors. Early on the following day the caterans set out for Ardeonaig. The archer and his sons had posted themselves at well concealed points, and received the visitors with flights of arrows, slaying them all as they were crossing the burn. The piper was killed as he was retreating, and his body fell into this pool. The story relates that McKendrick, the *stalcar*, or arrowmaker, resided in Mains Castle.

CILL MA-CHARMAIG—*The cell of my Cormac* ; the site of the old church and churchyard of Ardeonaig.

CROIT NAN CNAMH—*Croft of the bones.*

CROIT A' MHUILINN—*Croft of the mill.*

CROIT NA H-ATH—*The kiln croft.*

LECHKIN—*The hill-side.*

RADHAR CRUINN—*The round outfield.*

SOCACH—*The snouted place.*

BRAEINTRINE—*The top of the Third.* There was a " Middle Third " in Ardeonaig.

TOMOUR—*The dun mound* ; *C. tom,* and *odhar,* dun.

CROMALLTAN—*The little crooked burn* ; *G. crom,* crooked.

CROFTINREOT—*The croft of the bog-myrtle.* G. *Croit an roid.*

BEULINA—*The mouth of the ford* ; G. *beul,* mouth, and *ath,* ford.

BEALACH—*The pass.*

TOMBANE—*The fair mound.*

CROIT NA BEALLAIDH—*The croft of the broom.*

CROFT SHENACH, CROIT AN T-SHIONNAICH—*The croft of the fox.*

DRUIM NA DUBHCHAR—*The ridge of the dark turn.*

MEAL IANAICH—*The fowling hill.*

DALCROY—*The hard field.* G. *An dail chruaidh.*

MARG DOW—*The black merkland.*

TOM BEITHE—*The birch knoll.*

TULLOCHCANN—*The (pretty ?) hillock* ; second part of name is obscure.

TOMCHARR—TOM A' CHARRA—*The mound of the standing stone.*

CAMUSCHURAICH—*The wherry bay.*

FUARAN TOM BEITHE—*The spring of the birch mound* ; near source of stream on east boundary of Camuschurraich farm.

LAG NAN CNO—*The hollow of the nuts.*

CRAGGAN BUIDHE—*The yellow rocky knoll.*

LEAC A' GHILLE REAMHAIR—*The flag-stone of the fat lad.* This is a rocky point jutting out into the loch.

CORRABHARRAN—*The little peaked top* ; the top of a prominent hill at Cloichran. G. *Corr Bharran.*

CLOICHRAN—*The stony or rocky place.* The farms of Camuschuraich and Cloichran formed a detached portion of the old parish of Kenmore. In 1769 there were six tenants in the former, and eight in the latter farm. At present Tullochcann, Camuschuraich, and Cloichran are let together to one farmer. Cloichran is the most back-lying farm on the loch side. It used to be called *Cloichran fuar,* " Cold Cloichran."

RIVER DOCHART AT KILLIN. IN FLOOD.

CREAG AN DUDAIR—*Rock of the trumpeter.*

CUILTEAN CHLOICHRAIN—*The nooks of Cloichran.*

ALLT NA BREACLAICH—*Burn of the spotted hill*; the mill of Cloichran was at the foot of this burn. It was called *Am Muilionn dubh*, The black mill, and the humming tune, or *port a beul*, "Tha am muilionn dubh air bhogadan," is said to have been connected with it.

BATHAICHEAN—*The byres or bow-houses.* The lairds of Glenorchy used to keep large herds of black cattle under the charge of bow-men. There appears to have been one of these bow-houses here.

CROFT NA FIANNAG—*The crowberry croft.*

AUCH—*The Field*; a high-lying farm on the ten merk land of Auchmore.

DOCHART[1]—*Evil-scourer*, from G. *do*, evil, and *cart*, cleanse.

AUCHMORE—*The great Field*; belonged to the Earls of Atholl, then to the Menzieses of Weem, and was acquired first on tack and afterwards in feu by the Campbells of Glenorchy. At one time it formed one of the eleven detached portions of the parish of Weem. Auchmore House is the principal seat of the Earl of Breadalbane. There are traces of fortifications at Firbush Point on Loch Tay.

KINNELL—*The head of the rock*; from *Ceann*, head, and *alla*, genitive of *all*, rock.

SLEOCH—*The rifted place.*

CLACHAIG—*The stony place.*

AONACH—*The deserted place.*

LAGFUIRT—*The hollow of the port or ferry.* G. *Lag a' phuirt.*

ELLANUAINE—*The green island*; a croft on Kinnell.

ELLANCOR—*The odd island*; Ellanuaine, and Ellancor are situated to the west of *Sraid Ghlas*, Grey Street, the row of houses facing the Dochart, at the end of Killin bridge. These "islands" may at one time have been surrounded by marshes.

CROFTINDEWAR—*The croft of the Dewar*; a triangular piece of land about eighty acres in extent, which belonged to the family of Dewars who were the hereditary keepers of the crozier of St. Fillan. It is now merged in the farm of Acharn.

ACHARN, ACHACHARN—*The field of the cairn.*

LIX, LICKS—*The hard slope.* Lix was divided into Lower, Middle, and Upper Lix.

LAIRIG ILIDH—*Ilidh's Pass*; the pass leads to Glenogle.

(1) Gual Dochart is on the east side of Auchmore. G., *gual*, shoulder.

ARDCHYLE,[1] ARDCHOILLE—*The high wood*; at one time connected with the MacGregors.

LIANGHARTAN—*The little flax enclosure*; G. *lion*, flax, *gartan*, garden.

LEDCHARRY—*The slope of the pillar-stone.*

EDRAVEANOCH—*Between the two middles.* G. *Eadar*, between, and *meadhain*, middle.

SUIE—*The seat* (St. Fillan's). G. *An Suidhe*. The Dewar of the Bell of St. Fillan had his croft at Suie.

LUIB—*The Bend*; the old inn here used to be called " Tigh na luib," the house of the bend.

CORRYCHEROCH—*The sheep corrie.* A gabled house on the east side of the burn, now in ruins, is said to have been at one time occupied by Rob Roy. A detachment of Argyllshire Militia which occupied Finlarig Castle in 1689 set fire to the house of Corrycheroch, which at that time belonged to James Drummond, Duke of Perth. Seven of the men engaged in this affair were shot by Macnab of Innishewan, who watched their movements from a hidden position.

LOCH IUBHAIR—*The yew loch.* Ewer was one of the Macnab lands.

PORT AN EILEIN—*Port of the island.*

INVERMONICHILE—*The mouth of the Monichile burn*; " Monichile " may mean *The moor of the wood*. This farm is now known as Benmore.

INVERARDRAN—*Confluence of the high streamlet*; from *dobhar*, an early Celtic word for water; diminutive, *dobhran*.

STRONUA—*The nose of the Cave*; from *uaimh*, cave.

STRONGHARBH—*The rough nose*; from *garbh*, rough.

ALLT NA PATLERAN—*Paterlan's burn*: Paterlan may have been an urisk.

CRIANLARICH—*The aspen site*: in Gaelic always with the definite article, *a' Chrianlarich*.

INNERHERIVE—Confluence of the bull (burn); burns have often the names of animals. G. *Tarbh*.

EWICH—*The yew place.* It has no connection with *éigheach*, crying or shouting.

ACHRIOCH—*The speckled field.*

LINNE NAOMH—*The holy pool* (of St. Fillan).

CONINISH—*The hound meadow.*

(1) A notable weaving business, the last of its kind in Breadalbane, was carried on at Ardchyle during the first half of last century by Donald McNaughton, who was succeeded by his son, Robert. Robert wove a plaid designed by himself for Queen Victoria from wool spun by the late Marchioness of Breadalbane. He afterwards became tenant of Black Mount Hotel, and later of Luib Hotel, in which tenancy he was succeeded by his brother, Donald McNaughton, now retired.

BEN LAOIGH—*The calves' ben.* The Coninish burn, which is the source of the river Tay, rises in Corrie Laoigh.

DAL RIGH—*The king's field* ; site of Bruce's battle with the McDougalls of Lorn.

LOCHAN NAN ARM—*The lochlet of the weapons* ; Bruce's men are said to have flung their weapons into this loch when retreating from Dal Righ.

TYNDRUM—*The house of the ridge* ; the ridge being the watershed between the east and west of *Alba.* The elevation of the watershed on the public highway to Dalmally is 1,025 feet above sea-level.

CLIFTON ; site of the village attached to the lead mines at Tyndrum. The village got its name from Sir Robert Clifton, of Clifton, who worked the lead mines at the time of the rebellion of 1745. The lands on which the village is situated are called *Achinturin.* Professor W. J. Watson states that the Gaelic name is *Achadh nan Tuirighnean,* the field of the Kings, and that the battle between Nectan, king of the Picts, and Oengus, son of Fergus, was fought here in A.D. 729. Colin Campbell, first laird of Glenorchy, built a tower in Strathfillan, probably here.

LOCHAN NA BI—*Lochlet of the pitch-pine* ; the little loch beyond the county march from which the river Lochy (Lorn) flows westward.

AUCHTERTYRE—*The upper part of the land* ; G. *uachdar,* upper, and *tìr,* land.

INVERHAGGERNIE—*Confluence of the whispering stream* ; G. *cagar,* whisper.

LOCHAN NA CRAOIBHE—*Loch of the tree* ; above Inverhaggernie.

LOCH MÀRAGAN—*The mother loch* ; the source of the Inverhaggernie burn.

DUINISH—*The black meadow* ; *dubh,* black, and *innis,* meadow. On Duinish is a little loch close to the river Fillan that used to be called, *Lochan Bagile.* The name is obscure.

DÙN-NA-MUCLAICH—*The fort of the rough or piggish ground* ; situated on Liaragan farm, and immediately above the Isle of Lochdochard.

LIARAGAN—Probably from *liath,* grey.

FEART—*Grave, burial-place* ; at shepherd's house between Lochs Dochart and Ewer. Compare *Dail na (bh) Feart.*

ACHESSAN—*The field of the little waterfall.* Lochessan is the source of the burn that flows past Achessan. It has an artificial island. Below the loch is *Creag na h-analaich,* the rock of resting, where persons or horses going up the hill took breath ; from *anail,* breath. There is a *Cnoc na h-analaich* below *Tom na moine,* the peat hill, from which the people of Acharn, Kenmore, brought their peats.

STRATHFILLAN gets its name from Faolan, the Irish saint, who founded a monastery here about the beginning of the eighth century. In Gaelic the strath is called *Sraithibh*, At the Straths. St. Fillan's church was at Kirkton, the Clachan of Sraithibh.

The estate of Crianlarich is owned by the descendants of Mr. Edward Place, of Skelton Grange, near York, who acquired lands in Glendochart at the beginning of last century. Auchessan belongs to Ian Francis Christie, Esq.; Portnellan, to Frederick Walter Christie, Esq., C.A.; and Lochdochart, to William Leslie Christie, Esq.

INNISCHEWAN—*Ewan's meadow*; once a possession of the Macnabs. The lands of Innishewan, Auchlyne, Croftchose, and Bovain were acquired in 1936 by Col. J. G. Crabbe, Duncow, Dumfries.

AUCHLYNE[1]—*The fat or pleasant field*; G. *Achadh loinne*, from *loinn*, rich, fat; the best farm in Glendochart. We get in Breadalbane such names as *An Dail ghionach*, The greedy plain, and in the Strath of Appin, *An Dail reamhar*, The fat plain.

CROFTCHOSE—*The croft of the nook*; G. *còs*, a nook or corner.

BOWACHTER—*The upper bothy*; G. *uachdar*, top.

BOVAIN—*The middle bothy*; G. *meadhain*, middle. The ancient seat of the Macnabs of that ilk.

ARDNAGAULD—*The height of the Lowlanders*; from *Gall*, a Scottish Lowlander.

CRAIGNAVIE—*The heavenly rock*; said to have been a preaching place of St. Fillan. *An Cnoc Beannaichte*, the Blessed Hill, on this farm, is situated above the road to Bovain, and a little to the east of an old lime kiln.

KILLIN—*The white Church*. G. *fionn*, white or fair. Professor Watson suggests the secondary meaning, holy, both for Killin, and Finlarig, which may have been a pilgrim pass.

The village of Killin stretches from the east of Craignavie to the Bridge of Lochay, and formerly consisted of several lands which had distinctive names. Monomore, next Craignavie, which in Gaelic means the Great Moor, was divided into Croftnamaish, Croftintobair, Croftcroy, and the Officer's Croft. *Croit na mèise* was probably the croft in possession of a family of Dewars who had custody of the *Mes*, or portable altar of St. Fillan. Croftin-tobair was the Croft of the Well, and Croftcroy *A' Chroit chruaidh*, The hard Croft. Barnacarry, *The top of the Weir*, lay east of Monomore. Stix, like the place of the same name near Kenmore, may have been derived from *Stuicean*, stocks. Balachroisg, the

(1) Auchlyne was held by Patrick Campbell of Achallader at the beginning of last century, and sold by his son, John, to the fourth Earl of Breadalbane, in 1825.

Town of the Crossing, lay about the centre of the village. The parish church is situated on Reinrune (G. *Réidh an Roinn*), the Clearing of the Point. To the east of Reinrune was *Marg an Luig*, The merk-land of the Hollow. The little burn running through the glebe is called *Allt Torraidh*, the Burn of heaping, probably because during floods it brings down quantities of gravel from the steep hill above.

Ceann a' Chabhsair, the End of the Causeway, was the name of a few houses near Bridge of Lochay. The land next Kenknock was *Marg a' Ghobhainn*, the Smith's merk-land, and above it was *Sron a' Chlachain*, The Nose of the Clachan. The burn here is *An t-allt Fuileach*, the Bloody Burn.

The Inn of Killin, now Killin Hotel, was known as *Tigh na Sràide*, The House of the Street, or Street-house. There used to be a prison in the " Street," and during the carrying out of improvements some fifty years ago one of the dungeons was discovered, and converted into a cellar.

Tom na Croiche, the Hill of the Gallows, is behind the School, and near it is a small mound called *Tom nan Aingeal*, the Knoll of the Angels, where the Baron Courts of Breadalbane used sometimes to be held.

EASTER KENKNOCK, on the west side of the river Lochay, is a two-merk land, which was formerly a detached part of the parish of Weem. It extends to 196 acres, and belonged at one time to the Menzieses of the Ilk. The name means *Head Hill*.

GLENLOCHAY—*The Glen of the Black goddess* ; takes its name from the river. This glen is distinguished from the one of the same name in Lòrn by the term, *Albannach*, of Alba.

MOIARLANNAICH—*The plain of the west-land* ; G. *magh*, plain, and *iarlann*.

DALDRAVAIG—*The field of the slut* ; G. *Drabhag*, a slattern.

MURLAGAN—Professor Watson derives this name from *murbhalgan*, the diminutive of *murbhalg*, a sea-bag inlet, which refers to a feature of the river at this place.

CORRYCHARMAIG—*The Corrie of Cormac*. It was in a little house at Corrycharmaig that Angus MacRonald-og died after being wounded at the battle of Coire nam Bonnach, *The Bannock Corrie*, on Sron a Chlachain, in 1646.

BOTHTUARNEY—*The bothy with the northern aspect*; G. *tuath*, north.

INNISCHEROCH—*The sheep meadow*; G. *caora* ; or from *caor*, a torrent.

INNISDAIMH—*The ox or stag meadow* ; G. *damh*, ox, or stag.

LUBCHURRAN—*The dub of the carrots* ; G. *lub*, a pool, or dub, and *curran*, carrot.

BEN NAN IOMAIREAN—*The Ben of the ridges.*

In Glenlochay—Creag Mhor in the Distance.

The Forest of MAMLORN — *The slow-rising hill of Lathurna* (Lorn), was at one time a royal hunting forest of the Scottish kings. In 1617 Sir Duncan Campbell, the first baronet, was appointed to the office of heritable keeper of the forests of Mamlorn, Bendaskerly, and Finglen. Owing to a dispute regarding the boundaries of Mamlorn with Menzies of Culdares the ground was carefully surveyed in 1735 by David Dowie. The plan has been preserved, and a number of the old place names are thus available.

The following names are taken from Dowie's map, and his own spelling is adopted :—

TUILM—*Rocky knoll* ; G. *Tolm.*

KERKLE—*The Circle* ; G. *Cearcal.*

LOCH NA MALLTENELL—*The loch of the gathering hill* ; G. *meall,* a lumpish mountain, and *tionail,* gather.

CRAIGNAHALICK—*Rock of the litter* ; from G. *alach,* brood ; may be *Cnoc na h-Eilig,* from *eileag,* a deer-trap.

TOMDOUNESS—*The mound of the water-fall fort* ; G. *Tom dun eas.*

MAMHAR—*The mam of Ar.* This name is difficult.

CORRYHESKERNEICH—*The sheltered corry* ; from G. *seasg,* dry, sheltered.

DERIMORE—*The great climb* ; G. *dìreadh,* climbing.

CORRIECHALL—*The corrie of the loss* ; G. *call,* loss.

STOBCLOICH—*The stone stob.*

PHREE CORRIEAN—*The forest of the bird corrie* ; G. *frìth,* forest, or moor.

CORRIE INTRECKIE—*Corrie of the snow* ; G. *Coire an t-sneachda.*

LOCHNABARIN—*The loch of the queen* ; G. *Loch na ban-righ.*

STRONLERIVE—*The ———nose* ; name is obscure.

CORRYBOUIE—*The yellow corrie* ; G. *Coire buidhe.*

CORRYBAYNE—*The fair corrie.*

CORRY ALTRUM—*The nursing corrie* ; lies between *Salich duie* on the southwest and *Sron nan ean,* the nose of the birds, on the north-east. The burn flowing from the corrie is *Allt-cheathaich,* the burn of the mist. A passage to and from the top of the corrie is shown in the plan. Corrie Altrum is the " Misty Corrie " which Duncan Ban praises in his song, " Coire Cheathaich."

LAIRIG MHIC BHAIDIDH—*The Pass of MacWattie* ; leads from the head of Glenlochay to *Abhainn Ghlas,* the Grey River, at *Tom a' Chaorainn,* the Rowan Mound, in Glenlyon. Several of the place-names on Dowie's map are mentioned in the songs and poems of Duncan Ban MacIntyre, who was for some time forester to the Earl of Breadalbane in the Mamlorn district. The poet resided at *Bad Odhar*, the Dun Copse, in Glenlochay.

BAD A' MHAIM—*The copse or thicket of the slow-rising hill.*

TOM A' CHROCHAIR—*The hangman's mound.*

CREAG NAM BODACH—*The old men's rock.*

KENKNOCK—*The Head Hill.* The Glenlochay Kenknock is known as " Wester " to distinguish it from Easter Kenknock at Killin. *Làirig nan lunn*, Pass of the staves, leads from Kenknock to Pubal in Glenlyon.

DALGIRDY—*The field of the Gaordidh.* The name was attached to the burn, and then applied to the field and the mountain, *Meall Gaoirdidh* ; may be derived from *gaoir*, noise.

TULLICH—*The hillock.*

TIRAI—*Land of good luck or joy.* G. *àdh*.

DUNCHROISG—*The fort of the crossing.* The " Crossing " here is to Glenlyon by *Lairig Bhreislich*, the Pass of ravings.

BORLAND—*The board-land or mensal-land.* G. *A' Bhorlainn.*

FINLARIG—*The white or holy pass* ; G. *fionn*, white or holy. The old road to the bank of the Lochay from Morenish passed over this pass at *Druim na lairig*, the Ridge of the pass. Finlarig,

RIVER LOCHAY AT KILLIN.

which was a ten-merk land, was divided into three portions, namely, the Upper Town, in which was the mill on *Allt na Baile*, Burn of the noisy torrent ; the Lower Town, or Mains of Finlarig ; and *Baile-cruinn*, the Round Town. Finlarig was surveyed by Dowie, who made the map of Mamlorn in 1735, and although his plan is not now available, the following places were noted on it :—Reinmore, *the Large Division* ; the Laigh Meadow, next Reinmore ; the Isle of Rann ; the Goose Park ; the Little Park under the green ; Margmore, *the Great Merk* ; the Laigh Park ; the Great Park for winter grass ; the Green ; The Down, probably " The Dun " (Dunlochay) ; The Three-merk Land ; The Wood above Bailecruinn.

The ruins of the Castle of Finlarig stand on a prominence to the east of a larger mound called Dunlochay, the site of a pre-historic fort. The castle was surrounded at one time by a moat. Judging from the present ruins the building was rectangular in shape, having a square tower on the south-west. The main portion, which runs east and west, is 55 feet long by 31 feet broad, but the extreme length of the building is 62 feet. The castle appears to have been four storeys in height. The walls vary in thickness from 3 feet to 6 feet. The kitchen was at the east end of the main building. The fire-place is almost 14 feet in width, and at each side are ingle-nook recesses. There was a spiral stair at the north-east corner of the building, and one also on the west side. Next the kitchen is a small apartment, from which a narrow stair led to a second storey, where the banqueting-hall had been. The only entrance to the castle now intact is on the south, and above the door-way there is a stone bearing the Royal Arms, and the letters,

I R
A R
1609

These are the initials of king James VI. and his Queen, Anne of Denmark, with both of whom Sir Duncan Campbell, the first baronet, was on friendly terms. Some old carved stones recovered from time to time are preserved within the ruins. They include rude representations of Sir Duncan himself and his second wife, Elizabeth Sinclair. Close by the castle is a pit with a heading-block, having a cavity for the reception of the head, where persons of gentle birth were executed. The common people were hanged on an oak tree. A branch from which the culprits are said to have been suspended was cut down some forty years ago, and showed a deep groove caused by the friction of the rope. Gruesome stories used to be told of the beheadings and the hangings at Finlarig in " Black Duncan's " time, but many of the details were probably inventions of the narrators.

ELLANRYNE, ISLANDRAN, EILAN ROWAN, G. *Eilean Reamhainn* may be connected with G. *roinn*, point or nose.

A portion of the haugh of Finlarig near the junction of the Lochay with the Dochart had this name. Close to the Lochay there is an eminence rising a few feet above the haugh, which appears to have been surrounded by a moat. It was here that the Macnabs of Bovain had their stronghold of Ellanryne, which was destroyed and burnt by the Campbells and the English in 1653.

LINNE LOCHAIDH—*The pool of Lochay*; the deep pool on the river behind Killin Hotel. A number of Atholl men were drowned here through the smashing of their boat some time about 1730. See lament for them in Highland Monthly, Vol. II., p. 285.

A' CHAITEAG SHIOMAIN, a pointed hill above Tirarthur; so called from its likeness to a heap of corn kept together by a straw rope. G. *sioman*.

TIRARTHUR—*The land of Arthur*; G. *Tìr Artuir*; an eight merk-land east of Finlarig. It included *Marag an eas*, the Merk-land of the waterfall; *Baile na dalach*, the *town of the haugh*; *Baile meadhaineach, Middle town*; and Milton of Tirarthur.

MORENISH—*The big meadow*; from G. *mor innis*; a thirty mark-land extending from Allt Tirarthur to Allt Edramhuch-daidh (Edramucky Burn); an ancient possession of the Crown;

CLACH AN T-SAGAIRT, MORENISH.

tenants' names are given in rentals of 1480. The chapel[1] at
Morenish was built in 1901 by Aline, wife of Sir Joseph White
Todd, Bart., in memory of her daughter, Elvira, by a previous
marriage.

Morenish was divided into the following lands :—

ARDMOYLE—*The bald height* : G. *Aird mhaol*. On Ardmoyle
is the little graveyard known as *Cladh Da Bhì*, where the
Royal branch of the Breadalbane MacDiarmids are buried.
Above it is *Tom a' chluig*, The mound of the bell.

BALLEMORE—*The great town* ; used to be known as *Baile
mór MhicGrigoir*, MacGregor's great town. A field on Ballemore
used to be called *Both an Tighearna*, The Lord's bothy.

TOMACHROCHAIR—*The hangman's mound*. A prominent
cliff on Tomachrochair is called *Creag a' mhionaich*, Rock of
the entrails, from the irony water oozing from the lime-stone.
Above the rock is *Cathair an Rìgh*, The King's chair, where there
is a natural seat commanding an extensive view. A little beyond
the head dike and near the gate leading to the moor is *Clach
an t-sagairt*, The priest's stone, a water-worn pillar, which
bears a remarkable resemblance to a priest. It is said that
persons who quarrelled were reconciled by joining hands over
this stone.

BLARLIARAGAN—*The moor of the grey meadows*. A lint mill
was erected on Blarliaragan in 1790, near to the meal mill on
Morenish Burn.

RYNACHUILG—*Cape of the sharp point* ; G. *roinn*, cape, and
colg, a sharp point. Above the public road there was a place named
An Caisteal, which may have been the site of the round fort
noticed by Thomas Pennant, and which he said was five miles
east of Killin. Tradition states that there was a " castle " on
Rynachuilg farm, situated near the loch.

EDRAMUCKY—*Between two swine burns*; G. *Eadar dá Mhucaidh*.
After the Campbells of Glenorchy acquired Morenish in 1602,
Edramucky was feued out to a member of the Lawers family
whose descendants held it until the eighteenth century. Duncan
Campbell of Edramucky, who married Anna, daughter of the
Rev. Patrick Campbell, minister of Kenmore, is believed to have
murdered Sir James Campbell, of Lawers, at Greenock, on 22
April, 1723. The two kinsmen had been drinking together the
previous night. They parted apparently on good terms, intending
to cross next day to Dunbarton, and travel home to Lochtayside. In the morning Campbell of Lawers was found dead in
bed with two bullet wounds in his head. Edramucky had
disappeared, and as he had a few days before purchased some
ammunition for a pistol, suspicion at once rested on him, and
a warrant was issued for his arrest. See *Edinburgh Evening*

(1) Sir Joseph and Lady Todd are buried within the chapel grounds.

Courant, 2 May, 1723. There is no evidence to show that Edramucky was ever captured, or brought to trial. When his family left Edramucky in 1736, " Lady " Edramucky went to live at Stix House, near Kenmore. The Castle of Edramucky was situated on the south of the present farm buildings, close to the burn, and about 200 yards from Loch Tay. The foundations of the building may still be traced, and a few ancient sycamores and elms, that lined the avenue leading to the castle, survive. Two fields on Edramucky bear the names, *Croit nam prinichean*, The croft of the pins ; and *Ach a' chùirt*, The Field of the court.

KILTYRIE—*The nook of parching corn* ; G. *cùil*, nook, and *tìreadh*. This derivation, which Professor Watson gives, is borne out by another name on the farm, *Glas Ghradan*, The green of the parched corn ; from *gradan*, corn hastily prepared for grinding by setting fire to the ears until the husks were burned. The grain thus hardened was ground into meal on the *brath*, hand-mill. See Armstrong's Dictionary. A rock on Edramucky was called *Creag Dochart*, The evil cleansing rock. Kiltyrie is a four merk-land.

CARWHIN—*The corrie of Cunna* ; G. *Coire Chunna*. This place gets its name from the saint who is commemorated at Cladh Chunna, at Invervar, Glenlyon. Carwhin was a twelve merk-land, and was divided into three portions, namely, Wester Carwhin, Easter Carwhin, and Carie. Wester Carwhin included *Tom Odhar*, The dun mound ; *Marg a Phuill*, The merk-land of the mud, or pool ; *Marg Dubh*, The black merk-land ; and *Marg na h-Ath*, The merk-land of the Lime-kiln. Easter Carwhin comprehended *Blar More*, The Big field ; *Croit a' Bhealaich*, The Croft of the Pass ; and Carwhin proper. *Druim a' bhaird*, The bard's ridge ; and *Blàran bòidheach*, The pretty field, are place-names on Carie. Professor Watson derives Carie from *càthar*, mossy place. *Eilean nam breaban*, The Island of the shoe or boot soles, is off Wester Carwhin. *Tom Mhòrair*, The mound of the great man, is a prominent knoll about half a mile above the public road. Behind it, Seumas Mor Mac Ghille Fhionntaig, the last smuggler on Lochtayside, had his still. *Tom na h-ulaidh*, Mound of the hidden treasure ; *Creag na Croiche*, Rock of the Gallows, are on Easter Carwhin. *Lag a' mhòid*, The Hollow of the Court, is below the Gallows' Rock. The House of Carwhin occupied the site of the old farmhouse, now in ruins, on Blairmore, near Loch Tay. It is said that there was a paved road from the house to the shore. The graveyard of the district lay at the east side of Blairmore, and is now enclosed in the wood.

CRANNICH—*The place of trees* ; a district which used to form a detached portion of Weem parish ; comprises the farms of Wester, and Easter Tombreck ; Craggantoll, Cragganeaster,

Balnahanaid, and Balnasuim. Crannich, an ancient thanage, was granted to Robert de Meygnes, ancestor of the Menzieses of Weem, by the Earl of Atholl, prior to 1327. It was purchased from the Menzieses by Sir Duncan Campbell, the first Baronet of Glenorchy, in 1602.

TOMBRECK—*The speckled mound.* Above the public road on this farm there is a grassy ridge called *An Caisteal*, The Castle, where there was probably a round fort in pre-historic times. All the stones have been removed.

CRAGGANTOLL—*The rocky knoll of the holes* ; so called from the great number of cup-markings on a rock behind the farm-house.

CRAGGANESTER[1]—*The rocky knoll of water-falls* ; G. *cragan*, a little rocky knoll, and *easdobhar*, falling-water.

BALNAHANAID—*The town of the Annat, or Mother-church* ; the ancient ecclesiastical site was situated in front of the present farm-house near Loch Tay. There is now no trace of the church, but stone-coffins have been turned up here, and some Stone Age implements. The meal mill of the district of Crannich was at Balnahanaid.

BALNASUIM—*Town of the souming.* At the south-east corner of this farm, above Loch Tay, is a small graveyard, called *Cladh Phobuil*, the people's graveyard. It was marked as " neglected " on a plan of 1769.

LAWERS—*The sounding one* ; name derived from the Burn of Lawers, which is very loud when in flood. G. *Labhar*, loud spoken ; Welsh, *Llafar*. The name extended from the burn to the district and to the mountain, Ben Lawers. Lawers was a forty merk-land, and was divided into Lawarmore, Lawarmead-haineach, and Cloanlawar.

CROFTINTYGAN—*Croft of the marten* ; G. *Croit an taghain.* Two names on this farm are, *Stuc-ianaich*, the fowling height ; and *An Caisteal Mor*, the Big Castle, situated above the public road.

TOMB—*The Mound* ; G. *tom.* The Church and Manse of Lawers are on Tomb, and also The Hotel, which used to be called *Tigh na Croit*, Croft-house.

DRIUMNAFEROCH—*The ridge of grazing* ; G. *feur*, grass. The School is on Driumnaferoch.

CUILTRANNICH—*The nook of bracken* ; G. *Cuil*, nook, and *raineach*, fern or bracken. The modern meal mill of Lawers and also the smithy were on Cuiltrannich. The *Sìthean*, the Fairy Hill of Lawers, is below the mill. Beside the *Sìthean* is Ewen Cameron's Lint Mill.

(1) A bronze axe-head 4½ inches long by 2½ inches broad at the cutting edge was found at Cragganester by James McLaren in 1934.

Z

EAST END OF LOCH TAY, FROM LAWERS.

BAILE MHUILINN—*Miltown.* This farm included the Parks of Lawers. The following place-names were recorded on Miltown, *Dail,* The plain field ; *An Garadh mor,* The big Garden ; *Tomeorna,* The Barley Mound ; *Allt Dubh,* The Black Burn. The old church built in 1669, now a ruin, the House of the Lady of Lawers, the Ferry-man's house, and the Steamboat Pier are on Miltown. It is said that one or two interments took place outside the church, but there are no gravestones.

MACHUIM—*The burial-place of the plain ;* G. *magh,* plain, and *tuam,* grave or tomb. Machuim is situated on east side of Lawers Burn,[1] and close to the loch is the little ancient graveyard of the district.

LAWERNACROY—*Lawers of the tree ;* G. *Labhar na craoibhe.* The Stone Circle is on this farm. Above the head dike' is a spring which is supposed to have health-giving qualities. *Croit an doruis* (The door croft), and *Bothan Dubh,* black bothy, are on Machuim.

DUALLAN—*The Black meadow ;* G. *An Dubh Ailean.*

LURGINBUIE—*The yellow shank ;* G. *lurgin,* a long leg or shank, and *buidhe,* yellow.

DRUMGLAS—*The grey or green ridge.*

MARGANTRUIN—*The merk-land of the stream ;* G. *Marg an t-sruthain.*

SHEANLARICH—*The old site or ruin ;* G. *Seann laraich.*

CRAGGANRUAR—*The delving knoll ;* G. *ruamhair,* delving.

The eastern portion of Lawers used to be called CLUAN LABHAR—*The meadow of Lawers ;* and the land was divided into Wester, Middle, and Easter Cluanlabhar. In old charters Cluan was sometimes written " Clene," which gave rise to the name " Glenlawar." Place-names on this part of Lawers are, *Leothad More* (Big Slope), *Leothad an Uilt* (Slope of the Burn), *Talamh Tarsuinn* (The cross-land), *Croit an Doruis* (the Door Croft), *Cul Chinn* (Back of the Head), and *Bruaich nan Con* (Bank of the Dogs).

The burns, of which there are several, are called, *Allt nan Clach* (Burn of the Stones), *Allt na h-Ath* (Kiln Burn), *Allt Uisge* (Water Burn), and *Allt Trom* (The Heavy Burn). The gallows of Lawers stood on a limestone rock on Easter Cluanlabhar, called *Tom na Croiche.* The hole into which the gallows was fixed was blasted away many years ago. A little erection beside the bridge on Allt Phaderleigh was built as a Baptist chapel. An occasional service is held in it, although the congregation attached to it has died out entirely.

FEARNAN—*The Alder place ;* old spelling, Ferna. Alder

(1) The Lawers Burn has its source in Lochan Nan Cat, " the Little Loch of the Cats." This dark tarn was the scene of a murder at the beginning of last century. See Trans. Gaelic Soc., Inverness, vol. xxv., p. 146.

trees grow along the shore in great numbers. Fearnan is a thirty merk-land, and extends from Allt Phaderleigh on the west to about half a mile east of Letterellan. It includes a pendicle on the north side of Drummond Hill called Kinghallin. The eastern march of Fearnan was never properly defined, and there used to be a stretch of debatable ground between it and the lands of Port of Loch Tay. The lands of Fearnan were :—Lagfern, Tomintyvoir, Ballimenoch, Balnairn, Schanlarich, Corrie-cherrow, Boreland, Croftnalin, Stronfearnan and Margcroy, and Kinghallin.

LAGFERN—*Hollow of the alders* ; lies next to Allt Phaderleigh ; place-names here are, *Leothad na Fàire* (Slope of the ridge), *Gortan nan gobhar* (Little enclosure of the goats), *Radhar na criche* (Outfield of the March). At Lagfern there is a rough stone slab, about three feet in height, which bears on each side a rudely cut Latin cross. It is said that the markets for the district used to be held here.

TOMINTYVOIR—*The Mound of the Big-house* ; G., *Tom an taighe mhóir*. There is no information as to the Big-house.

BALLIMENOCH—*Middle town* ; G., *Baile meadhaineach*. A place-name here was *Blar na tiobairt*, The flat of the tibert, or holy well.

BALNAIRN—*Town of the alders* ; G., *Baile an fhearna*.

SCHANLARICH—*The old site or ruin* ; G. *Seann laraich*.

MARKET CROSS, FEARNAN.

CORRIECHERROW—*The odd quarter* ; G. *Corra*, odd, uneven, and *ceathramh*, quarter. A little meadow near the loch on this old farm is called *An Innis*.

BORELAND—*The board-land* ; G. *A' Bhorlainn*.

CROFTNALIN—*Croft of the pleasant plain* ; G. *croit*, croft, and *àilean*, a green plain. The meal mill of Fearnan was on Croftnalin. It was situated in a hollow behind the Hotel, and a large boulder, still there, has a round pot hole on the top. Into this the first grain of the season brought to the mill was placed and blessed. The lade that supplied the mill with water was connected with a stream that passes behind Boreland Farm-house. Tradition states that a prioress of the nunnery of the Isle of Loch Tay engineered the aqueduct by which the water of several streams that run down the west slope of Fearnan was caught for the use of the mill. The track of this old aqueduct may still be distinctly seen. It is further related that on the night of the Lady of Lawer's death there was a great rain storm ; and the aqueduct broke its bank to the west of Boreland Farm-house. The flood formed the deep burn that flows past the school, and on that account is called *Allt an Tuilbheum*, The Burn of the flood-breach. The Hotel is also on Croftnalin, and is known as *Tigh an loin*, The House of the marsh. There was a brew-seat on the site of the Hotel garden.

STRONFEARNAN—*The Nose of Fearnan*. The old village and the manor house of the Robertsons of Strowan, who owned the lands of Fearnan for several centuries, were situated behind the little graveyard, which is known as *Cladh na Sròine*, The Grave-yard of the Nose. This graveyard was probably formed when that of Inchadney was closed in 1760 ; but one or two old recumbent stones suggest that there were burials here prior to that year. The right of burial in Cladh na Sròine is now confined to a few families of the name of MacLean, who have been long resident in this district.

The site of St. Ciaran's church and churchyard was on *Dal Chiarain*, Ciaran's Field, on the Boreland side of the road to Fortingall. The old holy-water stone of the church stands on the top of the wall beside the highway. The churchyard has been included in the arable land, but within the past hundred years burials appear to have taken place at this ancient and sacred spot. The steep brae on the road to Fortingall is called *Bhruthach Clach an sgriodain*, The Brae of the stone of the scree. In rainy weather this old track would be like the bed of a stream. The hill above Fearnan is called *Meall Greadh*, The Hill of the studs of horses. On the east side of the Fortingall road, at the boundary between the parish of Kenmore and that of Fortingall, is *Clach an Tuirc*, The Boar's Stone. It has several cup-markings on the top. *Tom Darach*, The oak-mound, lies east of Cladh na Sroine. Letterellan means, *The slope of Allan* ; G. *leitir*, a slope

LOCH TAY AND BEN LAWERS FROM THE MANSE OF KENMORE.

(always to water), *Ailean*. Above Letterellan is Margcroy, *The hard merk-land*, and below the road on the east side of Letterellan was *Croit na Cùilich*, The Croft of the Nook. *Clach a' Bhreitheimh*, the judge's seat at Fearnan, was built into the walls of a house (Lawers View).

PORT OF LOCH TAY. The ten merk-land of the Port of Loch Tay extends from the east side of Letterellan to the Rustic Lodge along the southern face and foot of Drummond Hill. This land, along with the Isle of Loch Tay and the salmon fishing on the loch, was gifted in 1122 by Alexander I., king of Scots, to the monks of the abbey of Scone. Before 1389 the Crown had assumed possession of the Port and the Isle, both of which were held at that time by Duncan, Earl of Fife. They were set on tack in 1467 to Sir Colin Campbell, first Laird of Glenorchy; and twenty-one years later his son, Sir Duncan, obtained from king James IV. a feu charter of the Port, and also of lands in Eddergoll, on the opposite side of Loch Tay.

ISLE OF LOCH TAY. G. *Eilean nam Ban naomh*, Island of the Holy Women. The ruins on this island, which are roofless and covered with ivy, consist of two contiguous buildings running east and west, and extend to a total length of 142 feet. The walls of the eastmost portion, which may be termed the main building, are 81 feet long by 31 feet broad outside. About 16 feet from the east gable there is a transverse wall, to the west of which there was a spacious apartment about 55 feet in length, which most likely formed the banqueting hall. The foundations of a wall, which runs almost the whole length of the centre of this apartment, would give support to the great expanse of flooring above, and, with transverse walls both right and left, would form extensive cellarage for the establishment. The western portion, which is scarcely in line with the main building, owing to the curve which the island takes, is smaller in breadth by about 7 feet. It has two divisional walls. The westmost compartment, judging from the breadth of the chimney, may have been the kitchen. The gables as they stand are about forty-five feet in height, and the walls about $3\frac{1}{2}$ feet in thickness. There are several loop holes in the walls. Those on the north side have been built up to half the thickness of the walls, and, as the unbuilt portion is on the outside, the stopping-up was made from the interior, a precaution which was probably taken when the buildings were subjected to Montrose's artillery.

To the south of the buildings lay the courtyard, oblong in form, and extending to about 850 square yards, and enclosed on the west, south, and east sides by a stone wall, the foundations of which may still be seen. This was probably " the barmekyn wall " built by Sir Colin, the first laird of Glenorchy. At the north-west corner, where there appears to have been an entrance, a square building protruded beyond the line of the wall.

There are three windows in the eastmost gable, each measuring about 12 inches by 20 inches, and from the situation of these the building seems to have been a four-storied one. The windows, small as they are, were secured by stanchions. Portions of the slates, half an inch in thickness, lie scattered around the island. A pit, perhaps the well, with built-up sides, is situated at the south-east corner of the courtyard.

At the beginning of last century[1] there were no monastic remains on the island, except two stones, the one bearing the figure of a cross, and the other hollowed a little on the side, perhaps for consecrated water.

The orchard[2] that belonged to the island is now included in Taymouth Castle gardens, and beside it was the village of *Ceann a' Ghàraidh*, The End of the Garden. A few sycamore trees of huge girth still mark the western boundary of an orchard which was let in 1702 to John Bane, who had the ale-house in the village. Part of the rent payable was " a thousand fruit." Any one found breaking into the orchard was to be incarcerated in the prison of Taymouth until he paid five pounds Scots, which was to be given to John " for his encouragement."

DRUMMOND—*At the Ridge*; G. *Druiminn*, from *druiminn*, locative of *druim*; the hill extends from Fearnan to Comrie, a distance of five miles. The open space on Drummond Hill is Rhevaurd, *The Bard's Slope*. It was at one time under crofts. To the west of Rhevaurd, on the ridge of the hill, is a deep ravine called, *Am Feadan*, The Whistle ; and below this and a little to the west is *A' Chreag Liath*, the Grey Rock, now called the Black Rock. Before the gardens were transferred from Taymouth to their present site, about 1800, the ground occupied by them was laid out under crofts which had distinctive names. Some of these names were, *Dail earba*, The Field of the roe ; *Croit a' chura*, The corner Croft ; *Lag nan ean*, Hollow of the birds ; *Lag a bhile*, Hollow of the edge ; compare *Cois a bhile*. An eminence at the left of the entrance to the Gardens was *Stuc Chorkil*, and the knoll beside the gardener's cottage, on the east of the public road, was *Cnoc a' bhathaich*, which means, The Byre knoll. Before 1813 the public road from the end of the bridge to Dalerb skirted the shore of Loch Tay.

DALMARTAIG, DALMARTENE—*The plain of Martain* ; the large field lying to the east of the Mains. Between the terrace and the bank of the river there is a low-lying field of nine acres, now under trees, that used to be called " The Elysian Fields."

CRAGGAN DAIDH, or CREAG AN AIGH, a rock on the north side of the road to Comrie Bridge, about a quarter of a mile east of the Mains' Crossroads, where it is said the Romans buried a pot of gold, when they were leaving the camp at Fortingall. Tradition relates that, every time the sun shines, its rays fall on the treasure. Many searches have been made for the gold, and even the face of the rock has been blasted away, but the treasure has never been found. The name may mean either *David's rock*, or *the Rock of good fortune*.

INCHADNEY, the name of the peninsula formed by the bend of the river below Taymouth Castle, and east of Dalmartaig. The church, churchyard, and manse of Inchadney, now Kenmore, were situated on the east side of the apex of the peninsula on a low-lying strip of land between the terrace and the river. There are various spellings of the name in old documents— 1491, Inchadden ; 1522, Inchaidin ; 1561, Inchekadyn ; 1579, Inchadin ; 1729, Inchaldne ; 1769, Inchadnie ; now Inchadney. Attempts[1] have been made to derive the name of this ancient ecclesiastical site from St. Aidan, and to explain it as *Innis Aidan*, Aidan's Meadow, which would give in Gaelic *Innis Aodhain*. Professor W. J. Watson states definitely that such a derivation is impossible. Old people called the place *Innis Chailtnigh*, The Meadow of Cailtnigh ; and the letter *l*, preserved in some of the former spellings, confirms Dr. Watson's view. The name seems to be derived from the same source as *Allt Chailtnigh*, Keltney Burn, just a mile and a half away. What " Cailtnigh " means it is impossible to say. The church of Inchadney appears to have been dedicated to the Nine Maidens, whose fair was held beside it about the 18th of July each year until 1575, when Sir Colin Campbell of Glenorchy, the sixth laird, removed it to Kenmore. The Nine Maidens were the daughters of St. Donald of the Glen of Ogilvy, in Angus, and lived in the eighth century. There are several dedications to these saintly maidens in Angus. The market continued to be held at Kenmore, until within the past sixty years, about the third week of July, and was called *Feill nam Ban Naomh*, The Market of the Holy Women. A little meadow, extending from the east side of the churchyard to Newhall Bridge over the Tay, was called *Lag a' Chlaidh*, the Hollow of the Churchyard. A great oak tree on the northern boundary of the churchyard was said to have been the tree under which Sir Walter Scott, in " Waverley," describes the burial of Colonel Wogan. The hero was, however, buried in Kenmore Kirk. " Wogan's tree " fell during a storm in the winter of 1936-37. The Holy Well of Inchadney is situated at the foot of the terrace, about five hundred yards to the north of the churchyard, and at the edge of the great meadow of *Poll Tairbh*, the Bull's Pool. Up to the middle of last century the well used to be visited by great numbers of people on the morning of *Bealtuinn*, the first day of May.

(1) See " The Gaelic Kingdom in Scotland " by Charles Stewart, Killin (1880).

AA

COMRIE—The Confluence ; G. *Cuimirigh*, from *comar*, confluence ; at the junction of the Lyon with the Tay. The lands
of Comrie were formerly a Menzies property and formed a
barony. They lay in the old parishes of Kenmore, Weem, and
Fortingall, and were acquired by the Breadalbane family about
the middle of the eighteenth century. Comrie Castle, on the
banks of the Lyon, now an ivy covered ruin, is said to have been
the first residence of the Menzieses of that Ilk in Perthshire. The
castle was destroyed by fire in 1487. It was afterwards repaired
and given to a younger son when the Castle of Weem was built.
Before the first bridge over the Lyon was erected in 1786, there
was a ferry at the Point with a ferry-man's house and croft
attached. The courts of the barony were held on a knoll to the
north of the Rustic Lodge, and in front of the Lodge, on the
south side of the public road, there are traces of a small circular
enclosure that is said to have been a graveyard. The lands of
Comrie consisted of the following :—Stron Comrie, Little Comrie,
Mains of Comrie, Auchleys (now Auchloa), and Laggan. Auchleys
has been explained as meaning " the Field of the beacon," from
auch, and *leus*, a flame. The shealings of Comrie were situated
at the foot of Schiehallion. For some years prior to 1862 the
Mains of Comrie was the home-farm to Taymouth Castle.

TAY. In Ptolemy's notes, *Tava* ; Welsh, *Taw* ; Gaelic, *Tatha* ;
the name of a Celtic river goddess, the Silent One. In Wales
we have the river Tawe ; and in Devon, the Tavy and the
Taw.

The following is an account of a peculiar phenomenon that
was witnessed on Loch Tay on Sunday, 12th September, 1784,
between the hours of eight and nine o'clock in the morning :—
" The water of the bay at the east end of Loch Tay ebbed about
three hundred feet, and left the channel or bed of the bay almost
quite dry where the water is usually three feet in depth ; and,
being gathered in the form of a wave, rolled on about three
hundred feet further to the westward, until it met a similar
wave rolling in a contrary direction. When these clashed
together they rose to a perpendicular height of four feet and
upwards, emitting a white foam on the top of the water. Then
this wave so formed took a lateral direction southward towards
the shore, gaining upon the land four feet beyond the high
water mark of the Loch at that time. Then it returned from
the shore to the lake, and continued to ebb and flow for about
an hour and a half, the wave gradually diminishing in size every
time it reached the shore until it wholly disappeared. It is to
be observed that during this phenomenon there was an absolute
calm.

" Upon the two following days, at an hour a little later in the
morning, there was the same appearance, but not in any respect
to the same degree

" The first who observed the phenomenon was one MacIntyre, a blacksmith, living in the village of Kenmore, who went to wash his face and hands in the bay, and was greatly surprised and frightened on observing the water retiring from him while at that operation. He immediately ran and alarmed his neighbours who came running, and saw the ebbing and the flowing above described.

" Upon ten o'clock of the same day, two men standing upon the bridge of Kenmore, which is upon the river nearly where it rises from the lake, observed the weeds in the bed of the river pointing towards the loch instead of downwards with the river, and that the stream of the river flowed into the lake, and not out of it."

The above description of the phenomenon was communicated at the time to the Antiquarian Society of Perth, and is preserved in the Museum of that city. The Rev. Thomas Fleming, minister of Kenmore, was preaching at Amulree on the day of the occurrence, but on his return home he obtained an account of it from eye-witnesses for the Royal Society of Edinburgh. Mr. Fleming's letter to the Society was published in the Old Statistical Report of Kenmore, which was written by the Rev. Colin McVean, in 1794.

INDEX.

Campbell, Elizabeth, 2nd, wife of Sir John C. of Glenorchy, p. 157.
Campbell, Elizabeth, daughter of 4th Earl of Breadalbane, p. 196.
Campbell, Elizabeth, daughter of James C. of Auchlyne, p. 246.
Campbell, Elizabeth, wife of Irvine of Drum, p. 358.
Campbell, Ewen, son of William C. of Lochdochart, p. 244.
Campbell, Gavin, 3rd Marquis of Breadalbane, p. 228.
Campbell, George, son of 3rd Earl of Breadalbane, pp. 185, 193.
Campbell, Henrietta, daughter of 2nd Earl of Breadalbane, p. 177.
Campbell, Hugh, son of James C. of Auchlyne, p. 246.
Campbell, Hugh, Ledcharrie, p. 245.
Campbell, Iain Og, hanged, p. 138.
Campbell, Iain Herbert, 8th Earl of Breadalbane, p. 228. See p. 233.
Campbell, Isobel, wife of James C. of Ardkinlas, p. 145.
Campbell, Isobel, daughter of William C. of Lochdochart, p. 244.
Campbell, Ivan, Col., son of 6th Earl of Breadalbane, pp. 228, 233.
Campbell, James, son of Colin C. of Glenfalloch, p. 222.
Campbell, James, son of Chas. C. of Lochdochart, p. 244.
Campbell, James, sheriff-sub. of Perth, p. 244.
Campbell, James, son of Dr. Chas. Ed. C. of Montreal, p. 244.
Campbell, James, minister, Kenmore, pp. 274, 319.
Campbell, James, elder, Kenmore, p. 303.
Campbell, James, minister, Kilninver, his daughter, p. 311.
Campbell, Janet, wife of Hugh McDougall, minister, Killin, p. 292.
Campbell, Jean, wife of Alexr. Comrie, minister, Kenmore, p. 268.
Campbell, Jean, wife of Robert Macnab, of Innishewan, p. 368.
Campbell, Jemima, daughter of 3rd Earl of Breadalbane, p. 185.
Campbell, John, son of Duncan C. 3rd of Auchlyne, p. 246.
Campbell, John, brother to James 3rd of Lawers, escort to France, p. 120.
Campbell, John, bishop of the Isles, pp. 118, 354.
Campbell, John, of the Royal Bank, Edinburgh, helps Dewar of Quigrich, pp. 71, 175.
Campbell, John (McGlasserig), poet, Morenish, p. 188.
Campbell, John, Lord Glenorchy, son of 3rd Earl of Breadalbane, p. 193
Campbell, John, Lord Ormelie, son of 4th Earl of Breadalbane, p. 196.
Campbell, John, Boreland, Fearnan, pp. 249, 355.
Campbell, John, Milton, Lawers, p. 249.
Campbell, John, minister, Killin, p. 293.
Campbell, John, in Portbane, p. 268.
Campbell, John, missionary, Ardeonaig and Lawers, p. 299.
Campbell, John, elder, Kenmore, pp. 302, 303.
Campbell, John, brother to James C. 2nd of Lawers, p. 239.
Campbell, John, schoolmaster, Glenquaich, p. 313.
Campbell, John, schoolmaster, Achianich, p. 314.

Campbell, John, claimant, Fort William, p. 329.
Campbell, John, innkeeper, Muttonhole, p. 331.
Campbell, John, a poor scholar, p. 331.
Campbell, John, Forty-shilling Land, p. 331.
Campbell, John, schoolmaster, Ardeonaig, p. 334.
Campbell, Juliana, wife of Murdoch Maclaine, of Lochbuy, p. 145.
Campbell, Juliana, wife of Sir Colin C. 8th of Glenorchy, p. 143.
Campbell, Katherine, wife of Finlay Macnab, 12th of Bovain, p. 97.
Campbell, Katryne, wife of Finlay Macnab, 10th of Bovain, p. 96.
Campbell, Louisa, daughter of Duncan C. 3rd of Auchlyne, p. 246.
Campbell, Louisa, daughter of John C. of Achallader, p. 246.
Campbell, Margaret, daughter of Duncan C. 3rd of Auchlyne, p. 246.
Campbell, Margaret, wife of E. of Glencairn, p. 124.
Campbell, Margaret, daughter of Colin C. 6th of Glenorchy, p. 124.
Campbell, Margaret, wife of Iain Og C., p. 139.
Campbell, Margaret, wife of John Cameron of Lochiel, p. 145.
Campbell, Margaret Lilias, alleged daughter of 3rd Earl of Breadalbane, p. 221.
Campbell, Lady Margaret, wife of Hon. Ivan C., p. 233.
Campbell, Margaret, daughter of Chas. C. of Lochdochart, p. 244.
Campbell, Margaret, wife of Daniel McNaughton, soldier, p. 331.
Campbell, Marion, wife of Patrick Macnab of Bovain, p. 94.
Campbell, Marion, wife of Gregor Roy MacGregor of Glenstrae, p. 128.
Campbell, Mariot, wife of Finlay Macnab, 8th of Bovain, p. 95.
Campbell, Marjorie, reputed daughter of Laird of Lawers, p. 176.
Campbell, Marjory, wife of Edw. Tosach of Monzievaird, p. 240.
Campbell, Mary, wife of John Min Macnab, pp. 99, 101 ; married Mal. MacGregor, obtains Ewer p. 104.
Campbell, Lady Mary, daughter of Earl of Argyll, wife of 6th Earl of Caithness, p. 175.
Campbell, Lady Mary, wife of Archd. Cockburn, p. 176.
Campbell, Lady Mary, daughter of 4th Earl of Breadalbane, p. 196.
Campbell, Norman, son of 6th Earl of Breadalbane, p. 228.
Campbell, Patrick, son of Alexr. C. of Lochdochart, p. 244.
Campbell, Patrick, minister, Kenmore, p. 268 ; married Marjorie Menzies, p. 268 ; reference to, pp. 305, 399.
Campbell, Patrick, minister, Killin, p. 283.
Campbell, Patrick, elder, Kenmore, pp. 266, 303.
Campbell, Patrick, minister, Kilninver, p. 292.
Campbell, Patrick, Glenlyon, takes tack of Morenish, p. 38.
Campbell, Patrick, vintner, Kenmore, p. 310.
Campbell, reputed son of Lord Ormelie, p. 176.
Campbell, Robert, son of Colin C. of Glenfalloch, p. 222.
Campbell, Robert, son of Alexr. of Lochdochart, p. 244.

cc

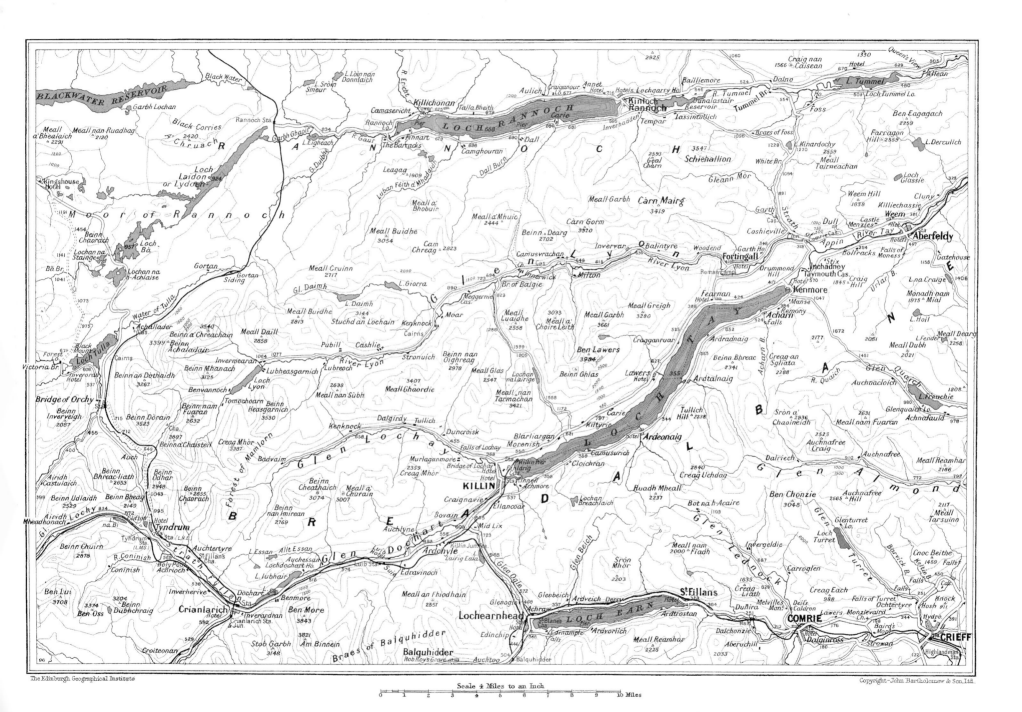

Scale 4 Miles to an Inch

0   1   2   3   4   5   6   7   8   9   10 Miles